SECRET MISSIONS TO CUBA

SECRET MISSIONS TO CUBA

FIDEL CASTRO, BERNARDO BENES, AND CUBAN MIAMI

ROBERT M. LEVINE

palgrave

First published 2001 by
PALGRAVE™
175 Fifth Avenue, New York, NY 10010 and
Houndmills, Basingstoke, Hampshire, England RG21 6XS.
Companies and representatives throughout the world.

Palgrave is the new global publishing imprint of St Martin's Press LLC
Scholarly and Reference Division and Palgrave Publishers Ltd (formerly
Macmillan Press Ltd).

ISBN 0–312–23987–4 hardback

Library of Congress Cataloging-in-Publication Data
Levine, Robert M.
Secret missions to Cuba : Fidel Castro, Bernardo Benes, and Cuban
Miami / by Robert M. Levine.
    p. cm.
    Includes bibliographical references (p.) and index.
    ISBN 0–312–23987–4
    1. United States—Relations—Cuba. 2. Cuba—Relations—United
States. 3. Benes, Bernardo. 4. Businessmen—Florida—Miami—
Biography. 5. Cuban Americans—Florida—Miami—Biography. 6.
Exiles—Florida—Miami—Political activity—Case studies. 7. Castro,
Fidel, 1927 - 8. Espionage, American—Cuba. 9. Cuban Americans—
Florida—Miami—Social conditions. 10. Miami (Fla.)—Social
conditions—20th century.
E183.8.C9 L46 2001
303.48′27307291—dc21   2001
                                                             021890

Design by Letra Libre, Inc.

First Edition: September 2001
10 9 8 7 6 5 4 3 2

Printed in the United States of America.

To the grandchildren of
Ricky and Bernardo Benes:
Allan, Eliana, Garrett, Seth,
Brett, Stephen, Nataly and Cydney

CONTENTS

LIST OF PHOTOGRAPHS

CHAPTER FIVE

CHAPTER SIX

PREFACE

S ecret Missions to Cuba reveals for the first time the full details of a
story sketchily known at best. Indeed, some of its events have never
appeared in print. The research in this book generated tensions as
it progressed. Participants differed pointedly one from another in recollections of activities in which they played key roles. Our story begins with
Bernardo Benes.

Benes arrived in Miami from Havana on Friday, November 11, 1960,
as a young lawyer and accountant in the wave of arrivals after Castro's
victory on January 1, 1959. The man "with a flair for public relations, a
cigar in his mouth, and an atrocious accent in English"[1] demanded full
participation by Cubans in the community. He not only lobbied for Cuban
exile causes but, from the early 1960s to 1978, spent long hours trying to
convince "Anglo" philanthropies, businesses, and other organizations to
reach out into the Cuban exile community. First, he advised, they should
form Hispanic (read: Cuban) divisions, and later bring local Cuban
Americans into positions of leadership.[2]

Starting in 1977, Benes made at least seventy-five private trips to Havana with the support of high officials of the Carter and Reagan administrations. He spent approximately 150 hours with Fidel Castro, and
thousands of hours with Cuban senior officials, mostly members of Castro's trusted Special Forces. The players in the secret negotiations had to
take extraordinary steps to hide their activities from the Soviets. They exchanged messages through the Cuban consul in Kingston, Jamaica, and
used code names ("Benito" for Benes; "Gustavo" for his business partner,
Carlos (Charles) Dascal; "Pedrito" for State Department official Peter
Tarnoff).

Benes's descriptions about his encounters with Castro reveal new
and sometimes startling insights into Castro's personality and character.

Despite the election of Ronald Reagan, considerably more of a hardliner toward Cuba than Jimmy Carter, Benes and Dascal continued to act as emissaries between the State Department and Castro's highest advisors, especially during and after the 1980 Mariel crisis. Later, in fact, Benes carried a message from the president to Castro, offering to open relations and end the embargo in exchange for ending Cuba's "Exporting the Revolution" policy. Had the Miami Cuban exile community learned of this gesture, a CIA-sponsored operation possibly linked to the administration's negotiations with Soviet Premier Mikhail Gorbachev, its members would have felt shocked and bitterly betrayed.

Among Benes's achievements, with the assistance of others, was Castro's agreement in 1978 to free 3,600 political prisoners; another was the Cuban regime's agreement to permit exiles in the United States to visit their relatives and to allow Cubans to visit their relatives in the United States. Washington spent billions of dollars to deal with Cuba, but Castro's decision to free his political prisoners and to permit exiles to visit their relatives—done with little cost to Washington—proved the most meaningful act in forty-two years of United States relations with Fidel Castro. Cuba benefited from the remitted dollars, but Cuban exiles, torn emotionally between their dual loyalties and desperate to reunify their families even briefly, benefited the most.

Benes and Dascal participated in the negotiations on their own since the United States had broken relations with Cuba. They remained in constant touch with top administration officials. Congressman Dante Fascell and Secretary of State Cyrus Vance acted as their main supporters. They worked closely with Peter Tarnoff, Vance's executive secretariat, at the State Department. Benes's missions to Cuba continued between 1977 and 1986. Agents of the Federal Bureau of Investigation and the Central Intelligence Agency also participated in this process.

As a result of his dialogue with Castro, however, Benes, in his own words, became "a pariah" in South Florida. After having seen him as a respected community leader, Cuban Miami suddenly rejected him. More than twenty years of vituperation left him disoriented and briefly suicidal. In his angry and depressed state, he became querulous, hard to deal with. He was subject to experiences that seemed Kakfaesque. On October 25, 1978, the Secret Service contacted Benes to say that President Carter, who was campaigning for Florida Governor Bob Graham's reelection, wanted to see him the next day. He was taken to the airport landing strip adjacent to Air Force One and asked to stand fifty feet behind a line of leaders of the Florida Democratic Party shaking hands with the president. When Carter reached the end of the line, he walked over to Benes. The president thanked him for his tireless efforts to help the cause of human rights.

But as soon as Benes went to his car, he turned on the radio. At that moment, a Spanish-language radio station was reviling him as a communist and traitor.

He remained under FBI protection, surviving at least one and possibly two assassination attempts, and wearing a bulletproof vest during the first year. His bank was picketed and firebombed, and, for the second time in his life, he lost almost all of his assets. For years he could not even visit Little Havana without people refusing to shake his hand or look him in the eye. In recent years, he has gained grudging acceptance from some but

P.1   President Jimmy Carter thanking Benes at Miami International Airport.
Miami *News* collection

remains despised by many, and is virtually stranded on the periphery of the Cuban exile community. Consider, for instance, what occurred as recently as August 14, 2000: This is the day when Benes heard that Joe Lieberman had been chosen as Al Gore's running mate. That morning, the news director of Radio Mambí, Armando Pérez-Roura, in urging the Miami Cuban community to not vote for Lieberman/Gore, stated that Cubans should not vote for Lieberman since "he is a Jew, just like Bernardo Benes, who seeks to dialogue with Castro."[3] Clearly, Pérez-Roura's statement is disturbing in several ways.

This book seeks to understand the nature of the Miami Cuban exile experience over four decades, using the trajectory of Benes's experience as a case study in community dynamics. His story provides a sadly cautionary tale: people who take risks in a charged atmosphere run the risk of falling victim to the emotional climate, especially when that climate encompasses rage and hate.

The following chapters unfold the history of the Miami Cuban community in the context of the disquieting, poisonous relationship between the United States and Cuba since 1959. It examines the pressures exerted on Miami Cubans both by their self-appointed as well as their elected leaders to conform to the Cuban militant exile lobby's line, even if it has at times included threats to the principle of free speech and accepted tactics of intimidation, bombings, and assassinations. Emotions run deep in Miami, fueled by the pain of having to adjust to a foreign culture and the sting of perceived betrayals. These went back as far as the near-constant practice of political corruption under the Cuban republic; when Batista overthrew its elected government in 1952; when President John F. Kennedy, earlier badly advised, withdrew promised support for the Bay of Pigs invasion in 1961. They also included actions by community "dialoguers" speaking personally with the hated Fidel Castro starting in 1978, and, having perhaps the greatest impact of all within Cuban Miami, Attorney General Janet Reno's order to have six-year-old Elián González returned to his father and federal agents sent to seize him early in 2000.

While most influential Miamians remained silent after Benes's efforts at dialogue, some thanked Benes privately. "I just want you to know that great men *must* do what they believe in. You have done it. I will always respect you for it," Robert A. Brandon of Coral Gables wrote to Benes.[4] Wood

McCue, for eight years the director of the Comprehensive Health Planning Council for South Florida under whom Benes served as an unpaid board member and, later, president of the national parent agency, said in an e-mail note when asked for comments about Benes that "Bernardo is one of my favorite persons and I consider him to be a brother."[5] Clerics—from Roman Catholic and Episcopal bishops to rabbis and evangelical Protestants—told him how much they appreciated his efforts to work on behalf of, in the words of Bishop James L. Duncan, "our Cuban brethren."[6] His family gave him continual support, even when things turned bleak.[7] "Anglo" community activist and County Commissioner Ruth Shack praised him in personal letters. Some Miami Cubans—including Lourdes Alonso and lawyer Ricardo Martinez-Cid—did too, but there were not many others. Hundreds of families asked him to help intervene in behalf of a relative, imprisoned in Cuba or threatened with deportation from the United States.

But only a tiny handful offered Benes support publicly. Among them included Ernest A. Iniguez, a Hialeah police officer who sent a mailgram to Myles Frechette at the State Department's Cuban desk, stating:

> Sir, a few individuals at present are enjoying an alarming degree of success in disrupting the community and putting innocent lives in danger. . . . Certain small newspapers and loud radio stations are perpetrating a hoax on the community expanding on a demonical lie. In the Miami area there is not a communist behind every tree and one out of every five ex-political prisoners is not a spy. I feel that the FBI and the State Department should come forth and deny the scale of those accusations and allow innocent citizens to continue their lives.[8]

Some time later, former United States Interests Section head Wayne Smith spoke in Spanish on Miami's radio station WQBA ("*Cubanísima*"), calling Benes a friend and in no manner a Cuban agent. "My personal opinion, since we live in free country, I have the right to have my personal point of view, is that all of this is absurd."[9] But no one stepped forward where it really mattered. During the twenty-two years since he returned with the first planeload of prisoners, Benes remained unemployed for twelve of those years.

Carrying out the research for this book produced moments of anguish. In November 2000, just when the manuscript neared completion, unknown robbers stole Benes's car from a downtown Miami parking space.

In the trunk were not only copies of the manuscript but dozens of valuable documents and notes from his files. Even more mysteriously, the car was found a week later—intact, without damage, and without anything missing. Could someone simply have photocopied the manuscript or the documents? Three weeks later the author's briefcase, containing important documents related to the study, was stolen from the outer office of a University of Miami administrator during an appointment. Then some photographs disappeared for two days before turning up in an unlikely place. Perhaps we have seen too many James Bond movies—or perhaps the book's contents made people worry.

Working on *Secret Missions to Cuba* has been unlike any of my previous book projects. The tensions the study generated were consistently unsettling, not to mention wholly unpredictable, and the fact that interviewees vociferously denied statements (which I had proof of) occasionally made me wonder if I'd landed squarely in the middle of an espionage/spy novel. Indeed, the process affected Benes as well. After re-reading a letter from an old friend and mentor who had been queried for information, Benes confessed that he began to cry because, in his words, "His letter made me aware of the extent of the injustice committed by Miami Cubans against me for being good. I am sixty-five, without income, and without real employment. I have not made one single penny this year."[10]

This book also seeks insight into the hearts and minds of more than 700,000 former Cubans and their children residing in Miami, assaulted in a way by headline-seeking media, by what sensitive Cuban Americans term "Cuban bashing" by holier-than-thou Anglos, and by Miami's complex ethnic tensions. How may we understand the trauma of the exile from Cuba and the reasons why Miami Cubans permitted themselves to be intimidated to the point at which speaking out in favor of dialogue with Castro, or any other "dissident" opinion, could and did lead to death threats, some of which were carried out? Bernardo Benes was only one of many who suffered because of the acquiescence of politicians and community leaders lacking the courage to speak out.

ACKNOWLEDGMENTS

M any people provided assistance in researching this book. Among them: Tina María Abich; Dr. José Raúl Alfonso; Lic. Moisés Asís; the late Jim Baker of Operation Pedro Pan; attorneys Jo Anne and Michael Bander; historian Margalit Bejarano; "Skip" Brandon; journalist Edna Buchanan; former National Security Advisor Zbigniew Brzezinski; oral historian Elizabeth Campisi; Israel Castellanos; academician Max Castro; scientist Leon A. Cuervo; Tom Cunningham, former president of Britain's Open University; diplomatic historian Justus Doenecke; Dr. José "Pepe" Edelstein; photographer and scholar Juan Carlos Espinosa; former president of Panama Ricardo de la Espriella and his wife Mercedes María; historian Luis Martínez Fernández; president of the University of Miami Edward T. Foote II; the Reverend Raúl Fernández-Calienes; Elena Freyre; Jossie García; Patricia García-Velez; Senator Jack Gordon; Jim Hampton of the *Miami Herald*; Harvard's Luiz Sérgio Hernández Jr.; educator Ofélia Martín Hudson; economist Antonio Jorge; and Dr. Diane Just of the Center for Latin American Studies. Also, veteran Miami journalist Howard Kleinberg; Nita Rous Manitzas of the Center for International Policy; J. L. Medina; Ambassador Ambler H. Moss, Jr.; Silvia J. Muñoz of Miami's Pedro Pan Association; Emílio Ochoa, one of the writers of Cuba's 1940 constitution; attorney Karen J. Orlin; Enrique Ovares, former president of the Cuban Federation of University Students; former Carter administration Latin American specialist Robert A. Pastor; Luis Pozo, son of the former mayor of Havana; Emilio Rangel; Sergio Rodríguez of the University of Miami administration; Susan Sachs; "Luis Salas," a Cuban American career military officer; Basílio V. Sifko; the former head of the United States Interests Section in Havana, Wayne S. Smith; librarian Sara Sánchez, Anita Stone, retired attorney Seth Stopek; psychologist José Szapocnik; former State Department official

Peter Tarnoff; Angel Fernández Varela, former chief officer of Radio Swan; Fred Wahl; Monsignor Bryan O. Walsh; General Vernon A. Walters; and several former employees of the FBI and CIA who wish not to be named. More than anyone else, Palgrave/St. Martin's editor Gayatri Patnaik deserves credit for understanding from the first this book's potential and for shepherding the manuscript through the editorial process. Along the way, she boosted my courage when it was needed, diplomatically handled undiplomatic moments, and never wavered in her conviction that such a potentially controversial book merited publication. I am also grateful to Sabahat Chaudhary for her end-of-the-line copyediting.

STATEMENT ON
CORROBORATION

Obviously, a book of this kind, especially when it deals not only with the recent past but also the present, needs to provide as much corroboration as possible. Some of Bernardo Benes's personal documents covering the years since 1960 were donated in 1992 to the Cuban Heritage Collection of the University of Miami Library, thereby making them available to scholars, and the remainder will be deposited after this book is published. They include hundreds of newspaper clippings, photographs, legal documents, lists of names and addresses, minutes of meetings, and long, detailed pages of notes taken with the permission of the Cuban officials with whom Benes was dealing, often with verbatim citations. During the negotiation years during the Carter and Reagan administrations, Benes wrote on a yellow pad the details of every meeting or telephone conversation with the date, the people involved and the subjects discussed. He has kept all these documents in chronological sequence. The Cubans gave Benes permission to take notes, and United States officials knew of his note-taking as well. They contain a wealth of information on the negotiations, including seventy-eight documents from the Carter years and twenty-nine during the Reagan administration.

Benes possesses one of three original copies made by the Cuban government listing thousands of claims for confiscated property and the amounts it was willing to pay provided the negotiations succeeded. Whenever the text quotes Benes without adding an endnote, I checked in every case the detailed notes taken by Benes either at the event described or immediately afterwards.

Benes's collection of evidence by itself falls short of providing sufficient proof. The 1977–78 mission under the Carter administration is easier to corroborate than the second mission during the Reagan years because the latter was entirely covert. Still, I have worked painstakingly to find corroboration and to spot untruths. Corroborative evidence backs Benes's entire detailed story.

Many have helped by providing feedback or by answering long lists of questions. President Carter's ambassador to Panama at that time, Ambler H. Moss, Jr., has not only read the manuscript but added details, such as a description of Benes's request to his office in the American Embassy in Panama to use a secure phone to speak with Peter Tarnoff at the State Department in Washington. Robert A. Pastor, President Carter's Latin American advisor on the National Security Council, also read the manuscript and made helpful comments. I spoke with Peter Tarnoff, "Skip" Brandon, and Zbigniew Brzezinski by phone and corresponded with William Aramony, and several others.

For the secret negotiations during the Reagan years, corroboration is even more difficult, because as a CIA operation, it was never revealed publicly. I have spoken, however, with a senior CIA official, now retired, who worked with Benes not only in Miami and Washington but also in Mexico, and with a senior FBI agent, also now retired, who worked on the negotiations. During a week at the United States Air Force Academy in which both I and General Vernon A. Walters, former deputy director of the CIA and ambassador-at-large, participated in a program related to Latin America, we had two talks about Latin America in general and about Cuba in particular. General Walters sent me a copy of his privately published and out-of-print memoirs after he returned from Colorado Springs; unfortunately, however, his book was published in the mid-1970s, so it does not contain information about Walters's secret trip to meet with Castro as part of the negotiation process. Fortunately, we spoke about it at length over the telephone, and he gave me permission to quote him.

I also contacted James Baker and George Shultz, both members of President Reagan's cabinet when, under the prodding of the CIA, a meeting was held to discuss the implications of offering Castro normalized relations in all areas as long as he abandoned his efforts to export his revolution abroad. Both Baker and Shultz replied that they had "no recollection" of the meeting, but one could argue that "no recollection" is not a hard-and-fast denial.

Former Florida State Senator Jack Gordon confirmed Benes's story—told in chapter three—about the Johnson and Murphy boots he brought for Castro to replace his Florsheims. I have spoken with members of militant organizations and with Cuban political prisoners who languished in jail for a decade and a half before Benes's negotiations won their release in 1978. I have interviewed journalists who interviewed Benes immediately after what he expected to be his triumphant return from Havana with the first planeload of released prisoners.

In mid-2000, Benes wrote to one of the Cubans with whom he had negotiated. He asked if government officials would clarify some points and permit me to interview them. The response was: "Fidel Castro prefers to dwell on the present and on the future, not the past."[11]

Several persons central to this book's themes have died since the events in which they played major roles. These include President John F. Kennedy; Senator Abraham Ribicoff; Representative Claude Pepper, Representative Dante Fascell, CIA Director William Casey, and Jorge Mas Canosa. President Ronald Reagan, suffering from Alzheimer's disease, unfortunately cannot be asked about the clandestine attempts to strike a deal with Castro.

CHAPTER ONE

BEGINNINGS

One day in August 1977, immediately before leaving for a vacation trip with his family to western North Carolina, a call arrived for Bernardo Benes from Ricardo de la Espriella, his friend from the time when he worked under contract to the United States Agency for International Development (USAID) and now Panama's vice-president. De la Espriella asked him to change his plans and come to Panama instead. Benes's first inclination was to turn down the invitation. But Benes had close ties in Panama because of his work as an advisor for home-building financing for USAID and for creating a United Way chapter there. In 1969, in fact, the Panamanian government awarded him the country's highest honor given to foreigners, the Vasco Núñez de Balboa Medal with the degree of Knight Commander. Ricardo de la Espriella later would be president of Panama until replaced by General Manuel Noriega in February 1984.

Feeling a sense of personal obligation, Benes changed his mind and accepted. He often flew to Panama on banking business, and it seemed reasonable to him that de la Espriella would want to see him. The true reason would turn out to be stranger in many ways than fiction.

The Benes family arrived in Panama City on August 21, 1977. They stayed at the Panama Hilton, intending to swim, sightsee, and relax. The morning after they arrived, they all went to the hotel's breakfast room, accompanied by Roberto "Mango" López, de la Espriella's chauffeur. During their meal, Bernardo's daughter, Lishka, went up to her room, but

1.1   Panama City, 1969, Office of General Omar Torrijos, meeting on housing needs. Those present include Torrijos (seated, middle); Florida Senator Jack Gordon; Henry Schoville, Director of Housing for the International Development Bank; Benes; and others. Bernardo Benes collection.

she returned quickly, a bit agitated. She said that Alberto Pons, Benes's Cuban-Panamanian friend, had called on the phone and had insisted on speaking with her father. Pons had left Cuba in 1952 when Batista had come to power and had become successful in Panama, obtaining a Mc-Gregor franchise and also manufacturing custom *guayaberas*, the elegant cotton shirts worn by men in lieu of suitjackets.

Benes picked up the phone in the breakfast room and, after the usual introductory small talk, was told by Pons: "Look, I want to invite you to lunch because some Cubans are here to see you." Benes recalls that he became confused, and asked Pons, "Which Cuba?" since for him now "Cubans" also meant Cubans from Miami. Pons replied that they were from Castro's government, and that they would meet at the Panamar, Benes's favorite seafood restaurant, at 1:00 P.M. Bernardo briefly considered declining but gave in to his curiosity. His family, accustomed to being disappointed by last-minute changes, went off by themselves with

1.2   Receipt from Panamar Restaurant. Bernardo Benes collection.

"Mango" López as their driver. But first López dropped Benes off at the restaurant. Benes figured that the Cubans had asked to see him because of his links to President Jimmy Carter, with whom Benes had been photographed many times during Carter's campaign in Florida.

Benes's change of mind to accept the invitation to lunch with some strangers turned out to be the most fateful decision of his life.

Benes arrived before the others and killed time chatting with Mr. Sierra, the owner of the Panamar and an old acquaintance. Then, at about 1:15, Pons entered with three Cubans. One was Antonio "Tony" de la Guardia, whom Benes had known from his days in the anti-Batista student movement. The second was introduced as José Luis Padrón, whom Benes described later as "of strong complexion and short." The third turned out to be Amado Padrón, Cuba's consul in Panama. They sat at a discreet corner table on a terrace overlooking the Pacific Ocean, ordered grilled lobster and *corvina* (sea bass), and talked for almost three hours.[1]

They discussed mostly trivial matters. The Cubans avoided topics of substance and were cautious in their replies to Benes's questions. At the conclusion of the lunch, Pons and the others invited Benes to dine with them that evening at Pons's home. This time Benes declined because of his family. Having eaten earlier with his wife and children, Benes arrived at Pons's house at 9:30 P.M., where the men chatted until six in the morning. This time, however, the conversation was far from cautious, dealing with issues ranging from the United States economic embargo to Cuban political prisoners.[2] The discussion between the Cubans and Benes in Panama lasted for almost ten hours. The Cubans seemed not to care about the conversation in particular. It was almost as if they were sizing Benes up, assessing his personality, his ambitions, and his weaknesses.

The rest of the vacation proceeded without incident or further contact. As soon as Benes returned to Miami, however, he contacted Larry Sternfield, a CIA agent he had met during his USAID work in Latin America. "Larry," he recalled saying, "who are they?" Sternfield arrived at Benes's bank eight hours later with photographs of Padrón and de la Guardia. The men, who Benes assumed were minor Cuban officials, were among the top members of the revolutionary regime's intelligence service, Sternfield observed. Padrón was "Fidel Castro's proxy and right-hand man internationally," and de la Guardia was Padrón's assistant. They were both officers in the elite Special Forces of the Interior ministry. Benes recalls that the news stunned him, and he asked Sternfield to advise him.

Sternfield told Benes to continue talking to the Cubans and to keep him informed about what was said. He added that Washington had given the green light for additional meetings.[3] Bernardo recalls that the issue of political prisoners touched him deeply, and that during the mid-1970s, he and journalist Humberto Medrano had taken out a full-page ad in the

Miami Herald denouncing Castro's government for its treatment of political prisoners. Reports by such groups as the International Society for Human Rights of inhuman treatment in Cuban prisons circulated widely but were ignored by Cuban officials. Luis Martínez, a prisoner in *Tres Marías* Prison in Oriente province, told of spending two weeks in punishment boxes, where he and seven other men were each forced into a cell space of no more than eighteen inches wide. Martínez and the others went on a hunger strike, spitting out or vomiting the food that guards forced into their mouths.[4] Even "regular" prison regimens in Cuba, where dissidents and others were jailed for political "crimes," were harsh—for men as well as for women.

Only Fidel Castro or perhaps José Luis Padrón knew why the Cuban intelligence agents had sought out Benes. What the Cubans wanted were persons sufficiently idealistic to act as go-betweens between Havana and Washington, who could accomplish this without news leaking out, especially to the Miami exile community. The answer possibly rests on the fact that Benes's civic activities in Miami were well known, and that in 1977 he was the second closest Cuban exile to the Carter administration, after Alfredo Durán, the Florida Democratic Party chair. In addition, Benes had played soccer at the University of Havana with Raúl Castro.

Also, Benes, as well as de la Guardia and Padrón, had spent a good deal of time in Panama. The Cubans used Panama as a convenient base of intelligence (and business) operations. Benes had been traveling to Panama since the early 1960s. Charles (Carlos) Dascal, his partner, shared business interests there—and after his talk with Larry Sternfield, Benes invited Dascal to accompany him on his trips to Cuba.[5]

Because Benes had asked his partner to join him, the Cubans presumably investigated Dascal, too. It is now known that when the Cubans found an acceptable individual to perform tasks useful to them, they not only rolled out the red carpet but they created opportunities to put their guests in compromising positions that could be used against them.[6] None of this happened during Benes and Dascal's visits—the Cubans knew they had nothing to hide—but as for Benes, they apparently found his ebullience, intelligence, and concern for human welfare to be attractive characteristics for a potential "dialoguer." Because he was an outsider in Miami, Benes's vulnerability and anxiousness to help made it easier to manipulate him into a false sense of importance. If this was the Cubans' reasoning, they had done their research well.

In various places—Nassau (at the Hotel Britannia), Mexico City (at the Hotel María Isabel), Jamaica (at the Pegasus), and Panama (at the Hilton)—Benes, Padrón, and de la Guardia continued to meet, joined now by Dascal, Benes's boss and business partner, whom Benes had invited along, in his words, for companionship and because Dascal was extremely perceptive. He had been Bernardo's brother's closest friend from childhood. In Miami, Dascal had become financially successful; the automobile franchise that he and Benes had obtained from the Ford Motor Company was the first Cuban-American-owned agency in the United States, and had expanded by the 1990s to become the forty-second top company in Miami, ranked by revenue.[7] Dascal chaired Continental National Bank, where Benes served as vice-chair. They were co-founders of the bank. Dascal later became chairman and chief executive officer, serving on the board of Florida International University's Foundation as well.

Once the secret meetings with Castro began in February 1978, Dascal played an equal role throughout the negotiation process as Benes's partner. Benes talked more about human rights issues; Dascal engaged Castro and his aides more on details and on the possibilities for business with Cuba if normal relations were restored. Castro enjoyed Dascal's presence and found him a good conversationalist.[8] According to a Carter administration official, Dascal tended to be more retiring, leaving to Benes the task of maintaining phone contact with Secretary of State Vance's Executive Secretariat, Peter Tarnoff, and others in Washington.

But in Miami, Dascal, an astute businessman and a shrewd student of Cuban–United States politics, avoided publicity and kept his role as quiet as possible. Benes, whose role in the dialogue and prisoner release was spread across the front pages of Miami newspapers and broadcast over the airwaves, became identified as the main target. Benes returned on the plane with the first group of released prisoners; Dascal quietly slipped back into South Florida without notice. As a result of his determination to be kept out of the limelight, Dascal rarely was attacked in Miami, and his role remained largely undisclosed.

After a few months of clandestine meetings, the Cubans began to suggest that Castro might be willing to meet with Cuban exiles as a measure to improve relations, and, during a five-day visit to Cuba by twenty-three New England businessmen, Castro informed the group that there might be ways to permit exiles to return to visit their families. In December, Representative Richard Kelly (R-FL) visited Cuba and conversed with Castro, who told him that he would like to do something to reunite exiles with their loved ones.[9] Less than a month after Benes's lunch with the Cubans, Havana and Washington opened "Special Interests Sections" in each other's capital cities, the first formal diplomatic link since relations between the two countries ceased on January 3, 1961. What neither the Benes-Dascal team nor the Castro government realized, however, was how seriously Cuba's military involvement in Africa bothered the Carter administration. President Gerald Ford refused to negotiate with Cuba at all, but Carter left the door open—provided that, as he told CBS's Walter Cronkite in a televised interview, Cuba withdrew from Africa prior to any normalization of relations.[10] Zbigniew Brzezinski, Carter's director of the National Security Council, took an especially hard line on Cuba's support of revolution in Africa because he tended to see foreign policy through the lens of the Cold War with the Soviet Union. When he considered problems in individual places—Cuba, Nicaragua, the Middle East—Brzezinski always thought first of how any new policy might give an advantage to Moscow.

Brzezinski showed tremendous concern for Cuban actions in Africa. In April 1978, 17,000 Cuban troops were stationed in Ethiopia alone. Taking the cue from his National Security Council director, President Carter said publicly, "There is no possibility that we would see any substantial improvement in our relationship with Cuba as long as [Castro is] committed to this military intrusion policy in the internal affairs of African people. There is no doubt in my mind that Cuba is used by the Soviet Union as surrogates in several places in Africa."[11] The National Security Council also worried abut the crisis in Nicaragua, where efforts to rid the country of the long-entrenched Somoza dictatorship had led to the emergence of the Sandinista rebels, fully backed by Cuba and the Soviet Union.

Castro's gambit to hold a public "dialogue" with non-militant Miami Cubans, as the press explained after the first released prisoners began to arrive in Florida, involved others besides Benes and Dascal. "In Kingston, Jamaica," *Miami Herald* reporters wrote later, patronizingly:

A bearded preacher whose black eyes held a zealot's glint behind thick rectangular spectacles visited an embassy to ask some questions. They didn't throw him out but he got a very cold shoulder. The diplomats already thought he was a pest. Back in Miami people were calling him a crackpot. In Washington, a slick-haired, jowly Carter administration official met a long-time friend for coffee and a chat. He had done the same thing often before, but this time the conversation made him uncomfortable. He immediately reported it to the National Security Council. . . . On his own [pastor Manuel Espinosa] had made two attempts the year before to contact Castro by sailing from Key West to Cuba, but his efforts had failed. On one of the trips he had been arrested and jailed for three days before being released. Ultimately, he succeeded in convincing Cuban officials to permit members of his congregation to visit. "I'm no saint, but I'm no crook either," the bearded Espinosa said when asked in Miami to explain what he had been up to.

The *Herald* reporters proved to be very perceptive about Espinosa. He ran his Hialeah church, they alleged, more as a business than as a place of worship. One of the first Miami Cubans to speak out publicly in favor of dialogue with Cuba, later he abruptly turned about-face, inciting hatred against Benes and the other *dialogueros* as communists and Castro agents. By broadcasting harangues over the Miami Cuban radio stations, Espinosa more than anyone else put the lives of Benes and the others who had gone to Cuba in jeopardy.

No one, of course, knew this in 1977. Final plans emerged after a trip to New York City and Washington by Padrón and del la Guardia, joined by Dascal and Benes. The secret mission to Cuba for the Carter administration, which Sternfield had authorized, began to take shape.

Early in January 1978, the Cuban intelligence officers José Luis Padrón and Tony de la Guardia visited South Florida. Jim Freeman, the FBI agent assigned to Benes and Dascal, wondered if it might be a good idea to invite the two Cubans for a weekend at the Boca Raton Yacht and Country Club. Benes agreed, and on Thursday night dined with them at the club which, Benes remembered, was still decorated for Christmas and filled with wealthy members and guests. After their meal, Padrón and Benes walked around the pool, taking in the extraordinary luxury of the grounds. According to Benes, Padrón said: "I don't know why my comrades work so arduously around Fidel. I do know I am on his side because he wants the best for the Cuban people." Then Padrón paused, dropping his voice. "After seeing this, I am convinced that any effort will be useless." What he meant, Benes figured out later, was that Cubans would never attain the quality of life and comfort he had seen in Boca Raton. When Padrón returned with Benes to the group, he had reverted to his old self, although he would remain closer to Benes than ever before. During another meeting, in New York City, he told Benes that his idol was New York Yankees center fielder Mickey Mantle. Benes and Dascal understood what Padrón meant: he wanted to see the Yankees play. So they went to a game against the Seattle Mariners and bought Yankee caps for Padrón and de la Guardia. Some weeks later, in Padrón's residence in Havana, Benes saw the cap prominently displayed on the wall along with other hats, mostly from military uniforms, from all over the world.

On February 12, 1978, Bernardo Benes and Carlos Dascal returned to Cuba after eighteen years in exile. They flew first to Jamaica, where a black Mercedes picked them up at the airport and took them to the handsome residence of the Cuban consul in Kingston, Ramón de la Cruz. For the next year and a half, all contact between the Americans and Cubans passed through the consul, who excelled as an intermediary. When they referred to Castro, they used the term "*El Tío*" (Uncle). No message ever passed directly between Havana and Washington or Miami.

"Adolfito," a special agent who had arrived on the plane with Padrón and de la Guardia, took Benes to a room. The agent removed Benes's glasses and placed a black moustache and toupée on him, then took photographs. Half an hour later, Benes and Dascal received Cuban diplomatic passports, which, they were told, could be used only for clandestine exit from the Kingston airport if needed.[12] He and Dascal were then flown to Havana in a sixteen-seat Antonov airplane marked CU–800. The two colonels, Padrón and de la Guardia, and "Adolfito" accompanied them. They did not land at Havana's José Martí International Airport but at Baracoa military airport near Santa Fé, west of the city of Havana. They landed at 9:00 P.M. Rain poured down. Several black Mercedes-Benz government automobiles were waiting for them in the dark. Two guards flanked each limousine. Benes recalls that the scene later reminded him of a similar one in the television series "Mission Impossible."

The cars raced through Havana and delivered Benes and Dascal to the Cuban State Security Department's Protocol House #1, at Santa María del Mar, a beach east of Havana. They remained there for only ten minutes and then were taken by Padrón and de la Guardia to the Palace of the Revolution, formerly the Ministry of Justice building. They entered via an underground garage facing south, into an elevator. When the door opened, Fidel Castro, in his customary olive drab fatigues, greeted them. Benes exited from the elevator first:

> "How are you, Benes?" Castro said, using the formal Spanish "¿Como está Usted?"
> "How are you, Fidel?" Benes replied, using the familiar "¿Como estas Fidel?"

Spontaneously, Benes said to Castro: "If you write me a check for one million dollars to repay the value of what you took from my father, we would understand each other better."[13] Castro responded by narrowing his eyes to the point at which one could not see his pupils, and Benes, realizing his gaffe, tried the opposite approach. "Fidel," he said, "you must remember from your Jesuit education the story of Moses' forty years in the desert. For me, it has taken only eighteen years of exile to reach the Promised Land."

Castro then introduced the Cuban exiles to his aide, Pepín Naranjo, whom Benes had known from his university days, and to General José Abrantes, his chief security officer and also a member of the Communist Party's Central Committee. Both would be present at some point in all of the fourteen face-to-face meetings with Benes and Dascal during the next seven months.[14]

CUBAN BEGINNINGS

Bernardo Benes's father, Baruch, was born in the city of Minsk, Belarus, in 1905. In 1923, a few months after his seventeenth birthday, he left the Soviet Union, where conditions under the Bolsheviks were worsening. His family had literally been reduced to digging up roots in the woods for food. Baruch, accompanied by a friend of his father's, crossed Europe and boarded a Havana-bound freighter at the port of Le Havre in northern France. They would rather have journeyed to the United States, but by that year anti-immigrant policies had begun to close the country's formerly open doors. Baruch arrived in Havana with $20 that his father's friend had given him, and traveled to the city of Matanzas, sixty miles east of Havana. He used the remaining cash to purchase cotton cloth from which he made handkerchiefs and other items, peddling them door to door on credit. With his business expanding, he learned some Spanish, changed his name from Baruch to Boris, and eventually prospered.[15] Despite his success, throughout his life, Boris remained a dour man, bearing a burden of which he would never speak.

Bernardo learned the full story of his father's family only in 1994. They had died in the Nazi concentration camps or in the German bombing of Minsk, and possibly because he felt so much pain, Boris attempted throughout most of his life to protect his children by remaining silent. At the time of his death, he believed that he had no living relatives, although much later Bernardo discovered a number of cousins in the former Soviet Union who had miraculously survived World War II. One of them, Galina Sinelnikova, a pediatrician, had seen a photograph of the Benes family in her late father's personal items in 1984 and had spent years attempting to locate members.

Bernardo's mother, Dora Baikovitz, emigrated in 1928 from Kovno, Lithuania, to Cuba, and met Boris in Matanzas. Bernardo, their third child, was born on December 27, 1934. The two older siblings were Jaime, four years older, and Ana, a year and a half older and red-haired like Bernardo. When Bernardo turned five the family moved to a house in the Matanzas Hill, on Milanés Street. Boris Benes had started to prosper, and his new house was one of two adjacent chalets with porches and wood columns. The other house belonged to Dr. Mario Dihigo, an influential physician. Boris Benes owned a leather warehouse at the intersection of Cuba and Compostela streets in Matanzas, which he kept even after he moved his family to Havana.

Matanzas, a quiet, provincial capital, offered a pleasant setting for a young child. The family would visit the surrounding Yumurí Valley and visit the Ermita de los Catalanes, a colonial-era Spanish church. The boy found the landscape to be extraordinary—a little river, full of bends and lined with Cuban palms, meandered at the valley bottom, and then there were the unforgettable Bellamar caves. Close to the Matanzas house was

Machado Park, at the entrance of the city. *Guajiros* (rural peasants) sold their produce at the city's plaza in weekly markets and troubadours played and sang *puntos guajiros* (rustic ballads). Boris Benes's economic success, after only ten years in a country where he arrived not speaking the language, was remarkable, especially considering that the Great Depression affected Cuba even more severely than it had the United States. Many, if not most of the thousands of Russian and East European Jews who came to Cuba in the early 1920s remained poor, living from day to day. For a number of years, Boris walked the streets as a peddler, until he managed to buy a two-door Ford and expand his business. Later, he found a way to manufacture the items sold by peddlers and thus become a supplier and ultimately an industrialist.

On Sundays, the family dined at a Chinese *fonda,* a modest restaurant named Los Tres Amigos, and the city's police band also performed concerts in the park that day. In 1940, the family went to see the Russian film *Balalaika* without their father, who was late in arriving from a trip to Havana. When they returned home, they found him wrapped in bandages from head to foot. He had fallen asleep while driving his car, and his life was saved only by the fact that a group of men from a baseball team traveling in a truck along the Central Highway found him immediately after his accident.

When Bernardo was still a young boy, Sander Baikovitz, his maternal grandfather, visited the Benes family from Lithuania. Trips of this kind were extremely rare, and presumably Bernardo's father paid the fare. This was the only time in his life that Bernardo would see any of his grandparents, and sadly, during his trip home, his grandfather caught pneumonia and died in New York, where he was buried.

Roughly fifteen Jewish families lived in Matanzas, then more of a town than a city. On alternate years they joined together at the Benes's home to observe the High Holy Days—Rosh Hashanah and Yom Kippur—as individual families tried to maintain their Jewish identity. Children, usually boys, were tutored in Yiddish, the language of East European Ashkenazi Jews. Bernardo and his siblings took weekly Yiddish classes and received a violin lesson from Alexander Prilutchi, principal violinist in the Havana Symphony Orchestra. Matanzas also had its scandals, like any small city. In one of the Jewish families, the wife came home, found her husband in bed

1.3 Matanzas, ca. 1936. Birthday party. Bernardo (first row far left), Ana (first row, fifth from left), and Jaime (sixth from left). Bernardo Benes collection.

with another woman, and murdered him. Other daily events—shopping for food once a day, deliveries of milk and eggs—were more mundane, distinctive of the slower life everywhere in Cuba but Havana.

The Benes children lived normal lives, although they heard epithets about "dirty Jews" and "Cuba is for Cubans." Bernardo visited the homes of his friends, most of them Roman Catholic. When he was three or four, he noticed that the houses all had pictures of Jesus on their walls. Jewish homes were different, of course, and it took a while for Bernardo to understand. There was no Jewish school or any synagogue in the city.

One day, when Bernardo was about six, his father announced that the family would move to Havana, where he just signed a contract to buy the "Perro" undershirt factory. They rented a large house in Guanabacoa, a small city close to Havana. The children entered private schools, including Edison in the neighborhood of La Víbora, and, in Guanabacoa, Colegio Lancha. After their move to Vedado, they attended the Colegio Añorga elementary school. Eventually, the Benes children attended and graduated from Ruston Academy, an elite American-run preparatory school. Almost all of its students were from Havana's wealthiest families or were children of diplomats or high-level foreign businessmen. In this regard, Cuba differed substantially from other Latin American countries, where the children of outsiders were typically unwelcome in prestigious private schools.

To graduate, the Ruston seniors took their examinations at the respected Instituto del Vedado. Because he graduated high school at the age of sixteen in 1951, Bernardo was too young to enter the University of Havana. Boris convinced Bernardo to study in the United States. Bernardo applied and was accepted to the University of Maryland, as his older brother Jaime had done before going on to a degree in chemical engineering at Case Western Reserve University (then the Case Institute of Technology) in Cleveland. But after traveling to College Park and buying all of his books and bedding, Bernardo found that he had been assigned to a makeshift freshman dormitory twenty-five blocks from the main campus. Chilled by the September weather, on the first day of classes, Bernardo packed up his things, gave his newly purchased lamp to his roommate of a day, and hitched a ride to his mother's cousin's house in Washington, D.C. The following day Bernardo flew to New York, and after visiting an uncle for several days, returned to Havana.

To deal with his underage status, he entered the University of Havana as a "free" student, an auditor who takes the final examination. In the morning he sat in on law classes, and at night he took courses in commercial subjects and accountancy. Ultimately, he received degrees both in law and public accounting. Although his family was completely apolitical, he became attracted to the reformist, social democratic *Partido Ortodoxo* (Orthodox Party). He admired Eddy Chibás and José Pardo Llada, the party leaders. Pardo Llada had a popular daily radio program at 1:00 in the afternoon and on Sundays, Eddy Chibás spoke at 8:00 in the evening. The tie was made even closer by the fact that his brother's best friend was the son of Roberto Agramonte, the Ortodoxo candidate for the presidency until Batista's coup in March 1952 terminated the elections scheduled for June.

After his last law school class, Bernardo usually headed straight for his family's club, the Casino Deportivo. Many members were Jews, excluded by unwritten custom from the so-called Big Five clubs of Havana's elite.

1.4   Benes receiving Bar Association Award from Fidel Castro, 1959. Bernardo Benes collection.

Cuban high society put family status even over political power: the Big Five also excluded Fulgencio Batista because of his mixed racial origins.

At the Casino, Benes and his friends swam for an hour, had lunch, and in the afternoon played poker or dominoes; sometimes they studied. At night they went to the movies or to baseball games. Like many Cuban youths, Benes developed a strong interest in baseball—*la pelota*, Cuba's national sport. In the United States, professional baseball barred black athletes until 1947; Cuban teams had been racially integrated since the beginning of the century. Benes started to watch games in Matanzas with his uncle, Enrique, at the Palmar del Junco stadium and later at Havana's La Tropical Stadium at the park run by La Tropical brewery. Ultimately, he rooted for Cienfuegos in the winter and in the summer for the Cuban Sugar Kings, a Triple-A minor league team in the farm system of the Cincinnati Reds. Bernardo followed the Sugar Kings to spring training at Central Cunagua, a sugar refinery in Camagüey province. After he developed a friendship with Bobby Maduro, the co-owner of El Cerro Stadium and the Sugar Kings, he found himself in need of Maduro's protection.

At one night game, after the police had been tipped off that students planned an anti-Batista demonstration in the stadium, they rushed in, found Bernardo in the stands, and marched him out of the stadium with machine guns poking into his ribs. Maduro had been watching this from his box and intervened in Benes's favor. His act of protection, which occurred a second time as well, consolidated in Benes a lifelong sense of affection for Maduro.[16]

Bernardo remembers the day the Japanese bombed Pearl Harbor. The first edition of the evening newspaper *El País*, on December 7, 1941, headlined the outbreak of war. Benes was home, ill with chicken pox. Another blow was the death of his uncle in Matanzas of a heart attack. The uncle, Israel Baikovitz, was his father's partner in the leather warehouse; for Bernardo, it was his first personal loss.

By emigrating to Cuba, Bernardo's mother and father had unknowingly saved themselves from the horrors of World War II and the Holocaust. Since the turn of the century, Cuba had provided refuge for thousands of Jews from the lands of the Mediterranean and from Central and Eastern Europe. From 1935 to early 1942 (except for the period immediately after the June 1939 arrival of the Hamburg-American Line S. S. *St. Louis*, the refugee ship that was turned away by both Cuba and the United States), Cuba opened its doors to Jews fleeing the Nazis, if they could pay off immigration officials. The new arrivals discovered, as had the immigrants who had come to Cuba earlier, that Cuba was a pleasant country with a live-and-let-live attitude toward people with light skin but that it also was deeply corrupt. Elections turned on false vote counts, bribery, and payoffs. Fred Wahl, a Polish refugee who lived in Havana from 1936 to 1940 before gaining entry to United States, explains what Cuban residents needed to do to obtain entry permits for relatives still trapped in Europe: "I went to the office of General Manuel Benítez, the head of immigration. I handed him an envelope with four hundred fifty dollars and the names of my family. He shook my hand and told me to wait fifteen minutes, after which time his secretary gave me the permits."[17] Fulgencio Batista, who, since the 1933 revolution, ran Cuba from behind the scenes, had appointed Benítez. Batista and his cronies received millions of dollars in graft, a way of life on the island.

Nevertheless, during all of this, the Benes family prospered. They lived in Vedado from 1942 to 1947. Then they moved into a large, handsome house in Santos Suárez, next to the home of Nicolás Castellanos, who became mayor of Havana when the incumbent, Manuel Fernández Supervielle, committed suicide in the face of growing opposition to his administration's failure to provide potable water for the city. When Castellanos asked Benes to sell his house to him, Benes agreed and exchanged houses with him, and a few years later the family moved again, this time to Miramar, one of Havana's most desired neighborhoods.

STORM CLOUDS

Two major political events changed everything during the early 1950s. In 1951, Eddy Chibás, the leader of the reformist Ortodoxo Party, committed suicide after he had denounced President Carlos Prío Socarrás's education minister, Aureliano Sánchez Arango, for corruption but then was unable to produce evidence supporting his allegations. Then, on March 10, 1952, Fulgencio Batista carried out a coup d'état, making himself chief of state. The reformists entered a period of disarray. The student federation held rallies against Batista, but the participants quickly disbanded when the police shot live bullets over the heads of the protesters. One of the young members of the Ortodoxo Party, a congressional candidate in the canceled 1952 electoral race, was Fidel Castro Ruz. He was born on August 13, 1926, to Lina Ruz and Ángel Castro. His father was a Spanish-born immigrant who owned a large sugar plantation in Oriente province. Castro, one of seven children in the family, grew up as a member of the gentry, attended Jesuit schools, played basketball and baseball fairly well (although not nearly well enough to be offered a major league contract as a pitcher for the then-Washington Senators, as rumors hold), and attended the University of Havana Law School. There, he strutted around with a .45 caliber revolver in a holster and was considered an arrogant dreamer, according to Benes and others, by fellow students.[18]

In 1948 Castro married Mirta Diaz-Balart, the daughter of one of Batista's closest supporters. They had one son, Fidel Castro Ruz Diaz-Balart, but divorced in 1954. Benes recalls that once Castro graduated he rarely practiced law, but lived on an allowance provided by his father.

Once, the story went, he received $40 to buy food for his family but used it instead to purchase the complete set of writings by Benito Mussolini.

In 1952, Castro precipitated a bizarre scene at the Supreme Court when he demanded to address the justices and then denounced Batista's recent coup. The young man insisted that Batista be sentenced to one hundred years in prison for usurping power over the country. Batista is said to have laughed at this, and chose not to jail the young man with influential in-laws.

Castro reemerged in mid-1953. With 165 poorly armed young men, on July 26, he led a surprise assault during the city's celebration of its patron saint on the Moncada Barracks, Cuba's second largest military encampment, in Santiago de Cuba in Oriente province. But the attack failed; twenty-two soldiers and eight rebels died. After the surviving rebels were captured, Batista's soldiers murdered fifty-six of them. Others were beaten or tortured. Castro stayed hidden, under the protection of the archbishop of Santiago, Enrique Pérez Serantes, an old friend of Castro's father, Ángel Castro, until he was captured and tried as the leader of the assault on the barracks.[19] During his trial, Castro acted as defense lawyer for his comrades and later in self-defense in his trial. Castro and his younger brother Raúl, one of the leaders of the attack, were taken to Boniato prison in Oriente province to await transportation to the Island of Pines. While there, Jesús Yáñez Pelletier, the prison superintendent, intercepted information about a Batista government plot to kill Castro. For refusing to participate, the army dismissed Pelletier, and ultimately he was forced into exile, only to return after Castro took power.[20]

Not long after he and Raúl arrived at the Model (pronounced Mo-*dell*) Prison on the Isle of Pines, built a decade earlier by dictator Gerardo Machado, Castro allegedly bragged in letters to his comrades that he was living well and enjoying the sun and air. He wrote drafts of his political program and denunciations of Batista's murders and corruption, and sent them to Jorge Mañach, the founder of the reformist ABC Party in 1933. Mañach, a well-known intellectual, enriched the text with erudite references to Greek and Latin classics and published it underground as *History Will Absolve Me*.[21] The book's title came from Castro's final words at his trial, "Condemn me, no matter, history will absolve me."[22] In his book, Castro advocated revolution, but in the form of social reform. The University of Havana, he noted, graduated an average of 200 physicians annually, for whom there were no jobs; in 1955 more than 3,000 physicians remained unemployed. *History Will Absolve Me* spoke to the middle classes,

> [to] the 10,000 . . . doctors, engineers, lawyers, veterinarians, school teachers, dentists, pharmacists, newspapermen, painters, sculptors, etc., who come forth from school with their degrees, anxious to work and full of hope, only to find themselves at a dead end with all doors closed and where no one hears their clamor or supplication.[23]

In 1955, Batista amnestied Castro and Raúl and permitted them to leave for Mexico.[24] Once again, Castro's ties to the elite rescued him. Raúl, who as a youth had been affiliated with the Cuban Communist Party (PSP) did not tell his brother for years, but he obviously was more of a hardline leftist than Castro, whose office even after the revolution (for a while) contained crucifixes and Roman Catholic memorabilia. In Mexico, for the first time, they met the idealistic, young Argentine revolutionary, Ernesto "Che" Guevara, whom they welcomed as a comrade and pressed into service as the group's physician. Anti-Batista exiles in Florida, led by former president Carlos Prío Socarrás, sent them enough money to purchase a barely seaworthy yacht, the *Granma*, at the port of Tuxpan on Mexico's Yucatán Peninsula. Eighteen months later, in December 1956, *Granma*, carrying eighty-two badly seasick rebels, reached the southern coast of Cuba, after a harrowing, weeklong voyage. Shore police, who fired on the boat, discovered them. Only twenty survived, including Castro, Raúl, and Guevara.[25] Some accounts claim that the survivors numbered twelve, a veiled reference to Christ's twelve apostles.[26] To show Castro's mettle, when the remnant band, unarmed and on the run, whined about their predicament, their leader supposedly replied: "Gentlemen. We have won! We are still alive!"

Castro's guerrilla exploits caught the imagination not only of his rebels but also much of Cuba's educated middle class, which had supported the reformist Ortodoxo Party before Batista's 1952 coup. Batista's decision to amnesty the Moncada attackers before the end of their prison terms showed that he did not understand the depth of opposition to his regime.[27] The brutality of his agents turned public opinion and distressed the United States. In the words of Wayne S. Smith, then a junior Cuba-watcher at the State Department's Bureau of Intelligence and Research:

> Batista always controlled tremendously superior forces. The problem was within the corrupt and incompetent regime itself. Batista's police overreacted to insurgent pressure by torturing and killing hundreds, innocent and guilty alike. Bodies were left hanging from trees and alongside roadways.[28]

Cuba under Batista had become infested with American gangsters, casinos, nightclubs, and prostitution. Although most members of the upper class minded their own business, secluded in their private clubs and social circle, some exhibited a kind of languid arrogance that seemed to match the times. Few protested when Batista's police openly (and randomly) rounded up suspects of anti-regime activity and beat or murdered them. University classes went on, punctuated by student protests and occasional closings by the police. The decade also witnessed a political polarization among elites. On the far right, the *Diário de la Marina* newspaper maintained its pre-war, pro-Franco, anti-liberal, and anti-Semitic stance. Salvador Díaz-Versón, a journalist and author, founded Cuba's Anti-Communist League, although during World War II, when the Soviet Union became an ally, he shifted its tone to support the war effort. Batista's government followed conservative economic polices that aided United States investors on the island, but his administration was more corrupt than ideologically consistent. In the center, the Ortodoxo and other reform-minded parties remained helpless because Batista had canceled elections. And on the left, communists and socialists opposed Batista but mostly with words, not action. Open anti-Batista protest came mostly from university students, and, in September 1957, in the form of a joint uprising at the Cienfuegos naval base joined by civilians in the town. Batista's forces surrounded the area and smashed the rebellion, using everything from tanks to B–26 bombers.

Benes joined some of the student demonstrations during the late 1950s on the steps of the University of Havana. A friend, José Antonio Echeverría ("Manzanita") brought him into the University Students Federation (FEU), the student group opposing Batista. Bernardo's role was not central; however, as a law and accounting student, he helped raise funds for the movement. Benes also befriended two other student members of FEU:

Osmel Francis de los Reyes, a black law student from Guantánamo, and René Anillo, from Pinar del Rio. When on March 13, 1957, FEU leaders launched a failed attack on Havana's presidential palace, Bernardo hid Osmel in his sister Ana's house for half a year. The friends then had to leave Cuba, and when they married their fiancées, Bernardo signed proxies for them.

A turning point for Benes occurred during his final year of law school. Just before the end of his final semester in 1956, Osmel Francis told him that Professor Ramón Zaydín wanted to see Bernardo and Osmel at Zaydín's law offices on 162 Cuba Street in Old Havana. Zaydín and his cousin, Carlos Márquez Sterling, had been two of the drafters of Cuba's respected and socially progressive 1940 constitution. During World War II, Zaydín won election as senator from the Camagüey province and later served as a member of Cuba's United Nation's delegation.[29] By the 1950s, Zaydín himself had earned a reputation as one of the most lucid and charismatic law professors at the University of Havana.

Not knowing why he was being summoned, Bernardo imagined that he was in some kind of academic difficulty. Instead, Zaydín asked him if there were any other lawyers in his family. Benes replied in the negative, and engaged in further small talk, explaining what his father and brother did for a living. Then Zaydín asked him to join his law firm.

Benes replied that he would be honored. Zaydín told him that he would earn $75 a month, plus half of the billings of cases Benes brought in. At first, while waiting for his law degree, he mostly cleaned Zaydín's unkempt office and filed papers. Zaydín's public opposition to Batista had lost him clients, but by the end of the year Bernardo had earned $15,000, a small fortune for such a young man. He started out with his father and brother's businesses as his clients. In time, he became the attorney for Cuba's National Association of Textile Manufacturers, the Association of Tourism Merchants, and did pro bono work for Jewish organizations, including the Patronato, the main cultural and social center for affluent Cuban Jews. He and Zaydín also represented some real estate developers, some of whom built condominiums, then an innovative form of ownership.

In addition, Benes became a close friend of attorney Rafael Rubio Padilla. Whenever Benes faced an ethical issue, he would go to Rubio for advice. Rubio was a devout Roman Catholic with an impeccable sense of

fairness; to this he added a broad view of culture and a knowledge of
world affairs. The two men became so close that when Bernardo's parents
died decades later in Miami, he asked Rubio Padilla to give their eulogies.

As a teenager, Bernardo began to date Raquel "Ricky" Gurinsky, the
daughter of a well-to-do department store owner in Güines, a town in Havana province, who lived in Havana's Santos Suárez neighborhood. After
five years of courtship, they married, on February 23, 1958, the day before
Cuba's national celebration of the start of the war for independence from
Spain. Benes recalls that he selected the date because he and Ricky could
celebrate each year until late, because the next day would be a national
holiday. Ricky and Bernardo eventually had three children—Joel in Cuba,
Lishka and Edgar in the United States. Ricky provided constant emotional support to her husband throughout the ups and downs of his life,
even though the stress frequently left her exasperated.

The wedding ceremony occurred at the Patronato, the Jewish community in the suburbs of Havana dedicated in 1953 as the *Casa de la Comu-
nidad Hebrea de Cuba* (Jewish Community House). Because the facility
had been designed to serve the affluent Jewish families who had moved to
the suburbs rather than the less affluent Jewish residents of Old Havana,
it was built in the fashionable Vedado district. To a certain degree, it replaced the Centro Israelita, in the old city, where most of the impoverished Jewish immigrants had lived for decades (and where poor and
elderly Jews still live). The Patronato, as it was called, was a modern community center, with a social hall and meeting facilities. Construction costs
for the Patronato, designed by Aquiles Capablanca, one of Cuba's leading
architects, ran to almost a million dollars. To the affluent among Cuba's
Jews, it symbolized their rise from poverty to economic success and their
newly won civic respectability.

Among the guests invited to the opening of the Patronato had been
President Fulgencio Batista. Benes does not remember if the reason for
the invitation was that Batista was popular among the Jewish leaders or
that he was president of the Republic. The truth probably encompassed
both possibilities. Cuban Jews had been suspicious of Batista's predecessor
Socarrás's "Cuba for the Cubans" slogan, and Grau had tolerated the
anti-Semitic journalist (and congressman) Primitivo Rodríguez.[30] Many
of the most highly successful Jews in Cuba chose not to act against news

of atrocities by Batista's police and welcomed the sense of stability that at least superficially pervaded the country. At first, many liked Batista. His mixed-race origin made him tolerant of minority groups, unlike other Cuban politicians, who came from the white upper class and in many cases held racist views.

But by the mid-1950s, the dictator's support had started to ebb. In 1957, Batista forced a presiding judge, Manuel Urrutia Lleó, into exile for refusing to sentence a group of Castro supporters. In July, security police shot and killed Frank País, a leader of the 26th of July movement. Strikes erupted in three of Cuba's eastern provinces, and thousands marched in protest against the police violence. Castro called for a nationwide general strike in April 1958, but except in Santiago de Cuba, it failed. Batista, sensing the time was ripe for a counteroffensive, launched it in the Sierra Maestra. But by August, Castro's guerrillas had routed the government's forces. The tide had turned.

Others organized to oppose Batista as well. In the Escambray Mountains in Las Villas province, FEU student revolutionaries Fauré Chaumón and Rolando Cubela organized a guerrilla movement under the *Directorio Estudantil 13 de Marzo*. Eloy Gutiérrez Menoyo (who, according to Wayne Smith, "had the reputation of being something of a brigand") formed another rebel movement, the "Second" Escambray Front"[31] (*El Segundo Frente del Escambray*). Havana witnessed bombings and unrest, while eastern Cuba became the site of increasingly successful assaults on government sites. José Miró Cardona, former president of the Havana Bar Association, formed an independent underground anti-Batista group composed mostly of professionals sympathetic to Castro but not linked to his guerrilla movement. In November 1957, seven anti-Batista groups formed the Cuban Liberation Council, but Castro pulled out after a month because—as he admitted years later—he did not believe that his own group could control all of the others.[32]

Novice United States Ambassador Earl E. T. Smith—a political contributor to the Republican Party from Palm Beach, not a career diplomat—accepted Batista's arguments that his use of force was to combat communism, but a lengthy debate in Washington ensued on what to do about Cuba's violations of its defense agreements, which forbade the use of military weapons against civilians. Finally, on March 18, 1958, three days after Batista suspended constitutional guarantees, Washington banned arms sales to Cuba.

In that same month, Cuba's Joint Committee of Civic Institutions, representing forty-two religious, professional, and fraternal organizations, demanded Batista's resignation. He would be replaced, the committee's statement explained, by a provisional government "comprising citizens of outstanding prestige."[33] Some within the United States Embassy saw this as a possible opportunity to ditch Batista yet keep the government out of the hands of the guerrillas, but Ambassador Smith had become a personal friend of Batista. The Joint Committee was ignored, and the passing months witnessed a further downturn in Cuba's political stability.

Rebels under the command of Raúl Castro kidnapped nineteen civilians from the United States and Canada, employees of a foreign-owned mining company, and thirty enlisted men, including eleven marines, from a local American garrison. The hostages were released, but the action chilled the sympathy many United States members of Congress had felt for the revolutionary 26th of July movement. In November, hijackers who claimed to be members of Castro's anti-Batista offensive took over a plane during its flight from Miami to Varadero. They forced the pilot to fly to Oriente province and land, but the rebels there, who apparently knew nothing about the incident, refused to light the airfield. The plane crashed into Nipe Bay, killing most of the passengers, including the wife and three children of a Cuban-born American citizen. In mid-December, Batista delivered his children's passports to the United States Embassy for visas.[34]

Still, no one could have predicted what would happen next. The Benes family maintained their closeness even after Bernardo's marriage. Boris, Dora, and Bernardo's sister and her family occupied the same luxury apartment building in Miramar as Bernardo and Ricky, and his brother Jaime lived three blocks away. Uncles and cousins formed an extended family and frequently visited. Everything seemed fine but for the ominous political instability facing Cuba.

It must be remembered that Cuba's political atmosphere after the end of the Second World War reflected hope among the citizenry— Cuba had the highest literacy rate in Latin America and the second-highest standard of living—for social justice and functioning democratic institutions. The middle class put its hopes in reformist politics. The problem was that in Cuba officials themselves were almost universally corrupt, and that impunity increased as one rose in government circles. Reformist yearnings came to an abrupt halt with Batista's 1952 coup but revived again in support for Castro's 26th of July movement. Castro, after all, had been an Ortodoxo himself, and his pre-1959 position advocated nationalist reform, not socialism. Benes recalls Ramón Grau San Martín's pre-1952 regime:

> When the Cuban congress allocated millions of dollars for breakfasts for needy schoolchildren, the funds ended up in private bank accounts in Miami. Old currency notes earmarked to be burned ended up in private hands. Much of this money ended up in Key Biscayne real estate, building Miami Stadium, and other projects. The highest officials demanded bribes for contracts and tax breaks and sometimes stooped to extortion. When this got out of control, murders followed.[35]

Benes's parents had known about his membership in the student anti-Batista movement and wanted him to resign, but after he refused, they did not press him further. In fact, he worked as a volunteer in the financial section of the *13 de Marzo* organization, helping to raise funds. The reason for his parents' insistence that Bernardo not become an activist stemmed from the long-standing political passivity of Cuba's Jews, a conscious decision not to risk "making trouble" lest they be targeted as disloyal. Even among Jewish youths born in Cuba, the large majority shunned politics. Nor did most university students in general join the anti-Batista cause. Out of 15,000 students at the University of Havana, only between 1,000 and 1,500 probably participated.[36] Fidel Castro had also studied at the University of Havana, but before Benes. What no one knew—or remembered—was that in 1948, his final year of secondary school, Castro had applied for admission to Harvard College but was turned down.[37] As a law student, Castro spoke passionately about justice and nationalism but was never considered a communist, especially given the religious influences in his early life.

By 1955, the core student opposition to Batista had became more heated. Student leaders within the FEU organized the *Directorio Estudantil Revolucionario,* dedicated to the political overthrow of the dictatorship.

In March 1957, radical members of the FEU's *Directorio* carried out their plans to invade the presidential palace in an attempt to assassinate Batista, but failed. In retaliation, four of Benes's good friends, including Fructuoso Rodríguez, were gunned down in Humboldt Street. The president of the FEU, José Antonio Echevarria, also killed near the university, was buried in his hometown of Cárdenas. A large number of students, including Benes, by then a new lawyer, attended, as well as members of state security forces watching and taking down names. Batista's police regularly singled out activists for beatings or worse. The police murdered many students, some only suspected of activity in the movement.

In the last days of Batista's regime, Havana seemed much as it had been before. The dictator's police held the upper hand, and tourism, always at its height during the late fall and early winter, flourished. Actor Errol Flynn visited Havana in December and later fibbed that he had been in the mountains during the fighting. Some nightclub bands played banned songs associated with the rebel cause, including "*Mamá, son de la loma*" (Mama, they're from the hill), which the 26th of July's clandestine *Radio Rebelde* had taken as a kind of a theme song. People bet on when Batista would fall.[38]

THE COMING FLOOD

With Fidel Castro's forces controlling much of eastern Cuba, the United States State Department began to become actively involved in Cuban affairs, despite Ambassador Smith's inertia. United States and Cuban subsidiaries employed a tenth of all Cuban workers and controlled the power utilities, oil companies, and the most prosperous mines and sugar plantations. In February 1958, the United States Justice Department indicted former Cuban president Carlos Prío Socarrás and others for raising funds to launch an invasion from United States territory to overthrow Batista. In December, William D. Pawley, a friend of the Eisenhower administration, met secretly with General Batista to try to persuade him to accept exile in Florida, but Batista refused. His regime tottered. Days later, a Cuban air force pilot flew his B–26 to Miami and requested asylum. At 2:30 in the morning of New Year's Day, 1959, while Che Guevara's troops were taking command of the city of Santa Clara, Batista and his closest relatives and cronies flew from Camp Columbia airbase to the Dominican Republic. Throughout the night, various other flights took Batista's friends and high officials to Miami, West Palm Beach, New York, Mexico City, New Orleans, and Jacksonville. Batista's brother Panchín, the mayor of Havana, left too, as did mobster Meyer Lansky, by then suffering from ill health. Batista made no provision for the thousands of other Cubans who had worked for his regime.[39]

Among the "souvenirs" he took with him into exile, some claimed, was the twenty-carat diamond in the *Capitólio*, the seat of government. Meanwhile, revolutionary soldiers took control of the capital city and Fidel Castro took the Moncada Barracks in Oriente province, where his insurrection against Batista had begun on July 26, 1953. Havana celebrated Three Kings' Day amidst a heady atmosphere of excitement. A column in Havana's widely read *Diário de la Marina* compared Castro and his guerrillas to the Three Kings who had visited Bethlehem. As in the past, the journalist wrote, the Three Kings "came from the Oriente (East) and had beards." The Cuban Three Kings wore olive green, sent "by God to return good fortune to this island."[40]

A provisional government took power in the vacuum left by Batista's flight. Former Judge Manuel Urrutia became president, and José Miró Cardona, the former president of the Havana Bar Association and a respected professor of law, became prime minister. Fatigue-clad rebel soldiers, still carrying their rifles, occupied the posh offices and clubs in the city and relaxed. Warily, the United States recognized the new government on January 7. The next day, Fidel Castro, who had set out a week earlier in a slow, armed caravan from Santiago de Cuba, a distance of nearly 750 miles, arrived in Havana in triumph.

Castro made his first speech at the same Camp Columbia from which Batista had departed. The first thing he did was to proclaim the victory of his 26th of July movement—distancing himself, by so doing, from the other three anti-Batista groups: the *Directório Estudiantil*, the "Second Front of Escambray," and *la Organizacíon Auténtica*. The key phrase in his speech was "¿armas para qué?" ("arms for what?"). This shocked the other major anti-Batista forces because it meant that they would be disarmed. Castro also demanded that the United States return the Batista regime's "war criminals," one of the earliest acts increasing tension between Washington and Havana. Still, for Cubans, his charismatic appeal seemed to be universal, regardless of what he said.

January 8 also marked the Havana opening of an Italian play, "The Coming Flood" (*El Diluvio que Viene*). In retrospect, the play's title proved prophetic. That same day, while watching Castro's speech on television at Camp Columbia (where Castro was surrounded by his rebel forces), Boris Benes warned his family that Castro was a communist and said that he feared for Cuba's future. Boris confessed that he had witnessed a similar event forty-two years before in his native Russia. On January 19, eleven days after Castro's entry into Havana, Raquel Benes delivered her first child, a boy she and Bernardo named Joel Eduardo. Shortly afterward, at a rally of 800,000 people, the largest ever held on the island, Castro warned that the revolution would seek economic as well as political freedom, and condemned the meddling in Cuban affairs by the United States.[41] Boris's three children argued with their father, having been, like most Cuban youths, swept up in the euphoria surrounding the revolution. They saw Castro's movement as one that would bring social and economic justice to the Cuban people. Bernardo, in fact, received a permit (the fiftieth to be issued) given to former members of the Revolutionary Student Directorate, permitting him to carry a gun. He never obtained one, but it was a sign that the new Castro government considered him trustworthy. Only months later did the Beneses realize that something was very, very wrong with the 1959 revolution.

Castro's first cabinet had a "social democratic" orientation, with little hint of communist influence. His former professor, José Miró Cardona, was fair-minded and highly capable as prime minister. A woman, Elena Mederos, was named to the social welfare ministry. Every single member of the cabinet had belonged to one of the three revolutionary movements opposing Batista. None was communist or even a known communist sympathizer. The Communist Party (PSP) had never participated actively in the revolution and had been outlawed since Batista's 1952 coup. Behind the scenes, however, Castro waged a tactical struggle with the communists, including his brother Raúl. For the time being, Castro prevailed, claiming that his revolution was nationalist, not socialist. Secretly, however, he kept in close contact with the PSP, meeting at a house in Cojimar (a fishing village popularized by Hemingway), and even while arguing publicly that he opposed communism, he privately relied on party leaders for advice about important government policies.

On February 13, however, the façade of shared power began to unravel. José Miró Cardona resigned as prime minister and was replaced by Fidel Castro himself. Miró Cardona went into exile a year later. In mid-March, Cuba nationalized the telephone company, an affiliate of the International Telephone and Telegraph Company (IT&T). Also in March, officials began to demand that the United States give up its base at Guantánamo, and Cuba stopped cashing the nominal checks from Washington for its lease. The revolutionary government reduced prices for medicine, lowered rents by as much as half, and created the Cuban Film Institute (ICAIC).[42]

In March 1959, the anti-Batista *Directorio 13 de Marzo*'s leaders asked that Benes be appointed to the position of legal counsel to the Ministry of Finance under Minister Rufo López Fresquet. Although the minister assumed that Benes was a communist, the first under-secretary, José M. Illan, convinced his colleagues of their mistake because he knew the Benes family. Bernardo, in fact, had won the first post-revolutionary prize in the annual Angel C. Betancourt Contest given by the Havana Bar Association for the best book published in the legal field. Fidel Castro had presented the prize personally to Benes.

The manuscript, typed by his fiancé Ricky, analyzed the role of accounting practices in corporate law. Benes received the award (plus a hundred pesos) before an audience of thousands of lawyers attending the annual Lawyers' Day convention held on June 8, at the Havana Hilton, since nationalized and renamed the *Habana Libre* (Free Havana) Hotel.

Some practices survived the revolution. Early on in his government post, a tax law was enacted that denied members of nonprofit organizations not on a new official list the right to deduct their membership fees from their taxes. When he learned that the Patronato could apply, Benes took care of it in a week. Even in the "people's" Cuba, connections helped.[43]

On April 15, 1959, Castro flew to the United States, where he spent eleven days, less than four months after his movement's seizure of power in Cuba. His public appearances received extensive (and mostly positive) coverage in the press, probably as much for the novelty of the bearded revolutionary with his army fatigues and cigar than anything else. He and his entourage traveled along the eastern seaboard. President Eisenhower, who did not want to meet him, arranged for a golfing trip to Augusta, Georgia. Castro visited Princeton and Yale, where he was greeted politely, and Harvard, where Dean McGeorge Bundy told a cheering crowd of about eight thousand that Castro had been turned down in 1948 but that if wanted to enroll, there would a place for him in the class of 1963. In Washington, Castro met with Vice-President Richard Nixon, although no statements were released following the meeting. Castro did almost all of the talking, explaining his government's intentions to end unemployment, eradicate poverty, and transform the nation. Nixon listened and said nothing. He did, however, write a confidential memorandum to Senate Majority Leader Mike Mansfield (D-MT), summarizing his reaction:

> When Castro arrived for the conference he seemed somewhat nervous and tense. He apparently felt that he had not done as well on "Meet the Press" as he had hoped. He was particularly concerned about whether he might have irritated Senator [Frank] Smathers [D-FL] for the comments he made with regard to him. . . . [Castro] used the same argument that he was simply reflecting the will of the people in justifying the executions of war criminals and his overruling the acquittal of Batista's aviators. In fact, he seemed to be obsessed with the idea that it was his responsibility to carry out the will of the people whatever it might appear to be at a particular time.[44]

Perhaps the most telling was Nixon's assessment of Fidel Castro's personality. Nixon's curious writing style notwithstanding, his memorandum's conclusion reflects shrewd insight into Castro's future:

> My own appraisal of him as a man is somewhat mixed. The one fact we can be sure of is that he had those indefinable qualities which make him a leader of men. Whatever we may think of him, he is going to be a great factor in the development of Cuba and very possibly in Latin American affairs generally. He seems to be sincere, he is either incredibly naïve about Communism or under Communist discipline—my guess is the former and I have already implied [that] his ideas as to how to run a government or an economy are less developed than those of almost any world figure I have met in fifty countries.[45]

Soon after Castro returned home, his agrarian reform law, technically based on an article in Cuba's 1940 Constitution, took effect. It set limits on the size and quantity of land holdings and expropriated the remainder, offering compensation on the basis of the land's assessed value—which had not been adjusted to real value in several decades. Since foreigners owned three-quarters of Cuba's productive land—five American sugar companies together controlled more than two million acres—the law hit them hardest. The regime expropriated more than 70,000 acres of land owned by American sugar companies, and 35,000 acres in Oriente province owned by the United Fruit Company. Confiscated land was handed over to cooperatives or distributed to individuals at no cost. The pace of the revolutionary government's decrees increased rapidly. On July 16, Castro accused President Urrutia of impeding the progress of the revolution. Urrutia resigned immediately and went into exile in Venezuela. Osvaldo Dorticós, the lawyer who had drafted the agrarian reform legislation, took over as president. He had been Raúl Castro's candidate and, since 1953, a member of Cuba's Communist Party.

In November, Che Guevara, the newly appointed head of the National Bank of Cuba, sold all of Cuba's gold reserves in the United States, to ward off possible confiscation by the United States in retaliation for Cuba's seizure of American property. Guevara deposited the money in Canadian and Swiss banks. In 1959, 26,527 Cubans entered the United States; in the next year, 60,224; in 1961, 49,961.[46] Smaller numbers went to such countries as Spain, Mexico, Venezuela, and Colombia. Raúl Castro explained the mass departures as "the normal exodus that takes place when the people take the power in their own hands and liquidate exploitation and the privileged classes. Their departure does not damage the revolution, but fortifies it as a spontaneous purification."[47]

During the revolution's first year, the four-decade-old Communist Party (the Partido Socialista Popular) worked diligently and quietly to expand its influence. Generally, communists sought positions in the intelligence and military communities. Ironically, the communists did not participate in the anti-Batista struggle, but as soon as the dictator fell from power they emerged, volunteering for revolutionary work, pressuring Castro to accelerate the pace of revolutionary change, and keeping the Soviet Union abreast of events. The revolutionary regime faced many challenges: for one thing, every important position in government and in the armed forces had to be filled almost immediately. Out of the revolution's reorganization came a new intelligence service, which within a few years would be bolstered by KBG "advisors" from the Soviet Union. Later on, Castro threw the Soviet agents out for about a year (they returned, however, to leave again in 1990 with the collapse of the Soviet Union). By then, Cuban agents had become polished, thorough, and innovative. When someone of any importance was to come to Cuba for a visit, the intelligence service performed background checks so detailed that the guest could be manipulated to the advantage of the Cuban government.

Benes and the other anti-Batista Cubans who considered the revolution Cuba's best chance for social justice and national pride stuck it out as long as they could. One of his first cases as a lawyer in post-revolutionary Cuba was to recruit Osmel Francis to join him in defense of a mutual friend, Elpidio Núñez, who owned a bus company, *Omnibus Aliados* (*Ruta 4*), and had been arrested and jailed for allegedly murdering one of his company's bus drivers during the Batista years. Hearings started at 10:00 P.M. in a poorly lit cellar in the La Cabaña fortress. Osmel Francis, Bernardo's former law school fellow student, headed the defense, and Núñez was acquitted, a rarity in the early days of the Revolution.[48] Even though his side won its case, Benes was dismayed at the way the trial proceeded because the revolutionaries were sidestepping the procedures of Cuban law.

During the first eighteen months of the Revolution, during which Benes remained in spite of the growing numbers of upper-echelon Cubans abandoning the country, Castro had established himself as even more authoritarian than Batista, although he defended his actions in the name of the Cuban people, and many of his actions were cheered. His revolutionary tribunals sentenced thousands of Cubans to prison or death by firing squad, acts that angered and embittered those Cubans who had gone into exile. The United States withdrew its military missions from its embassy in Havana. Private beach clubs were opened to the public or taken over by government agencies for their own use. The regime lowered rates for utilities and prices for medicine.

The provocation, which was inevitable given the direction the revolution was going despite Castro's personal vacillations, came in mid-October when Castro named his brother, Raúl, head of the army. Days later, Commander Húber Matos, rebel military chief of Camagüey province, told Castro that he would resign because he could not serve in an army "that was coming under communist control." In a letter to Castro, Matos, a strong ally of Castro in the anti-Batista struggle, said that resignation was his only honorable course. Said to be furious, Castro ordered Matos seized and sentenced to twenty years in prison. Only one higher official of Castro's forces had ever acted similarly: Pedro Luis Díaz Lanz, commander of the Cuban rebel air force, had flown his plane to the United States in June 1959 because Raúl Castro had recruited Spanish communists to indoctrinate the armed forces.[49] At the same time, anti-Castro groups outside Cuba began to raise funds to purchase arms and ammunition. On March 4, 1960, a French freighter, *La Coubre*, loaded with Belgian weapons possibly destined for Algeria exploded in Havana harbor, although the bombers remained unidentified. After Shell Oil, Esso (later renamed Exxon), and Texaco refused to refine crude oil shipped from the Soviet Union, Castro confiscated their refineries. He seized all American banks, including branches of Chase Manhattan, the First National Bank of Boston, and City Bank of New York. Schools run by the Roman Catholic Church shut down. Cuban authorities warned citizens of a possible invasion by the United States armed forces. Parents put children to sleep in bathtubs, considered the safest place in the event of falling bombs.[50]

In mid-September 1960, Fidel Castro made a defiant visit to the United Nations in New York City. Refusing to stay in luxury quarters, he moved his entourage to the Theresa Hotel in Harlem, where he received a number of heads of state, including Nikita Khrushchev, Egypt's Gamal Abdel Nasser, and Prime Minister Nehru of India. He also met with Malcolm X. If this was meant to catch the attention of the world press, it surely did. On his return to Havana, Castro announced the creation of the Committees for the Defense of the Revolution (CDR) on every block of every town and city in Cuba. These were groups of revolutionaries with the power to denounce neighbors and send them to trial for antigovernment sentiments, and they functioned as the backbone of Cuban internal security. An Orwellian atmosphere began to descend on the island.

In early October 1960, Fidel Castro made several additional announcements that alarmed observers. The Soviets, who seemed as mystified as the United States State Department during this period, sent a special emissary, Aleksandr Alekseev, to Cuba to assess the revolution. Alekseev unhappily reported to Moscow that the communists, including Carlos Rafael Rodríguez, the editor of the communist newspaper, "were exaggerating their control over the Cuban revolution."[51] But Che Guevara and Fidel Castro met with Alekseev and promised good relations, although they preferred not to provoke the United States further. Alekseev remained on the island, becoming the KGB station chief and, in the words of Alexsandr Fursenko and Timothy Naftali, "Fidel Castro's favorite Russian."[52] To cultivate Castro, who puzzled the Soviets because they felt that he was very different from his brother Raúl, Nikita Khrushchev personally asked Castro for permission to have his speeches published in Russian. Castro was delighted, and Alekseev paid him $385 for one article published in Moscow. Castro was reported by Alekseev to have been "visibly moved," and told the Russian that "If everything I say is published . . . I will become a millionaire!" "You couldn't have chosen a better time," Castro told Alekseev, "because I just borrowed ten pesos from Guevara for cigarettes." Seven months later, Castro received $8,000 from the Soviet Union's Central Committee of the Communist Party for a collection of speeches.[53] Benes, however, still believed that the revolution might fulfill its potential in restoring democracy, so he and Ricky stayed.[54]

An event during the long holiday weekend around October 10, 1960, commemorating the start of the nineteenth-century struggle for independence from Spain, proved another turning point for Benes's capacity to live under the revolutionary regime. Up to that point, he and many others saw the revolution as a welcome antidote to Batista's dictatorship. Bernardo and his wife; his sister Ana; her husband, Dr. David Anders; and a few other couples traveled by train to Santiago de Cuba at the eastern point of the 750-mile-long island. At the Versailles Hotel, where they stayed, the group ran into Castro's brother, the chief of staff of the revolutionary army, Raúl Castro Ruz, with his wife, Vilma Espín, an alumna of Bryn Mawr College in Philadelphia and a fervent revolutionary. Raúl Castro had played soccer for four years with Bernardo at the University of

Havana. The encounter was cordial, and the group spent a long time standing around the swimming pool and conversing. One of the members of the party was Raúl Mausovicius, Benes's closest friend, who told jokes to keep the atmosphere light.

Inevitably, however, politics came up in the conversation. Bernardo told Raúl in passing that he sensed that living conditions were becoming harder, and that he had heard that there were *alzados* (anti-Castro guerrillas) in the Escambray Mountains in central Cuba. Castro replied: "Don't worry, Bernardo, we will . . ." and suddenly squeezed his right fist before Benes's in an angry gesture that sent chills through Benes's body. When the conversation ended, Benes told his wife that they must return to Havana, that Raúl's angry clenched fist signaled the end of their comfortable lives in Cuba. Ricky disagreed, arguing that there was nothing to worry about. Bernardo countered: "I know Raúl, and I am afraid that things are going to be very bad for us."

No sooner did they return to Havana than three new decrees were announced, on October 14, 15, and 16. They showed that Ricky's optimism had been ill-founded. On the first day, all large factories in Cuba were confiscated. The next day, a "housing reform" act canceled the right to own more than one house. On the third day, death sentences by firing squad were announced publicly against Cubans who had fought against Castro's guerrillas.

The seizure of all privately owned factories, of course, affected Boris Benes. The revolutionary government confiscated his *Tejidos y Confecciones Perro, Textilera Tricana,* and Gold Seal Hosiery.[55] Security police locked the doors of his plants, refusing to let him enter even to remove his personal effects from his office. Then his son Jaime, whose industrial dyeing plant, *Operadora Colortex,* faced constant challenges from his employees' labor union, left Cuba for the United States in October 1960. Bernardo, for the time being, continued to work at the Ministry of Finance on Cuba Street, spending the rest of his time at Zaydín's law office.

Jaime's flight, however, triggered a new round of troubles. The trade union leaders, many of them communists, accused Bernardo of somehow engineering Jaime's departure, and they began to harass him. The G–2 (State Security) police would speed through Old Havana's narrow streets, tires screeching, and stop in front of the Treasury Department and with great commotion look for Bernardo. According to Bernardo, agents barged into his third-floor office on three consecutive mornings. They entered residential neighborhoods the same way, interrogating people at all hours of the day or night. Jaime's decision had been no different from that of hundreds of Cuban industrialists and businessmen by that time, but the security police seemed especially interested in his case. Finally, Bernardo figured it out: they hadn't cared about Jaime's factory as much as they wanted his two imported Peugeot automobiles.

At first, they interrogated Bernardo only at his job, but soon they started coming to his apartment in the same building where his mother and father lived, at Eighth Street between Fifth and Seventh avenues in Miramar. This was when the family reluctantly decided that they had to leave Cuba. The Beneses were bewildered by the attitude of the regime. Boris Benes thought that he had enjoyed excellent relations with his 500 factory workers. There never had been a strike, nor had either Boris or Jaime ever been served with a complaint or taken to court.

Since Bernardo worked for the Cuban government, regulations required that he file a request for exit papers through his department. Instead, after leaving his office for lunch, he headed to Havana's international airport, without luggage, and caught a Pan American Airways flight to Miami. He told only two people: Ramón Zaydín, his boss; and his friend, Bobby Maduro. The baseball-team owner sent one of his employees, who also worked in the customs department, to see Bernardo through the steps for getting a flight and being permitted to board. This was November 11, 1960, a Friday. The next day, not restricted by the need for exit visas, Ricky and Joel flew out, and Bernardo's parents followed soon afterward. They would have been stunned beyond belief to know that the government from which they were fleeing, which they considered a temporary annoyance, would survive more than forty years in power, forcing them, along with hundreds of thousands of others, into what would turn out to be permanent exile.

Twenty-five-year-old Bernardo Benes arrived in the United States alone, was met by no one, and spent the night disconsolately at the Tropic Hotel, a small hotel on Collins Avenue in Miami Beach. He had brought with him a check for $210 sewn into his suit's shoulder but nothing else. Ricky and their eighteen-month-old son arrived the next day. His parents came shortly afterwards. They stayed at the hotel and made contacts with other family members and friends who had arrived earlier. Bernardo's uncle, Enrique Baikovitz, introduced Bernardo to Jack Gordon, president of the Washington Federal Savings and Loan Association and his second cousin by marriage. Because of Bernardo's experience in law and accounting, Gordon gave him a job as a clerk in the audit department. Ten days after he had landed in Miami, he was working for $65 a week. He would remain at the S&L for fifteen years, rising quickly to the post of vice-president and becoming the major bridge-builder in the Cuban American community. During his first dozen years as an exile in Miami, he supported anti-Castro causes, more than once raising money to help finance attacks on Cuban soil, lobbying in Washington, and working to bring the political leaders of the exile enclave together. Once Benes understood, by the mid-1960s, that Castro would not fall easily, his priorities changed to fighting to integrate Miami Cubans into the city's "old boy" power structure.

Some Cubans who had fought for the revolution to overthrow Batista and restore democratic ways stayed longer, because they felt it was their duty to moderate the revolutionary movement. Leon A. Cuervo, a young scientist from a prominent Havana family who had supported the 26th of July movement, took a position with INAM, the National Agrarian Reform Institute. Years later, he recalled that the first shock he received occurred when a military tribunal's not-guilty verdict at the conclusion of a trial of pilots for treason was rejected by Castro, who appointed a new tribunal that reversed the verdict. When Dr. Cuervo told fellow scientists at INAM that he feared the effects of a Cuban alliance with the Soviet Union, a colleague behind his back reported his words directly to Raúl Castro. The only reason Cuervo was not arrested, he believes, is that a friend, a communist since the 1930s, intervened on his behalf. Beginning in 1961, Cuervo's wife kept their children out of their small private school, because indoctrination had started. Still, the Cuervos felt it was their duty to remain. But when Castro overturned labor union elections in 1961 because not a single communist had won office, the Cuervos finally gave up and flew to Miami.[56]

What Benes and other Cuban exiles did not know when they took up residence in Miami, however, was that many would resent efforts to integrate Cubans into Miami's "Anglo" power structure. The United States government, moreover, openly as well as covertly would expend enormous sums of money to fund right-wing groups within the community and to stir up anti-Castro hostility. No such aid came for building bridges or for helping the émigrés overcome their psychological ties to the pre-1959 Cuban regime.

CHAPTER TWO

CUBAN MIAMI

The total number of Cuban-born residents in the United States before the late 1950s had always been modest, probably fewer than 20,000, even though Cubans fleeing Batista's police state after his 1952 coup swelled the number of Cuban exiles. In Florida, Tampa, not Miami, had the largest population of Cubans, followed by Key West. Just as Florida had given refuge to Cuban exiles as far back as the nineteenth-century wars for independence from Spain, during the mid-1950s, Miami had become a place of intrigue where exiled Cuban politicians plotted against Batista. The ousted president, Carlos Prío Socarrás, financed conspiracies, using Miami Beach's Lucerne Hotel and his own home in South Miami for meetings. One of the visitors was Fidel Castro, released from prison by Batista because of the influential family connections of Castro's wife, Mirta Díaz-Balart.[1]

Cubans fearing arrest and imprisonment—especially officials of Batista's police, armed forces, and government—were the earliest to depart. Batista himself lived in a palatial home in Daytona Beach as well as in Portugal, France, and Spain until his death in Madeira in 1973. A quarter-century later, someone found dozens of boxes of papers in a trash bin rented by the dictator's surviving family. They included bills from his years in exile suggesting conspicuous consumption: two weeks at the Waldorf Astoria hotel in New York at $250 a night; proof of vaccination for two poodles traveling with him to Switzerland, evidence of land deals and properties in Spain, and a list of cash-gift recipients, including a number of customs agents in various ports of call.[2]

For Miami, everything changed after 1959. For affluent, property-owning Cubans, Castro's actions dashed hopes almost immediately; and the increasing indoctrination, denunciations, and mean-spirited bureaucrats, especially by 1970, encouraged tens of thousands more to leave. By 1980, nearly 700,000 Cubans had sought refuge abroad—nearly 10 percent of Cuba's population.[3] Since the early 1960s, Miami had become the center of the Cuban exodus. In 1966, the Cuban Refugee Center estimated that some 2,500 towns and cities had taken in Cuban exiles. Puerto Rico and northern New Jersey's Elizabeth–Union City area had the largest communities after Miami, the former because Cubans could easily get by in Spanish.

In Miami, however, by mid-1960, the Catholic Hispanic Center (*Centro Hispánico Católico*), the only agency providing help to the newcomers, became overwhelmed. Given the long lines of desperate families each day, resources began to run out. Irish-born Monsignor Brian O. Walsh of the Miami Roman Catholic Archdiocese, who would become a hero for his handling of the crisis, called a meeting of community leaders—the "movers and shakers" in his words. But the only agreement reached was that the city and county could not handle the problem, and that the State of Florida should intervene. But when Monsignor Walsh contacted Governor LeRoy Collins, the state's chief official told him to seek aid from the federal government because state aid was limited by statute to $100 a month per family.[4]

President Dwight D. Eisenhower, viewing the Miami crisis in terms of the unexpected arrival in the United States of the Hungarian Freedom Fighters in 1956, sent Tracy Voorhees, who had headed the Hungarian refugee relief effort, to Miami. A public relations man from New York City, Voorhees displayed little sympathy for the exiled Cubans. When Monsignor Walsh pleaded for family assistance, Voorhees, before a group of community leaders, responded, "If the Cubans want to stay in Miami, I will buy each one a tin cup and let them stand on street corners." His December 1960 report to Eisenhower, according to Walsh, recommended that the Miami Cubans be given one-way air tickets to any city in the United States outside of South Florida.[5]

As soon as Eisenhower left office in January 1960, the new president, John F. Kennedy, sent Abraham Ribicoff, his Secretary of Health, Education, and Welfare, to Miami. Ribicoff became appalled at the state limit of $100 a month for family assistance; he immediately arranged for funds to subsidize Operation Pedro Pan, the children's rescue airlift from Havana and to provide aid to families and loans to needy youths to permit them to attend college. The federal government, however, did not provide any funds for building low-cost housing or for rehabilitating the hundreds of dilapidated and often abandoned buildings in the area that would become known as Little Havana, nor did the government do anything to provide job training or orientation. The remainder of the assistance for those arriving in destitute conditions fell to the Roman Catholic Church and, to a lesser extent, to Jewish and Protestant charities.

What awaited new arrivals was a sprawling subtropical city remarkably similar to Havana, except for the lack of Cuba's stately colonial architecture. Miami provided the same sultry climate as Cuba's, as well as seasonal tropical storms and hurricanes, palm trees, and miles of waterfront. Miami real estate prices rose rapidly after World War II came to a close. In 1952, Miami reached a population of 247,262, its surrounding metropolitan area (Dade County, stretching south to the entrance to Florida's Keys) holding an equal number of residents. Air conditioning had been invented, although most homes still relied on ceiling fans to combat the heat and humidity. Commercial airlines, including Eastern, National, and Pan American Airways, put fleets of propeller DC-6s and Constellations into service to transport passengers from the Northeast to sunny South Florida. Many servicemen, who before being shipped out had been trained in South Florida, returned to start businesses or to study under the GI Bill.

The cities of Miami, Coral Gables, Hialeah, and Miami Beach all were mostly white (except for Miami's Overtown) and mostly Protestant (Jews and other minorities were barred from many fashionable hotels and resorts). African Americans, descended from slaves as well as from immigrants from the Bahamas, worked in the segregated city as servants and laborers. Schools were segregated, as well as public toilets and Miami's buses. Miami in 1952 had fifty-six elementary schools for whites and thirteen for "coloreds." A few thousand Hispanics, mostly Cubans, had settled in Miami over the decades. An estimated 10,000 Cubans lived in Miami in 1958, 3,500 of them residents and the others mostly young people fleeing Batista's dictatorship. Miami was a segregated city. Blacks lived north of downtown in Liberty City, Overtown (formerly Colored Town), and Opa-Locka, and in the far south of the county, in the area around Cutler Ridge. Jews settled in Miami Beach in the sections not closed to them, mostly in the then-crumbling Art Deco district and across the Miami River from downtown in Riverside, a declining neighborhood along South West Eighth Street. Roman Catholics remained a small minority in the city through the end of the 1950s, especially in Coral Gables, a planned community built in the 1920s for affluent "WASPs" who would come down from the North to live in a balmy paradise.

As noted earlier, many of the earliest pre-Batista exiles managed to take care of themselves. Grau San Martín's Minister of Education supposedly shipped sacks of money to Miami. Some close to Batista did so even before Fidel Castro entered Havana in January 1959 in the midst of a tumultuous general strike. Many, however, did not. Landowners, industrialists, managers and other employees of expropriated businesses, and revolutionaries who had opposed Batista but now saw the revolution as having been betrayed, became *personae non grata* in their own country. The majority of wealthy Cubans had not taken precautions. Boris Benes, worth millions, at the last minute bought $15,000 in American currency, paying seven or even eight to one in pesos that nominally held equal value as the dollar.

At first, the large numbers of Cubans pouring into Miami overshadowed all else. Nearly 35,000 left Cuba during 1959. Almost all were highly educated. Their departure robbed Cuba of its most skillful technicians, professionals, and administrators, a blow that would be felt in Cuba's economy. Members of the initial wave of exiles who came between 1959 and 1962 were overwhelmingly Caucasian and from the upper echelons of Cuban society. A journalist likened it to an exodus from Cambridge, Princeton, New Haven, and Palo Alto.[6]

Not only did many wealthy Cubans connected to the Batista regime get money out, but also, even during the 1960s and 1970s, some managed to beat the system. They smuggled in jewelry that was theirs or that had been exchanged for goods left behind, or cashed in treasury bonds and transferred the payout to banks in the United States, or sent funds to contacts in other countries. Batista cronies connected to the Cuban State Development Bank (BANDES) were said to have "withdrawn" millions of dollars for themselves in late 1958, and in November 1959, when Fidel Castro replaced Felipe Pazos, the president of Cuba's national bank, with Marxist Ernesto "Che" Guevara, a run on banks led to the withdrawal of between $50 million to $60 million in pesos.

The extent to which some Cubans arrived well-heeled to the United States will probably never be known, but based on interviews with individual exiles, especially those who left Cuba first for third countries, it may have been that a higher percentage of new arrivals brought assets with them than the prevailing wisdom claimed.[7] Many high government officials and members of the elite, for example, had bank accounts in the United States for years. And even without foreign accounts, there were ways to take out money. Some enterprising persons packed up their family photo albums and, in some cases, valuable paintings and other artwork, wrapped them in brown paper, and mailed them from their local post office to friends outside Cuba. Even so, most of the exiles came with nothing but the clothing on their backs and, for members of the elite, their family contacts.

For the majority, bringing out assets from Cuba became increasingly difficult. Those who carried pesos with them found that they were unable to exchange them at the 1:1 rate that had prevailed on the island, and when Castro issued new currency, the old pesos became worthless. During 1960 and 1961, moreover, there were not many individuals remaining in Cuba with funds to buy the luxury homes, furnishings from businesses, or automobiles left behind by the emigrés.

Culture shock came from not speaking English, but many of the initial exiles had visited the United States or done business with American firms and therefore had a sense of American culture beyond their knowledge of Hollywood movies. There had been some anxiety among middle-class Cubans during the 1950s: Cuban per-capita income had remained relatively stable, and Cubans were losing ground to the booming American economy.[8] Yet those with the deepest understanding of the American system were those who took it for granted that Washington would not permit Castro to stay in power, and almost none of the first exiles came to the United States intending to remain.

One of the most dramatic aspects of the crisis was the Pedro (for Peter) Pan airlift of Cuban children to Miami.[9] Rumors had spread in Cuba that children might be shipped to the Soviet Union for indoctrination or, in the case of older youths, to the cane fields. The dramatic airlift of elite children whose parents could not leave with them offered a poignant example of the family dislocations caused by the 1959 revolution—even though, at the same time, Pedro Pan served Castro's interests by ridding him, in the end, of the airlifted children's parents, a thorn in his side and potential opponents of his government had they stayed. It also showed the parents' determination to risk separation from their own children to provide them opportunities for a better life.

It started in December 1960 when James Baker, the headmaster of the Ruston Academy, contacted Bryan Walsh. Quickly, they arranged for the initial flight of 200 children from Havana. After the United States Embassy closed, the operation continued quietly. Sometimes documents were falsified to lower the age of youths who otherwise would have been forced to remain because they were of military age.[10] The airlift continued until late 1962.

Assisting behind the scenes were Polita Grau, the former First Lady of Cuba, and her brother Ramón. From their Havana home, they secretly distributed improvised invitations on United States letterhead stationery inviting the children to come. A brave woman, Polita had been involved as a student in the effort to overthrow dictator Gerardo Machado in 1933 and had supported Castro until he began seizing private property. For her role in Pedro Pan, Polita served fourteen years in Cuban prisons "for conspiring with the CIA to topple Fidel Castro." She remained in jail until finally released under Castro's 1978 amnesty, negotiated by Benes and Dascal.[11]

Funding came from the CIA and other United States government agencies, which provided five dollars a day per child for maintenance. By the time the flights ended, 14,156 unaccompanied minors had arrived via Pedro Pan. If they did not have relatives, they were placed with foster families in Miami and elsewhere until their families could join them. When the numbers became too large for foster placement, the Miami Catholic archdiocese set up five camps, Matecumbe (later renamed Boys' Town), Florida City, Kendall, Jesuit Boys' Home, and St. Raphael. In addition, Maurice Ferré, a wealthy Puerto Rican industrialist born in Ponce and who in 1973 became mayor of Miami, donated a house near downtown Miami that became known as the Cuban Boys' Home.

Among former Pedro Pan children who became well known were radio newsman and Miami City Commissioner Tomás Regalado; Raúl Bezos, father of the founder of Amazon.com, Jeff Bezos; singer Willy Chirino; businessman Armando Codina; and volatile Miami Mayor Joe Carrollo. Some of the children had relatively positive experiences. Fourteen-year-old Silvia Muñoz lived at the Florida City camp, a single street with rows of duplexes. Each housed twenty to twenty-five girls with a Cuban couple in each as house parents. Muñoz remembers that her house parents were detached, while other couples were more loving. "Overall," she remembers, "everyone in the camp was very good to us and tried to minimize our heartaches as much as they could."[12]

Some of the accommodations, however, were substandard. Matecumbe, near the Everglades, was isolated and mosquito-ridden, and children cried themselves to sleep. In some facilities, cases of negligence and abuse were reported. None of the children who arrived via the airlift had ever seen segregation, and they were shocked when they saw blacks barred from public places in Miami.

Some children sent to foster homes around the United States found themselves in places where no one could understand their language and from which they remained totally cut off from their families. In some cases, Pedro Pan children were never reunited with their families, because the Cuban government denied exit permits to their parents even forty years later.

The Hebrew Immigrant Aid Society (HIAS) ran a concomitant airlift for Cuban Jewish children.[13] Jewish Family Services, a private agency, also helped. Protestants also ran small versions of Pedro Pan for children whose parents belonged to their congregations in Cuba. The United States government paid for the foster homes and the overall relocation process.

Pedro Pan notwithstanding, leaving Cuba after mid-1960 became extremely difficult. Airline tickets after 1960 had to be purchased in dollars. The exiles were harassed by mean-spirited militiamen, who sometimes subjected departing passengers to strip searches, while processing their papers. The Cuban government limited passengers to five dollars in cash and a suitcase. The government confiscated the rest of their belongings—their houses, their cars, and their businesses. Young men of army age were forced to remain. The exiles were ridiculed in the Cuban press as *gusanos* (worms, a term used in Cuba for lowlifes), and Cubans were told by government media that the exiles lived in misery, exploited by the capitalists who ran American life.[14] Nonetheless, more and more Cubans sought to flee.

New arrivals received identity cards issued by the U. S. Justice Department and were required to notify the attorney general of any address changes. Each year in January they had to register, even if they had not moved. The Cubans were not eligible for municipal welfare, although a federally funded refugee center housed in the old *Miami Herald* building provided cash, social services, medical examinations, and surplus food from 1962 until it closed in 1974.[15] The federal government ceased paying medical bills and giving financial aid to Cubans who had been in the United States for more than three years. The Catholic Hispanic Center, established by the archdiocese of Miami in 1959, also provided assistance, as did the Protestant Latin American Emergency Committee, the Greater Miami Jewish Federation, HIAS, and several other voluntary relief agencies.

The United States during this time faced an economic recession that was felt more severely in Miami than elsewhere because of its dependence on seasonal tourism. Most jobs available to the exiles who had come without resources were menial. Cubans who had been professionals were blocked from practicing in the United States unless they passed qualifying examinations in English. This became one reason why some Cuban professionals chose to go to Puerto Rico, where they could take their examinations for certification in their own language. For several years, angry exiles who had been attorneys in Cuba picketed the Florida Bar Association for its refusal to administer the bar examination in Spanish. Physicians, many of whom had to take jobs as hospital orderlies or lab technicians, eventually were able to sit for examinations that permitted thousands of them to practice medicine in Florida under a program at the University of Miami Medical School headed by Dr. Rafael Peñalver. The University of Miami also provided certification programs for former teachers and administrators to be accredited in order to teach in local public schools. Those who came after 1961 represented a broader social and economic spectrum. Many were professionals and businessmen whose homes and businesses were seized in the name of the revolution, but others were semi-professional and middle-class people who found that they could not live in Cuba under Castro. Some were people of mixed race who in the segregated American states were considered blacks. Political events, however, on both sides of the Straits of Florida made leaving Cuba much more difficult. President Dwight D. Eisenhower had refused to meet with Castro when he came to the United Nations in April 1959, and when the State Department demanded compensation for nationalized American businesses, Castro stepped up his anti-American tirades and secretly began to acquire arms from the Soviet Union.[16] President Eisenhower's reduction of the United States quota for Cuban sugar in response to Castro's seizure of American oil refineries badly hurt Cuba's economy. Meanwhile, Miami Cubans soon realized their political influence, although they remained within their Spanish-language enclave. But "the old hegemonic order was ruptured and the way paved for a novel set of definitions about what the city was and should become."[17]

By 1970, the federal census listed 560,628 Cubans in the United States, 252,520 residing in Florida. Officials working with private charitable organizations across the country pressured new arrivals to settle outside of Miami; by 1972, exiles resided in cities and towns throughout the United States in every state in the union, with even Alaska receiving one resettled exile.[18]

The exodus transplanted most of Cuba's professionals, researchers, and entrepreneurs. In the words of an observer, "they brought the best of home with them. Centro Vasco restaurant—since fire-bombed and closed for booking a 73-year old Cuban singer who apparently didn't denounce Castro sufficiently—moved lock, stock and barrel from Havana to Miami. The Jesuits moved their Belén Prep School, as did the University of St. Thomas. Havana's elite charity, the League Against Cancer, moved its fund raising balls to Miami area country clubs."[19] The exclusive Big Five social clubs replicated themselves, although not with the lavish facilities that they had enjoyed in Havana. Many of their members brought their elite values and behaviors with them to South Florida.

They established a Miami enclave dedicated to preserving the past in as complete manner as possible. Miami Cubans today speak a version of 1950s Cuban Spanish that has been supplanted by a new vernacular in Cuba. For years, the only Cuban music heard in Miami was classics from before 1959 or the music of such Cuban exiles as singers Olga Guillot and

2.1 Broken-down housing for new arrivals, early 1960s. Robert M. Levine collection.

Celia Cruz, who had joined the exodus. Enclave members also maintained their interpersonal networks, thereby making it far easier for the initial Cuban exiles to become successful financially than the waves of later arrivals, who ranged in origin from middle-class down to the poor and therefore lacked connections that opened doors. At the top of the social and economic ladder, professional groups replicated themselves: the Interamerican Business Association, the most important, and the Association of Cuban Banks, founded in Cuba in 1949 to represent the top forty banks on the island, re-formed in Miami in 1992 as the Cuban Banking Study Group, dedicated to "overseeing an orderly development of [Cuba's] banking industry after the long-awaited demise of Castro and the expected transition to a free market economy.[20]

Most of the exiles from Cuba came with nothing more than a suitcase and in some cases had cameras, watches, or jewelry confiscated by Cuban customs officials. By mid-1960, private and public agencies in Miami had become overwhelmed. New arrivals were placed in run-down, roach-infested downtown hotels, or in decaying properties in South Miami Beach.

Eventually, most settled in the neighborhood of Riverside, across the Miami River stretching west from downtown Miami, an uneven and declining district made up of small houses, walk-up apartments, and such businesses as automobile repair shops and stores selling cheap furniture. Husbands and wives walked the pavement seeking employment. Former medical doctors found jobs as orderlies. Accountants were hired during tourist season as valet parkers at Miami Beach hotels. Former industrialists ended up as janitors. In many cases, married women exiles—who had never worked in Cuba—found jobs (as housecleaners, or baby sitters, or in textile factories) more readily than their husbands did. This created stress, inverting the status hierarchy by which elite Cuban families had lived before 1959.

In 1962, Ricky, three-year-old Joel, and Bernardo Benes traveled to Toronto to apply for United States residency. As Cuban refugees, they were not eligible for residency status in Florida without first leaving the country. Seven years later, Benes's personal network had become so useful that Claude Pepper, the Democratic congressman from Miami (and a member of the board of Benes's Washington Federal Savings & Loan), introduced a private bill (H.R. 3532) in Congress to grant Benes citizenship.

Pepper's law office had secured a deal with Washington Federal to handle 50 percent of the closings on every mortgage granted by the Savings and Loan Association. Benes needed citizenship to represent the United States in Latin America under a contract his bank received from USAID under the Alliance for Progress to counsel Latin American officials about how to set up S&Ls, and he received his citizenship papers on August 20, 1969.[21] By then, Benes had become prominent enough in Miami that newspapers ran stories about his achievement.[22]

The overwhelming number of Cuban arrivals not only stayed in Miami, but they transformed it. In addition to the assistance first from Cuban émigré-owned banks and later local banks in general, builders and other entrepreneurs became eligible for federal loans, administered through the Small Business Administration. This helped Cuban businessmen in Miami and elsewhere open banks, construction companies, restaurants, private schools, and retail and wholesale stores.

Things differed for those with professional skills or contacts. The banking industry illustrates how the first wave of Cubans made their way in Miami, in most cases to affluence after a relatively short period of time. In 1959, Dade County, stretching from just below Hallandale and North Miami Beach to Homestead and Florida City at the entrance to the Florida Everglades, boasted 23,019 business establishments served by only thirty-eight banks.[23] The number of businesses had doubled since 1948, but others of the so-called Sunbelt cities had prospered more during the period. Most of the new start-ups employed fewer than four persons and comprised over half of all Miami businesses in 1959. Miami, dependent on seasonal tourism, attracted fixed-income retirees from the Northeast, not young families. The atmosphere did not seem propitious for an economic boom or even gradual urban improvement.

The influx of Cubans and the formation of Cuban enclaves (in Riverside, which became known as Little Havana, Miami Beach, and later Westchester and Hialeah) in which Miami Cubans could conduct their affairs in Spanish created numerous opportunities for growth not previously foreseen. Banks played a major role. In Cuba, banking had provided capital for investments in agricultural financing, the construction industry, and tourism (as well as opportunities for the corrupt to skim money). Some Cuban bankers had grown very wealthy, although they had to compete with foreign banks that had come to Cuba at the beginning of the twentieth century. Near the end of Batista's government, runs on some banks started, and as many as $50 to $60 million (in pesos) were withdrawn and removed from the country.[24]

In August 1960, Cuba's revolutionary government confiscated and nationalized most foreign-owned banks. Some, although by no means all, bankers managed to take some of their assets with them when they departed Cuba for Miami. By 1966, the number of banks in Dade County had jumped to sixty-seven, none owned by exiles. Miami's economy, in spite of a nationwide recession between 1960 and 1962, surpassed earlier rates of growth. One reason was that the Cuban bankers working in existing banks helped new arrivals start up business by offering small loans to exiles based simply on personal ties before the revolution in Cuba.

In 1974, Benes and Carlos Dascal opened the first Cuban American bank, and the going wasn't easy. As lower-class Cubans arrived, they preferred to cash their checks at local Cuban markets because they did not have bank accounts; in turn, these markets, usually cash-poor, would "float" checks to their own bank on Friday. They would then cash the checks during the weekend and deposit the cash on Monday so that they would clear.[25]

Consider the case of banker Carlos Arboleya. When he arrived in 1960, he could not find a bank job because others had come before him and the industry was still small. He took a temporary job as an inventory clerk in a shoe factory. Within a year and a half, the talented Arboleya had risen to vice-president of the firm, and he used his position to hire, by his estimate, forty-two or forty-three bankers to work making shoes. Five years later, he received offers from thirteen banks in Miami to come and work for them.[26]

Many of the other bankers whom he had hired later became presidents or executives of banks as the economy grew. During the early 1960s, a story circulated throughout Miami that there was a shoe factory that employed only Cuban bankers. The story was only partly false. In time, Cuban bankers joined up with "Anglos" to consolidate their holdings.[27] Sensitivities remained. To make non–Spanish speaking customers comfortable, some "Anglo-Cuban" banks forbade their Cuban employees to converse with one another publicly in Spanish.[28]

Still, many remained doubters. In 1965, Miami's Mayor Robert King High commented in *Time* magazine, "no community can assimilate any great number of people who come here with limitations of speech and no money."[29] Mayor High's statement may have been correct under usual conditions, but he overlooked the energy generated by a growing enclave based on close networks of family ties and supported by radio and television stations, newspapers, schools, and social organizations—all copies of what had been left behind—and the fact that such an enclave slowed assimilation and fostered separatism.

What helped was the fact that the emergence of a prosperous and dynamic Cuban Miami exceeded all predictions. Monsignor Bryan Walsh recalled the prevailing pessimism when the Disney Corporation opened Disney World in Orlando. "[Potential investors] knew that 80 percent of the tourists who came to Florida came by car and Disney World would be like a Chinese wall—nobody would drive further south. The state of Florida put a low priority on building major highways into South Florida. The second factor was the jet plane. It became just as cheap to fly to Jamaica or Puerto Rico, where you can get two weeks of sunshine guaranteed, than to fly to Miami, where you may get two weeks of rain if you're unlucky. Had it not been for the Cubans, Miami would have been a dead duck."[30]

Efforts to improve ties with non-Cubans in Miami were overshadowed by the higher profile given by the press and media to more than sixty groups operating out of Miami dedicated to overthrowing Castro's government. In January 1961, an Anti-Castro Cuban Alliance was formed, uniting most of the independent organizations. Its leaders included former officers from Castro's militia, and its goal was to engage in anti-Castro activities. By then, the first Spanish-language radio stations had started broadcasting. In time, the political endorsements of the "Cuban" stations carried more weight than the endorsement of the *Miami Herald*. Norman Díaz was the first Spanish-language broadcaster. He started in 1960 on station WMET, leased by Abel Mestre, the former co-owner of Havana's CMQ. Some of the new Spanish-language radio stations were started by Anglos, who then hired exiles with experience in radio to create twenty-four-hour-a-day Cuban programming.

Radio personalities at times warred among themselves rather than attempting to achieve exile unity. Two of the largest and most vocal anti-

Castro groups in Miami—the Revolutionary Movement of the People and the Democratic Front—merged, forming the National Revolutionary Council. José Miró Cardona, Castro's short-lived prime minister, headed this new group. But it soon collapsed.

As early as 1960, exile militants working closely with several United States civilian and military agencies had initiated preparations to invade Cuba. The Eisenhower administration had approved various covert plans to overthrow Castro and his government.[31] Recruits were sent for training into the Florida Everglades and countries in Central America. Cuban exiles from all walks of life volunteered. When President Kennedy took office, he learned about the measures underway. He accepted them but submitted a reorganized plan that led to the creation of Brigade 2506, an invasion force of volunteer soldiers advised by U.S. military personnel and contract advisors. Flavio Bravo, Blas Roca's second-in-command in the PSP, flew to Moscow to tell the Kremlin that Kennedy seemed to be much more aggressive than Eisenhower about Cuba, and that if thousands of anti-Castro rebels managed to penetrate Cuban defenses, Cubans would be "living in a period like your crusade against the *kulaks* [peasants] in 1927–30."[32]

After the invasion had started, however, reacting to advice from advisors that it would likely fail and that the United States should not become directly involved, Kennedy canceled the plans to provide air cover by United States military planes unless the Cuban exile forces established their beachhead on Cuban soil. As a result, the exile volunteers who launched their April 17, 1961, invasion of Cuba's Bay of Pigs and Girón Beach stood no chance. The Cuban exile force had no jets, but mostly old B–26s shot down by the Cubans. The invasion brigade was confronted by 20,000 Cuban troops and defeated in three days when their ammunition ran out. Eighty died in the fighting and another 37 drowned. Cuban soldiers captured 1,189 others. The fiasco represented a major victory for the Soviet bloc, although some of the claims made by the Cubans about having known about the invasion preparations, step by step, as they unfolded, proved later to have been false. Two years later, Castro revealed to Soviet Premier Khrushchev that "the Cubans [had not been] very good at infiltrating the Cuban émigré movement abroad." They did not know, it turned out, about the activities of their greatest enemies: Manuel Ray

(Minister of the Interior in Castro's first cabinet before Ray defected), José Miró Cardona, and Tony Varona.[33]

This was no solace for the anti-Castro rebels captured during the invasion. One group of prisoners was taken from the beach in a sealed truck, under conditions so bad that some of them died en route to prison. The survivors of the invasion received thirty-year sentences in Cuban prisons, and seven were executed as Batista-era war criminals. The Bay of Pigs failure permitted Castro to publicly justify his new alliance with the Soviet Union, and it provided an anti-American rallying point that would be exploited for decades. The KGB took control of the Cuban security service. Cuba requested and received enormous amounts of weaponry from Soviet bloc countries, especially Czechoslovakia, the USSR, and China. This included 125 modern tanks, anti-tank guns, 167,000 pistols and rifles with ammunition, and 428 field artillery pieces.

Now openly protected by the Soviet Union, Castro's hold over the 7 million residents of Cuba tightened and permitted him to barter the surviving Bay of Pigs veterans in December 1962 in exchange for $53 million in food and medical supplies from the United States. The members of the exile community who pressured Washington into negotiating with Cuba and paying the ransom emerged as heroes. This would not always be the case with similar events in later years.

President Kennedy and his wife, Jacqueline, traveled to Miami's Orange Bowl in December 1962 to greet the returned invaders. Before a crowd estimated at between 35,000 and 40,000 exiles, Kennedy received the Brigade 2506 flag twenty months after the failed invasion and declared: "I can assure you that this flag will be returned to this brigade in a free Havana."[34]

In the wake of the Bay of Pigs debacle, Kennedy reiterated to the National Security Council and to the Joint Chiefs of Staff his determination to drive out Castro. He suggested that plans be made for reconstruction of Cuba's "civil affairs and military government" after a successful invasion. He approved the return of covert actions to rid Cuba of Castro, including support of José Miró Cardona's government-in-exile in Miami. The CIA launched an operation named Candela, which aimed to kill Fidel Castro on July 26, the anniversary of the attacks on the Moncada Barracks. Cuban and KGB agents uncovered the plan and set out to liquidate the Candela network. This, as well as CIA plans to create pretexts for future armed invasions of Cuba, escalated hostilities considerably, not only between Cuba and the United States but elsewhere. In mid-August, Nikita Khrushchev ordered the construction of the Berlin Wall. And a few weeks later, on September 4, Castro asked the Kremlin for eight divisions of surface-to-air missiles, 388 missiles in all.[35] By mid-1962, Soviet technicians had been posted all over Cuba to supervise the construction of the missile sites.

The Cuban Missile Crisis erupted in October 1962. After it was defused, avoiding nuclear strikes on the United States and the Soviet Union by the thinnest of margins, the strained relations between Washington and Havana that had existed since the Bay of Pigs worsened considerably. Castro halted all direct flights to Miami, causing a sharp temporary decline in the number of new refugees. Those who managed to get to the United States did so clandestinely or via third countries, especially Spain, Venezuela, and Mexico. These exiles, however, were labeled aliens by the United States government and therefore fell subject to the immigration restrictions imposed by the Immigration and Naturalization Service. Castro's anger at John F. Kennedy—and at the covert actions Kennedy approved against the Cuban regime—caused many to believe stories spread after Kennedy's assassination about Castroite involvement in the plot.[36]

WAVE UPON WAVE

Historians and demographers debate about how many "waves" of Cubans came after Batista's fall. At the least, there have been seven, added to the one formed by the small group of Batista cronies who saw the handwriting on the wall, as it were, and fled before Castro's victory. Batista and his closest cronies flew to the Dominican Republic after midnight on December 31,1958–January 1, 1959. The main initial wave came between early 1959 and late 1962. Perhaps 5,000 of these first arrivals had been officials of Batista's government and members of his entourage. The rest were those driven out by the revolution's confiscations and threats. Many anti-Batista exiles in Miami, New York, and other cities returned to Cuba from 1960 to 1961, only to leave again for the United States three decades later. The two defining moments for the first wave of refugees was the failed Bay of Pigs invasion in 1961 and the Missile Crisis a year later. In the aftermath of these events, all but the most idealistic stopped believing that they would soon return to Cuba and reclaim their affluent homes and businesses as they had expected. Hatred of Castro became even more deeply felt.

The second wave came between October 1962 and September 1965. Sixty thousand Cubans came legally during this period, as well another 6,000 who entered the United States by illegal means. Some came from Cuba; others came from third countries, where they first had gone: Spain, Mexico, Jamaica, and Venezuela, mostly. There they obtained a U.S. visa or a "visa waiver" issued by the U.S. State Department. The release of 1,117 captured prisoners from the failed Bay of Pigs invasion as well as their families brought the total to more than 4,000 men, women, and children exchanged for a ransom in dollars paid by the United States. Although relations between Cuba and the United States worsened, Castro stayed very much in power.

By the third wave (September 1965 to April 1973), the arrivals tended to be working-class Cubans heeding Fidel Castro's speech to the annual meeting of the Committee for the Defense of the Revolution in which he said that any Cuban wishing to leave the island could do so. This led to the Freedom Flights, beginning on December 1, 1965, and continuing until April 16, 1973, bringing at least 340,000 more exiles representing a cross-section of the Cuban population.[37] Still another wave arrived during Mariel in 1980 and throughout the 1980s and after, mostly in the form of rafters, called "boat people" by the media.

Most Cubans settling elsewhere eventually fared well, but only in Miami did they attain political and economic predominance. They came to South Florida in overwhelming numbers and were highly educated and experienced in business. Miami, part of the rapidly emerging Sunbelt but economically on its periphery, at the same time awaited development. Although it did not seem so at first, Miami's opportunities for growth on one hand and the arrival of the Cuban influx on the other would change the identity of Dade County forever. By 2001, in the 2.1 million population of newly dubbed Miami-Dade County, only 21 percent were "Anglo."

Another way of looking at the impact of the influx of Cubans to Miami is to realize that more than 665,000 Cubans poured into Miami between 1960 and 1977, while at least another 125,000 more arrived during the Mariel boatlift in 1980, and tens of thousands more subsequently. Although the initial wave of Cuban arrivals considered themselves exiles, not immigrants, and expected to return to a Castro-free island in a matter of weeks or months, Cuban Americans in South Florida still shared many traits with immigrants from other Latin American countries. These included the Spanish language and, among most community members, Roman Catholicism. Other traits, however, differed considerably. By the late 1970s, Cuban Americans had become the wealthiest group of Hispanic origin in the United States, surpassing all other Latino communities around the country in economic prowess. By the next decade, they had reached positions of power in government, finance, manufacturing, construction, and education. Interestingly, the desperate exiles who arrived during Mariel—and who were castigated by Castro as *escoria* (garbage) and by Miami Cuban radio as "bullets aimed at Miami"—over time assimilated more completely than any of the other waves of arrivals from Cuba.[38]

The arrivals faced several kinds of barriers and problems. For one, their values conflicted with the ways people were expected to behave in their adopted society. Preserving their cultural identity (*cubanidad*) remained an unswerving ideal. Another barrier was circumstantial: lack of fluent English, or specific training, or transferable skills and licenses earned in Cuba. Discrimination posed a third barrier, especially among Cubans of Asian or African background. Some (and sometimes all) of these obstacles contributed to low self-esteem, isolation, depression, homesickness, or cultural confusion.[39]

The stories of exiles who did not settle in Miami differed substantially from those who did. The experience of the Muñoz family was typical, although in Cuba they were not members of the elite but the middle-class. Silvia's mother arrived at the end of 1962, but her Spanish-born husband could not leave Cuba for another five years. Mother and daughter lived in a tiny rooming house with no sink; meals were comprised mostly of Spam and powdered eggs distributed by the refugee center. They shared a hallway refrigerator and a bathroom with three other (male) roomers. Silvia's mother finally found work as a seamstress and later in a woodworking company, although she had an accident there and sliced off her thumb at the joint. When Silvia married at seventeen, her mother moved in with an American family as a nanny. After her father arrived, he worked in a Cuban grocery store six and a half days a week until well into his seventies.[40]

A few exiles chose to leave Miami. María de los Angeles Torres recalls: "Feelings against Cuban exiles were mounting. My father wanted to revalidate his medical license and felt that he would have better job opportunities outside of Miami. My mother was critical of the pretension and consumerism that characterized [Miami exile] life, particularly around the "'doctors' wives clubs." So my father applied through Catholic Charities for relocation, and we were sent to Cleveland, Ohio." But the American heartland wasn't as receptive as what the family had wished for. They found Americans as cold as the winter weather, and racist. The day following President Kennedy's assassination, children yelled at María and her sister as they boarded their school bus: "You dirty Cubans, you dirty Cubans, you killed our President." The next day, they found their bicycles smashed. The family moved to Texas, only to encounter segregated public facilities and hostility to Hispanics.[41]

Many others shared the Torres' experience, but not Cubans who remained in Florida. The steady arrival of tens and then hundreds of thousands of Cubans to Miami energized the economy in other ways, mostly in the providing of services delivered by Spanish-speaking dentists, hairdressers, plumbers, accountants, and the like. Grocery stores expanded, as did the number of private schools in the city. When the children from Cuba arrived, the Dade County school system refused to offer instruction in Spanish, even if the newcomers spoke no English at all. Partially in response (as well as to preserve social status), dozens of private schools sprang up, some transporting names from schools in Cuba such as the elite academies, Belén Jesuit, Edison, and LaSalle, other schools serving refugee children who did not speak English, like the Demetrio Pérez's Lincoln-Martí school chain. All of this generated revenue, some coming from the burgeoning municipal tax base, some from private agencies such as Roman Catholic charities. In addition, the federal government provided more than $180 million in aid between 1961 and 1965, in addition to the cost of the Freedom Flights, estimated at $300 million at least.[42]

The story of La Progresiva Presbyterian School is one of a school wholly transplanted from Cuba to Miami. Founded in 1900 by American missionaries in Cárdenas (in the province of Matanzas), the school was confiscated by the Castro government in 1961 and renamed the Marcelo Salado school, named for a revolutionary youth killed fighting Batista's forces. Today, Elián González studies at that school in Cuba.

With her husband, the Reverend Ernesto Sosa, curriculum director María Sosa, a 1935 Progressiva alumna, reopened the school in Miami in 1971, in the heart of Little Havana. Class size—from pre-kindergarten to high school—ranges from seventeen and twenty students, and most spend their entire school lives together. Students pay what they can, and those who do not have the means receive grants from the United States Presbyterian Church.[43]

Entire neighborhoods became revitalized, and by 1977 there were more Cuban-owned businesses in Miami than the total of all businesses in 1959. In the ensuing years, many of these businesses attracted interest from Latin Americans, who felt comfortable negotiating in Spanish with Miami Cuban business executives and financiers. From its start as an enclave economy, Cuban Miami by the 1990s had attracted more than 330 multinational companies, 29 binational chambers of commerce, 49 foreign consulates, and 20 foreign trade offices. Miami became a magnet not only for escapees from Cuba but also for immigrants from all parts of the hemisphere. By the late 1980s, Miami started to refer to itself as the "Crossroads of the Americas."

On the whole, Cuban Americans overcame the obstacles of transition far better than most other new arrivals. They successfully constructed a social, political, and moral community while simultaneously adjusting to a foreign culture and managing to maintain a good portion of what they brought in their hearts, if not their suitcases.

A NEW WORLD

Arriving in November 1960, Bernardo Benes came to a city already populated by tens of thousands of Cubans who had arrived earlier. But he quickly surmounted any disadvantage this might have posed. By luck, banker Jack Gordon was a distant cousin by his first marriage. Gordon, an astute businessman, realized that it might be useful to employ one of the new Cuban arrivals. He asked his bank's personnel director, George Hirsh, to interview Benes, and after Hirsh gave the green light, hired Bernardo to work as a clerk in the audit department.

The job allowed Bernardo to move his wife, child, and parents, together with his sister, brother-in-law, and niece to a dilapidated two-story, three-bedroom house in South Miami Beach on Euclid Avenue and Fourteenth Place. The house became so crowded—especially when additional guests arrived—that Bernardo and his brother-in-law had to sleep outside on a little patio. When it rained, they came in and slept on the floor. One took a number to use the two tiny bathrooms. Ricky, now pregnant with her second child, received no news from her parents and sister in Cuba. Bernardo found out what had happened but did not tell his wife, who learned the truth when her sister arrived months later. She told Ricky that by early 1961 it had become so difficult to leave Cuba that would-be exiles had to convert pesos into dollars on the black market, taking tremendous losses in the conversion rate but gaining enough to provide for family members until they could depart. One day, Ricky's mother and father were both arrested for illegal trading in currency. They were sent to jail: her mother spent six months in a mostly women's prison in Guanajay, and her father served nine months in the notorious La Cabaña Fortress prison. When released, Ricky's mother found that her home had not yet been confiscated. This was good fortune indeed because she had hidden their passports in the freezer; without them, it would surely have proven more difficult to flee from the island.

Otherwise, things improved for Bernardo's career in the United States. Within a year of hiring Bernardo, Gordon, a liberal and champion of underdog causes, promoted him to his assistant. Because Benes kept bringing his friends to the bank for interviews, in short order Washington Federal had the highest percentage of Cuban employees of any business in Miami. At first the Cuban community did not generate much money, because few people had any, but they developed a loyalty to Washington Federal that lasted for years. One of Benes's hires—the father of Magda Montiel Davis, a pro-dialogue activist who decades later would be vilified as had been Benes—started out as a porter but worked his way up to a managerial position. He would often take Joel Benes and Jonathan Gordon, the son of his boss, to baseball games and introduce them to old-time Cuban baseball players who had come to Miami.

The story of Benes's new life in Miami illustrates not only the story of a man driven by the desire to make a new life for his family and the entire Cuban exile community but the remarkably singular nature of the community itself. During his first two decades in South Florida, Benes applied tireless energy to many causes: restoring, at least as far as possible, the way of life his family had enjoyed in Cuba; pressuring the "Anglo" elite to admit talented Cuban Miamians to historically exclusionary volunteer and community organizations; fulfilling his personal need to be appreciated and accepted as an insider by the Cuban community; and helping assuage the isolation felt by his community-within-a-community—that is, the 10,000 or so Cuban Jews who faced prejudice not only as Cubans but also as Jews.

The first time Benes's name appeared in the press (the *Miami Herald* incorrectly called him Eduardo Benes) was in 1961, when he attempted to transfer his friend Bobby Maduro's Cuban Sugar Kings—since moved, with little financial success—to Jersey City after Castro banned professional sports. Benes had been the lawyer for the Sugar Kings when they were a farm team of the ironically named pre-Castro-era Cincinnati Reds. Maduro, who owned the team, was the son of a wealthy and respected owner of an insurance company. The Maduros lost everything in 1959, when further franchise moves failed. Benes and Gordon approached Miami Mayor Robert King High for help to transfer the Jersey City franchise to South Florida, which had been without a team since the minor-league Miami Marlins had moved to San Juan. Having the Sugar Kings in Miami would do little but restore a sentimental link, but Miami civic leaders showed little interest in offering a subsidy (Benes and Gordon had asked for $50,000) and low rent for Miami Stadium.[44]

The group favoring bringing Cuban baseball to Miami wrote to Cuban players in the major leagues: Orestes Miñoso, who played the outfield in 1961 for the Chicago White Sox (and cringed when sportscasters called him "Minnie" Minoso), and the Washington Senators' Camilo Pascual, but the effort failed. Bobby Maduro, a decent and honest man, lived in poverty in exile. At the end, when he was hospitalized for a brain tumor, his room looked out at the sadly deteriorated baseball stadium that would be named for him after his death.

Jack Gordon realized that good public relations with the Cuban ex-iles, some engaged in starting businesses to cater to the growing Cuban community in Miami, would lead to further bridge-building activities. In addition to Benes's regular banking duties, Gordon made his new vice-president his Minister without Portfolio. Benes was allowed to pursue the bank's interests by devoting much of his time to community activities.[45]

Meanwhile, pressures for property-owning Cubans to depart the island continued to increase. In the first phase of the revolution, Castro's police and G–2 (State Security) agents imprisoned more than 40,000 people and executed a few thousand more. On April 16, 1961, Castro proclaimed himself a Marxist-Leninist and boasted that Cuba was now a socialist na-tion. Exiles in the United States and abroad still expected Castro to fall, but some realized that their absence would be long lasting, and began to take steps to help themselves and others in their new communities.

Benes, arguably the most public of the members of this emerging group, prodded Miami's power structure to open its doors for Cuban refugees. Benes encouraged his growing network of friends and acquain-tances to bankroll them. His business strength, however, which lay in his creativity and his role as financial advisor, would make some of his friends, and associates who listened to him, wealthy, but would not benefit Benes himself.

Others whom he befriended turned on him, cutting him out of the very deals that Benes had brokered. For example, Washington Federal Savings and Loan financed what may have been the first condominium in the United States. Leonard Turkel, his landlord and next-door neighbor, put up the building, at the corner of Española Way and Pennsylvania Avenue in Miami Beach. Seeing this, Benes decided to get into the condominium business himself. Raising the money for this new kind of venture was achieved in the old-fashioned way—through networking with friends and relatives. He would play dominos until two in the morning with friends and tell them how he had closed condominium deals while at Zaydín's law firm. A group of his listeners followed Benes's guidelines and successfully built four condominium apartments. But they failed to include Benes as a business partner in their venture, and though he had originated many of the ideas, he saw none of the profits.

On a separate occasion, Benes briefly became involved with the first Cuban American automobile dealership in the United States, as a result of his friendship with Bill Aramony, director of the United Way in Miami and later national director in Alexandria, Virginia. Benes contacted Aramony and asked him if he knew any senior official from General Motors or Ford. A few days later, two representatives of the Ford Motor Company arrived in Miami and had a long lunch at the Bilbao Restaurant with Benes and Carlos Dascal. Three days later, Benes, Dascal, and a few other investors had become owners of Midway Ford. They then hired a former sales manager of a large Chevrolet dealership in Miami to run their dealership, which proved to be an unwise decision. Once again, Benes had come up with the idea, brought the right people together and gave them freedom to run the business, to his financial detriment. He left the agency with a bitter taste but chose not to fight in court.

Benes's community activities extended beyond his work for Continental National Bank. From the start, the tiny Benes home became a meeting place for Cuban Jews. Many of the Jewish Cubans who arrived in the first wave were shocked by the indifference shown to them by Miami's Anglo Jewish institutions. One rabbi, Mayer Abramowitz, opened his home and synagogue to them, but few others followed suit. Since the thousands of Jewish Cuban exiles had no Spanish-language synagogue, some of them living in their third homeland after fleeing to Cuba from Europe, they wandered up and down Lincoln Road meeting friends as they walked. Existing Jewish houses of worship provided assistance only sporadically. In the case of the Benes family, thanks to Jack Gordon, Joel was invited to attend Temple Beth Sholom's nursery school, while its rabbi, Leon Kronish, gave Ricky a job for twenty-five dollars a week escorting children on the school bus. The Benes family also received synagogue membership without having to pay dues. Most other Cuban Jews, however, did not receive similar favors.

During the 1960s, Benes and others looked to establish a synagogue for Jewish Cuban exiles, most of whom had settled in Miami Beach. "As I told you personally," Benes wrote to Rabbi Kronish, "I feel that I owe some kind of 'protection' [for] the elderly Jewish people [who] came from Cuba."[46] "We are a naïve people," Benes told a reporter. "We expected to be greeted with love, not with its opposite—indifference."[47]

In 1969, Benes became president of the Cuban-Hebrew Congregation. Its executive director, Ofelia Ruder, published a monthly informational bulletin, *The Jew-Ban*, a name (also spoken as *juban*, to identify Jewish Cuban refugees), that was coined innocently but as time passed became an embarrassment to members of the younger generation.[48]

At a speech that same year before the South Florida Economic Society, Benes compared the Berlin Wall to the Florida Straits, which separated 225,000 Cubans (that year) from their homeland. Just as Germans in East Berlin risked their lives to escape and often fell to the bullets of border guards, Cubans risked their lives on flimsy boats and in makeshift vessels to reach the mainland.

Benes worked passionately to build bridges to the "old boy" network in Miami and also worked hard to overthrow Castro. He lobbied his friend Claude Pepper to introduce the first bill in Congress denouncing the Castro regime. In 1967, Congressman Pepper invited Benes and three other Miami Cubans (Luis Botifoll, former Cuban Premier Jorge García Montes, and ex-President Carlos Prío Socarrás) to Washington to lobby for his anti-Castro bill. Benes testified before the Senate Judiciary Committee at hearings on the "Communist threat to the United States through the Caribbean."

Senator Strom Thurmond, then still a segregationist Dixiecrat from South Carolina, swore him in. One of the first questions directed to Benes was about his political affiliations. He replied that he belonged to no political party or organization in the United States but that he was anti-Castro because Castro "is a communist and communism represents immorality." He also told the committee that in his view more capital had fled Latin America after the Castro takeover in Cuba than the $2 billion spent under the Alliance for Progress. This has left Latin American countries internally weakened, he noted, and vulnerable.[49] The Pepper bill, stating the principles on which United States–Cuban relations should be governed, was approved by Congress on August 16, 1967.

Benes was well acquainted with Latin America. One of his major activities at the bank was as a contract advisor to the State Department's USAID program to export the savings and loan concept abroad as a means to provide home mortgages for Latin Americans of modest income. This program formed part of President John F. Kennedy's Alliance for Progress and in the end proved highly successful.

In addition, Benes's Washington Federal Savings and Loan began to invite groups of Latin Americans for three-week training courses on S&L institutions. More than 500 Latin Americans, and some Asians and Africans, received training in the program. USAID officials learned about this and contracted Benes to write a training manual in Spanish. It was published jointly by USAID and the Inter-American Development Bank in Spanish and distributed throughout the hemisphere. A Portuguese edition translated and published by the Pontifical Catholic University of Rio de Janeiro was distributed in Brazil. In the United States, savings and loan associations failed because regulations restricted them to non-adjustable mortgages, and because, in some cases, individual S&Ls speculated imprudently. The main reason was that when inflation reached double digits under President Carter, S&Ls lost money on every mortgage they issued. By contrast, many Latin American governments regularly adjusted loan payments to the cost of living, thereby providing the flexibility needed to make S&L plans work. Across the region, especially in Chile, Paraguay, Brazil, and the Dominican Republic, the S&L process became highly successful, financing tens of thousands (and ultimately millions) of homes for modest-income families. The Brazilian arrangements were made through the *Banco Nacional de Habitação*, one of three agencies offering housing loans, even under the country's military government, from 1964 to 1985.

As early as 1966, USAID funds from Washington were channeled through the S&Ls established by the men trained at Benes's bank, yielding 20,000 conventionally financed homes in Latin America. Benes spoke ebulliently to Larry Birger of the *American Savings and Loan Weekly* in a 1966 interview: "This is a tremendous weapon against the Reds," he said, using Cold War rhetoric. "Any Latin who owns his home will be thinking twice about pledging future allegiance to the Communists."[50]

Despite his fast pace as a banker and entrepreneur, Benes spent enormous amounts of time at volunteer work in the community, and found hundreds of jobs for unemployed Cubans. His interests ranged from relief aid for newcomers at the Cuban Refugee Emergency Center in the old *Miami News* building, in 1962 renamed the Freedom Tower, to establishing the Latin American division of the United Fund of Dade County. He became the only Spanish-speaking member of Miami's Welfare Planning

Council. He raised money for the State of Israel. He founded a Miami "Interamerican" chapter of Hadassah, the Jewish women's charitable organization.[51] He created a group, Medical Operation Amigo, which sent volunteer social workers and health officials to Peru and Nicaragua in the aftermath of natural disasters. The first group, headed by Dr. Modesto Mora, went to Peru in June 1970 after mudslides had destroyed thousands of homes. The support of Congressman Claude Pepper made this trip possible. According to Benes, Pepper spent ten hours on the phone to Washington agencies, and the next day enough equipment was shipped to Peru to operate a portable hospital. A few years later, the same arrangement was made twice to fly doctors and nurses to Managua, Nicaragua, to assist victims of earthquakes, mudslides, and flooding.

Although he became a registered Democrat, Benes generally kept his political views to himself. But his older brother, Jaime, then living in Charlotte, North Carolina, and working as a textile engineer at a plant owned by relatives, wrote a lengthy letter to the Charlotte *Observer* that reflected his brother's outlook, since the two were close and always in contact with one another. Jaime Benes, in the name of the "Cuban refugees in Charlotte," complained that a series of ten articles published in the paper had been too soft on Castro. He wrote:

> No attempt is made to report the actual living conditions of the Cuban people under the worst regime that any Latin American country has known. By inference, [the articles] made [Castro's Cuba] look better than Batista's government. The Cuban people never had any animosity or hate against the American people, and the fact that the end of tourism marked a decline in business for organized prostitution does not imply that the Cuban people thought that the American tourists were the only cause of prostitution . . .
>
> There was never malaria in Cuba, so Castro could not have eliminated it. The new "doctors" are not real, as they have made a doctor out of any second or third-year medical student with a six-week accelerated course. The polio immunization never took place, as the Russian polio vaccine did not prove itself to be any good and caused some deaths. . . . Life in Cuba has become a nightmare, as one never knows when the dreaded G-2 or militia will come in the middle of the night and haul you to one of the many prisons. Cubans call their ration cards Passports to Hunger, as they cannot even get what is rationed. With all these things tormenting the Cuban people . . . it is not surprising that Castro can only rely on the 14-to-19 year-

old group, which he has been brainwashing and indoctrinating for the last three years. This group would fight against any invasion, but the rest of the Cuban people would not fight against any invasion, either of Cubans, Americans, or Latin Americans.[52]

Once perceived as a voting bloc, Cubans in Miami began to receive preferential treatment from immigration authorities. At first, Cubans received visa waivers by the United States Embassy as parolees—exiles from a communist government—even though immigration quotas were filled. Five years later, under the Johnson administration's Cuban Adjustment Act of 1966, Cubans received the most preferential status ever given to arrivals from other countries. This new Immigration and Naturalization Service regulation extended resident status to Cubans a year and a day after their legal entry to the United States, giving them, as residents, the precious "green card" permitting them to work legally. Even those who did not come with visas but who stayed in the country for more than a year were covered by the Adjustment Act. Arrivals from every other country in the world had to wait much longer, filing for admission. This was easy for some—those with American-citizen spouses or children— but very difficult for everyone else, who had to prove financial independence or have backing from an American firm. Moreover, although the Adjustment Act was intended as a temporary measure to prevent bottlenecks in the processing of the flood of Cubans who had entered between 1960 and 1962, it has never been repealed, although President Bill Clinton altered it in the mid-1990s by turning back would-be refugees who did not reach dry land. As a result, Cubans seeking to enter the United States continued to have privileges extended to no other group, although certainly they received uneven treatment at best once they settled in, and most chose to remain within the psychological safety of the Miami-Cuban enclave rather than to pursue complete assimilation.

In frustration and anger at Cuba's downward spiral into a socialist state, Cuban exile groups in Miami from the beginning sought to keep their struggle against Castro from ebbing. In 1964, the Bacardí Rum Corporation, headed by José "Pepín" Bosch, provided funds for a referendum to select representatives to a broad-based exile front, named the *Representación Cubana del Exilio* (RECE). Jorge Mas Canosa, who would ultimately achieve national influence as head of the Cuban American National Foundation, soon emerged as one of the front's leaders. But the RECE did not accomplish its goal of representing all Miami Cubans—never a community that shared the same opinions—and so its influence waned.

In 1965, speaking at the base of the Statue of Liberty, President Lyndon Johnson announced that any Cubans who so wished would be admitted to the United States. This paved the way for the Freedom Flights, which started on December 1 of that year. Also, Cuban officials permitted relatives of refugees to leave from the port of Camarioca in Matanzas province, bringing in about 2,866 new arrivals. A "memorandum of understanding" signed three months later, in December 1965, by officials of the Johnson administration and the Cuban government, with the assistance of the Swiss Embassy in Havana, authorized two daily flights from Varadero airport east of Havana to Miami. The air bridge served to reunify families and bring others permitted to leave Cuba to enter the United States. From December 1, 1965, to April 6, 1972, 3,000 to 4,000 exiles flew to Miami every month. Males of military age, however, were barred from emigrating, and those with skills had to remain at least until replacements were found and trained. Sometimes this meant waiting two or three years while being forced to perform manual agricultural labor until the visas were granted. More than 300,000 additional Cubans came to the United States before the flights stopped in the spring of 1973.

Most of the new arrivals had relatives of Cubans already in the United States, not necessarily in Miami. Benes, remembering his own lonely arrival in 1960, formed a volunteer women's auxiliary from the Cuban Hebrew Congregation, which he helped found, to operate a reception center and snack bar in Building 69 at Opa-locka airport, where the flights were to arrive. Later, women from other religious organizations joined the effort. He arranged for food and soft drinks and coffee to be donated by local firms and given to the new arrivals. He worked so fast that the reception center was open on the day of the first flight from Cuba. Benes remembers how appreciative the new arrivals were. A woman who must have been in her 90s, came up to Bernardo at the booth and told him: "I have prayed to God to let me live long enough to have one more Chester." Benes realized she was talking about cigarettes, and quickly produced a pack of Chesterfields for her.[53]

Many of the arrivals were elderly or infirm relatives of Cubans in Miami. Most of the rest came from lower-middle and working-class backgrounds, although the educational levels of even these exiles were higher than the average for the entire Cuban population. Exiles during this period were predominantly urban and Caucasian, with the exception of as many as 8,000 Cubans of Chinese origin. Still, many jokes came at the expense of the Miami Cubans and their insularity, and that they were transplanting Cuba to South Florida. One involved Benes. A Miami Beach newspaper reported the following tale:

> Banker Bernardo Benes, whose American adventures have been chronicled in *Fortune* Magazine, is one of the most successful Cuban refugees in Miami Beach. But it takes a while to get adjusted. When a reporter called Benes yesterday, his secretary replied, "Dr. Benes is out of the country." Asked where he had gone, she replied with a charming accent, "To Washington, D.C."[54]

Often, things did not go smoothly. Some Miamians invented pejorative terms for Cubans. Many resented the fact that Cubans received government help whereas other national groups—especially the tens of thousands of Haitians who had fled to South Florida—did not. Members of some of the other larger Latin American communities in Miami complained that the Cubans ignored their problems and hired only fellow Cubans. African Americans, only recently given equal rights in the United States, resented that fact that even menial job advertisements frequently required a knowledge of Spanish, and they became dismayed when Cubans purchased gas stations, laundries, food shops, or hotels and then replaced the black employees with Cubans. Benes attempted to help by volunteering to be the first Cuban on the board of the Greater Miami Urban League. He met with City Commissioner Athalie Range, publisher Garth Reeves, Urban League president T. Willard "Tal" Fair, William Wynn, and other leaders from the African American community to find ways to deal with the situation. His main effort was to persuade School Superintendent Johnny Jones, an African American, to require Spanish in inner city schools, but over time the efforts to make African American children bilingual failed. In 1966, Benes developed the city's first "sweat equity" duplex, designed by architect Richard Rose. The pilot project succeeded. Within a

few months, a duplex apartment in Liberty City, built by the families themselves, was ready for occupancy. But Miami's city leaders did not follow
through, and it remained, at the time, the only such duplex built in Dade
County.

In June 1966, Director Marshall Wise of Miami's Cuban Refugee Center gave a talk to the Inter-American Business Men's Association entitled
"The Cuban Exile in Miami: Asset or Liability?" In it, he not only summarized his center's accomplishments but also ventured some guesses
about the future. They turned out to be prophecies.

Since the refugee program had opened in January 1961, he said,
113,000 of the 204,000 refugees processed by his center were resettled
into 3,000 communities in every state in the country. That half of the arrivals were sent elsewhere might seem surprising, but many, if not most,
returned to Miami later. Wise then told his audience that "refugees" was
not an apt term; that in fact they were political exiles "asking only an opportunity to live in decency and with dignity."[55] Then he addressed the
issue of "assets" and "liabilities." From the standpoint of the employer in
need of skilled help, he said, the Cuban exile is an eagerly sought asset
"because of his ability and willingness to work." To the "unskilled, uned-
ucated and insecure American employee at the lower end of the employment ladder, the Cuban exile is a distinct liability because he threatens
the shaky security of this 'last-to-be-hired' and 'first-to-be-fired' type of
worker." To the "self-serving, malcontent resident who believes it's un-
American to speak a foreign language in public, or even speak English
with a foreign accent, the exile is a liability that he doesn't understand
and resents. . . . To the local exploiting employer, who won't, or says he
can't, pay a decent minimum wage . . . the exile is an asset he can easily
exploit and use."[56]

Wise continued his back-and-forth characterizations of assets and liabilities; all dependent on whether the sayer is a "crier of doom" or an optimist open to tolerance. Then, concluding his talk, he addressed himself
directly to the Cuban members of his audience. His words, read thirty-five
years later, were on the mark:

> You have been welcomed and accepted here, you have been criticized for
> your shortcomings, praised for your virtues; attacked by some, and de-

fended by others. God knows that your virtues far outweigh your short-comings, and you who are the leaders carry on your shoulders the responsibility to keep it that way. You must counsel with those who might get into trouble with the law and set them straight. Tell them that in a democracy the laws apply equally to the rich as they apply to the poor, and that they apply equally to guests in this country as they apply to our own citizens. You must also counsel with groups, professional, political, or otherwise, who might be considering taking harsh actions against society or segments of our society . . . just for the temporary advantage of a few. More active participation in general community activities will enhance the image and prestige that you have built at the cost of humiliation, tears, and sacrifice.[57]

When Marshall Wise died some years later, only eight people attended the funeral, held in Miami.

Not all Anglos shared Wise's compassionate insights. They displayed resentment against the now-established Cuban émigré community. Some complained that the Cubans showed little interest in contributing to the larger community while they isolated themselves within their enclave. Later, when the Cubans in Miami achieved a majority of the population, others would complain further that the exile community intimidated those who would dissent against the policies of the exile leaders, especially when elected officials seemed single-minded in their work for Miami Cubans and against Castroism first and foremost. Some of the discord among Anglos stemmed from differences in their way of life. The long-time residents complained that the Cuban families had many children who always made noise. "The noise and the late hours of the Cubans," the Miami Beach *Sun* complained, "have caused landlords to evict some people and at times older residents have complained to the police."[58] Cuban Jews, who had flocked to Miami Beach, complained that their landlords, often Jewish as well, gouged them. "We had a better rent situation in Cuba," one said.

Beyond Miami Beach, the anger spread over the proposed county bilingual ordinance throughout Dade County, especially in the southern part of the county where few Cubans had settled. Rumors claimed that the Cubans intended to make Spanish Miami's "official language" and that all students would be forced to study Spanish in the public schools. The recent racial integration of Florida schools raised tensions even further. In the same 1967 issue of the Miami Beach *Sun,* a Miami Beach resident revealed, in a letter to the editor, how the language and school issues had turned inflammatory: "The unpleasant fact," he wrote, "is that public school officials in Miami Beach have been and are ignoring the problems present every day. . . . Nerves are being rubbed raw, tension is mounting, and minor incidents are breaking out with increasing frequency. Teachers and administrators for the most part are turning their backs on the scene. . . . Only a bigot or fool would allow the present situation to continue. Only an idiot would allow it to continue."

The bilingualism crusade continued. Three years later, in a polite letter co-signed by a Protestant minister, the Reverend Floyd Knox, Benes protested to the Dade County school superintendent that budget cuts were drastically reducing programs for teaching English to Spanish-speaking students. This was happening, the letter said, even in places like Riverside Elementary, in Little Havana, where 96.8 percent of the students spoke no English. Benes added that he had just learned that for some years the school system had maintained a "Citizens Advisory Committee for bilingual education," but that it had never met. Benes told the school board that federal funds were available to convert a public school into a "model demonstration bilingual school in Dade County."[59]

Political differences also loomed large. Traditionally progressive, especially the retired residents from the Northeast, the Miami Beach elite was shocked by the political attitudes of many of the new arrivals from Cuba. It was not unusual to find Cubans who wanted to "bomb the hell out of North Vietnam or kill every communist on earth," a Miami Beach resident said.[60] In 1960, only one Spanish-language newspaper published in Miami, the *Diario de las Americas,* owned by Nicaraguans but soon considered the newspaper of choice for the Cuban exiles. A few years later, Batista's associates started *Patria,* edited by Armando García-Sigrid, a former politician, and Ernesto Montaner, a pro-Batista poet in exile. *Patria* and similar free newspapers (revenue came from advertising and subsidies) fulminated against the late President Kennedy's unkept promises to the exiles and called local politicians foolish liberals. The established English-language newspapers in Miami began to experiment with pages printed in Spanish—the *Miami News* was the first to print an entire page in that language. In 1987, the *Herald* founded *El Herald* (renamed *El*

Nuevo Herald nine years later) to serve the hundreds of thousands of Miamians who read Spanish but not English.

Benes countered the right-wing press by explaining exile motivations to his Anglo associates. As chair of the Greater Miami Coalition's committee on services to Cubans, he said: "I'm sorry to say that many of us are ignorant about what's going on in the world. . . . Many Cubans here have a naïve and uninformed opinion of world politics. They exist in prejudice. If they would have known about [Alabama's segregationist governor] George Wallace they would have voted for him." But Benes chided the Miami Beach establishment for its attitudes, too. "We pay taxes just like all other people," he said. "Sooner or later the politicians will have to listen to the Cuban residents and citizens on the Beach."[61] Interestingly, in the same article the reporter quoted another Cuban exile, Moses Behar, who had left Cuba so early in 1959 that he had managed to escape with money and jewelry. Within ten years, Behar had become a major apartment-house owner on Miami Beach and claimed to notice "no animosity at all" between Cubans and Anglos.

As a banker, Benes invited counterparts from Latin America to seminars in Miami given by invited representatives of the Import-Export bank in Washington. Continental also promoted Cuban culture and made-in-America products. The bank invited manufacturers of Cuban-style cigars to show their wares in the hopes of garnering publicity for the industry. Food editors from the local press were invited to judge a contest for the "best Cuban sandwich," held in the bank's lobby. During the hot and humid weather from May through November, male employees were permitted to wear guayaberas, the lightweight Cuban shirts often made of linen, rather than coats and ties. In 1980, the bank collected 15,000 toys for distribution on Three Kings' Day on January 6 to poor children in Miami. During the Mariel exodus, bank officers picked up thirty-five refugees from the Orange Bowl football stadium, where they were residing temporarily. At the bank, Benes and Cesar Camacho, the bank's attorney, provided orientation sessions about life in Miami. An employee who played the piano entertained patrons in the lobby at lunchtime with music written by the Cuban composer Ernesto Lecuona.

Some civic groups honored Benes for his efforts. Miami's Evangelism Task Force selected Benes as "one of [our community's] outstanding business and

community leaders." "To further assist you in your task," the letter concluded, "we are sending you a New Testament in today's language."[62] If af-
fronted by this gratuitous act of proselytism, Benes did not show it, accepting
the recognition graciously. Benes was one of the few Cuban Americans to acknowledge the fact that the growth of the Cuban enclave drove black workers from their jobs since once they bought or opened a business, Cubans
almost invariably hired other Cubans.

Ethnic and racial tensions, however, kept Miami divided, especially between Cubans and blacks as well as Cubans and Anglos. As early as 1967,
relations between the Cuban community and the *Miami Herald* started to
deteriorate. In an effort to seek improvement, Benes provided the newspaper with a list of dozens of Cuban attorneys, certified public accountants, architects, engineers, and other professionals for the *Herald* to
contact and use as community resources. Included on the list were Raúl J.
Valdes Fauli, later mayor of Coral Gables; Julio Villeya of the Latin
Builders' Association; Aurora Botifoll and Madre Margarita Miranda of
the praiseworthy Centro Mater; and the presidents of the Big Five Cuban
social clubs that, along with many other social groups, had been re-created
in Miami. The list included students from the University of Miami, officers
of the Cuban Lions, Kiwanis, and Rotary Clubs; journalists from the Spanish-language press. There were educators, including Eduardo Padrón of
Miami Dade Junior College (as it was then called), the Latin Chamber of
Commerce, and the Havana Optimist Club. He listed the leaders of what
he termed the "exile Revolutionary Organizations," including Alpha 66,
La Verdad sobre Cuba (Truth about Cuba Committee); Brigade 2506;
RECE; ABDALA (a group of young anti-Castro militants), and the *Comité
Ejecutivo Libertador.* Benes's list numbered more than one hundred persons,
comprising a detailed census of the most prominent members of the Cuban
American community, organized by specialization (engineer, journalist,
volunteer leader, etc.). When Anglos said that they knew no Cubans to
appoint to their boards, Benes simply gave them a copy of his list. Most ignored the effort, but three Anglo community leaders responded enthusiastically to the list: County Manager Ray Goode, United Way's William
Aramony, and Wood McCue of the Health Planning Council.

Benes devoted extensive effort to issues related to Miami's Jewish community. In 1967, when Israel preemptively attacked Syria and Egypt in

2.2 Alpha 66 truck in Miami anti-Castro demonstration, early 1960s. The sign on the door reads, referring to Castro's calling exiles "scum": "We are not scum; we are from Alpha." Robert M. Levine collection.

what became the Middle East's Six-Day War, Benes mobilized, within the first twenty-four hours, more than twenty Cuban-owned businesses in Little Havana to sell paper ribbons reading, "The dollar of dignity, in support of the people of Israel, from the Cubans of Miami" for $1. Some 4,000 Cubans, most of them not Jewish, bought and wore the blue-colored ribbons. Benes then set up a series of meetings of Cuban organizations to explain and discuss Middle East events. One of the attendees—who later sent a congratulatory letter to Benes—was former Auténtico Party congressman Primitivo Rodríguez, a man of Lebanese descent who had been one of the most outspoken anti-Semites in Cuba during the 1950s. In his letter, Rodríguez praised the "brave and heroic" Israeli military forces, and added an apology "with profound sincerity," for his past statements over the years.[63] During one of the last of his trips from Havana, following a trip to Israel, Benes convinced the elderly leaders of his former synagogue—the sanctuary, which had been mostly converted into government offices, was now termite-ridden and crumbling—to permit him to carry four Torah scrolls, a yarmulke, and prayer shawl to Florida. Castro personally approved Benes's request to carry these religious articles back to Miami. When he returned to his home in Miami, Benes, for reasons he could not explain, took one of the Torahs and put it in his bed, "as if it were an exile in need of comfort." He caressed it and began to sob.[64]

MILITANCY AND VIOLENCE

By the late 1960s, some people—not those listening to Spanish-language radio stations, however—sensed that exile stridency might be diminishing. Dr. Miró Cardona, the former head of the Cuban Revolutionary Council that welded together warring exile factions to field the invasion at the Bay of Pigs in 1961, had become a professor at the University of Puerto Rico. Manuel Artime, the onetime Castro captain and exile leader who ran training bases in Nicaragua and Costa Rica, by 1968 had gone into lumber business, importing wood from Central America. The more militant of the anti-Castro groups and individuals, however, never abandoned their goals. On April 12, 1974, an unknown sniper killed an exile leader, José Elias de la Torriente, the first incident in a new wave of exile political violence.

On October 6, 1976, a Cuban airplane crashed after an explosion near Barbados, killing seventy-eight passengers, many of them young Cuban athletes. Luis Posada Carriles, an anti-Castro activist trained by the CIA, and Orlando Bosch Avila, were charged by Venezuelan officials with the bombing, although both men were eventually acquitted. Posada Carriles later claimed that hardline anti-Castro groups in Miami had funded his anti-Castro terrorist acts, but he later retracted his story. Some years later, still at liberty, he appeared on a special telecast on Miami's Spanish-language Channel 23. Interviewed at an unidentified location, Posada Carriles admitted that the airplane bombing had been a "big mistake" from a human point of view, but he assigned responsibility to the Cuban government, adding that some of the passengers had been intelligence agents from Cuba and North Korea. He added: "That sabotage was the most effective blow that has been delivered to Cuba." According to the usually reserved Miami Herald, which described Posada Carriles as a "master of disguises" and an "assassin," during the time he spent in jail he received regular visits from such distinguished Miamians as Mayor Maurice Ferré.[65] In fact, United States government agencies in the United States had been assisting militant exile Cubans for more than two decades. Posada Carriles, after escaping from a Venezuelan prison, joined Colonel Oliver North in El Salvador to run weapons to the Nicaraguan contras.

Documents examined after the fall of the Berlin Wall and the breakup of the Soviet Union, including the Archive of the President of the Russian Federation and the Russian Ministries of Defense and Foreign Affairs, reveal that even before Castro's victory, as early as spring 1957, the Eisenhower administration feared that Fidel Castro was a potentially "dangerous nationalist." This led a high-ranking CIA delegation to the Oriente province, the locale of Castro's early years, to investigate Castro's character and personality.[66]

Only four months after his taking power, Fidel Castro came to the United States on a triumphant tour that ultimately raised more questions than provided answers about his motives. On April 15, 1959, Castro disembarked at Washington's National Airport at the invitation of the American Society of Newspaper Editors. While many applauded—writer Norman Mailer called Castro a "modern Cortez"[67]—the American Secret Service spent the eleven days of Castro's visit trying to protect him from pro-Batista assassins. Two years after the failed Bay of Pigs invasion, exiles in flotillas of fast boats began attacking the Cuban coast, with CIA backing. The new flow of monetary resources and the presence of large numbers of CIA and other agency operatives in Miami raised the morale of the hardliners and kept their organizations alive. Only in 1972 did the raids stop. In that year, Bay of Pigs veteran Manolo Reboso was appointed to the Miami City Commission, the first Cuban-born American citizen to hold public office.

Acts of violence continued to occur. In February 1975, exile Luciano Nieves, who had said publicly that he favored peaceful coexistence with Castro, was shot and killed. Six months later, publisher (and former Batista supporter) Rolando Masferrer, died in a bomb explosion. In December, bombs exploded at Miami's FBI headquarters, two post office buildings, a bank, and Miami International Airport. Not long afterwards, the news director of WQBA, Emilio Milián, had both legs blown off by a bomb that exploded in his car.[68]

In the following year, 1976, a former president of the Bay of Pigs Veterans' Association, Juan José Peruyero, was shot dead in front of his house. When the United States and Cuba announced on September 1 that each would establish "interest sections" in their respective capitals to facilitate communication, exile leaders organized a protest parade, the "March of Dignity," down Biscayne Boulevard denouncing Castro. Approximately 12,000 marchers participated.

Benes expended much of his efforts working within Cuban Miami. In 1962, he had helped obtain financing for the newly proposed Pan American Hospital, with the help of a group of twenty-two Cuban doctors and their spouses, headed by Modesto Mora, Benes's physician. No banks accepted the loan applications for funds to begin construction until Washington Federal S&L—headed by Jack Gordon and aided in the effort by board member Congressman Claude Pepper—funded the construction of the first hospital in South Florida for the Cuban community. Officially, doctors, nurses, and staff were supposed to be bilingual, but from the beginning, the preferred language was Spanish, and the hospital was part of a fast-growing network of institutions in the community serving the refugees. Benes fostered links to almost every Anglo institution in the city, speaking at luncheons, cultivating the heads of charitable organizations, and pleading for invitations for Cubans to join.

In 1969, Benes took on Dade County's ordinance limiting government employment to resident citizens. Benes's later efforts to enact a bilingual ordinance—that allowed, for example, warning signs to be posted in both English and Spanish—had passed by an 8–0 vote of the Dade County commission, but not without community protests. He had prevailed in negotiations with Jackson Memorial Hospital because the hospital administrators themselves realized that more Spanish-speaking staff had to be added.

The early 1970s witnessed the relationships between Miami Cubans and their Anglo neighbors deteriorating. Benes began calling himself "the token Cuban," implying frustration that his efforts to integrate Miami Cubans into Anglo businesses and government had fallen short. He warned, for instance, that if the public schools did not give black students the ability to communicate in Spanish, they would be at a severe disadvantage seeking employment in an increasingly Spanish-speaking region.

In a newspaper story by the *Herald*'s Mike Baxter, the reporter observed that Benes requested that the schools recognize and accept a pluralistic culture in Miami—as opposed to "making the refugees' assimilation into the American culture their highest goal."[69]

Yet, the response was underwhelming. School board member (and later congressman) William Lehman suggested that "enthusiasm" by teachers and students could resolve any problems. Dr. Paul Bell, administrative director of the school system's division of educational planning, replied, "I think maybe there's a lack of understanding on the part of Dr. Benes and others of what actually is being done and what could be done."[70] Miami's Anglo leadership—and remember that these were still the days when old timers pronounced the name of the city "Miam-uh"—could not understand why the Cubans did not act like other immigrant groups. The Cubans, they complained, resisted assimilation by preserving their own culture and demanding that the majority accommodate them, rather than accept the fact that they were here to stay, and that they would benefit economically and socially by becoming Americanized. Many immigrant groups, of course, chose this path, not only in Florida but also across the United States.

By this time, Benes had become close to Alvah H. Chapman Jr., the president of the Miami Herald Publishing Company. Chapman worked behind the scenes to aid Benes in his efforts to bring Cubans into positions of service and leadership, but he did not interfere with his newspaper's day-to-day reporting, some of which appeared mean-spirited to Cuban readers.

Benes jousted with Charles "Chuck" Perry, the first president of Miami's new Florida International University, part of the state's university system. Just as the private University of Miami in the 1930s and 40s consciously restricted the number of Jews on its faculty, FIU, in its first decade, seemed oblivious to the presence of Hispanics in the community. When a news item announced the appointment of a black Miamian, W. D. Tolbert, as FIU's first "urban agent" (to plan for the training of community workers), Benes chided Perry in a personal letter: "I am enclosing a copy of a clipping from the *Miami Herald* telling of the appointment of Mr. W. D. Tolbert as the University's first 'urban agent.' Would you consider having a Spanish speaking 'agent?' I can supply you with beautiful candidates."[71]

A year later, Benes informed Perry the following in a confidential letter: "over the past months I have been noticing a great increase in criticism of the University from the Spanish-speaking, mainly Cubans . . . who feel that [it] is not being responsive in adequately reflecting the name 'International.'" Benes followed up by bringing thirty Cuban professionals to a meeting at Perry's office. Perry responded by calling the assertion an "Ill-founded rumor" and pointed out that FIU currently enrolled 900 "Cubans." He also called attention to FIU's new program, which trained Cuban-educated certified public accountants to pass the Florida Board of Accountancy's CPA examination.[72]

Benes also tackled less serious issues. In a prank designed to publicize his bank, Benes took on an even more hallowed Miami institution—the National Football League Dolphins. When Rafael Ortega, the son of his friend, Tony Ortega, was signed by the Dolphins but injured his knee, Coach Don Shula told him that he would not play. Tony complained to Benes that Shula was being unreasonable, and that his son was clearly capable of playing. At the next home game, Benes hired an airplane to fly a banner above the Orange Bowl reading: SHULA, PLAY ORTEGA. CONTINENTAL NATIONAL BANK, THE FIRST CUBAN AMERICAN BANK. The Dolphins' defensive coordinator asked Ortega if he knew who was behind the episode. Ortega's response was: "No, but I'm opening an account in this bank tomorrow."[73]

In 1977, Benes co-founded and served as president of the Comprehensive Health Planning Council of South Florida. Under his tenure, the council established the Public Health Trust to run Jackson Memorial Hospital, a network of community health-care centers, and to see that all hospitals in the county had Spanish-speaking staff able to communicate with patients. Benes had occasionally visited emergency rooms and observed anguished Spanish-speaking people unable to communicate with doctors and nurses, and vowed to make certain that this would no longer happen.

CHANGING TIMES IN CUBAN MIAMI

By the mid-1970s, other Cuban voices had started to garner the limelight. Benes had become overexposed publicly, and new groups garnered publicity, in many cases less willing than Benes to compromise. Dade County adopted an ordinance refusing the use of any public building—including the Convention Center—for groups from Cuba or sympathetic to its communist regime. In 1980, the most powerful Cuban Miami group of all, the Cuban American National Foundation (CANF), would be established under the forceful leadership of Jorge Mas Canosa. This organization, well funded and highly effective in its lobbying efforts, became influential not only in South Florida but also in Washington, D.C.

According to some of his former colleagues, Benes's selection as candidate Jimmy Carter's Latin coordinator for his run for the presidency reduced his influence further. The public exposure of Benes as a promoter and fundraiser for a candidate considered excessively liberal—in this community that had turned into a conservative, Republican bastion—generated resentment among Miami Cubans. Some Democrats never trusted the commitment of Florida Democrats to the national party's goals: many were, in Congressman Claude Pepper's words, southern racists and "Republicans in disguise."[74]

During the 1980s, Miami had virtually changed overnight. Many Miami Cubans distanced themselves from the new arrivals from Mariel, knowing that some of them were criminals or mentally troubled. However, Spanish-speaking businessmen welcomed *marielitos* as employees, especially in factories and warehouses because without working papers or green cards, these new arrivals could be exploited into working long hours, without being paid overtime or benefits, and they realized they were powerless to complain.

Still, Miami Cubans during the 1980s showed their pride in being American. Driving around Little Havana and Westchester and Hialeah, one saw Buicks and Chevys in the driveways of the more modest homes, and Lincolns and Cadillacs in front of the more affluent ones. "Anglo" yuppies by then had turned to Hondas, BMWs, and Porsches. A decade later, "*Yucas*" (an acronym for Young Upwardly Mobile Cuban Americans") coveted Lexuses, Jaguars, Infinitis, and even Lamborghinis, sold at Miami's automobile dealerships for the rich.

By the mid-1990s, Washington's attitude toward the Cuban issue had changed. On the political side, after the shooting down of the Brothers to the Rescue planes, the Clinton Administration accepted the provisions of the Helms-Burton Act tightening the embargo, although to assuage the anger expressed by most of the United States' closest allies, the hardest-line mandates were not enforced. Policies affecting newly arriving Cuban refugees, however, did change. In 1994, the number of Cubans arriving in unseaworthy boats and rafts reached unprecedented proportions. Cuba's economy, suffering from mismanagement and lack of Soviet bailout revenue, had hit its lowest point, and rioters protested openly in Havana on August 5. The rafters were motivated by the past history of the United States in welcoming Cubans, and through August, no one in Washington suggested otherwise.

But the arrival of approximately 33,000 *balseros* (rafters) during August 1994 forced a dramatic reassessment of United States policy. It was obvious that Castro, not the Clinton administration, controlled the migration. Castro told CNN reporters, in fact, that in light of recent hijackings of state-owned vessels, Cuba would not deter anyone attempting to leave. Thousands responded by boarding makeshift vessels and setting out to sea. The fortunate encountered smooth seas, or were rescued by the United States Coast Guard.[75] Another Mariel, or worse, loomed on the horizon.

Although the 1966 Cuban Adjustment Act remained in force, the federal government effectively overrode it by issuing a new policy dealing with Cubans crossing the Florida Straits seeking refuge in the United States. Further problems ensued when the Guantánamo Naval Base—constructed for a population of fewer than 5,000—filled up with 33,000 Cuban internees, as well as 14,000 Haitians.

The State Department offered the refugees opportunities to return, but Cuban authorities refused to accept them, although about 1,000 escaped and sneaked back into Cuban territory. The Defense Department sought a quick solution to the problem, since the badly overcrowded base required nearly 8,000 military personnel to run the camps at a cost to taxpayers of $1 million a day. All food and supplies had to be shipped in, and drinking water was available only from overtaxed desalinization plants. Marines, according to Colonel Luis Salas of the Pentagon, "were literally putting up the tents that would handle each additional shipload of migrants even as the ships were entering the harbor."[76] Tensions rose further when one large group was shipped to the Panama Canal Zone, where they

2.3 Rafters in the Florida Straits. Robert M. Levine collection

ultimately rioted and destroyed their camp, leading the Panamanian government to refuse to extend the agreement. United States military personnel did not expect this, because conditions in Panama were actually better than in Guantánamo. But nearly two-thirds of the interned population was comprised of young, single males, who considered the United States military personnel unsympathetic and hostile to them. Because month after month passed with no word about what would be their fate, rumors spread of forced repatriation to Cuba.

Even after negotiations between Havana and Washington created a visa system and eased the tensions, rafters continued to arrive. Some were smuggled in after paying high fees to boat captains who took them to the Bahamas or elsewhere to await undercover transportation to Florida. This, in turn, led to an even more controversial "wet/dry" policy. *Balseros* who made contact with dry land on the American mainland would win resident status after being processed and checked. But boats interdicted at sea—even only a few yards from shore—would have their passengers returned to Cuba to face ostracism or worse. Filmed episodes of rafters disembarking from their boats and being pushed back into the water by Coast Guard officials using fire hoses and other forceful means were telecast on the evening news. Anger continued to rise, but the impasse continued.

By 2000, Miami's population of Cuban origin largely remained culturally torn between their Cuban heritage and their American way of life. "I feel embarrassed by my own Spanish," one young woman said at a forum on the meaning of Generation Ñ, the second generation of Cuban Americans, "but we insist that it be spoken at home, even if it comes out as Spanglish."[77]

Differences in life experience from generation to generation enhanced the emotional difficulties. Families who came soon after Castro's takeover experienced tensions among their children and grandchildren. Exiles leaving Cuba during the island's "Special Period" of economic deprivation, caused by the loss of Soviet subsidies and the tightening of the embargo, shared more characteristics of economic, as opposed to political, refugees. These included not only rafters but also the 20,000 Cubans who were annually granted entry visas as part of an arrangement with the United States. All of them were "children of communism," with some still adhering to socialist beliefs. How these people would fare remained difficult to predict.

CHAPTER THREE

MISSION TO HAVANA: THE CARTER YEARS

F idel Castro's victory over Batista's corrupt dictatorship not only dramatically affected relations between the United States and Cuba; in the words of a foreign policy analyst, "its principal effect was to dynamite the logjam in U.S. policy toward Latin America."[1] Almost overnight, Washington officials and journalists thrust Castro's revolutionary government into the cauldron of the Cold War. The United States awoke to the threat posed by revolutionary Cuba to the entire region, especially in countries ruled by strongmen dictators in league with a tiny elite. This, experts theorized, would leave the rest of the immiserated population vulnerable to Castro-like movements, or, in the case of fragile democracies like Brazil, where rural peasant leagues threatened to topple the ruling landed oligarchy, it would create the pre-conditions for the spread of revolution within the hemisphere.

In March 1960, President Dwight D. Eisenhower, upset by the circus-like atmosphere of firing squads, impromptu military tribunals, and Castro's angry harangues against "Yankee imperialism," agreed to fund an invasion of Cuba "designed to take care of Castro." Seven months later, in October, John F. Kennedy, running for the presidency (who surely had been briefed on Eisenhower's action), accused the Republicans of "blunder, inaction, retreat, and failure" in Latin America, and called for arming "fighters for freedom . . . who offer eventual hope of overthrowing Castro." His opponent, Vice-President Richard M. Nixon, who knew about all of the anti-Castro measures, called Kennedy's statement "dangerously irresponsible." He could not reply in any greater detail because he had been sworn to secrecy.[2] In the final presidential debate before Kennedy's narrow victory at the polls, Kennedy warned again of the danger of Castroism and urged policies that would "win the hearts and minds of Latin America's poor."[3] In 1961, President Kennedy created the Army's Special Forces (the "Green Berets"), elite army troops trained to fight "Castro-type guerrilla insurgencies" but they ultimately only saw action a few years later in Vietnam. But the Bay of Pigs invasion failed, as did CIA efforts to destabilize Castro's government.

Events then occurred in the United States that would lead to new kinds of foreign policy initiatives abroad. In autumn of 1963, Cuba's United Nations delegation used third parties to inform the State Department that it would consider opening confidential talks on normalization of relations. William Atwood, an advisor to the United States Mission to the United Nations, held several meetings with the Cubans, and advanced to the point at which Atwood was informed that the Cuban ambassador to the United Nations would meet with him to discuss a date for talks to be held in Havana. President John F. Kennedy, on his own, asked the French journalist, Jean Daniel, to deliver a message to Fidel Castro during a scheduled interview. Reportedly, Castro greeted the news—that Kennedy was willing to negotiate—with elation, and responded by saying that he was willing to make concessions. Just as Daniel prepared to depart Havana for Washington, the world learned that on November 22, 1963, John F. Kennedy had been gunned down in Dallas.[4]

Under the presidency of Lyndon B. Johnson, despite accusations that the CIA was attempting to kill Castro and to implicate Cuba in the Kennedy assassination, the Cubans made further gestures seeking negotiations. In July 1964, Castro held several long meetings with the *New York Times's* Richard Eder; allegedly, Castro told the reporter that both sides shared blame for their mutual antagonisms.[5] But Secretary of State Dean Rusk, still believing that Castro's government would not last, rejected the overtures because he did not want to signal weakness on the part of the United States.

Sometime during 1971, Bernardo Benes convinced Pepín Bosch, the chairman of the Bacardí Corporation and head of RECE, the Cuban-based umbrella group for anti-Castro organizations, to mount a radio transmitter on a yacht. Crew members would broadcast for twenty minutes each evening, starting with "El Canonazo de la Nueve," the cannon firing that heralded 9:00 P.M. all through Havana. These broadcasts would be loving, not confrontational. When Bosch agreed to cooperate, Benes contacted his friend Larry Sternfield in the CIA, asking for support. Benes narrates the rest:

> Two weeks later, [Sternfield] came back with a manila envelope and told me that his superiors had approved the transmissions to Cuba and that they had some new electronic device that allowed the yacht not to be identified by Cuban authorities. Before leaving my office, he said that they needed approval from the president, Richard Nixon. To my great surprise, I received a call a few days later from Larry, who told me that the operation had not been approved by the president. . . . This is how I became a *dialoguero*. I knew that the Cuban exile community lacked the power to become effective opponents of the Cuban government. We needed the support of the U. S. government, and if the president did not help us, I decided that we had to look for an acceptable and dignified coexistence with Castro. So I converted myself from belligerent to a *dialoguero*.[6]

The first formal negotiations between Castro's Cuba and the United States occurred in 1973, when the two countries signed an anti-hijacking agreement. Other events, however, pushed aside any further negotiations. In 1974, Secretary of State Henry Kissinger and Fidel Castro issued public statements suggesting that improved relations would benefit both countries.[7] But second-term president Richard M. Nixon abruptly resigned from office in August 1974, under threat of impeachment for the Watergate scandal; eight months later, the last United States military forces withdrew in defeat from Vietnam.

In the summer of 1975, Assistant Secretary of State William D. Rogers reaffirmed the willingness of the United States to improve relations, but the arrival of Cuban soldiers in Angola halted any possible progress to this end. President Gerald Ford labeled Cuba's involvement in Africa as "aggression."[8] Jimmy Carter, an "outsider" in the world of Washington politics, won the 1976 presidential election and entered the White House personally unconnected with the troubles of his predecessors Lyndon Johnson, Richard Nixon, and Gerald Ford. President Jimmy

Carter's passionate personal concern for human rights led him naturally to Latin America, riddled by military dictatorships and repression not only in Cuba, but also throughout the region from the Southern Cone to Central America.[9] Castro would exploit Carter's deep commitment to human rights, using the issue as a wedge to attempt to end the economic embargo and restore diplomatic relations.

The Carter administration inherited major problem areas in the hemisphere beyond Cuba. Right-wing dictatorships had become installed in Chile, Argentina, Uruguay, and Brazil. The Nixon administration starting in 1970 had worked to undermine the newly elected left-leaning Chilean government headed by Salvador Allende, first by economic pressure (Nixon told CIA Director Richard Helms to "make [Chile's] economy scream"), and thereafter by full-fledged support of the military coup that overthrew Allende in 1973. In the following year, the U.S. House of Representatives and Senate each issued damaging reports, one of which, *Alleged Assassination Plots Involving Foreign Leaders*, devoted over one hundred pages to reports of plots to kill Fidel Castro. Jimmy Carter, disavowing such tactics on his inauguration day in January 1977, asserted, "our commitment to human rights must be absolute."[10]

Carter's National Security Council's initial focus in Latin America was Panama. Six months of negotiations led to the Treaty on Permanent Neutrality of the Canal and transfer of United States control to Panama in the year 2000. With the Panama Canal issue on its way to resolution, President Carter turned to the knotty Cuban question. In the year preceding the presidential election, Carter, then governor of Georgia, had visited Miami to meet with local Cubans. Alfredo Durán, a lawyer and Bay of Pigs veteran as well as an active member of the Florida Democratic Party, assembled the guest list. This was the first time Benes would meet Carter. The forty-five-minute meeting was held in the editorial offices of *Réplica*, a successful magazine that began as a newspaper to counter the far-right-wing newspaper *Patria*, controlled by pro-Batista interests. In Cuba, Max Lesnik, *Réplica*'s publisher had been the leader of the youth wing of the reformist Ortodoxo Party to which Castro had belonged.

Jimmy Carter considered human rights and the plight of Castro's political prisoners to be the primary issues blocking improved relations between the two countries. After Carter became a formal presidential candidate, Benes became chairman of the campaign's Hispanic Committee in Florida. During the campaign, candidate Carter suggested that relations with Cuba could be improved "on a measured and reciprocal basis"; he was the first president to say so since 1959. Robert A. Pastor, Carter's Latin American specialist on the NSC, in his 1992 analysis of United States policy towards Latin America after 1976, noted, however, that "although encouraged by Carter's energy and ideas, many Latin leaders were skeptical that the United States would really consult them on key economic issues."[11] To dispel these fears, Carter initiated talks on sugar production and pricing, and pledged to negotiate an international sugar agreement.

Immediately following Carter's presidential inauguration in January 1976, Cuba-watchers began to notice a more relaxed relationship between Cuba and the United States, although there had been a wave of bombings and killings among exile factions. A year later, Cuba and the United States opened their "interests sections" in Havana and Washington, and in October, fifty-five teenage Miami Cubans belonging to the left-leaning Antonio Maceo Brigade were permitted to visit Havana for a month, to do volunteer work and to visit relatives which most of them had never met.[12] Four members of an evangelical Protestant church in Hialeah visited Cuba, followed by six larger groups over the next seventeen months. Senators Jacob Javits (R-NY) and Claiborne Pell (D-RI) visited Cuba in 1974, and Representative Charles Whalen (R-OH) became the first member of the House of Representatives to travel to Castro's Cuba. In 1975, Secretary of State Henry Kissinger held secret negotiations with Cuban officials to coordinate the policies of the two countries on the issues of air piracy and immigration.[13]

Following Carter's victory, speculation arose in Miami that Benes might be appointed to the Bureau of Latin American Affairs of USAID, the Agency for International Development.[14] He seemed to be a logical choice: he had worked on contract for the agency and had done extensive consulting with Latin American leaders on ways to finance low-cost housing. He was a delegate to the Florida Democratic Convention in St. Petersburg and, once the election was won, was invited to the White House to attend a ceremony proclaiming "Hispanic Heritage Week." Although he was not offered the job in the Carter administration, it enabled

Benes to keep his foot in the door. The stars seemed in alignment: Carter, more than anything else during his presidency, maintained a firm commitment to improving human rights.

Benes's missions to Cuba for the Carter administration can be divided into four stages. The first started in Panama in 1977 and continued through October 1978, during which he and his partner, Carlos Dascal, negotiated with the Cubans to create the basis for the release of Castro's political prisoners and to permit Cuban exiles to visit their families on the island. A visit with six Miami exiles in October 1978, to bring back the first group of released prisoners, comprised the second stage. The November and December "dialogue," largely for show, was the third; and continued talks with Castro up to the last days of Carter's presidency, the fourth.

Benes observed an interesting pattern as the dialogue missions evolved. The initial operation started with the consent and support of President Carter's National Security Council and the CIA, and concluded with supervisory authority shifted to the FBI and the Department of State. The FBI had proven to be vigilant, supportive, and efficient. Before and after each trip, Benes would call the FBI and describe what was planned and, on his return, what had occurred.

The missions had become a possibility when incoming Carter administration officials began to hint that the president might be willing to reconsider United States Cold War policy in place since the Bay of Pigs and the Cuban Missile Crisis. On February 1, 1977, during his confirmation hearings before the United States Senate, Secretary of State-designate Cyrus Vance told reporters that he would be open to talking with Castro if no preconditions were imposed. Moreover, he told the Senate that "If Cuba is willing to live within the international system, then we ought to seek ways to find whether we can eliminate the impediments which exist between us and try to move toward normalization."[15] Vance's statements angered Cubans in Miami. Carlos Arboleya, the Cuban American president of the powerful Barnett Bank, complained in the *Herald* that the United States should never talk with Castro as long as Cuban jails held political prisoners. Benes was quoted in the same article, saying that he believed that Carter would keep his promise "to consult with Cuban friends before taking [any] definite positions with respect to Cuba."[16]

The story of the dialogue—between Miami Cubans and Fidel Castro over the release of political prisoners and permission for other Cuban exiles to visit their relatives on the island—started in a manner as unconventional as it was unprecedented. Various Miami Cubans were contacted by representatives of the Castro government and invited to participate in talks that might lead to a "dialogue." In June 1977, the Cuban consul in Jamaica held a dinner party and invited Manuel Espinosa, the pastor of a Hialeah Protestant church. Presumably, this contact did not yield what the Cubans wanted, although Espinosa would play a peripheral role in the dialogue.

At their first meeting, Castro took ten minutes to tell Benes that he had read Benes's entire dossier, comprised of information about his youth in Cuba, his work in Zaydín's law office, and his career in the United States. Intelligence agents had even interviewed former employees of Boris Benes's "Perro" textile factory. The report, Castro said, concluded that the Benes family was honest, hardworking, and responsible. Castro was aware of Benes's relationship with Alfredo Durán, the Cuban American lawyer who was active in the state Democratic Party, as well as Benes's volunteer work for the Carter campaign. Clearly, few stones had been left unturned.

The first instance of the unprecedented dialogue occurred in Castro's private office. The space was divided into four areas: a living room with leather sofas and armchairs, an alcove with thousands of books on shelves, a conference area, and a bathroom. All of the other meetings took place at the Cuban Special Forces' Protocol House #1, at the end of Fifth Avenue in the western portion of the city, although after the tenth trip, Benes and Dascal were housed in different places. Frequently, the sessions ran into the early hours before dawn. Benes later estimated that he spent a total of 150 hours in conversation with Castro during both the Carter and (more briefly) Reagan years.

At their first meeting on February 14, 1978, Castro expounded on Cuba's foreign policy, a sore point for the United States government. He explained why Africa held more interest for him than Latin America, where rigid social structures and organized interest groups (trade unions, the Church, corporations, the armed forces) made rebel activity more difficult. Africa, by contrast, was "poor and lacked such forces." When asked about the Nicaraguan Sandinistas, Castro replied that he was not impressed by their potential to take power.[17]

Castro accompanied Benes and Dascal to the Santa María del Mar Protocol House. They sat in a black Soviet-made Zyl limousine, while Castro expounded on his revolution's greatest achievements: education, health care, and the Cuban people's national consciousness. He spoke at length about President Kennedy's Peace Corps, and said that he was thinking of starting a similar organization in Cuba.

The following day, they flew back to Miami. Benes and Dascal met Padrón and de la Guardia again, this time on March 20, 1978 in Mexico City, where the CIA's Larry Sternfield had been posted as political attaché in the U. S. Embassy. Sternfield left them in a hotel room, adjacent to the embassy, where the Cubans, Benes, and Dascal reviewed the issues for literally twenty hours; they explained, for the last time, what Castro would and would not be prepared to do.

Reviewing his encounters with Castro in retrospect, Benes admits that sometimes he and Dascal offered Castro advice or made offhand comments that *El Comandante* may not have appreciated. At their first meeting, they had made small talk about some of the students Benes had known in the FEU, the anti-Batista student group, and about General José Abrantes's brother, who had died in an airplane accident. Also at the first meeting, when it was well past midnight, Benes rose from his chair and absent-mindedly started meandering around Castro's office, while talking. Benes walked over to Castro's desk and, still talking, began to page through one of the books on the desktop. Then, he sat down in Castro's chair. José Luis Padrón later told Benes that at the point during the meeting that he had stood up, Abrantes had taken his pistol out, because he knew that Castro kept a gun in his desk and was afraid that Benes was looking for it so he could kill Castro. Benes, who has never touched a gun in his life, moved quickly back to his chair and stayed there.

When Castro asked Benes why he hadn't stayed in Cuba to change the revolution from within, *El Jefe* added that he supposed it was because making money was too important for Benes. Bernardo recalls that he responded angrily: "You ruined our family financially. But this is not what turned me against you. What did this was the way you lined people up against a wall and shot them." To this, according to Benes, Castro replied:

"I was very sorry to have to do that, but we had to set examples. It was the only way to consolidate . . . the revolution."

Once, when they were taken to the Hotel Internacional on Varadero beach, which in pre-1959 times was perhaps the grandest hotel on the island, Benes noticed that the wooden chairs had rusty, protruding nails. When they met Castro in Havana, Benes, referring to the deteriorated condition of the hotel, said to him: "Being poor is shit. Why don't you appoint someone from Special Forces to get things fixed up?" Six months later, José Luis Padrón became the country's Minister of Tourism.

At another meeting, Castro sat with one leg crossed over the other and Benes noticed from the sole that his boots were Florsheims. He commented on this, saying that they were "middle-class" boots. Castro replied that they were "good American products." Benes then told him that he could do better and asked for his shoe size. Castro shouted "Pepín!" and ordered his aide, Pepín Naranjo, to go to the trunk of Castro's car and check his shoe size. The next time Benes visited Castro, he gave him a pair of Johnson & Murphy boots worth $650, which Castro accepted with pleasure.[18] Benes recalled that Castro spent at least ten minutes admiring them.[19]

The Cubans insisted that the embargo be lifted, and they offered the possibility of joint ventures between the Cuban government and foreign investors. They spoke about "freezing" Africa, not pulling out their troops but halting the fighting. In short, they wanted to know if President Carter was interested in accelerating the negotiations. They explained how important it would be for them to obtain American technology.

Notably, the Cubans took extreme measures to assure that these meetings remained secret. The reason was obvious: Castro and his aides feared what might happen if Soviet Intelligence found out, although to Benes and Dascal, they always boasted that they had full independence politically. Benes recalled that there were so many measures taken to keep the Soviets in the dark that he and Dascal started referring to their treatment as the "Timoshenko Operation," which they arbitrarily named after World War II Soviet Field Marshal Semyon Timoshenko.[20] José Luis Padrón, knowing that Benes would tell Castro this, asked Benes, as a favor, to not do so. In fact, Padrón and his comrades never liked the Soviets, whom they dubbed "bolos," as in "ball and chain," but they had to restrain themselves from showing any animosity.[21]

EL PRESIDENTE CHAPULTEPEC · EL HOTEL CON AFECTO · THE HOTEL THAT

3.1 Notes taken by Benes at secret Mexico City meeting. Bernardo Benes collection.

Padrón commented on the impoverished life faced by many Cubans, and praised them for their stoic patience, stating that Cuba's great capital was its political influence in Third World countries. He complained about the high price of oil and the resulting impact on poor countries, Cuba included. Padrón added, as if an afterthought, that the Cuban exiles could not be ignored by Cuba, just as Israel could not ignore the Palestinians.

Many of their conversations revolved around the issue of releasing Cuba's political prisoners. Benes gave Padrón a message from Max Lesnik and Roger Redondo asking that Eloy Gutiérrez Menoyo be released. Menoyo was a Spanish-born Cuban whose family, Republican stalwarts in Spain's civil war, had fled to Cuba when Eloy was eight. As a youth, Menoyo became an anti-Batista activist and rose to command the Second Front of the Escambray in central Cuba. After Batista's fall, however, his group was ignored by Castro and disarmed. In 1961, Menoyo arrived in Miami by boat, and eventually founded Alpha 66, a paramilitary organization dedicated to harassing Cuba in any way possible, including hit-and-run raids in boats. Captured later during one of these raids by Cuban forces, Menoyo was jailed for twenty-two years when the negotiations started. José Luis Padrón kept apprised as much as possible with events in the United States. Sometimes, especially after reading about a harsh anti-Cuban speech or about the activities of the Cuban exiles, Padrón wavered. Whenever he expressed doubt about the meetings between Carter administration figures and the Cubans, Benes and Dascal told him that the proof that Washington was serious was that the story of the secret trips had not been leaked. They told the Cubans about the upcoming meeting with Brzezinski and that the National Security Director had shown interest in continuing the talks. At the conclusion of the meeting, Benes and Dascal met and was debriefed by Larry Sternfield, and then flew to Washington to deliver a memorandum prepared by the Cubans, as well as one written by Benes.[22]

The Cubans' memorandum was to be delivered either to President Jimmy Carter or Zbigniew Brzezinski at the National Security Council. Brzezinski, Benes affirms, received it on March 24. In addition, Benes's memorandum read:

During the period from March 20 to 22, 2001, we met in Mexico City, with logistical support by the CIA Director in that country, with Fidel

Castro's personal envoy José Luis Padrón, and his aide, Antonio de la Guardia. After 20 hours of conversations, the following summarizes the most important points of the negotiations.

a. Fidel Castro has appointed José Luis Padrón to represent him in conversations with representatives of the United States government, with the purpose of discussing all and each subjects of interest for both countries. These meetings must be *clandestine,* and for that reason only the two involved countries must know about them, not the Soviet Union. (This paragraph was textually dictated by José Luis Padrón.)

b. Padrón suggested that Dascal and Dr. Benes should attend the first meeting to help establish the necessary rapport amongst the parties.

c. Padrón is very anxious about the delay from the United States in answering the message sent earlier.

d. Padrón spoke on liberating, through an *ad hoc* commission, during 1978 over one thousand political prisoners and at the end of 1979 to release all the remaining ones.

e. Padrón repeated over once that this step by Castro was a response to my request and appeal since the beginning of these conversations in August 1977 and to support President Carter and Dr. Brzezinski's policy on human rights.

f. Padrón discussed with us what he considered the advantages for the United States in acknowledging the Cuban Government's position on human rights with reference to the possible release of political prisoners as soon as these meetings take shape and their results begin to be obvious."[23]

Benes and Dascal met Dr. Brzezinski on March 9, 1978. The meeting lasted forty minutes. Reviewing his notes, Benes recalls the encounter:

As soon as he saw that my memorandum to him was signed by "Dr. Benes," Brzezinski replied that his wife was a niece of the deceased former Czechoslovak President Edward Benes. I replied that I probably was not related to his wife's uncle because I am Jewish, my father came from Russia, and President Benes was a Roman Catholic born in Czechoslovakia. I added, though, that I had met Valentin, President Benes's son, in Buenos

Aires. When I said that, Brzezinski suddenly became enraged, striking his fist on his desk with such force that the objects on it trembled. "President Benes had no son!" he roared. "His closest relative was my wife, his niece![24]

Benes tried to pacify Brzezinski by explaining that their meeting was more important than family matters. Brzezinski, however, seemed to think Benes's response sophomoric, and continued in a sour mood. But he read both memoranda carefully, commenting about the role of the United States in the world, on the budget cuts for military defense over the prior fifteen years, and on the need for the United States to remain strong, powerful, and to fight for human rights.[25] Brzezinski invited Benes and Dascal to a second meeting which occurred later. Benes felt disheartened, however, and worried that the documents would be thrown into a drawer and be forgotten. Brzezinski, the Carter administration's leading "hawk" on Cold War issues, had kept bringing up Cuba's presence in Africa, and the presumed role of the USSR as a stumbling block to any further opening of the United States' position. "If the Soviets want to play with us," he stated, "we will play with the Soviets."[26]

For their part, the Cubans had incorrectly insisted that Benes and Dascal deal with Brzezinski, not Secretary of State Cyrus Vance. As military men, they assumed that the civilian Vance was a figurehead, and that Brzezinski, known for his strong stand on the Soviets, had more influence. Their inability to comprehend the way the cabinet system worked enabled their faulty judgment. Brzezinski worsened matters by refusing to believe Benes and Dascal's assertion that the Cubans had taken strenuous measures to ensure that the Soviets knew nothing about the negotiations. Brzezinski asked for corroboration of the dates of the trips and wanted to know who Padrón was. Essentially, he remained skeptical throughout the entire process as it unfolded.

Unbeknownst to Benes and Dascal, what had happened was that the Carter administration had finally come to a rough agreement about its Cuba policy, which made Benes and Dascal superfluous. As the doors began to close for them, Benes and Dascal, in anguish, visited Congressman Dante Fascell, whom Benes knew well. Fascell, representing a Miami district and therefore very interested in Cuba, chaired the Interamerican Subcommittee of the House Foreign Relations Committee, and later would chair the committee itself.

3/24/78

MEMO

TO: DR. Z. B.
FROM: DR. B. BENES

SUBJECT: MESSAGE FROM PRESIDENT OF CUBA FIDEL CASTRO, TO PRESIDENT CARTER AND/OR DR. Z. B.

During the period of March 20th to 22nd in Mexico City, with logistic support from CIA director in that country, we met with personal envoy and confidant of Castro, Jose Luis Padron, and his assistant Antonio de la Guardia. After 20 hours of meetings, the following is a summary of conversations:

A) NEGOTIATIONS

1) F. Castro has appointed Jose Luis Padron to represent him to meet with U.S. representatives in order to discuss all and any matters of interest to both countries. These meetings to be CLANDESTINE and, therefore, only the 2 countries will be aware of its existence, NOT THE SOVIET UNION (the former paragraph dictated by Padron).
PERSONAL COMMENT: This message is the most positive thing coming out from Cuba in last 20 years. It is a complete change of behavior of the Cuban Government

2) To establish credibility on the above message it will be easy to arrange, through Padron, a direct phone communication of F. Castro with President Carter or D. Z. B.

3) Padron suggested, in order of priority, the following meeting place: A) New York City B) Mexico

3.2   Page of memorandum from Benes to Zbigniew Brzezinski, March 24, 1978. Bernardo Benes collection.

Fascell listened to their story for about ten minutes, picked up a phone on his desk and, in front of Dascal and Benes, said: "Mr. Secretary, I have two friends here from Miami who told me something very important. I would appreciate it if you could see them today." After listening to who Benes and Dascal were, Vance agreed to see them in his office at five o'clock.

Vance's reaction differed substantially from Brzezinski's; he welcomed the two Miamians cordially and spoke with them for two hours. As the meeting concluded, Vance, using his intercom, instructed his secretary to ask Peter Tarnoff to join them. Tarnoff held the position of Vance's special assistant, someone who in Cuba might be called the Foreign Minister's *Jefe de Despacho* (chief of staff). Tarnoff was a career Foreign Service officer with a quick sense of humor, and he, Benes, and Dascal worked closely together for the next thirty months until the Mariel boatlift, a major embarrassment for candidate Carter. Even on vacation, Tarnoff called Benes—in Benes's hyperbolic words: "During these thirty months, I talked more to Peter than to my wife."

During one of their trips to Havana, Benes and Dascal brought with them a videotaped documentary they had ordered from Miami's Spanish-language TV Channel 23's Néstor Penedo. They paid Penedo and told him that they wanted to use it to convince Spanish businessmen to invest through their bank, Continental National. The video, which Benes still possesses, would survey the achievements of the Cubans in Miami over the past eighteen years. Esteban Lamelas, a Miami Cuban television announcer, recorded the soundtrack. According to Benes, Castro and his staff were astonished when they watched it. Castro sat at Benes's side, squirming and uttering comments throughout. The video showed buildings and factories built by Cubans; it depicted Miami Cubans playing dominos in Little Havana, socializing at their country clubs, holding elaborate *quinceñera* balls for their fifteen-year-old daughters, and going about their daily lives. Castro may have been thinking to himself: "How is it possible with all the racism and all the crime in that country? Look [at] what those Cubans have done."[27] One section of the video showed David Egozi's Suave shoe factory, with the narrator observing that it produced sixty thousand pairs of shoes a day. Castro jumped up and declared, "Benes, that is a mistake. He meant sixty thousand a year." Benes replied,

"No, Fidel, the figure is per day, just as the announcer said." The shoe factory, in fact, employed three thousand workers and was the first Cuban-owned business to become listed on the New York Stock Exchange. When the tape ended and the lights were switched on, Benes saw Castro staring ahead, a depressed look on his face.

Castro took pride in his belief that he understood the United States well. He read everything he could find, often making observations about people or issues that were sometimes so specific that ordinary Americans might not even have know them. On the other hand, his overall view of the country ninety miles from his shores reflected the rigid Marxist framework that he had internalized. Put simply, Castro saw what he wanted to see. One day he spoke with the two Americans about California's Proposition 13, the anti-government, anti-tax measure. Castro called it a "populist liberal movement," an example of the people expressing their dissatisfaction with capitalism. Benes surprised him by explaining that the movement was ultra-conservative and that, if passed, "Prop 13" would sharply reduce expenditures on social services, among other California government programs.

At another meeting, Castro offered an interesting, if misogynist, comparison. "Cuba," he said, "is like a beautiful woman broken down by pregnancy. The commercial treaty we have with the Soviets helps us considerably." Lifting the United States embargo, he said, would be important but not vital—more of a friendly gesture that anything else. "We cannot choose between lifting the blockade and continuing trade relations with the Soviet Union, which benefits us. The USSR pays us forty-five cents per pound of sugar, although the world price is seven cents. The same thing happens with Soviet oil. The Soviets have applied a moratorium on our debts and are building the first thermonuclear plant in Cienfuegos for us, which will produce more electricity than all other plants in Cuba combined." "But we know," he added, "that American technology is the best. For the time being, we have to be satisfied with second-rate quality."

Castro also revealed evidence of his impressive memory. On one Sunday, Padrón, de la Guardia, Benes, and Dascal were at the Protocol House eating lobsters while waiting for Castro. He arrived at 2:00 P.M., in an impetuous mood. "We don't have much time today because at four I have to sign some papers with 'El Gallego.'" "The Galician" turned out to be Spanish Prime Minister Adolfo Suárez. Using no notes, Castro delivered a de-tailed, exhaustive summary of what would be discussed, citing figures on economic themes from Cuba's electric power output, to cows, hens, sugar cane and citrus. He used no notes. At 6:00 P.M., two hours after his sched-uled meeting with the Spanish leader, he departed.

By July, Benes and Dascal sensed an improving atmosphere. Peter Tarnoff told them that he and his colleagues in the State Department were very satisfied with the prisoner release negotiations. On July 12, Tarnoff telephoned Benes with a verbal message to be delivered to Padrón from Secretary of State Vance in Geneva. It stated that the United States wanted to hold higher-level meetings but that the date could not be spec-ified yet.[28] The next day, Benes and Dascal had lunch at Miami's Ameri-can Club, with Jim Freeman and Joe Dawson, the two FBI agents who were providing logistical coverage for their trips. Four days later, Benes called Ramón de la Cruz, the Cuban consul in Kingston, and was told that the final list of prisoners to be freed would be made available to Benes soon. They agreed on the procedure; the Cubans would deliver each list to Benes as it became ready. Benes would then make two copies, one for the FBI and the second for the United States Immigration Service. De-tails were discussed at length in Washington and in Miami, with major roles taken by "Skip" Brandon, the head of the FBI's Cuba desk at its Washington headquarters, and Joe Dawson, who once traveled to Cuba with Brandon, while Benes was already there on one of his trips and spoke with the chief of Cuba's immigration department and other senior officers about the prisoner release.

On July 26, the anniversary of the beginning of Castro's guerrilla movement, Peter Tarnoff called Benes from Washington to ask Benes to inform Castro that President Carter and Secretary of State Vance had proposed that David Aaron, Brzezinski's deputy in the National Security Council, and David Newsom meet with Padrón to initiate official-level talks. At the same time, Castro's speech on July 26 in Havana violently attacked the United States and its foreign policy, casting doubts among the Americans that anything significant would be accomplished. Yet, bringing in David Aaron to the talks was, Benes observed later, the first time someone associated with Zbigniew Brzezinski had reentered the pic-ture, so Benes remained optimistic. The meeting was proposed for Florida and would revolve around the topics of Cuba's role in Africa and issues concerning Puerto Rico and the movement there for independence from the United States, which Cuba backed but that Puerto Rican voters never endorsed.

Sometimes the four main negotiators met in Miami. On August 13, 1978, while the operation was still covert, Padrón, de la Guardia, Benes, and Dascal had breakfast at the Casablanca Cafeteria on Calle Ocho in Little Havana. The waitress saw Benes and greeted him: "Congratulations, Dr. Benes!" Startled, Benes replied: "Congratulations for what?" "Today is Fidel's birthday," she said. The other three, in Benes words, "went bananas," since two of them were Castro agents.[29] On another occasion in Miami, Benes and Dascal learned a lesson about the irrational loyalty to Castro by his disciples. During the visit of a Cuban State Security official, a colonel, Benes and Dascal learned of the death of the mother of one of their friends. They decided to go to the woman's home to pay their condolences, and the colonel joined them. During their conversation, the woman asked the colonel how he could not believe in God, because that was so important to her as she sought consolation. "Look," he replied, "I have been in similar situations. The difference is that I think of what Fidel Castro would do in my situation. That is enough for me."[30]

This proved to be a turning point. Benes and Dascal continued to talk with Fidel Castro (aides to Castro told Robert Pastor later that Benes was the only person who could hold his own with El Tío word for word.)[31] According to the Carter administration, the members of the Cuban "team"—Robert A. Pastor, Peter Tarnoff, David Aaron, and David Newsom, rather than Benes and Dascal, negotiated the specifics of the prisoner releases after mid-1978. Sometimes members of the team traveled alone; other times they went in pairs, and finally, in August, all of the Americans met with the Cubans in Cuernavaca, Mexico, to seal the arrangement. Benes's role, Pastor said, ended when the Carter team entered the negotiations, although Benes disagrees vehemently.[32] Actually, Benes and Dascal continued meeting with officials from both countries and for many months after the start of the prisoner release until the last days of the Carter presidency. Like Wayne Smith, Pastor had received only partial information.

On their trips to Cuba, Castro continued to play the host to Benes and Dascal just as before, because he thought they could be useful in establishing the "dialogue" with Miami Cuban exiles. He also probably found Benes useful as a go-between. So, Benes and Dascal traveled again to Havana to meet with their Cuban contacts. They were assured that the proposal for a meeting with United States government officials had met with their approval. Benes then flew to Panama, where he used a high-tech, secure red telephone in the office of Carter's ambassador, Ambler H. Moss, Jr., to brief Tarnoff about his meeting with Padrón and de la Guardia. Tarnoff made a series of jokes about how nervous Benes seemed using the high-tech device. He also confirmed the time and date for the proposed meeting, which would be held in Atlanta, not Miami, at the advice of the FBI, presumably for security reasons.

According to the Cubans, the Atlanta meeting failed because of the distrust and arrogance of the Americans. On August 12, 1978, Padrón complained bitterly to Benes and Dascal that David Aaron said that President Carter had asked him that morning if the Cubans were serious. Furious, the Cubans almost walked out, but they relented, meeting with Newsom and Aaron. Benes and Dascal were then told that the administration was considering the United Nations as a possible forum for further discussions. President Carter understood that Congress would have to approve any changes in the status quo, and a less-than-comprehensive agreement at this time could prove to be a political liability. It was explained further that while some issues seemed easy to resolve—Panama Canal's status, for example, and the right of the Puerto Ricans to hold a plebiscite on independence—Carter, facing the presidential election in November during which he would seek a second term, needed to distance himself from anything that might backfire politically.

Padrón later reported to Benes and Dascal that David Aaron had told the Cubans that President Carter had asked him that morning "if the Cubans were [really] serious and responsible in their intentions." Aaron also said that the United States would not consider further negotiations until Cuba pulled its troops out of Africa. This insulted Padrón and de la Guardia, although Benes believes that the main discord emerged out of cultural differences between the Americans and their adversaries. Benes and Dascal had been able to avoid bringing up the history of animosity between the two countries, but the Americans seemed well aware of it and often cited past grievances. To the Cubans, Castro's vitriolic attacks on the United States during his marathon speeches simply reflected his trademark revolutionary zeal. To the Americans, hearing Castro attack "the Yankee imperialists" time and time again impeded their ability to be flexible. At Benes and Dascal's meeting on August 15 with Castro and his aides, Castro warned that the mood would have to be constructive, without threats from either side. "These conversations can definitely improve the international situation," Benes remembers vividly Castro's concluding remark on the subject: "But if we are harassed, ¡joderemos! [We will fuck them]."

Castro expressed frustration, furthermore, over what he considered the dual position taken by United States officials: one coming from the Oval Office (and the National Security Council), the other from the Department of State. He encouraged Dascal and Benes to convince Peter Tarnoff to visit Havana to help the situation. What he wanted, Castro said, first and foremost was cooperation on economic development, both industrial and agricultural. Other issues—Guantánamo's status, for example, or Puerto Rico's independence—would hold less urgency.

To protect the secrecy of Benes and Dascal's visits, their Cuban hosts discouraged them from walking around on their own or meeting old acquaintances. However, Benes asked to be put in touch with Osmel Francis de los Reyes, the anti-Batista student activist he had hid in his sister Ana's apartment for six or seven months in 1957 when he was on the run. Osmel had remained in Cuba and avowed his loyalty to the revolution. Finally, Benes was permitted to have lunch with his old friend. Osmel, after drinking too much, said to Benes: "I don't know what you are doing here, because I know you do not support the revolution. Why are you here?" At that point, Tony de la Guardia carried Osmel away, who was drunk and feeling triumphant. When de la Guardia returned, he said to Benes: "This never happened." To Benes, it seemed a depressing and touching spectacle, a confirmation that Cuba's police-state atmosphere under Castro differed little from that under Batista.

Once Benes asked Castro why *Granma*, the government's official newspaper, was so boring. "The problem is that editors and journalists are afraid of the Communist Party Central Committee. So they watch their step." He added: "I agree with you, but read *Juventud Rebelde*, the evening paper. You'll see that it's more interesting."[33] Another time, waiting for a meeting to begin, Benes started talking with some members of the Cuban Communist Party. He told them that he thought that racism still existed in Cuba. They declared the observation to be nonsense. During the meeting, the topic came up about the usefulness of opening communications between Cuba and leaders of the American Black Power movement. Pushing back his chair, one of the men who had spoken with Benes earlier about race declared: "*Chico,* there are too many Negroes here already!"[34]

On one occasion, Benes tells of standing in the living room talking with Castro and Abrantes. According to Benes, he said: "Fidel, why do you still have three hundred agents in Miami? How many times can they send you a photograph of the FBI headquarters or of Homestead Air Force Base or a recorded transcript of WQBA ('*La Cubanísima*')? Abrantes responded quickly. "Yes, but most of them are volunteers." It appeared, Benes thought, that Abrantes was trying to justify to his boss the costs of his spy operations in Miami.

Castro's personality quirks colored the meetings with Benes and Dascal. Although he showed up on time, if in the mood, he would extend the conversation for hours. His mood could vary: sometimes tempestuous, other times sympathetic, although he never dominated the agenda. Even Castro's closest and most highly placed comrades spoke on cue and rarely, if ever, took the initiative. By contrast, Dascal and Benes interrupted Castro at will. Benes always believed that because he and Dascal were Cuban, like Castro, they could understand one another better than foreigners—Americans or Russians—could. In the end, Dascal and Benes spoke more than the Cuban leader. Castro never appeared with his women friends nor with his brother, Raúl, although he occassionally told Benes that Raúl had sent his personal regards.

During some of his trips, Benes visited some of the important places from his youth. He traveled to Matanzas, where he had been born, and visited the house that his family, in 1941, had left to his father's dentist. The man still lived there and was the head of the Committee for the Defense of the Revolution (*Comité de Defensa de la Revolución,* or CDR) on the block, but was friendly, inviting Benes in for coffee. He visited the last apartment in which his family had lived before leaving Cuba, which was now the home of the first violinist of the Cuban National Symphony Orchestra, a Romanian, who was very kind and hospitable. But the building itself stood in ill repair. He visited his father's textile factory in Santos Suárez and another factory, Textilera Tricana, next to the Coca-Cola plant that also had belonged to his family. There, he encountered two pre-1959 employees, a receptionist named Isabel, who remembered Benes, and the chief mechanic Leocadio González, who, Benes said, was "part of our family." The three of them looked at one another and were deeply moved.

Once, Benes and Dascal were taken to Lenin Park, built on the ruins of an old sugar factory in southeast Havana and dominated by a huge statue of the father of the Bolsheviks. The modernistic amusement park, aquarium, and carnival-style rides seemed sharply out of place, because Cuba, and especially Havana, has always been quintessentially Spanish in architecture and feel. Another day they went to *La Bodeguita del Medio,* a tiny restaurant twelve steps from Cathedral Square in Old Havana. Benes's law office had been a block away, and the visit brought back bittersweet memories.

On another occasion, Benes passed by a huge, ugly modern building being constructed on Havana's Fifth Avenue in the suburb of Miramar. It turned out to be the new embassy of the Soviet Union. On subsequent visits, he noticed that it was growing taller and taller. When he told this to FBI agent Jim Freeman in Miami, Freeman asked him for the number of stories. Benes replied, jokingly: "Jim, I learned that every time they add another story, two KGB agents climb to the top with a pair of very powerful binoculars. They look northward trying to see your building at Biscayne and Thirty-ninth Street. The day they see it, they will tell the architect to stop adding more floors."[35]

A telling moment occurred when Dascal and Benes were taken to *El Carmelo.* The restaurant held many memories for the émigrés: special sandwiches, tasty filet mignons, caramel ice cream sundaes. But then they looked at the menu: fish croquettes, sausage sandwiches, no-brand beer, and no-brand cola. Benes recalls that he was hungry and could have eaten just about anything. But the food was terrible and the physical appearance of the restaurant had deteriorated badly as well. Before the revolution it had been famous for its elegance and the waiters were consummate professionals. Now, *El Carmelo* had the bleak look of a dingy Third World cafeteria.

When Benes dropped in at the University of Havana Law School, he noticed the flag of the Soviet Union behind the speaker's podium. He asked his host at the time, Carlos Alfonso, why there was no Cuban flag. Alfonso looked embarrassed and ran to find a janitor. "The janitors say that yesterday there was a celebration of the anniversary of the 1917 October Revolution."

In August 1978, during a visit of José Luis Padrón and Tony de la Guardia to Miami, the first concrete sign appeared that the negotiations might bear fruit. Since his meeting in Panama, Benes knew from Larry Sternfield that his talking partners were from the highest levels of the *Tropas Especiales* (Special Forces) that reported directly to Castro. The Cubans exclusively discussed the question of a prisoner release, knowing that Benes and Dascal would pass the information to the FBI and to their contacts in Washington.

In response, while Benes and Dascal were in Washington, they were given a message for Padrón regarding the details of the prisoner release. That same day, David Newsom asked Benes if he knew Senator Richard Stone (D-FL). Benes replied that he had participated in several community activities with Stone in Miami, and that Stone's father-in-law, Bill Singer, was a friend because Benes had appointed Singer chair of the newly created Public Health Trust for Miami's Jackson Memorial Hospital. As a senator, Stone consistently took an anti-Castro line, probably because of his growing constituency of Cuban and Nicaraguan Americans. Newsom and Tarnoff suggested that Benes visit the senator in his office, and ask him how he would react to a hypothetical lifting of the embargo on food and medicine for Cuba. Benes called ahead, made the appointment, and caught a taxi to the Senate Office Building.

From Benes's notes of the meeting:

Stone was waiting for me with cups of Cuban coffee on his desk.
    "Bernardo, I congratulate you. I know everything about what you have been doing."
    "Dick, I don't know what you are talking about."
    "I receive updates on your activities."
    "That's bad, since you are not supposed to know anything. This is supposed to be a secret."

They then sat down and drank their coffee. Neither said anything more about Benes's trips. Answering Benes's question, Stone said that he favored permitting food and medicine to be shipped to Cuba. Then he added that he would like to meet José Luis Padrón. As the meeting concluded, Benes asked Stone if he remembered any Cuban political prisoner's relative who might have asked him for his assistance. After a moment, Stone recalled that Miguel Sales's mother had asked that he help release her son, a poet, from prison in Cuba. As soon as he left Stone's office, Benes found a public telephone booth in the corridor and called the Cuban Embassy in Jamaica. He asked for Consul de la Cruz and informed him that Senator Stone was interested in Sales's release and hoped that the message would be passed on to Castro. It was a Friday afternoon; on Monday, Benes was back in Miami Beach playing dominos with friends, as they usually did on Monday evenings, when Ramón de la Cruz reached him by phone: "I have received a call from Castro's office with the news that Miguel Sales is free." The next morning, Benes called Stone, who said that he was amazed. Castro had delivered a swift message to one of his most prominent adversaries in the United States Senate, only seventy-two hours after Stone's request.

During the two formal dialogue sessions, one held in November and the other in December, Benes stayed at the crowded Riviera Hotel. Benes only took notes and did not speak at the gatherings. One day, as he was returning to the hotel on the bus, a woman with her three children approached him. He recognized her as María Victoria Lahera, a law school classmate. The lobby was noisy, and Benes knew that State Security agents were present. Suddenly, Maria Victoria began to speak like a ventriloquist, with her mouth almost closed: "My friend of old times! Do something to take me out of here. I cannot stand it anymore."

Then, instantaneously, she returned to her normal speaking voice. At that moment, Mercy Fraginals, another former law school classmate, approached and repeated the ventriloquism game. But Benes could do nothing for them. He could not escape from the lobby to go to his room until he passed though a gauntlet of Cubans hoping to tell him their stories and appeal for his help. It took Benes a very long time to make his way through the lobby and he felt depressed by the outpouring of requests for his help.

During another trip, Castro mentioned to Benes that he appreciated what the Soviets had done for Cuba. At that moment, Benes opened his briefcase and took out a copy of part of the *Congressional Record* he had coincidentally brought with him. It was a transcript from a hearing held by Senator Frank Church (D-ID) on CIA activities in the Caribbean. On page 379, Benes had outlined in yellow the testimony of a witness identified as a Mr. Tarabochia. In it, he said that in 1969–70, the Soviet Union had taken effective control of the DGI (Cuba's counterpart to the CIA) and forced the removal of its head, Manuel Piñero Lozada. The reasons for this were many, but the principal reason was that Piñero had caught "a number of Soviet advisors to the DGI conspiring to replace Fidel Castro with a party member presumably felt to be more amenable to orders from Moscow." The embarrassment caused to the Soviets was not only humiliating but also costly because, as a result of this involvement, Castro demanded the removal of all Soviet advisors to the DGI.[36] This was one reason why the Soviets presumably did not know about the secret negotiations between Havana and Washington. Benes showed a copy of the transcript to Castro, who read it carefully and confided to Benes that the story was true. His final reply is unprintable.

Further negotiations, however, fell short of restoring normal relations or easing the economic embargo. The State Department publicly remained mute. After the first released prisoners returned to Florida on October 21, 1978, Foggy Bottom spokesmen denied that there had been any coordination between the Carter administration and the negotiations and added, in the words of an unnamed State Department official: "Basically the feeling is that defining who can and cannot come makes it not much of a dialogue. And unless they [the Cubans] are prepared to talk about the lack of democracy in Cuba and human rights, we don't feel the meeting will be particularly meaningful."[37] Benes retorted that "only active terrorists" had been excluded from the dialogue.

Castro told Benes that he had wanted Peter Tarnoff and Cyrus Vance to visit personally to continue negotiations, but the process stopped as soon as the prisoners were released. President Carter's major goal—normalization of relations with Cuba based on Cuba's acceptance of the Helsinki agreement on human rights and other reforms—remained unfulfilled. Cuba and the United States remained too far

apart and too stubborn to take that step. Castro and Padrón told Dascal and Benes that they did not hold out high hopes for full-scale cooperation, and that Brzezinski was a dreamer if he thought Cuba's
revolution would fall if pushed. Revolutionary Cuba "could survive another twenty years of Washington's 'hardline,'" they stated. Yet the dialogue itself broke new ground, initiating a process of engagement
between the United States and Cuba that lasted through the Reagan
years.

United States officials knew about the meetings because Benes and
Dascal reported every detail of their conversations to the FBI and State
Department. The United States government has never publicly acknowledged that it had known about the talks, Congressman Dante Fascell recalled later, "But Benes was entirely on top of the table in everything he
did. Carter permitted the discussions, and some of the exile hard-liners
gave their blessing privately. It was a major undertaking in a very rough
political climate."[38] Congressman Fascell never revealed the identities of
the "hard-liners" to whom he had referred.

During some of his visits to Havana, Benes and Dascal met with
Wayne Smith, while on other trips, their contacts in Washington in-
structed them to speak with no one. Smith had first been posted to Ha-
vana as a junior officer in the United States Embassy (when Castro took
Havana), and in 1964 had been political officer on the Cuban desk at the
State Department.[39] Smith recalls these events:

> One day, Benes called from Varadero. . . . He invited me to bring my son
> down to spend a couple of days at the beach. I readily agreed and drove my
> son down. While there, Padrón and Carlos Alfonso (at least that is the
> name I remember), the head of CIMEX, appeared for lunch. Meeting
> Padrón at that particular point was most useful to me, as he quickly became
> my most important back-channel contact in the Cuban government. I met
> de la Guardia subsequently and came to know him well.[40]

Benes suggested on one occasion at the Interests Section to invite José
Luis Padrón and Tony de la Guardia to lunch. When Smith said that his
cook had the day off, Benes telephoned Padrón's office. Sometime before
1:00 P.M., a car pulled up filled with top-quality food. Padrón, de la
Guardia, and Carlos Alfonso joined Smith and his guests for lunch. Benes

told Smith that Miami had many caterers but that in Cuba they had just created the first one.

In one of the final sessions prior to announcing that a public dialogue would take place between Cubans and Cuban exiles, Fidel Castro issued to all present one of his famous warnings. "We want to work constructively," he said. "But if they fuck us, we shall fuck them twenty-four hours a day. We are willing to talk about anything, but in an atmosphere of decorum. We will not stand to be humiliated."[41]

The results of the final negotiations were announced publicly on September 6, 1978, in Havana. Castro, in an unprecedented stroke of public relations, authorized Benes to select ten Cuban American journalists and photographers (seven from Miami) to travel to Havana in November. They would cover the "dialogue," considering ways for Cubans living abroad to visit their relatives who had stayed on the island and to discuss the possible release of political prisoners. The only Cuban American named during the press conference was Manuel Espinosa. But the announcement was window-dressing: Benes, Dascal, and Castro had already worked out all of the details. Peter Tarnoff, in a telephone conversation with Benes a day later, pointed out that the publicity given to the dialogue in the American press would likely complicate things, and that the *dialogueros* should never be mistaken as spokesmen for the United States government. "It must be made clear," Tarnoff said, "that Cuban exiles attending the dialogue may negotiate nothing, absolutely nothing, in the name of the United States." The Cuban government must know, he added, that all Cubans in the United States who are citizens remain subject to the 1917 Logan Act. The Cubans, Tarnoff said, impatiently expected decisions to be made without delay because they did not understand the complicated steps needed to achieve consensus in the democratic framework of the United States.[42]

Two days later, Havana and Washington agreed that Peter Tarnoff, David Newsom, and David Aaron would attend a meeting set for September 20 and 21 in Mexico City.

Cuban officials then announced the imminent release of Eugenio Zálvidar and Tony Cuesta, anti-Castro militants captured in May 1966. In March 1963, Cuesta had led a group he called "Commando-L," shelling a Soviet freighter on Cuba's north coast. Two years later, in November

1965, he had attacked the home of then-Cuban president Osvaldo Dorticós, but the shells missed and destroyed an aquarium thirty yards away. When Cuesta faced capture, he tried to blow himself up, but he managed only to become blind and to lose his left hand. That Castro would be willing to release him, as well as forty-seven others, signaled a remarkable change in attitude, or so it seemed.

The entire set of negotiations had taken eighteen months. President Carter knew about them and sometimes argued about developments. Carter's principal motivation to see the project through was humanitarian—he prayed that a way could be found to release Cuba's political prisoners. Fidel Castro, in fact, repeatedly praised Carter as a distinguished human being, a paradoxical attitude given Castro's own human rights record. Cyrus Vance, Carter's Secretary of State, supported the negotiations, but National Security Advisor Zbigniew Brzezinski, who always perceived Cuba in the context of the Cold War with the Soviet Union, had opposed them. Representative Dante Fascell stepped in to bring Benes and Dascal back into the process—albeit with no authority to do anything but talk—and gave reports of their meetings to both Vance and Brzezinski. Most importantly, Fascell had arranged meetings "with the right people so there would be no misunderstandings."[43] The voluble Benes remarked bluntly, "without the cooperation of that little Italian congressman, I would not have been able to have brought back the first group of political prisoners."[44]

The talks had involved at least fourteen charter flights between Miami and Havana that brought Benes and Dascal face-to-face with high-level Cuban officials, including Castro himself. To finance their Lear-jet taxi service, the two Cuban Americans spent at least $140,000 of their own money before Castro agreed to release the prisoners. No one ever reimbursed them. The Cubans did, however, play perfect hosts. As soon as Benes and Dascal arrived, they received fresh pineapple juice at the VIP lounge at the airport. They were transported in Mercedes Benz cars with their own drivers. Benes gained weight because gourmet chefs cooked for them.

The trips took their toll in various ways. Acting impulsively, Benes had purchased five paintings of a Cuban artist through an unnamed intermediary. This provoked an angry confrontation with a Cuban security official. The incident revealed that his luggage was being searched, something that made Benes very uncomfortable. He found himself caught up in the tedium of constant flights, constant meetings, and Fidel Castro's insistence on speaking hour after hour.

Occasionally, humor broke out despite the weightiness of the negotiation process. Once when Abrantes, Padrón, de la Guardia, and Naranjo were with Benes and Dascal at the Protocol House at Santa María del Mar, Castro arrived. He invited Benes and Dascal to walk with him on the beach, five or six blocks from the guesthouse. On their way, under a full moon, at about ten in the evening, some women hotel workers boarding a bus spotted Castro. They poured out of the bus, some through the door, others through the windows (a few got their large rear ends stuck, Benes recalls, and had to be pushed from behind). They exited the bus, running toward their leader, screaming like bobbysoxers, "¡Fidel!" ¡El Comandante!" Some attempted to hug and kiss him. Castro permitted this to occur for several minutes, at which point General José Abrantes, the head of State Security, said, "We have to go back to work," and marched the women back to the bus. Benes then remarked: "Fidel, they may think you are their idol, but it is also possible that you set this up to impress us." Castro remained impassive, although it was likely that the event had been spontaneous. Benes, Dascal, Castro, and the others stood under a coconut tree and talked until five in the morning.

Another anecdote illustrates the underside of Cuban life under Castro. One day, Benes decided to thank his driver, a State Security lieutenant. He had bought some cheap transistor radios on Miami's Flagler Street for less than five dollars each and decided to give one of them to the driver as a gift. "Look," Benes said. "I want to leave this with you as a souvenir." According to Benes, the military chauffeur replied, "Doctor, you don't know how welcome this is because next week my daughter will celebrate her fifteenth birthday and I have nothing for her." Benes observed later: "These words made a very strong impact on me. If a person who had been working for the revolution in the internal security forces since 1959 couldn't even buy an inexpensive gift for his daughter's *quince,* the most important day in a Cuban girl's young life, the inevitable conclusion is that something is wrong. They know that the system is wrong, they know this now even more than before. Something as trivial as a small transistor radio, in a place where there are none, is a miraculous object."[45] The incident, Benes realized later, opened his eyes about the revolution. The driver, who had spent twenty years in the service of his ideal, lived in poverty, accepting it as his duty to the new order.

On August 31, 1978, prior to one of their trips, Dante Fascell gave a message to Benes to be delivered verbally to Castro. It said: "Thank you for your message, which looks positive and contributes to the solution of these problems we are analyzing. We continue to work for that goal. This is an extraordinary way to improve relations, the release of Cuban political prisoners. Such acts are genuine, and good for both parties, for both peoples. I will not be an obstacle for the process to move ahead."[46] The message, of course, remained a secret exchange between Castro and Fascell.

THE LONGEST DAY

As the date of the first prisoner release approached, the negotiations in Havana drove Benes and Dascal to the point of emotional exhaustion. To facilitate the prisoner transfer, Padrón in Havana and Tarnoff in Washington approved Benes's request to invite five additional Cuban Americans from Miami to accompany him. The charter flight would leave Miami in the evening of October 20, 1978, and return within twenty-four hours. Benes set the itinerary, which included breakfast with a large group of prisoners at the Combinado del Este Prison. The only pending item to be approved was Benes's request to meet in private either with Eloy Gutiérrez Menoyo or Húber Matos—the former military chief of Camagüey province jailed for his protest that too many communists had been added to the government—the best-known prisoners on the island.

Besides Benes, the members of the six-member committee included the Jesuit priest, Guillermo Arias; cigar manufacturer, Orlando Padrón; Reinol González, a political prisoner freed ten months earlier and now living in Miami; a construction engineer, Rafael Huget; and his close friend and Cuban baseball legend, Bobby Maduro. Shortly before their departure for Havana, Consul Ramón de la Cruz telephoned Benes and said that Castro wanted two additional persons to join the group: the Reverend Manuel Espinosa and Jorge Roblejo Lorié, a former Brigade 2506 member and the founder of a group in Miami called "El Comité de los 100" (The

Committee of 100). The six deliberated for a half-hour and came to a unanimous decision. Benes then called de la Cruz back and told him to "Tell El Tío [Castro] that we don't mind having Espinosa and Roblejo Lorié, but they would have to travel to Cuba by themselves. We refuse to have them fly with us." El Tío presumably received the message. Two hours later, de la Cruz called back to say that the Cuban government had accepted the group's decision not to add to its membership.

On Friday, October 20, the night of their departure, when Monsignor Bryan Walsh had blessed the members of the commission on the runway of Miami International Airport in front of a small army of journalists and press photographers, Benes became overcome with emotion and burst into tears. He had already been the target of attacks from within the exile community, and he felt alone and afraid.

The Eastern Airlines charter flight landed at Havana's Rancho Boyeros airport, now José Martí International Airport, and its passengers were taken to the press-filled VIP lounge. Although the six commission members sat together at the front of the room, all questions were addressed to Benes. After an hour, the commission members were taken in separate cars to El Laguito, a residential neighborhood in Havana whose homes had all been expropriated from former owners and now housed diplomats, high government officials, and foreign dignitaries. Benes and Bobby Maduro were given a bedroom in one of the houses, and then Benes was taken to meet briefly with Castro and Padrón. Benes and Padrón spent the rest of the evening with Tony Cuesta and his new wife and, by the end of their meeting, formally agreed that he and all of the released prisoners would endorse the planned schedule of interviews and, for those who wanted to go, departures from Cuba.

The next morning, cars arrived to take the commission members to the Combinado del Este prison so that they could have breakfast in the dining hall with the soon-to-be-released prisoners. Media representatives from Cuba and the United States were present. Emotions ran high—"It was a dream, a human rights triumph," Benes thought, "to have cameras inside the infamous Combinado del Este penitentiary." In response to his request to see either Matos or Menoyo, the Cubans selected Menoyo. So informed, Benes took Menoyo's close friend, Rafael Huget, with him. The encounter occurred in the prison warden's office. Menoyo hugged Huget with intense emotion. After some trivialities, Benes presented Menoyo with a letter from Roger Redondo, a *guajiro* (man from the countryside) and former comrade in the Second Front of Escambray who had fought for years for Menoyo's release, and showed him a photograph of Andrés Nazario Sargén picketing in front of Continental National Bank. They were beginning to converse when the New York Times's George Volsky barged into the room. Benes asked him to leave, saying that the meeting was private. Volsky did, but returned ten minutes later, followed by most of the rest of the press corps. The event became, in Benes's words, a disorganized press conference in which Eloy Gutiérrez Menoyo had the opportunity to express his viewpoint. He took a belligerent stance: in front of Benes, he pointed to the three military officers standing at the side. "These men don't even know their names, because they change them every day," referring to their roles as informers and intelligence officers.

The event at the prison backfired. Both the Cubans and the Miami exile community became enraged. Gutiérrez Menoyo's angry words were captured on film and later broadcast on Miami's Spanish-speaking Channel 23 by Nick Pimentel. To Benes's consternation, Menoyo stated that no dialogue was necessary—that Castro could have released the prisoners on his own. The statement made Menoyo a hero among Miami militants and embarrassed everyone involved in the negotiations.

After Menoyo finished, Benes and Huget returned to the dining room where the prisoners were eating breakfast with the visiting foreign journalists. A few minutes later, the same colonel who had taken Benes to see Menoyo whispered in Benes's ear that Castro wanted to meet him at the Protocol House #1, where they frequently met. They took the colonel's car and during the thirty-minute ride, Benes worried about how Castro would react to the news of Menoyo's impromptu press conference. After waiting for about ten minutes, an irate Castro entered, sweating, his beard covered with spittle. The usual cadre of Abrantes, Padrón, de la Guardia, and Naranjo accompanied him. Castro asked Benes sharply: "What happened with Menoyo?" Immediately, the colonel snapped to attention, struck his chest with his right fist, and said, "Chief, it was my fault." "Shit," Benes said to himself. The officer's courage had likely saved Benes from a clash with Castro at the most delicate stage of the prisoner negotiations.[47]

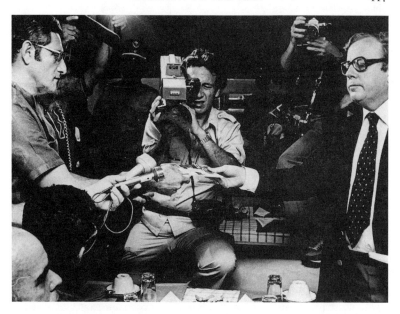

3.3   Press coverage of first prison visit, October 1978. Bernardo Benes collection.

Because of Menoyo's tirade, he did not return with the prisoners but was made to serve another eight years.[48] When finally released in 1986, he returned to Miami and announced the creation of a new organization, *Cambio Cubano* ("Cuban Exchange") based on the principle that dialogue with Castro was the only way to make progress toward normalizing relations with Cuba. In response to Menoyo's change of heart, Fico Rojas, leader of the Bay of Pigs (Brigade 2506) Veterans' Association, warned: "We will consider as traitors to Cuban liberty those who have supported and participated in dialogues with the *tiranía castrocomunista* (the Castro-communist tyranny)."[49]

In Havana, at three in the afternoon on October 21, the group of six reconvened at their guesthouse. Fidel Castro arrived a half-hour later and was introduced to each of the visitors. He gently touched the white collar of Father Arias, a priest at Miami's *Colegio de Belén*. Talk proceeded without incident until George Volsky and the rest of the journalists shoved their way in at four. During the commotion that followed, Helga Silva, then a *Miami News* reporter, snapped the picture that traveled around the world, and infuriated Miami militant exiles. The photograph showed Orlando Padrón offering one of his Miami-made cigars to Castro, with Benes sitting in the middle. Miami Cubans, who hated Castro for seizing their country and confiscating their property, felt outraged when the photograph appeared in the press. Orlando Padrón would pay for this later in the form of no fewer than four bombs placed at his small factory in Little Havana.[50]

When the meeting convened later in the day, Castro followed the scheduled format. Addressing the members of the exile commission, according to Benes's notes, Castro made the following points: he favored "expeditious procedures" for the release of more prisoners and for the reunification of Cuban families divided by exile; he understood that not all of the Cuban exile community in the United States was "counterrevolutionary"; his agreement to release prisoners was a gesture recognizing the "Cuban community abroad, but that sixty percent of the prisoners would likely want to remain in Cuba." Finally, Castro stated that Cuba would welcome a visit of thirty to fifty Cubans living in the United States to talk.

Perhaps the most touching event during the committee's visit was Bobby Maduro's visit to the *Cementerio de Colón* to take flowers, provided by the Cuban government, to the tomb of his late son, who had died at thirteen of leukemia. Benes knew that Maduro longed to visit his son's cemetery, and was the main reason Benes invited him to be a member of the exile commission. To be able to put flowers on the grave, Benes said later, Maduro swallowed his hatred for the Castro regime for twenty-four hours.

At about 5:30 P.M., according to television cameraman Emilio Rangel, who was covering the event for Miami's ABC affiliate, Channel 10, Benes was sitting next to Castro when a military aide whispered into Benes's ear. Rangel then heard Benes say: "Fidel, the prisoners are waiting at Rancho Boyeros airport." Castro answered, "Let them wait." Benes retorted: "Yes, but the problem is that some of them have been waiting for fifteen years to leave."[51] They adjourned the meeting, drove to José Martí airport, and boarded their Eastern Airlines charter flight.

Returning to Miami at the end of "the longest day" were forty-six political prisoners and thirty-three relatives. Before their departure, Castro met with Benes and others and discussed plans for the next sets of releases. Benes asked especially that Tony Cuesta be placed in the first group because of what he had suffered. Benes admitted to Castro that he had raised the $11,000 for Cuesta's Cuban incursion in 1966 by organizing a baseball game of exiled Cuban ball players from the old Habana and Almendares teams. Two of Benes's exile friends, Dr. Martiniano Orta, a physician, and Bebo Acosta, had asked him to raise money to buy boats for the anti-Castro Comandos L, headed by Cuesta.

Players arrived from all over the United States and Latin America, and New York Yankee star Joe DiMaggio threw out the first ball. The net gate receipts were given to Cuesta's commando, Herminio Diaz. But the attack on Cuba failed: Herminio was killed after landing in the Havana suburb of Miramar, and Cuesta lost his sight and one of his arms. He was taken prisoner. No one who had attended the baseball game knew where the money raised would go.

During one of his last trips before going public, Benes managed to meet Cuesta in a hotel in Santa María del Mar. Benes had never met him but explained that he had raised the money for the incursion and told him about the secret negotiations going on as well. Cuesta, according to Benes, agreed to take over the leadership of the negotiations over the prisoners—at least in principle. They met one more time, in the final hours of October 21, 1978, prior to their return flight to Miami. The meeting occurred at the penthouse of the Riviera Hotel in the presence of Cuesta's wife, his mother-in-law, one of his assistants, and José Luis Padrón. With them as witnesses, he agreed to take an active role in the repatriation process once he arrived in Miami.

The first group of released prisoners, including Cuesta and accompanied by Benes, flew to Miami and, immediately after landing, boarded busses for the Dade County Auditorium. With Benes's assistance, Cuesta got off the bus to the cheers of about half of the ten thousand people who had been waiting inside and outside the locale. The other half of the attendees, however, screamed at Benes and tried to block the entrance to the auditorium. Inside, the crowd cheered the returnees. Benes was taken aside by officers of the Dade County Sheriff's Department and warned that threats had been made about him, but he joined his wife and Monsignor Bryan Walsh inside. *The Washington Post* offered its description of the events:

Benes accompanied the ex-prisoners on their 38-minute flight to Miami, where they were taken directly by bus to an emotional reception at the Dade County Auditorium. The standing ovation as they entered the hall grew loudest for Antonio (Tony) Cuesta, the best known of the group, who was captured in 1966 on an infiltration mission. Blind and one-armed, he was guided into the hall by his wife of one month.[52]

According to another newspaper account, the choice of the auditorium, in the heart of Little Havana, had been an afterthought. With only a few days to prepare for the arrivals of the prisoners, it was found that more desirable places, including the city's Dinner Key convention center, were booked. The problem was that the crowd of up to 3,000 people had to remain in their seats while their loved ones were seated in a special section on the side. But as they approached their seats, members of the audience rushed forward to embrace them and the crush almost caused a riot. In the midst of the celebration, ominous signs suddenly appeared. Outside, a man assaulted someone carrying a banner in favor of "dialogue" until the police took the attacker away. The police later denied that any arrests had been made.[53]

Shocked by what the law enforcement deputies had confided to him, Benes learned further that, in the midst of the emotionally charged atmosphere of the first prisoner release, twenty or so well-organized picketers began walking daily in front of his bank carrying signs calling him a traitor and a Castro agent, for his "crime" of dealing directly with the Cubans; they demanded that customers close their accounts immediately. Benes asked a *Réplica* photographer to take photographs of the people picketing and that same afternoon showed them to Castro. In all of his previous meetings with the Cuban leader, Benes had never heard him laugh. But when Castro saw the photos of the picketers, particularly Andrés Nazario Sargén of Alpha 66, he laughed uncontrollably for several minutes until Benes said, "It may seem humorous for you in Havana, but it is not humorous to have this every day in front of your office."[54]

Attacks in Miami on the dialogue continued to escalate, especially over the Cuban exile radio stations, which characterized Benes's acts as vile treason. Even public reassurance that Benes had acted in a trustworthy manner from the head FBI man in Miami went unheeded. That Castro had agreed to free thousands of political prisoners and to permit exiles to visit their families in Cuba was ignored. Even some of the political prisoners who had been released earlier and made their way to the mainland opposed the meeting when the details came out. "People don't care about the dialogue," artist Siro del Castillo said. "What they want to do is go to Cuba."[55] Militant anti-Castroites fumed in anger. One of the *dialogueros*, Gerardo Moreno, the owner of a Miami bakery named Master Cake, returned to find large stickers saying "*Contra los Traidores*" ("Down with Traitors") pasted on his store windows.[56]

Tensions remained at fever pitch. For the first time, Benes violated his promise to himself that he would always take the high road in contrast to the organized exile groups and the Spanish-language media. In a press interview at the auditorium, in the words of *The Washington Post* correspondent Merwin Sigale, Benes "criticized those exiles who opposed his negotiations or any other dealings with the Cuban government."[57] The confrontation had been inevitable, but now Benes rose to his own defense. This would be used against him for years as the barrage of "Castro lover" taunts and threats continued. He told reporters that he wanted to turn over future negotiations to others. "I am delivering a package," he said. "That's finished."[58] His "longest day" had concluded in a jarring manner that he could never have anticipated.

The next day, Benes met with Cuesta. Dr. Orta and Bebo Acosta were present, expecting Cuesta to reiterate his acceptance of the offer to head negotiations for the further release of prisoners. Instead, he vacillated. Two days later, when the picketers started to appear in front of Continental National Bank, Cuesta walked in and informed Benes that he would "stop the pickets," if Benes would arrange an interview for him with Secretary of State Cyrus Vance. Feeling used, Benes declined, stood up, opened his office door, and told him: "Our meeting is over."

Benes never saw Cuesta again. Presumably he had consulted with other exile leaders, who advised him not to get involved with the *dialogueros*. Attacks in the Spanish-language press against the negotiations continued ceaselessly, even though every month, more released prisoners arrived to freedom in Miami. Benes's "crime" had been to speak directly with Castro. Journalist Fernández Caubí responded angrily to *The Washington Post* story that quoted Benes as having said that the accord represented the largest step toward the liberalization of a communist regime since 1917. He wrote:

> Fidel Castro has freed [a certain] number of prisoners, but his regime has not liberalized a drop. His satrapy is now a satrapy with fewer prisoners (Thank you, Fidel) but it continues to be a satrapy, even though a number of fools believe that he has changed his ways (Thank you, Bernardo).[59]

CHANGED LIVES

The dizzying events revealed the cost of being an outsider to Benes. Some of the anti-Castroites, including Spanish-resident and intellectual Carlos Alberto Montaner, Miguel Alvarez, a friend of Menoyo's, and Dr. Justo Carrillo, an economist and former Castro militant, in the midst of the furor against Benes, attempted, Benes believes, to remove him from the leadership of the dialogue and to substitute one of themselves. During one of Padrón and de la Guardia's visits to Miami before October 1978 to talk about the upcoming dialogue meetings in Havana, Benes invited Justo Carrillo to lunch with them at Miami's Bilbao Restaurant. A few days later, Carrillo invited Benes to the same restaurant, and brought several others, including lawyers Pedro Ramón López and his wife Teresa Saldice with him. Abruptly, they asked Benes to step aside in the dialogue process because he was "not a very important person and too controversial to continue." Benes played dumb, telling Carrillo that he didn't know what they were referring to.[60]

Meanwhile, talks continued about the public dialogue meeting in Havana between Castro and the exiles, scheduled for November. At a private meeting at the Palace of the Revolution with Benes and Dascal, Castro explained the conditions for inviting "some members of the Cuban community abroad"—the people he had always called *gusanos*. Benes and Dascal, he said, "could invite anyone they wanted," but he added that he had made five "*compromisos*" (prearrangements): his usual favorites: the Reverend Manuel Espinosa and Jorge Roblejo Lorié; representatives from three pro-Castro groups in New York, "Areito," (formed in 1974 by a group of Cuban American university students who leaned toward supporting Cuba's revolution), the Antonio Maceo Brigade, and the United

States affiliate of the *Casa de las Américas,* the Cuban publisher and cultural center.[61] This time, Castro got his way.

Plans for the "dialogue" group took shape after the first prisoners returned. It comprised approximately seventy-five exiles, including the five named by Castro. Benes had invited about fifteen members of the group, and although he was not named, the media perceived him as the group's coordinator. Still, nothing had been publicly said at that time about Benes's and Dascal's earlier roles, or about President Jimmy Carter's agreement to permit Fidel Castro to claim that the new spirit of cooperation was unilateral, engendered by Castro himself.[62]

On November 18, the first of two dialogues started. The "Committee of 75" comprised Cuban exiles selected from a list provided by the Cuban government as well as about fifteen names added by Benes. They ranged from diverse points of the political spectrum, including some veterans of Brigade 2506, but most members had belonged to moderate organizations or had not spoken out publicly against Castro's regime.

After the group arrived in Havana, Benes went to his hotel room, and a State Security colonel, Carlos de Armas (nicknamed "*Lingote,*" a nugget of gold, but in Cuban slang also for the name for someone stupid) knocked on the door and came in. De Armas told Benes, "*El Jefe* wants to see you in the Protocol One House." He said that Benes should wait at the Centro Vasco Restaurant on Third Street and Second Avenue in Vedado.[63]

When Benes went to the lobby, he encountered some people who had walked all the way from Matanzas—more than sixty-two miles—to see him. One was his father's former barber, who wanted Benes to help his son leave Cuba. Although others desperately wanted to speak with Benes also, de Armas was waiting outside in his car. They drove through the city and went to the Protocol House. They arrived at eleven in the morning; the dialogue was to begin that evening. Benes and Castro talked about the agenda, prepared by Benes, and Castro said that he agreed with it. Toward the end of the meeting, however, Castro warned, "Benes, don't turn this evening into a 'spectacle.'" Benes recalls that he responded rudely, to the shock of everyone else in the room: "Fidel Castro Ruz, *le roncan los cojones* [you need to have balls] to tell me not to make a 'spectacle' at the dialogue, when Fidel Castro Ruz has caused more spectacles than anyone in the twentieth century."[64]

TOTAL DE NUCLEOS...............49

EX-RECLUSOS...... 49

RECLUSOS 4

ACOMPAÑANTES.................. 90

TOTAL DE PERSONAS 143

D 129 RAFAEL J.P. PUERTAS ARENCIBIA
129.1 JOSEFINA GARCIA MORENO
129-2 VIVIANA PUERTAS GARCIA

D 130 FLAVIO R.DIAZ FIGUEROA
130.1 ISABEL DE NERY ACOSTA DOMINGUEZ
130.2 ISABEL DE NERY GONZALEZ ACOSTA
130.3 FELIPA DOMINGUEZ SIMON

C 131 CARIDAD ROQUE PEREZ
131.1 NANCY DE LA CARIDAD PEREZ SOLA

D 132 GILBERT CHAPPOTIN BARREDA
132.1 YARA AGUIRRE MAROT
132.2 BELKIS CHAPPOTIN AGUIRRE
132.3 LAZARO GILBERTO CHAPPOTIN AGUIRRE

D 133 CAROLINA GARCIA VEGA

D 134 GUILLERMO F. GARCIA GRANDIO

D 135 CARMELINA CASANOVA VALDES

C 136 JOSE SANCHEZ FERNANDEZ

C 136.1 RAMON MESTRE GUTIERREZ

D 137 RAUL A. CURBELO HERNANDEZ

3.4 Partial list of prisoners to be released, 1978. Bernardo Benes collection.

The dialogue turned out badly. Delegation members divided into factions, suspicious of one another. Although Benes confined his role to taking notes, someone, he believes, sabotaged his chair, so that the first time he sat in it, he fell to the floor. The exiles were put up at the Riviera Hotel and received VIP treatment, and any of them who had relatives were permitted to have reunions with them. But the group's members immediately began to argue among themselves about what positions to support in the dialogue. Open animosity flared: once, while Benes was talking with a group of Protestant ministers, he was shoved hard by one of Espinosa's men. Tensions ran high and continued that way throughout the meetings.

As reporters revealed later, cliques within the committee "criticized each other privately and, later, in print."[65] At their first meeting with Foreign Minister Ricardo Alarcón, the members of the committee argued so much that Alarcón began laughing. Even the seating arrangements were hotly disputed. Individual members of the committee felt intense emotions. Castro removed his pistol from its holster and put it down, saying "I guess we don't need this here." A woman began to cry, shocked by Castro's gesture, and later admitted, "My God, what are we coming to?"

The *Herald*'s coverage of the event revealed that some of the Cuban Americans from Miami had "privately expressed concern that they might be threatened when they returned by anti-Castro activists who oppose any dealings with the Communist government."[66] Commission members, another newspaper story reported, spent an entire day denying that a rift had occurred within the group over Benes's offer to send a chartered plane to Havana with gifts of pens and stationery as Christmas gifts for 3,500 political prisoners. He was to be accompanied by Orlando Padrón, the Cuban Miami cigar manufacturer, and eight other men who had donated a total of $5,000 for the flight and gifts, including Cesar Alvarez, a prominent attorney in Miami. Padrón later would be "rewarded" by having his cigar-making factory bombed several times. Cuban authorities, however, at first refused to give landing clearance for the plane. Later, they relented, and delivered the gifts. They also permitted a small girl, Lisette Díaz, to see her grandfather for the first time.

The nominal president of the dialogue group, which called itself "Operation Cuban Reunification," was the Reverend José Reyes, the forty-seven-year-old pastor of Miami's Palm Springs Baptist Church, who had been selected because he was not as controversial as Benes (for his appearance in photographs with Castro) or Espinosa (who was distrusted by many of the visiting delegation). When asked, the Reverend Reyes adamantly denied any rift over the matter within his group. "It's a matter of discipline and that is all," he said. "If each member were to do what he pleases, it would be chaotic." Benes refused to comment to reporters.[67] Many of the members of the delegation did not know for sure whether they were really negotiating or not: they had no knowledge of the Benes-Dascal talks.

In December 1978, the full story broke in *The Washington Post* and was immediately picked up by other newspapers across the country. Bernardo Benes was named as one of the men who, over the course of many secret trips to Havana over a period of eighteen months, had been the go-between who brokered the arrangement leading to Castro's announcement. "Diplomats and politicians eventually will parse the meanings, whatever they are, of Castro's moves. But for now, his announcement stands as one of recent history's larger and more positive human-rights episodes."[68]

The *Post* story by Ward Sinclair pointed out that Benes, whom Sinclair described "as a man with flaming red hair and a paunch exposed by a half-opened tropical short shirt," had fled Cuban communism eighteen years earlier. Earlier in 1978, Sinclair wrote, Benes had "returned home by invitation to sit with Castro and negotiate over prisoners and their families." The journalist added: "Benes refuses to provide details of his encounters with Castro and his secret trips to Cuba, undertaken, evidently, with approval of the Carter administration." He quoted him: "'I am just not going to talk about details—nothing until the last prisoner is out,' Benes said the other day. 'It is still a very sensitive situation. But I think the impact of this is going to be tremendous. It is the biggest step in liberalizing things that any communist nation has taken since 1917.'" Meanwhile, some Cubans responded with alacrity: Benes, believing in the humanitarian possibilities of his mission, had spent hours talking with Castro one-on-one. This was gravest offense possible in the eyes of the militant exiles.

CHANGED LIVES

Benes admitted later that he breached the secrecy of his many trips to Havana by speaking about once a month with John McMullen, the *Herald's* executive editor. He did this as protection in case anything happened to him, like one of the characters in a Dick Francis novel, to ensure that his side of the story would be known. After the discussions reached closure, Benes continued to report directly to Peter Tarnoff and kept in contact with Wayne Smith at the United States Interests Section in Havana, although Smith did not participate in any of the conversations with Castro. Tarnoff frequently told Benes that Vance was keeping up with events and was pleased.

In his *The Washington Post* article, Sinclair revealed that Benes's extraordinary expense of time during the negotiations had cut into his time for business, but he reported that Benes's Continental National Bank "appears to be thriving." Only four or five depositors had closed their accounts during the entire period of picketing, while many more opened new accounts. Another reporter noted that only in Benes's bank did one of the teller windows serve free Cuban coffee. The journalist concluded his story:

> Tears welled up in Bernardo Benes's eyes, when he said 'Many times, I felt lonesome, but my son Joel—he's 19, studying at the University of Florida— urged me to continue on, I needed that a lot. But I believed in what we were doing—there are still Don Quixotes in the world. I feel 50 feet tall now. After this Cuban process, I think all the political prisons in the world will open their doors."[69]

Overwhelmed by euphoria, after so many months of intense meetings, Benes permitted his imagination to soar.

As time passed, the Cubans continued to maintain contact with Benes, sending him the monthly lists of prisoners to be released from the Cuban Interests Section at the Czechoslovakian Embassy in Washington.[70]

On November 21, Benes met again with Castro, some members of the Communist Party's Central Committee, and the first meeting's participants.[71] He also met with Major García Entenza to work out arrangements to interview the released prisoners at the United States Interests Section. Castro's remarks, written down verbatim by Benes, indicate as much about Castro's own self-view as anything else:

- "If you are satisfied, we can conclude this event; if not, we will continue until you are satisfied. The Revolution has never been demagogic or theatrical,[72] though at times it has looked like it";

- "We are inclined to the idea [for creation of] an autonomous government agency to deal with the complex problems related to the Cuban community abroad";
- "[We are thinking of creating] a commission to lobby in the United States. This is a matter you have to decide";
- "[We want to] create mechanisms to maintain the dialogue. We are in agreement that this mechanism has been already created."

Here, one might argue that Castro may have convinced himself that the dialogue would convince the United States to soften its hard stance on relations. If so, he failed to comprehend the unabated anger among those he had driven from their homeland. The rest of his remarks—ranging from naïve and self-serving to wishful thinking—addressed points raised by the exile committee, according to Benes's handwritten notes:

- "There is no reason for more Cubans to go into exile";
- "The fear of loss of *patria potestad* (parents' rights) had precipitated the Pedro Pan exodus; we know this";
- "We should restore diplomatic relations";
- "We should have these dialogues with other countries";
- "We should resolve the economic blockade. . . . This is your problem," Castro told the exile delegation, "although I advise you to analyze the best timing for any activities on this subject. We don't want concessions; neither do we want the lifting of the blockade as a concession to us. The blockade hurts your group's efforts to convince others";
- "We expect not to have another 'Camarioca'";
- [We want] to create a pool of books and technical materials";
- "Perhaps we can send Cuban writers abroad";
- "[Bringing up] the right to vote and to participate in mass organizations shows [on your part] a great deal of audacity [but] we will study [the idea]. If our international experts approve it, we will view [the subject] with sympathy."
- "We will consider the publication of a newspaper or magazine to be distributed among the Cuban community abroad."

Finally, Castro speculated out loud on motives. The United States government might not approve trips to Cuba by émigrés, he said, because of intimidation from exile terrorists, who had threatened to continue their bombing attacks. "We have to be realistic, not idealistic," he said. For the time being, then, priority given to individuals requesting to visit should be given according to a humanitarian basis. He added:

> "We will permit starting January 1979 tour groups of Cubans traveling abroad, and in the future we will also allow individuals to travel to Cuba. Passports will be issued liberally. We will not exempt those who left illegally. When we issue you a permit, this will be [proof] that you will be respected in our country. All of this [however] gives us problems. A few years ago, receiving a letter from a relative in the United States was not socially acceptable. Much worse the gifts. Packages—we must try to avoid the sending of packages because of the bomb threat. We will create special stores in which Cuban Americans can buy products to give to their relatives in Cuba to avoid the problems of transportation and customs duties. Visitors will not be permitted to enter with packages."

Uncannily, Castro previewed some of the methods that would be employed more than a decade later, under Cuba's "Special Period" of belt-tightening. His suggestion about "special stores" for visitors anticipated Cuba's creation of a parallel tourist economy based on dollars, something that would widen the already enormous gap between Cubans on the island and visitors. He permitted more than 100,000 Cubans to visit their relatives in the United States.

He also commented to the visiting dialogue members on the Helsinki accord's statements about the principle of family reunification, in reaction to a copy given to him by Benes during the first of the two public dialogues.[73] "This cannot happen now," he argued—assuming against all sense of reality that Cuban exiles would want to return home to revolutionary Cuba. "We don't have houses; we don't have a single apartment available in the city of Havana. [But] we are building 30,000 housing units each year; [we will build] 50,000 in 1980 and expect 100,000 in 1985. [But] moral and economic problems will not permit us to promote a massive repatriation to Cuba; besides, we are a very austere country."[74]

Castro went on to express the terrible emotional burden of the loss of the Cubana Airlines plane blown up off the coast of Barbados by exile terrorists. "We still bleed about this," he remarked. "Can you imagine one plane full of your people visiting our island being blown up by one released prisoner the day after his release. . . . Their violence," he concluded, referring to the militants, "is their blindness. The only thing we can do is explain clearly our position [and what we are trying to accomplish with our revolution]. What else can we do?"

At the conclusion of the meeting, Benes felt that the Cubans seriously wanted to improve relations, and when Castro had asked in an anxious tone why Alfredo Durán had not participated, Benes thought this proved that Castro hoped to restore normal relations with the United States. Benes expected that the prisoner release was to be used as a springboard to larger issues. Padrón had told Dascal and Benes that during the negotiation sessions, Castro's thinking had suddenly turned 180 degrees: "I have never heard him speak to outsiders with such a sincere and clear manner that he used with you. Tell Dr. Brzezinski," Padrón concluded, "that this meeting marks the beginning of a Cuban New Economic Policy." This was a reference to Lenin's New Economic Policy of the 1920s that Brzezinski, a scholar of East European and Soviet history, would well understand. It also confirmed the suspicion, held by United States officials, that Castro's concessions on visitations and prisoner release constituted a ruse: that his real goal was to improve Cuba's economy through lifting of the embargo.

In his November 21, 1978, statements, Castro had said that 3,238 prisoners were being held for crimes against the state, as well as 425 convicted for crimes committed during the Batista regime. This totaled 3,663 prisoners. The initial agreement promised to release 400 prisoners a month, starting between December 20 and 25, so the first group could be home by Christmas. The actual arrangement turned out to be much more difficult to put into place. The costs of the flights would be in the hundreds of thousands of dollars, and it was unclear who would pay. Suspicions and distrust remained on both sides. The United States State Department warned that any opening of relations between Washington and Havana would depend on resolving the "important obstacle" of Cuban troops in Africa. Justice Department spokesman John Russell announced that as soon as the names of prisoners to be released were made available, department agents would have to be flown to Cuba to process the "parole visas" that would be issued. The timing when the lists would be made available turned out to be a sticking point and caused delays.[75] While the agreement had called for the transfer of 400 prisoners monthly through September 1979, nearly a year since the agreement was announced, an average of only 120 prisoners had come monthly. In a memorandum to White House official Philip Wise, Benes and Alfredo Durán blamed the Justice Department for being too slow to issue the promised parole visas.

Monsignor Bryan O. Walsh published a letter supporting the dialogue in the Miami Catholic Archdiocese's *The Voice*—its official publication. In it, Walsh made "an insistent and evangelical plea to the United States to respond favorably to Castro's offers, opening as soon as possible the doors for a rapid and understanding reception."[76] Three weeks later, a translation of the letter was made public in Havana.

Separately, Benes pointed out that the released prisoners in Cuba were living under "deplorable conditions of neglect, discrimination, despair" while waiting for the paperwork to be processed. In addition, more than 5,000 former prisoners remained in Cuba because no arrangements had been made in Washington for their settlement once they arrived in the United States. Benes focused his anger against Attorney General Griffin W. Bell, who seemed to be deliberately slowing down the processing of the paperwork that was necessary for the prisoners to leave Castro's island.[77] *The Washington Post* quoted Benes as saying sarcastically, "I understand why Secretary Bell is proceeding so slowly. He must have reviewed the entire list of released prisoners but found none named Bell."[78] Justice Department agents spent more than six weeks processing the first list of released prisoners and in the end screened out only one person. In response to congressional pressure, Bell sent additional FBI and INS personnel to interrogate prisoners in Cuba, but he refused to give up "his personal, case-by-case litmus tests."[79]

At 2:00 A.M. on December 10, Fidel Castro, clad in his usual military fatigues, held a press conference at Havana's Palace of the Revolution. Speaking before an applauding group of 140 exiles, he disclosed the names of 400 additional political detainees eligible for parole and announced that he would release 3,200 more within six or seven months. Castro stated that he would not release six United States citizens jailed in

Cuba on political charges, including one named by the *Herald* as a CIA agent. Others had been jailed for hijacking and terrorist crimes.

Washington officials had their concerns as well. The Justice Department expressed the fear that some of the released prisoners might be intelligence agents. Benes replied acidly: "[Castro] said that if he wanted to put agents into the United States, it would be much easier to slip them over the Mexican border on any night of the week."[80]

The Miami exiles had been flown to Cuba to sign a five-page document formalizing the agreements made earlier. Benes, whom the reporter called "the informal leader of the exiles," said he was "flabbergasted and extremely happy with the agreements signed after a nine-hour session starting the day before."[81]

On December 27, 1978, Howell Raines of the *New York Times* published a front page story captioned "Banker is Proud of Role in Freeing Cubans." Written in patronizing, almost belittling language, it started:

> Bernardo Benes, the master do-gooder of this city's "Little Havana" district, is as red-haired as a stump on fire and, these days, so proud of himself that he could just pop. For Mr. Benes has finally carried out the orders he got 10 years ago in "an illumination from God" that he must help free the political prisoners in his native Cuba. And what God directed, declared the effusive Mr. Benes, Jimmy Carter made possible . . . "You might say that I was a Lonely [sic.] Ranger or a Don Quixote," he added in his serviceable but less-than-flawless English.

Benes, Raines wrote, had become "the most prominent—and in anti-Castro circles the most hated—member of Miami's community of 430,000 Cuban exiles." "Benes's bank," the article went on, "has been picketed and telephone threats have been received. 'I forgive those Cubans who have started an unbelievable defamation campaign against me,' Benes replied, with a grand wave of his Havana cigar." Alfredo Durán, the Cuban-born chairman of Florida's Democratic Party and the highest ranking Cuban American advisor to President Carter, had said initially that he saw Benes's plan to rescue the prisoners as "another of Bernardo's fantasies." One of the first things Castro asked Benes was, "Why didn't Durán come?"[82] Fantasy or not, the Carter administration had endorsed the idea.

THE AFTERMATH

The return of the black-clad former prisoners carried with it a wealth of poignant stories. Miamians learned of the marriage in *Combinado del Este* prison of Alfredo Izaguirre, a former newspaper editor who had been in jail for seventeen years for allegedly attempting to kill Fidel Castro, to María de los Angeles Munero, a twenty-six-year-old specialist in psychiatric testing from Havana. She had met Alfredo while visiting her own father over a period of eight years in the same prison. At the wedding ceremony, which had been approved by the Cuban government before the prisoner release deal, the groom's mother, Rosa Rivas Izaguirre, was permitted to attend—it was the first time she had seen her son since 1961, when she had joined the exodus to Miami. Rosa Izaguirre had come to Havana as a member of the delegation sent to sign the final prisoner release agreement. The wedding took place in the prison's waiting room and the ceremony was attended by the bride's parents and grandparents, as well as Benes. She spent her wedding night with her mother-in-law, while her father and new husband were returned to their cells.[83] At the conclusion of the meeting with the exile delegation, Castro announced that he would release Izaguirre and Polita Grau, one of the founders of Operation Pedro Pan and sister of Cuba's former president, because of pleas from Izaguirre's mother and Grau's son.

When the prisoners, after much delay, began to be released, not all went to Miami. Venezuela and Panama also accepted a total of nine hundred of Castro's prisoners, with the stipulation that the new residents would initially be supported by relatives in Miami and by Panama's Cuban émigré population of about one hundred. Among the prisoners who chose not to go to the United States was Ramón Mestre Gutiérrez, a member of the Cuban Senate during Batista's dictatorship. Formerly the wealthy owner of a successful construction company, Mestre took a job in Havana as an insect exterminator, preferring to remain with his family. Some of the other prisoners who went abroad had been considered *plantados* (political prisoners who maintained their defiance of Castro by refusing to wear prison clothing and who suffered terrible conditions in jail because of their attitude). Cuba-watchers estimated that about six hundred political prisoners still sat in Castro's jails, and that between 70 and 80 percent

3.5   Wedding in Havana prison, 1978. Bernardo Benes collection.

of the political prisoners on the islands, who had served their sentences, would also leave if given the chance.[84] The *Miami Herald's* editors welcomed Castro's release of the political prisoners. An editorial speculated, "Maybe, just maybe, [Castro] would like to soften his contentions with the United States just a little to take attention from his meddling in Puerto Rico as well as Africa. Perhaps he just wants to stop feeding prisoners he knows have committed no real crimes and are of little danger to his locked-up island."[85]

Continental National Bank issued leaflets for the families of prisoners explaining the process by which the special visas would be issued, and provided the address of the United States Special Interests section to which families could write for information. In March 1979, the bank mailed a plea, in English and in Spanish, for assistance to every one of its customers:

> Recently, many political prisoners and ex-prisoners have been arriving to this country from Cuba trying to become members of our community. Their condition and needs upon arrival are well known to all of us, and their

main necessity is to find a job. Continental National Bank of Miami wants to help them, and we are asking your cooperation. If you have an opening in your business, please complete the attached form and return same to us for processing. Your help to this human cause will be greatly appreciated.[86]

As a result, Benes found himself being called a traitor and a communist repeatedly, and received threats on his life. He was stunned. Further, no one of influence in Miami stood up and publicly spoke out against the defamation campaign. The bridges Benes had painstakingly forged in Miami during the 1960s and early 1970s had totally crumbled.

Interviewed more than a decade later, Andrés Nazario Sargén, one of the founders of Alpha 66, explained why he had been one of the leaders of the vilification of Benes that lasted throughout the 1980s. "When an American citizen talks to Castro or helps a person in Cuba in any way," Sargén told the Herald's Meg Laughlin, "it gives Cubans in Cuba hope, which postpones their need to risk their lives to overthrow him—which hurts the cause. . . . I don't dislike Benes personally," he concluded. "He was serving the interests of the U.S. government at the time. But he is the enemy. He is a traitor." Domingo Moreira, a member of the board of directors of the Cuban American National Foundation, formed in 1980 as a powerfully effective lobby for hardline legislation against Castro, stated: "The way Benes was ostracized and called a traitor was to be expected. His motives could have been humanitarian, but he was authorized by the Carter administration to suggest there would be policy changes that would alleviate tensions with Cuba. This was unacceptable."[87]

Only one antagonist more than a decade later came to regret the campaign to make Benes into a social leper. Salvador Lew, owner of the radio station WRHC, said on the air that he was sorry. "At the time," he explained, "I believed Benes was part of a group of Castro agents. But later I got information to disprove that. I made a mistake. Benes did what he did for all the right reasons."[88]

Anxiety rose as exiles struggled with the dilemma of dual identity: were they first Cubans or Americans? Would they remain outsiders in one culture or integrate into both? The secret trips leading to the return of the prisoners and the opening of doors affected the community in unforeseen ways. "A community held together by an unquestioned tradition of belligerent opposition has been shaken to its foundations. Politically, this has left a vacuum in Little Havana," two astute journalists wrote. "Traditional hard line leaders are in disarray. By traveling to Cuba, hordes of their countrymen mock the exile covenant of militant hostility toward Castro."[89]

Worse, the press revealed that bickering had plagued the "now-famous dialogue in Havana. . . . The tourist-travel arrangements the new exile leaders helped establish have proved hopelessly inadequate," the *Herald* said, "a bureaucratic rat's nest of shoestring finances, canceled flights, federal investigations and missing funds." The article, featuring a five-column wide photograph of Benes sitting with a cigar-chewing Fidel Castro, continued:

> Exiles pay $850 to visit Cuba for a week, a price that includes a night in a hotel in Jamaica where nobody wants to go, and seven days at a Havana hotel where nobody wants to stay. In addition, the visiting exiles are spending thousands of dollars on gifts, some of them purchased in Miami, others bought at profiteering shops in Havana where a dollar buys 73 cents worth of goods.

"The exile community today is still in a state of shock," a sociologist from FIU declared. Miguel A. Alvarez, president of the Bay of Pigs Veterans' Association, announced that he "[was] totally, categorically opposed" to the dialogue."[90] Seven years earlier, Alvarez had participated as a member of the committee chaired by Benes to raise funds for Miami's memorial to the Bay of Pigs fighters who had died in the invasion.

A second, larger group of *dialogueros* from Miami and elsewhere—168 in number—attended a second session in Havana, but by then the novelty had worn off and little of significance occurred. For Benes and the Cubans, more important was the need to schedule the next level of meetings to discuss ways of achieving normalization. But the months dragged on with little visible progress. Crestfallen, Benes turned his attention northward. By this time, he felt that he had made it into the White House–State Department loop. In April, he informed Florida's Governor Bob Graham that he had spent five hours talking with Carter chief of staff Hamilton Jordan on subjects ranging from public health to energy policy. On September 14, he attended an all-day briefing session at the State Department and White House with such senior officials as Ambassador Robert Strauss, Zbigniew Brzezinski, Hamilton Jordan, Stuart Eizenstadt, and President Carter. After he returned to Miami, Benes received a note from Assistant to the President Sarah Waddington thanking him for meeting with the president's senior advisors[91] and giving him the telephone number of Phil Wise, whom he could contact whenever he wanted to get in touch. Benes then met with former Costa Rican president Daniel Obduber, and asked him for a position paper about Cuba. He received in the mail the text of a proposal from President Obduber offering to head a delegation of Latin American heads of state to mediate between Washington and Havana. This was the seed for the creation later of the "Basketball Team," a group of five Central American heads of state organized in order to visit both Castro and Reagan to help broker improved relations between Washington and Havana.

If Benes had made it into the loop, however, he remained on its periphery. A few days after taking office as director of the Cuban Affairs desk for the Department of State, Myles Frechette—later United States Ambassador to Colombia—notified Benes that he would like to come to Miami and spend two days "meeting with prominent Cuban Americans." Benes offered to host a cocktail party in his home for forty or fifty people, and Frechette accepted. Bernardo then set the date and invited the people. One day before his flight to Miami, Frechette canceled his trip, blaming an "emergency" in his office. Each of the invited guests were called and told that the party had been canceled. Then, later that same day, Benes's office received yet another phone call, saying that Frechette would be arriving after all, but on a different schedule.[92] Things would continue to be difficult. According to the Carter administration personnel working on the Cuban negotiations, Benes's usefulness had wound down—although Benes passionately denies the assertion, arguing that his and Dascal's mission went on in secret, and that the Cubans listened to them more than to the accredited diplomats. Formally, though, responsibility for the details of the negotiations had shifted to Peter Tarnoff, Robert Pastor, David Newsom, and David Aaron, assistant at the National Security Council to Zbigniew Brzezinski. There was some overlap, without mutual debriefings. Tarnoff, for example, made one secret trip in 1978 and three in 1980, the first one prior to Mariel.[93]

Why did the successful negotiations to release the political prisoners and to allow exiles to return to the island to visit their relatives not lead to more substantial results? The major reason may have been the lack of trust on each side. The Cubans probably understood that Benes and Dascal were, in the realm of Cold War power politics, simply messengers. The Cubans kept demanding to meet with senior officials of the Carter administration. The breakdown, from the Cuban viewpoint, was when David Aaron, Zbigniew Brzezinski's assistant at the National Security Council, refused to schedule any high level meeting. The Carter administration team attempted to convince the Cubans to pull out of Africa and pursue negotiations at a higher level—one of the main points, as well, on Benes and Dascal's agenda since the beginning of the talks.

According to Pastor, some cooperative agreements resulted, on search-and-rescue missions and anti-drug trafficking measures, but "on the crucial security issues, no progress occurred."[94] Benes recalled that there had been jealousies between the "amateurs" and "professionals" once Pastor and Tarnoff entered the negotiations, separately from Dascal and Benes. He offers this example:

> One day I went to the Miami International Airport to fly to Panama, as I did then frequently. When I arrived at the counter, I met Robert Pastor. He and other government officials were engaged in negotiating the Panama Canal treaty with Omar Torrijos. Very naively, I asked Bob where he was going. He responded: "To the West Coast." I usually believe whatever people tell me, but this time, somewhat dubious, I decided to tell a white lie. I waited until Pastor left and told the airline dispatcher, "I am flying to Panama with Robert Pastor and I'd like a seat next to him if possible." She accommodated me. During the trip, neither one of us referred to Pastor's "change of plans."[95]

The Carter administration never presented a united front over its Cuban policies. The president himself yearned for better relations if they could be linked to improvements in human rights, but Brzezinski and his allies distrusted the Soviets and the Cubans too much to act in a positive manner. Brzezinski firmly believed that Castro was no more than a puppet of the Kremlin. In fact, Castro likely had no intention of improving human rights in Cuba beyond his release of his political prisoners. But his acceptance of the terms of the 1978 accord, permitting Cuban exiles to visit their relatives on the island, was probably the most meaningful agreement between the United States and Cuba from 1959 to the present day.

Some Miami Cubans were grateful to Benes. One wrote:

> My family and I profoundly thank you for your dedication to this momentous effort during which you represented our Cuban community. You did this on behalf of the men who remained for years in Cuban prisons. We send you our best regards for health and happiness in the future.[96]

The *Herald* described what its reporters called a typical scene of Cuban exiles arriving in Havana on family reunification trips:

> With hampers [filled with] medicine and cosmetics, watches for every wrist, fan belts for the old pre-revolution Chevy. Thin people wore half a dozen layers of clothing, stuck fistfuls of ball-point pens and bubble gum in the pockets and undressed and unloaded it all into the closets and larders of their loved ones.[97]

On October 24, the lead *Miami Herald* editorial endorsed the "dialogue" as "the surest way to reap the humanitarian fruits of Castro's non-humanitarian moves." Calling Benes's critics shortsighted, the editorial noted, "the Cuban exile banker had been severely criticized by some in the exile community for his behind-the-scenes negotiations with the Castro government. Those exiles equate any contact with Castro with treason," the editorial continued, "and they have vilified Mr. Benes for paving the way for the prisoner releases now under way."[98]

MARIEL AND MISSED OPPORTUNITIES

Castro desperately wanted the United States embargo to end, although whether he really intended to make concessions or offered them—by releasing political prisoners, for example—only to hide his intentions remains to be seen. Probably his cynicism and opportunism determined his moves more than anything else. Castro told Benes that he respected Jimmy Carter more than any other American president as a device to take advantage of Carter's sensitivity toward human rights.

And sometimes Castro simply denied the truth. He denied that his revolution used theatrical devices, yet, in actuality, it relied heavily on coercive mass psychology and theatrics. The actions of his Special Forces and other police agencies, not to mention the neighborhood "Rapid Action Brigades" and the policy of encouraging children to denounce their parents for anti-revolutionary acts, hung over the lives of Cubans on the island and controlled their lives. Nor were his pronouncements usually reliable. Castro's public statement in 1978 that there would not be a "second Camarioca" not only proved false but led to an exodus of far greater proportions.

Castro's decision to permit exiles from the United States to visit their Cuban relatives had yielded an unexpected effect: over one million returnees, carrying gifts of consumer goods, medicines, and equipment, made Cubans on the island aware of their impoverished state two decades after the 1959 Revolution. Many were shocked by the appearance of the *gusanos*—official propaganda had depicted them as victims of American capitalism, but the men and women who landed at Cuban airports wore fine clothing and looked remarkably prosperous.

The crisis began in 1980 when Peruvian patrol boats sank two Cuban fishing vessels off the Peruvian port of Callao. Immediately, relations between Lima and Havana worsened, exacerbated by Cuban police beating back a group of Cubans seeking refuge in the Peruvian Embassy in Havana. To retaliate, Castro ordered his police to cease guarding the embassy. As soon as the police left, hundreds and then thousands of Cubans entered the embassy grounds to seek asylum and assistance in emigrating. Within days, more than 10,800 desperate and disillusioned Cubans jammed the embassy, lacking supplies of food or water. Thousands of others camped out in the swamps around the port of Mariel, waiting for permission to leave. Embarrassed and resentful, Cuban officials opened the door for emigration, although many dissidents seeking to leave were harassed, sometimes viciously, mostly by police and civilians at the port of Mariel.

Hundreds of boats, large and small, headed across the Florida Straits to pick up passengers and bring them to the United States. Some refugees in Miami sold possessions or took out second mortgages on their homes to buy a boat. Perhaps fittingly, the man who took command of the flotilla that eventually brought 129,000 Cubans to Florida was Napoleón Vilaboa, a car salesman and one of the members of the 1978 "Committee of 75." He traveled back and forth across the Florida Straits in a forty-one-foot fishing boat named after Oxun, the Yoruba goddess of love.[99] The first two boats reached Key West on April 21, bringing 55 refugees. By the third day, 2,746 arrived. President Jimmy Carter, looking at the humanitarian side, welcomed all of the arrivals with "an open heart and open arms."[100] Carter, running for re-election, also declared that his heart was with the Cubans seeking to leave. In Castro's eyes, this *patada a la lata* (unexpected blunder) showed Carter to be a fool—Brzezinski's puppet.

The Carter administration released $10 million in emergency refugee funds to reimburse the voluntary agencies that were working night and day to take care of the newcomers. But the exile community, in Pulitzer Prize-winning Liz Balmaseda's words, also declared a state of emergency, unofficially. They distanced themselves from the new arrivals, and re-coiled when the mostly young and dark-skinned *marielitos,* some named Vladimir or Vassily or Irina, used socialist words like *compañero* (comrade). They had grown up under communism and expected the American government to give them jobs, housing, and sustenance, as they had come to expect it in Cuba.

Immediately prior to Mariel, Benes thought that perhaps Peter Tarnoff might be able to help reopen negotiations with Castro on other, even more important, issues. Tarnoff had kept in touch with the two Cuban American emissaries after most of their trips.[101] He had told Benes and Dascal that he respected Padrón as a serious and competent professional. Tarnoff met Cuban officials at the highest level and became part of the negotiations. On January 2, 1980, Castro delivered a belligerent pro-Soviet, anti-Chinese, anti-American speech to a large rally in Havana. Tarnoff told Benes that no one in Washington had expected this, and that the effect was to reduce the influence of members of the cabinet who still wanted to negotiate further. Brzezinski allegedly had said that he wanted to bring Castro to his knees, but that he would support negotiations if they continued. Castro probably never realized the chilling impact of his speeches, or, if he did, appeared cynical. Benes and Dascal did not return to Havana until early May, over a minor topic: a dispute over exit permits for released former prisoners who had taken shelter during Mariel in the United States Interests Section.

When the Mariel boatlift ended, Tarnoff suggested to the Cubans that better relations might evolve if they announced their willingness to take the Mariel Cubans who had changed their minds and wanted to return to Cuba. In return, the FBI would cooperate with the Cuban Interests Section in Washington on such subjects as the murder of "Pechuga," a Cuban delegate to the United Nations who was gunned down on a New York City street. But again, nothing came of the overture. During this trip, however, José Luis Padrón informed Dascal and Benes that Castro might be willing to entertain multilateral talks, which had been proposed by Benes to Panamanian strongman, Omar Torrijos. General Torrijos, who was extremely bright and highly popular among his countrymen, carried out in a relatively brief time (before his death in a helicopter accident) perhaps more effective social reform without the use of coercion than Castro achieved with his enormous security apparatus. Benes remembers the first time they met:

> He took me walking, with only a single bodyguard, through the *Chorrillos* (shantytowns) of Panama City. He stopped people on the street, entered their shacks, and listened to the residents explain their problems. He did this for hours. Later, the *barrio* in which we had visited received extensive improvements, and became a model example of urban renewal.[102]

Working through de la Espriella, Benes initiated contact, leading to almost daily telephone calls. The "Basketball Team" idea emerged from these conversations: five high-level leaders from the Caribbean Basin— Torrijos, Costa Rica's Daniel Obduber, Carlos Andrés Pérez of Venezuela, Alfonso López Michelsen of Colombia, and José Francisco Peña Gómez, the head of the Dominican Republic's *Partido Revolucionario,* would fly to Cuba and Washington in Torrijos's personal plane and somehow convince both governments to end their belligerence.

On May 5, 1980, during a follow-up visit to Panama, Benes received a midnight call at de la Espriella's home from José Luis Padrón in Havana. "*El Tío,*" he said, "agrees to see the Basketball Team." Benes then asked his host the registration number of Torrijos's aircraft, so that he could obtain clearance to land in Havana and in Washington. But the Panamanian head of state, despite a secret meeting with Benes at El Faralón, a

3.6 Orange Bowl Tent City during Mariel, 1980. Bernardo Benes collection.

3.7 Page from Cuban computer printout listing claims to be paid after normalization. Bernardo Benes collection.

secluded government-owned residence in the mountains of Panama, to discuss the details of the mission, undermined the Basketball Team plan. Then and there, Torrijos decided to visit Castro himself. Benes, working with Daniel Obduber, tried to revive the multilateral project, but its time had passed. Cyrus Vance had stepped down as secretary of state, replaced by Edmund Muskie, who knew virtually nothing about the years of secret negotiations. Muskie's main concern was the continued presence of Cuban would-be émigrés who were given sanctuary at the American Interests Section, and Castro's growing petulance. Although Tarnoff and Padrón continued to keep channels open, Carter's failure to win re-election shut the door.

One of the most interesting documents to emerge from the negotiations was a 315-page computer printout bound between printed covers titled *Reclamaciones Norteamericanas por orden Alfabético General* (*American [Property] Claims in Alphabetical Order*).[103] Copies were handed out by the architect Osmani Cienfuegos, brother of the revolutionary hero Camilo Cienfuegos. The book listed every request by a United States citizen or corporation for payment for seized property, and indicated, among other information, what the Cuban government would be prepared to pay if normal diplomatic relations were restored. Amounts promised varied between $487 claimed by the Society of the Divine Word, to a few thousand dollars for individual homes, to nearly $2 million for sugar plantations and factories, and included four claims from the Chase Manhattan Bank for properties worth a total in excess of $8,500,000. The Coca-Cola Corporation claimed $41,037,460, of which the Cubans were prepared to pay somewhat less than $30 million. The Cubans were ostensibly prepared to pay back a good portion of every claim. Castro, on one occasion, told Dascal and Benes that he was disposed to pay indemnities to the more than 6,000 American companies confiscated in the early 1960s, whose claims had totaled $2 billion.[104]

During the same trip to Havana, Benes asked his hosts for their priorities if the economic boycott were to be partially lifted. Padrón delivered the list, and at the top was the American blacklisting of any cargo ship that moored even once in any Cuban harbor. Then came a long list of items, in descending order: spare parts, asphalt, textiles, paper, nickel, oil, ceramics, cement, metals, computers, shoes, and other products. Next-to-last on the list were medicines, and, at the very bottom, food.[105] Castro clearly put industrial development before the Cuban people's immediate needs.

Benes's last statement to the press as the dramatic encounter came to a close proved to be naive. "Once the prisons have been emptied," Benes said, "I believe the government's liberalization policy will proceed very fast. It is a logical, historical step." He also added in his interview that Castro had told him that he felt constant pressure from Cubans whose families lived abroad, and that he was glad to work with Jimmy Carter, about whom Castro remarked: "Carter is the first American president who has not been hostile toward Cuba."[106] Yet even though the prisoner release and the agreement on family reunification became Carter's most important human rights' achievement, normalization of relations never occurred. Cuba refused to budge on the security issues considered paramount by Brzezinski and others in Washington, as well as on the American insistence that Cuba take steps unilaterally rather than in tandem.[107]

One event occurred somewhat later which illustrated that Benes had not given up on his efforts to play a role in international affairs. In the words of Ambler H. Moss, Jr., the Carter administration's ambassador to Panama:

> He was on an airplane from Panama to Miami and seated next to his old friend Ricardo de la Espriella. Knowing that the Carter Administration was desperate to get Shah [Mohammed Reza Pahlavi] out of the United States as a step to free the American hostages, he asked Ricardo if Panama would take him. Ricardo gave a noncommittal answer. At that, Bernardo went to Peter Tarnoff with a message to Cyrus Vance that Panama would take in the Shah (big news if true, as all our NATO allies had turned him down and Mexico didn't want him back.)
>
> With that, I received a call from Peter on that same red telephone [that Benes had used before] to check it out. Ricardo, back in Panama, denied that he said that to Benes, but both of us thought that maybe if Carter asked Torrijos, man-to-man as a personal favor, it might fly. It eventually did. Hamilton Jordan came to Panama, we went to see Torrijos, and he agreed immediately. That was the start of another saga, but it doesn't involve Benes.[108]

Benes's recollection differs. He remembers that he met Ricardo de la Espriella at Miami International Airport while the Panamanian was returning from Washington to attend a meeting of the World Bank. De la Espriella told him that Secretary of State Vance needed a place willing to grant the shah asylum; Benes then suggested that Panama take him in, de la Espriella said that he would speak with Omar Torrijos about it.[109] Benes telephoned Peter Tarnoff, who initially assumed that Benes was joking. After his three-hour flight to Panama, de la Espriella found Ambassador Ambler Moss at his home, waiting for him. Moss asked for confirmation of what had been said and contacted Washington. Twenty hours after the airport conversation, President Carter's chief of staff, Hamilton Jordan, arrived in Panama, and working with Moss, completed the arrangement. Some days later, the shah was installed in a house on Contadora Island owned by Gabriel Lewis, the former Panamanian foreign minister.[110]

The reason that the shah's place of residence was so important was that it had become an issue in the negotiations between Iran's Foreign Minister Sadegh Ghotbzadeh and the Carter administration over the release of the American hostages held in Tehran. The Iranians accepted Panama because there the shah could not, they believed, easily interfere in Iranian affairs. But to the chagrin of the State Department, three months after arriving in Panama, the shah left in a chartered airplane for Egypt. That night, Omar Torrijos called Washington, saying that the Iranian government had contacted him that the hostages would be turned over to the Revolutionary Council if the plane could be made to turn around and return to Panama. But in the words of the *New York Times's* Tad Szulc, who accepted Benes's version of the story, "Torrijos viewed the offer tendered by Ghotbzadeh with skepticism. 'Screw them,' Torrijos said. 'I don't trust them.'"[111] Torrijos's response summed up, as well, the reason that caused many United States officials to be skeptical about the negotiations with the Cubans: they did not trust them either.

The Mariel boatlift notwithstanding, most of the returned prisoners assimilated into their new lives without further contact with Benes. Some, however, remember him with reverence. During the 1978 dialogue, Luis Pozo, son of Justo Luis del Pozo, Batista's mayor of Havana, was taken from his prison cell in Combinado del Este to the office of State Security because Benes had asked to interview him. Released with the other prisoners, Pozo spent four months in Havana and then left for Miami in March 1980 by chartered plane. Benes walked with him through customs and then drove immediately to Pan American Hospital, where Pozo's mother lay in a coma. After an hour, during which time his mother did not respond, Pozo was taken to Miami's Tropical Park, where his family and friends awaited him. All of this, Pozo remembers, Benes arranged.[112]

Summing up the atmosphere in Miami during the 1978–1980 period, *Herald* journalist Liz Balmaseda wrote:

> For the exile community, these were critical years. After two decades, our leaders finally had broken into the political establishment, their influence moving beyond Miami and toward Washington, DC. Exile businesses were thriving. Corporate boards were Cubanizing. There was too much to lose with unflattering associations . . . but the Miami exile community picked up Castro's vocabulary. The *marielitos* were called "scum," delinquents, social misfits, parasites, bums . . . words propagated by some of Castro's most strident opponents in exile. In their haste to save their own image, exiles bought into Castro's labels.[113]

Ultimately, the final result of the 1978 negotiations—the release of almost all of Castro's political prisoners and Cuba's agreement to permit more than one million trips of exiled Cubans to reunite, if briefly, with their families—would be more successful than Benes could have dreamed, but at enormous personal cost to himself. Castro's agreement on exile visits, even if it was a calculated move to earn dollars for his beleaguered economy, arguably represented the most welcome action in behalf of Cubans on both sides of the Straits of Florida since 1959.

Later, United States officials involved in the 1978–1980 events minimized the role played by Dascal and Benes. At best, these officials painted the role of the two Cuban exiles as that of "honest brokers," or "emissaries." David Aaron's demand that Castro move first by withdrawing Cuban troops from Africa angered the Cuban leader because he had expected gestures of good faith, not preconditions. To the extent that Benes and Dascal informed Castro and Padrón and the other high Cuban officials of the reality of life in the United States, they performed an invaluable, unprecedented service. Washington's belief that Castro was simply a puppet of the Soviet Union reflected Cold War thinking, and Benes believes that if the Cuban dictator had been listened to with genuinely open minds there would have been broader room in which to negotiate. In the end, however, both sides—Havana and Washington—used Benes and Dascal as pawns in a much larger game. Benes's family, and his monetary and emotional sacrifices, meant little to professional diplomats and politicians with agendas of their own.

CHAPTER FOUR

THE REAGAN YEARS
AND BEYOND

The 1980 Mariel boatlift brought tens of thousands of desperate Cubans to Florida and further hardened the anti-Castro policy of the United States. Mariel was not only difficult for its participants, but also for the Cuban families who stayed behind while family members left. In the mid-1980s, Cuba again shut its doors, refusing to honor its 1978 agreement of permitting exiles to visit. Some Cubans committed suicide in despair over the departure of their children or other close relatives, and Cubans who lined up to apply for visas at the height of Mariel were insulted by hecklers, splattered by eggs thrown at them, and in some cases were forced to wear signs reading, "I am a worm." Many received beatings, and one or two were beaten to death.[1] Many Mariel arrivals initially fared badly in the United States, too, although over time they adjusted.

The *marielitos*, as they were called, comprised more than 120,000 Cubans, a small percentage of which included convicted sexual deviants, homosexuals, men with long criminal records, and the mentally disabled, and some were simply released from confinement and placed on boats ready to leave Cuba. After this fact became known publicly, the welcome for the Mariel arrivals soured quickly. Mention of the "boat people" caused panic and fear, making it even more difficult for the innocent 90 percent to adjust. In addition, most of them were racially mixed and, at best, from the former lower-middle class. They came for the most part seeking greater opportunities—more consumer goods, more freedom to travel—but they also acknowledged some of the benefits of the Cuban revolution: health care, literacy training, sports programs, and Castro's "gutsy nationalism." This, as well as their non-elite status, turned most Miami exiles against them. Even though the *marielitos* injected fresh cultural life into the Cuban enclave, for years they bore the stigma of outcasts.[2]

In January 1981, during the transition from the Carter to the Reagan administrations, Benes had brunch at state Senator Jack Gordon's house in Miami Beach. Journalist Jack Anderson, who had written about Cuba and who was close to Gordon, also had been invited. After a long discussion about Cuba, Anderson offered to arrange a meeting between Benes to talk with Richard Allen, the new director of the National Security Council.

On February 20, one month after President Ronald Reagan entered office, Benes met not with Allen but with Roger Fontaine, the new National Security Council's Latin American specialist. For the sake of discretion, Fontaine and Benes met in Anderson's Washington office in Anderson's presence (who committed himself to secrecy). They conversed for over four hours. Benes did most of the talking; Fontaine asked questions but otherwise sat taking notes. Benes suggested that Fontaine consult the dossier on him that Peter Tarnoff had said had been compiled. The Cubans had one on Benes too, but obviously it was inaccessible—unless the CIA was at that time more skilled than it seemed.[3]

The main part of the meeting reviewed Benes's contacts in Cuba and discussed how the dozens of meetings had been arranged. Although Fontaine gave Bernardo his home telephone number, Benes never heard from him again. Richard Allen left his post on the NSC, and soon after Fontaine followed suit.

What transpired thereafter differed significantly from the events of 1977 and 1978. During the entire period of Benes and Dascal's fourteen meetings in Cuba, they had remained in constant touch with Carter administration officials. Now, Dascal would drop out and Benes would play a diminished role. He would be assigned to a companion, who would maintain exclusive contact with Reagan administration officials.

In August 1981, Benes met José Luis Padrón in Panama. Padrón delivered an odd message, to be delivered to Jim Freeman, deputy chief of the

FBI in South Florida and head of the department for Cuban affairs. "The Cuban government," Padrón said, "is disposed to contribute five thousand dollars for you to donate to charities if you permit Alpha 66 to continue its anti-Castro activities." "For us," he told Benes, puffing at his cigar to keep a straight face, "Alpha 66 is one of the best agents Cuba has in the United States. We have captured all of its infiltration agents since 1970. Fidel is not very concerned about the United States; he sleeps very well. Like President Reagan, he is taking off all of August for a vacation. He is disposed to talk, but he is not in a hurry."

Benes struggled with himself over whether he should become involved in this process more deeply. He was embittered by the abuse he had received from Miami Cubans. Furthermore, he needed to improve his personal finances. In mid-1981, he and Dascal flew to Washington to try to obtain a license for a new Spanish-language radio station. During their stay, Dascal, on an impulse, picked up the telephone and called the State Department, requesting to speak with Secretary of State Alexander Haig. According to Benes, the following dialogue ensued.

"Who is calling him?" asked the receptionist.

"It is Carlos," said Dascal, and left the telephone number where he could be reached.

The call briefly turned the State Department upside down. Officials thought that the call might have been from "Carlos the Jackal" (Ilych Ramírez), the Venezuelan international terrorist linked to murders and bombings across the world. Calling back, a State Department staffer determined that this "Carlos" was Carlos Dascal. Haig transferred the call to General Vernon A. Walters, the ambassador-at-large and fabled troubleshooter from his days as an enlisted man after World War I to his becoming deputy director of the CIA. Walters had known of the earlier negotiations and agreed to see Benes and Dascal. They had an animated conversation, with Walters pumping them about what they had learned in Cuba. Days later, he called and invited them to his modest home in Palm Beach, which he shared with his sister and brother-in-law.

Walters had first met the Cuban dictator when Castro returned to the United States in 1960. Known for his sharp mind, wit, and multilingualism, Walters was the only general officer in the United States Army not to graduate from high school (he had attended Jesuit schools in Europe,

however) and made his career both in military intelligence and as a negotiator with foreign leaders.

President Eisenhower had refused to meet with Castro because, as he
told Walters, the films he had seen on television of Castro's firing squads
had made him sick to his stomach. He informed Walters that he would
tell Vice-President Nixon to see him, just as he had instructed the previous year, but that the primary responsibility for escorting Castro would be
Walters's. Castro's English was rudimentary, and a television interview he
had given turned out to be disastrous because of the language barrier, so
Walters conversed with him in Spanish.[4]

Following the Benes-Dascal meetings with Castro and his high officials, General Walters was asked by President Reagan to assess the possibilities of negotiations with Castro.[5] On January 20, 1982, General
Walters met with Benes and Dascal, who were visiting Washington.
When they arrived, an aide informed them that an emergency had occurred, and that the meeting would be postponed until six that afternoon.
They spent the rest of the day talking with the lawyers who would represent Benes and Dascal before the Federal Communications Commission,
then entered Walters's office at the new scheduled time. The general received them, immediately asking: "And when do we go to Cuba?"

Walters then introduced his aide, Commander Lee Martini, and explained that the four of them would travel to Cuba as long as Castro and
Padrón would meet with them. The trip would be completely secret, and
would have to be approved by the White House. Benes suggested that
Walters contact the FBI chief, William Webster, who agreed to arrange
the trip pending further approval. The general told him to return home
and speak with Jim Freeman, the deputy chief of the Miami FBI. Freeman told Benes that to preserve secrecy, he would travel as "Gustavo,"
Walters would be "Joseph," and Martin would be "Michael."[6] Benes
would arrange for General Walters to be served meals of fresh fruit, especially papaya, his favorite. Benes and Dascal would go ahead to Havana to arrange the meeting, and the others would meet at Fort
Lauderdale International Airport.

Following Mariel, Cuban–United States relations had sunk to a low.
The Reagan administration did not link foreign policy to the human
rights concerns of Jimmy Carter, nor was Cuba a top priority except in the

case of Cuban assistance to leftist guerrilla groups in Africa and Central America. The mutual understandings between Havana and Washington that had began in 1977 ended abruptly with the politically charged Mariel exodus in 1980. The Cold War gripped Washington. Cuban Americans who applied under the Freedom of Information Act for information about the records of the Pedro Pan flights received rejection letters from the CIA stating, "The CIA may neither confirm nor deny the existence or nonexistence of records responsive to your request. Such information— unless, of course, it has been officially acknowledged—would be classified for reasons of national security under Executive Order 12356." So Cubans in the United States became trapped in a national security conflict that fueled anticommunist militancy in Cuban communities (in the United States) and made questioning official policy evidence of disloyalty.[7]

Benes and Dascal flew to Cuba on January 22 to establish the final details for their trip with General Walters. Padrón pledged secrecy and dictated two paragraphs to Walters about his government's willingness "to discuss, at proper levels, problems constituting the essence of differences in bilateral relations." They returned to Miami, read the message to Walters on the telephone, and waited for White House approval.

No one returned the call either to Dascal or Benes. Some weeks later, they learned that Vernon Walters had traveled to Cuba in March accompanied only by his aide, Commander Martini. The two military men had flown from Miami on a charter plane arranged for by the FBI.

What they did not know was that Walters had met with Padrón and Castro, and that Walters had found Castro to be initially very pleasant. When the Cubans met Walters at the handsome house in which he would be staying, Walters joked, "Is this a gift from the departed wealthy class?" Castro remained friendly, even deferential, to his guest. The general was fed papaya, his favorite fruit, three meals a day. Castro invited Walters to join him snorkeling, and remarked that both of them had studied under the Jesuits. General Walters, however, never one to pass up a good line, replied "*Pero yo me quedé fidel*" ("But I remained faithful," a wry pun on the Spanish word *fiel*, derived from "*fidel*"). Overall, however, Walters left somewhat confused. Castro kept repeating that "everything is negotiable," but then he would add the stern comment that "I have a sacred responsibility to the revolution and to the Cuban people." Castro clearly gave Walters very mixed signals, so the meetings produced nothing concrete and, for the time being, the discussions ended.[8]

Wayne Smith, the head of the United States Interests Section installed at the American Embassy in Havana, recounts a different story. Press accounts revealed in early December that Secretary of State, Alexander Haig, had met in Mexico on November 23, 1981, with Cuban Vice-President Carlos Rodríguez—without notifying Smith, to his discomfort. Smith claims that he discovered from friends in the State Department, as well as from the Cubans, that the meeting failed because Rodríguez believed that Haig's information about Cuba was, according to Smith, "in many cases incorrect" and that Haig demanded deeds, not words.[9] To Benes, this show of American clumsiness typified what he called the *Boniatillo* factor: no matter how hard a Cuban tries, he cannot explain fully to a non-Cuban diner why the sweet-potato custard is so special. Rodríguez and Haig simply represented two different worlds, whereas Benes and Dascal believed that as Cubans they understood Castro and his aides perfectly.

Smith further claims that after Walters' visit with Castro, the Reagan administration "started putting out the version that he had . . . found the Cubans so totally unbending and unwilling to negotiate that there was no point in trying; rather, we'd have to rely on force and pressure. . . . This," Smith concludes, "was a lie . . . the Cubans refused nothing."[10]

Worse, Smith argues in his memoirs, the Cubans did everything possible to convince the Americans of their sincerity and willingness to negotiation. Walters' visit, he says, was simply "a charade aimed at giving the impression of a willingness to talk where in fact no such willingness existed." To bolster his assertion, Smith observes that although Walters' trip to Havana had been secret, the administration "carefully leaked word through diplomatic circles that he had been there. By April, his visit had been reported in the press. This was all in preparation for the new measures [that] the administration intended to impose against Cuba."[11]

The process then passed into its second phase, which got off to a shaky start because the Reagan administration enacted measures to damage Cuba's economy further by allowing a 1977 fishing treaty to lapse, making it more difficult for United States citizens to travel to Cuba. Further, it did nothing to shorten the wait for the released political prisoners who required permit visas for entry to the United States. At the end of 1981, the Washington administration simply refused to issue any more visas. Smith's explanation is damning: "The Reagan administration's indifference to the fate of those ex-prisoners was consistent with its whole approach to human-rights violations in Cuba. While talking incessantly of human-rights violations, it made not the slightest effort to alleviate suffering."[12] The Carter administration, he points out, achieved the release of thousands of political prisoners and reunited tens of thousands of families. The Reagan administration's refusal to issue visas and its lack of concern with the remaining Cuban political prisoners would be criticized by the Human Rights Commission of the Organization of American States in 1984.

Benes continued his involvement, although Dascal left to pursue business interests in Miami. In October 1982, Benes accompanied Panama's new president, Ricardo de la Espriella, who had been invited to Washington by President Ronald Reagan. De la Espriella had invited Benes to come along, and Ricky Benes invited herself because she wanted to visit her daughter at the nearby University of Maryland. Ricardo's wife, Panama's First Lady Mercedes María de la Espriella, recalled that that she was furious because Ricky, not she, was the first woman to disembark from the American presidential airplane, and therefore appeared in the television coverage.[13]

President de la Espriella and his entourage visited Vice-President George H. W. Bush at Blair House and reviewed a military parade at the Pentagon. De la Espriella and Benes were so close that at 4:00 A.M., after Benes was awakened by de la Espriella's aide and told about the content of the speech written by his foreign affairs staff, Benes awakened de la Espriella, and they worked together to rewrite the text which was delivered the next day at the National Press Club.[14] Later, they ran into David Newsom, president of Catholic University, who had met Benes and Dascal in 1978 when they introduced Newsom, then a high State Department official, to Padrón and de la Guardia in New York City. The visit concluded with a half-hour interview with President Ronald Reagan which mostly consisted of pleasantries. When Bernardo and Ricky returned to Miami Beach, they hosted an informal dinner at their home for the Panamanian president. The guests included former Florida Governor

Ruben Askew; former United States Ambassador to Panama Ambler Moss; Jeb Bush, the son of then Vice-President George H. W. Bush; Representative Dante Fascell; President Gregory Wolfe of Florida International University; and Edward T. Foote II, president of the University of Miami.[15] No Miami Cubans attended. The Secret Service provided surveillance and monitored through the large electronic devices that had been placed in every room. No one, of course, could have predicted that de la Espriella would be deposed by Manuel Noriega two years later on February 13, 1984.

In retrospect, Benes noticed an interesting pattern as the dialogue mission evolved. The operation started with the consent and support of President Carter's National Security Council and the CIA, and concluded with supervisory authority shifted to the FBI and the Department of State. Before and after each trip, Benes would call the FBI and describe what was planned and, on his return, what had occurred. The FBI proved to be vigilant, supportive, and efficient. Once, however, at a meeting held in Nassau, in the Bahamas, however, he had forgotten to contact them. Benes and Dascal had stayed at the Britannia Hotel. Two days later, in Miami, Benes received a visit from the Mexican-born FBI agent nicknamed "Taco," in charge of Cuban affairs in Miami: "Listen," the agent told him. "The fried eggs you ate for breakfast at the Britannia Hotel needed a little more cooking."[16] This was the first and last time that Benes and Dascal neglected to inform the United States government about their activities.

PROJECT CUBA:
THE BONIATILLO FACTOR

In May 1983, on a campaign trip to Miami, a motorcade accompanied President Ronald Reagan from the airport to Little Havana, where he ate at Esquina de Tejas, making it famous forever in Cuban Miami tradition. For lunch, he ordered the $3.75 daily special #1—chicken, *moros* (black beans with rice), fried plantains, and flan with American coffee. His guests at his table included Jorge Mas Canosa; the restaurant's owner, Juan Vento; Roberto Cambo, chair of the Hispanic unit of the Reagan-Bush campaign; and Carlos Salman, Dade County's Hispanic campaign head. "What stirred me the most was that he said that he was sorry the

Cuban people could not enjoy the same food we were enjoying today," María Rosa González, coordinator for Hispanic affairs at Jackson Memorial Hospital, told reporters.[17] Reagan was then whisked away to the Dade Country Auditorium, where Benes had brought the first planeload of released Cuban political prisoners five years earlier. Jorge Mas Canosa, speaking Spanish, introduced the president. Mas Canosa endorsed the administration's aggressive policy in Central America, and urged the United States to abrogate an agreement with the Soviet Union stating that the United States would not invade Cuba unless Soviet missiles were stored on the island. In a rousing speech, Reagan told three thousand Miami Cubans: "If we cannot act decisively so close to home, who will believe us anywhere? Let us pledge ourselves to the freedom of the noble, long-suffering Cuban people." He also called Castro the head of "a new fascist regime," a variation of the usual anti-communist wordage. He did not mention the pardon he had granted a week earlier for the convicted Watergate burglar, Eugenio Martínez, a Miami Cuban exile. He concluded his speech by saying, in heavily accented Spanish, "*Viva Cuba Libre. Cuba Si, Castro No.*"

The *Herald* reported that Reagan had used "perhaps his most blistering language yet on Cuba and communism." Across the street from the auditorium, a banner proclaimed: "Our paramilitary training camp is ready to train freedom fighters to preserve democracy. Cuba should be free again. We need your cooperation." Another sign, designed by an ironworker who called himself 'a founder and fighter' of Alpha 66, showed a sketch of a dead Fidel Castro. There were no counterdemonstrations. One small anti-Reagan group that had rallied earlier in that month had been broken up by angry Cubans, one of whom fired a rifle. The group notified the news media that it would not appear at the Dade County Auditorium because the Miami police had said "that they could not guarantee [their] security."[18]

The presidential motorcade sped up Flagler Street and turned north to the airport, and the campaign entourage took off in Air Force One, having spent less than three hours in the city but having scored a major public relations coup.[19]

The administration did nothing to follow up on the Cuban issue until a year and a half later. In November 1984, the Reagan administration brought it forward, although not in the manner suggested by Reagan's assertive speech to the Miami Cubans. Instead, his administration initiated steps for secret overtures to Cuba's government possibly leading to normalizing relations, just as Carter had done in 1978. Dascal had dropped out of the negotiations, assuming a low profile perhaps in reaction to the opprobrium heaped on Benes by angry exiles. Benes, unlike during the Carter years, would have no direct contact himself with the United States government. Someone new assigned to the mission would be the intermediary, and would report through a third party to James Bloomfield, a graduate of the Naval Academy in Annapolis and retired CIA specialist on Cuba, newly contracted by the CIA to coordinate the planned operation.

The intermediary turned out to be Guillermo Alonso Bermudez, nicknamed "Guille" (also known as Guillermo Alonso-Pujol, Jr., since he was the son of Cuba's last constitutional vice-president under Carlos Prío Socarrás, 1948–1952). On November 19, 1984, Guille informed Benes that Jim Bloomfield would coordinate a new secret mission to Cuba. He also said that the "highest members of the White House inner circle" had approved Benes's role, although he offered no names. The CIA dubbed the program "Project Cuba," and planned the first meeting for February in Panama to prevent the information from filtering to the Soviets. José Luis Padrón, and anyone he brought with him, would represent the Cuban government. Vice-President George Bush or Attorney General Edwin Meese, Bloomfield, and a to-be-named top army or navy officer would represent the United States.

Guille approached Benes in Miami with the news that the Reagan administration wanted his assistance in talking to Castro again. Guille had been close to Benes before 1959; they attended baseball games together, and Guille had been invited to Bernardo's wedding. Benes rooted for the Cienfuegos team, and at the beginning of the 1950s, Guille had bought a 50 percent interest in the club. The two young men used to watch the games from Bobby Maduro's air-conditioned personal box at Havana's stadium. After Bernardo and Ricky's marriage, Guille rented the couple an apartment in a handsome building owned by his family, one floor below his own, and reduced the $175-a-month rent to $115 because Benes was just starting out as a lawyer. They constantly met until November 11, 1960, the day Benes defected.

Guille and one of his brothers remained in Cuba as political prisoners. His father, known by his friends as Don Guillermo, pulled strings throughout the world to gain his sons' release. When Guille came to Miami, he told Benes that he and his father had developed a very close relationship over many years with Colonel King, at one time the head of Latin American operations for the CIA. Don Guillermo knew the CIA well, and was the only Cuban émigré who publicly warned that the Bay of Pigs invasion would fail even though his eldest son, Jorge, was one of the invaders. Benes had CIA contacts at a lower level—he had some contact with agent Larry Sternfield, and he met twice with James Noel, the CIA station chief in Cuba. Benes was never on the CIA payroll, nor did he maintain regular contact with the Agency. But he did meet with Don Guillermo almost on a daily basis before the Bay of Pigs invasion on April 17, 1961. Benes often drove his rusty 1952 Ford to Fort Lauderdale to meet with the old man and his wife, Hortensia; he was intimate with the Alonso-Pujol family.

Once the mission began, Guille informed Benes that no one was to be told: not the FBI, not Congressman Dante Fascell, not Larry Sternfield, and not Panamanian Vice-President Ricardo de la Espriella. To reinforce the point, Benes was told that his home and office telephones would be wiretapped.

On Sunday morning, November 18, 1984, the National Security Council met in the White House to discuss "Project Cuba." According to Guille, five members dominated the conversations: Vice-President George H. W. Bush; Caspar Weinberger; James Baker; William Casey, the cigar-smoking director of the CIA; and, to a lesser degree, Secretary of State George P. Shultz.[20] Benes was to deliver a verbal message to Fidel Castro in person, and he was to travel only with Alonso-Pujol, who would serve as the contact with the White House.[21]

On November 22, 1984, Castro, through unknown channels but possibly the Cuban Interests Section in Washington, notified the White House of his acceptance of the preconditions for the meetings. He warned, however, that there must not be further "complications" in Nicaragua, which was then undergoing an armed struggle between the Castro-backed Sandinistas and the United States–backed government. Then the Reagan officials slowed the pace of the negotiations in terms of setting a date for the meetings. Weeks passed, and the Benes-Guille team kept active. Guille visited James Baker, President Reagan's chief of staff, at Baker's home the night before Christmas Eve. Baker said: "Fidel is a bright man to a superlative degree. He has great passion against the United States but he also is practical, and for this reason we are disposed to see if this can work. This is so explosive for this administration that not only must there be total and complete discretion, but also we must calibrate each step with the greatest possible care."[22] He also warned that he thought the mission had about a 20-percent chance of success, and that it was vital that President Reagan be kept fully informed.

Bloomfield told Guille that on a trip to Portugal, he had met with Baker and President Reagan. According to a memorandum written by Bloomfield, Baker confirmed to Bloomfield that the plan was still active. Everything would continue to be done with the greatest possible secrecy, and, presuming that Meese, Baker, Weinberger, and Casey agreed, a deal could be struck establishing relations with Cuba and lifting the embargo as long as Cuba agreed to "take care of Nicaragua" (by stopping aid to the Sandinistas) and to not intervene in Central America.[23]

On December 27, 1984—Benes's fiftieth birthday—Benes was in Cuba with Guille. Benes asked Castro if he might announce during his New Year's speech that all of the world's leaders should review their priorities and "divert funds spent on weapons to projects to fight misery, hunger, and disease." Nothing happened. The negotiations seemed to be going nowhere, although the Cubans' actions implied that they were still very interested. Benes continued communicating with Padrón, in coded messages somewhat oddly as "First Baseman"; Benes and Alonso-Pujol were "the Umpires" (Benes was "Home Plate Umpire"); Vice-President Bush the "Catcher" (Benes, the baseball fanatic, should have known that Bush played first base at Yale, but that was before Benes came to the United States); Attorney General Edwin Meese was "the Right Fielder." CIA agent Jim Bloomfield, "the Left Fielder," acted as liaison. Guille met with Secretary of Defense, Caspar Weinberger, on January 31 and again with Baker. The next day, Bloomfield told Guille that he retrieved the complete set of CIA dossiers on Cuba since 1959 in order to study them; he then spent until 12:15 A.M. speaking with Weinberger.

February, the month in which the meetings were to have started, saw a flurry of messages from Padrón suggesting changes in the plans. The "team" worried about Edwin Meese's political problems over the Justice Department's handling of the Iran-Nicaraguan Contra investigation.[24] At the White House, James Baker assured the coordination of the project, but his father-in-law died in California, setting everything back for a week.

Early in February 1985, Benes and Guille flew to Havana to meet with José Luis Padrón. He complained about the delay in receiving contact directly from the Reagan administration but added that he understood about such things: "in your country they are harder than for us." According to Benes, Padrón made a little speech:

> Both countries want security without surrendering flags, by looking for peace. Realism and pragmatism are essential in international politics. If the Soviets stop their four daily ships bringing oil, we will have to light the island with candles. Could we count on Venezuela after so many years of hostility? China is not Cuba. The Soviet Union has been very intelligent with Cuba, although they have made mistakes. When nations negotiate, each one has to compromise.[25]

Padrón also mentioned that Cuban intelligence had doubts about Jim Bloomfield; in fact, Cuban intelligence wondered whether Bloomfield existed at all. Padrón, however, said that he was ready to visit the United States, and talk further.

On March 13, 1985, Guille informed Benes that Bloomfield had encountered some difficulties on other matters that would prevent him from meeting with President Reagan. Bloomfield also said to Guille that he could tell Benes—but absolutely no one else, especially the Cubans— that the previous week's CIA flyovers of Cuba, as well as intelligence reports, had revealed that Cuba was preparing to ship large quantities of weapons, airplanes, and helicopters to Nicaragua for the Sandinistas. He warned Guille that Castro would have to cease doing this once negotiations started.

A few days later, Jim Bloomfield called Guille and immediately put Attorney General Edwin Meese on the line. Meese thanked him for all of his efforts to help solve the Cuban problem and explained the reasons for the delay in the initial arrangements. "You may say to Padrón," Guille recalled Meese saying, "[that] events not directly linked to this but in some parallel degree have delayed us much more than we expected, but we are working to deal with them so that the talks can be held."

In late March of 1985, Treasury Secretary Donald Regan, a former Marine and a Merrill Lynch executive, met with Alonso-Pujol and also thanked him in President Reagan's name for his efforts. Jim Bloomfield, he said, had kept him informed. The next day James Baker met with Guille, and said that Benes and Guille's reports represented "the most complete report[s] in the sense of understanding what is in Fidel's and Padrón's minds" that he had read. Baker told his visitor, however, that further delays would have to be expected. He then met with CIA director William Casey, who essentially said the same thing. To assure Padrón that nothing was wrong, Benes and Guille flew to Havana again on April 2.

Padrón, by this time, also faced difficulties behind the scenes. Castro had started to purge government officials and the Communist Party apparatus. Padrón assured his guests that the purge had nothing to do with any preparations for détente with the United States. He also cautioned that, in his opinion, improvements in relations would have to proceed slowly, with exchanges of small concessions creating a more relaxed atmosphere. If the United States interpreted this approach as a weakness on Cuba's part, then the whole effort would abort. "Remember," he said, "with Brzezinski's cooperation, we could have achieved much of this goal. Because of his resistance, Mariel happened."

Guille and Benes hurriedly asked Padrón if Castro could accept the start of Radio Martí. Padrón answered: "It would be a setback, a hostile act to which we would respond." He also warned: "Intelligence agents have reported that Bernardo Benes and Guillermo Alonso-Pujol Jr. have been traveling between Cuba and Washington, D.C. We must issue some misinformation to handle this and be more careful."[26]

In April 1985, Padrón informed Benes and Guille at the Protocol House that he had met privately with Castro the previous night, and that El Jefe remained suspicious that the initial meeting with Reagan administration officials had not materialized in February, as promised. Castro also allegedly told Padrón that he did not trust the fact that Benes and Guille never traveled in official planes: unless you do, Castro said, your credibility with our side *se jode* [is fucked]. Castro showed frustration at the tone of General Walters's trip and a subsequent meeting held in Mexico City with Carlos Rafael Rodríguez. On the ride to the airport, César, their driver, remained "silent and circumspect."[27]

Further problems surfaced. Jim Bloomfield told Guille that the National Security Council had approved $14 million in aid to the Nicaraguan Contras. After this happened, Bloomfield purportedly informed the White House of his deep opposition to the measure and the continuation of delays in moving forward. A day later, Donald Regan called Bloomfield to the White House to explain his memorandum. Bloomfield found the meeting so depressing that, according to Guille, he went to his house and wrote a letter resigning from his post as head of Project Cuba. James Baker then went to Bloomfield's defense, insisting that Edwin Meese schedule a meeting with the president. On that same day, April 17, Meese spoke with President Reagan for two hours and then called Jim, telling him that the president did not want him to resign; he promised that Reagan would call him. Three days later, Bloomfield spoke on the phone for an hour and a half with Guille. He told him that Reagan had refused to accept any resignations at this stage in the process, and that he wanted to assure Padrón and Castro of the administration's good faith. After further conversation, Padrón told Benes and Guille that although he was angered by the $14 million grant to the contras, Castro's position on negotiations remained the same as before. The Cubans, Padrón said, had kept their side of the bargain. Nothing had been said about General Walters's secret trip. The ball was in Washington's court, and *El Comandante* was growing increasingly annoyed.

In mid-May, Guille learned from Bloomfield that the true reason for the delay was that despite full approval from his most important aides, Ronald Reagan had still not given his assent. Aides found him increasingly distant. Reagan had appointed Donald Regan as Secretary of the Treasury, although he barely knew him, and he never briefed Regan about his job. Donald Regan commented later about the seeming dysfunctionality of the administration at this point:

> In the four years that I served as Secretary of the Treasury, I never saw President Reagan alone and never discussed economic philosophy or fiscal and

monetary policy with him one-on-one. From first day to last at Treasury, I was flying by the seat of my pants. The President never told me what he believed or what he wanted to accomplish in the field of economics. I had to figure these things out like any other American, by studying his speeches and reading the newspapers.[28]

Bloomfield reported another complication. Vice-President Bush had started to hesitate, worrying about a conservative backlash that might hurt his plans to run for president. White House speechwriter, Pat Buchanan, he added, as well as General Walters opposed negotiations. Then, a dramatic breakthrough seemed to occur. Afraid that things would fall apart, Bloomfield sent Benes and Guille back to Havana to carry a message from President Reagan. It would offer full diplomatic and trade relations with Cuba, with no restrictions, and a reestablished sugar quota for Cuba. All that Castro had to do would be to immediately cease his assistance to revolutionary movements around the world.

When Benes and Alonso-Pujol arrived at the executive area of Miami International Airport to board their chartered plane, several customs officials interrogated them rudely, confiscated their passports, and stopped their flight. Guille called Bloomfield and told him what had happened; the next day the passports were returned with profuse apologies.

Early in the morning of May 15, 1985, in Havana, Benes received a message from José Luis Padrón telling him that Castro was disposed to talk, and that they would meet at ten that night. When the time came, Benes and Guille were taken directly to Castro's office. Benes asked Castro who in his government knew about this mission. Castro replied: "Chomy" Miyar, Osmani Cienfuegos, Raúl Castro, José Luis Padrón, and Carlos Rafael Rodríguez. When Benes heard Rodríguez's name, he became startled, because Rodríguez had close ties to the Soviet Union. Castro then told Benes: "We know the Soviets much better than the Americans do, because we know their priorities and how they operate." He meant this as an assurance that the Cubans would be able to act independently.

Benes then repeated his message, which had been delivered to him verbally but which he had written down. He started, speaking in the name of President Ronald Reagan: "Mr. President, I would like to name an ambassador to Cuba, normalize relations, and end the economic embargo. I will approve a sugar quota for Cuba. All I ask is that you stop your country's effort to export revolution abroad." Castro looked shocked and told Benes that he wanted 72 hours to think about it. Two days later, Benes received a phone call from Padrón, who said that Castro was inclined to accept. Castro and Padrón were ready to receive him and Guille on May 18, 1985; *El Jefe* had spoken until 5:00 A.M with his top aides reviewing the oral message from the White House.

When they met together at 2:00 P.M., a Saturday, the first thing Castro asked Benes was whether the message "could be a fantasy of one or several officials." Benes replied that it was worth pursuing—that during the five years since their last meeting, Castro now had gray in his beard and that 2,500 days had elapsed since the initial meeting in Panama. Castro then told Benes that he realized that reaching a settlement with the United States would deprive Cuba of much of its influences in the Third World, especially in Latin America. "But I am disposed," Benes recalls that he replied, "to do it more for the sake of peace in the region which consequently will contribute to global peace." He went on to talk about Cuba's military objectives in Angola, about German socialist leader Willy Brandt, Israeli premier Golda Meir, Henry Kissinger, and other topics. He said that other governments in Latin America had offered to mediate but that he preferred to deal with the United States directly.

He continued: "Benes, tell your president that I accept this olive branch without reservation. As a token of my commitment, I will guarantee the Sandinistas"—meaning, rather dramatically, that he would stop backing the leftist government of Daniel Ortega in Nicaragua. Benes was excited, and returned to the United States with Guille. Benes recalls that when they landed in Miami at 6:00 P.M., he thought that the long Cold War with Cuba would end in a matter of days.

Others inside Washington doubted Castro's words. A high former CIA official who specialized in Cuba later replied to the question of whether he thought that Castro was sincere in his offer to pull out of Central America: "I think not."[29]

Now, fate intervened cruelly to undermine the mission. Castro allegedly accepted Reagan's offer on May 18, 1985. Benes, exhausted, arrived in Miami late that same afternoon, and believed that the prayed-for breakthrough had been achieved. But Benes would experience a rude awakening. The *Sunday Herald*, delivered early in the morning of the nineteenth, announced on its front page that Radio Martí would begin broadcasting to Cuba the following day, Monday, May 20. Using transmitters installed on Marathon Key, halfway between Miami and Key West, Radio Martí signed on the air on the 1150 kHz band with fourteen-and-a-half hours of programming. Officials of the new station were well prepared: for months, they had been monitoring Cuban broadcasts, reviewing Cuban publications, interviewing defectors and immigrants— all to find out what Cuban radio audiences lacked. "We had to find out what the Cubans were telling their population," explained Director Ernesto Betancourt, "and then determine what information should be made available to compensate for the omissions." Interspersed between regular programs, Radio Martí broadcast messages from Cuban Americans to relatives on the island.[30] In all, Radio Martí delighted hardliners in the United States and infuriated the Cuban government. Ironically, even though Castro remained infuriated, his own 26 of July movement in 1958 had launched its own clandestine station, *Radio Rebelde*, now the principal broadcast mouthpiece of the Cuban government.[31]

Benes scrambled to contact Alonso-Pujol to reach Bloomfield, who advised his two emissaries to inform Padrón that on June 15, Bloomfield had met at Camp David with William Casey, James Baker, and President Reagan. The president, Bloomfield said, wanted Padrón to come to Washington on August 15 with his aides via South Florida's Homestead Air Force Base, to be escorted by Benes and Alonso-Pujol on a United States military plane that would land at a CIA airport in Maryland. The United States negotiating team would be made of Casey and Bloomfield on a permanent basis, with Baker and Meese attending when free from other business. Benes and Alonso-Pujol would attend all sessions.

Guille and Benes returned to Havana with a message from the Reagan White House explaining why Radio Martí should not be an obstacle to the negotiations. Padrón, however, refused to accept the message. When Castro learned of the broadcasts, he had exploded with rage, accusing the Americans of insincerity. Starting up Radio Martí at the time it occurred, Padrón said, was inexplicable. "Not even banana republics led by underdeveloped people," he said, "could possibly understand this." He complained further that the United States had never responded to Cuba's protests over Radio Martí, and that its timing had signaled the United

States' desire to abort the project. Padrón further reminded Bloomfield that American officials had lied in the past: on the day of the United States invasion of Granada, when the new head of the Special Interests Section, Mr. Ferch, who presumably did not know the extent of the Granada operation, told Padrón that it was only a rescue operation, Padrón replied that he already knew that the Marines were bombing the Cuban construction camps. Ferch's response was: "Oh, my God!" Finally, Padrón said: "I regret that I and Fidel and Benes and Alonso-Pujol have tried to solve our differences, and they have taken personal risks. If the North Americans want to communicate, let them do it through formal channels. This [process] has created a tremendous impact on those of us who believed in it. It has made us look like tremendous *comemierdas* [assholes]." Padrón was so angry, Benes later wrote, that he did not give them an opportunity to divulge the contents of their message from Washington.[32] In any case, Benes told Padrón that he had left the message in a sealed envelope.

Benes later learned through a variety of sources, including senior FBI officials, that the overture to Castro had been wholly a CIA covert operation. He assumed that the details would always remain secret. Later that autumn, however, when walking to his seat at the Orange Bowl to watch a Miami Dolphins game, he stepped in front of Jeb Bush, the vice-president's son and a Miami resident, who was in the same row. Benes had passed Bush a dozen times before, but this time when Jeb stood up to let Benes and his son reach their seats, he asked Benes, "How are you, Mr. Ambassador?" Benes interpreted this as proof that Jeb had been informed about Project Cuba, arguably by his father, who had served as director of the CIA.[33]

The Cubans frequently complained that they had been unable to learn anything about Jim Bloomfield, and, at one point, Padrón doubted that Bloomfield existed. On his return from Havana, Benes called Larry Sternfield, the CIA agent with whom he had worked in 1978 during the Carter mission. Benes asked him Padrón's question: did Bloomfield really exist? Two weeks later, Sternfield called Benes, confirming Bloomfield's background as a retired CIA agent who had specialized in Cuban affairs. Cuban intelligence, he suggested, probably missed Bloomfield in its lists of CIA operatives because, years earlier, he had retired before coming back to work.

The new trips yielded some surprises. When they had met in 1984, Castro displayed disbelief when Benes and Guille told him that Mariel had aided the Republicans and damaged Carter politically. Benes claims that Castro was astonished, another indication that Castro never fully understood how American politics worked.

In early June 1986, Guille received a message that "James" (CIA Director William J. Casey) had requested the use of Benes's and Guille's contacts to arrange for a secret meeting with Casey's Cuban counterpart, General Germán "Luis" Barreiro Caramés. Barreiro was a member of the Cuban Communist Party's Central Committee and chief of counterintelligence. Like many of his fellow revolutionaries, including Castro, he had grown up in a prosperous family, attended the best schools, and graduated with a law degree from the University of Havana. Although he spoke little English, he had been in intelligence work since the age of fourteen and had once visited Miami. He received the top intelligence post when General José Abrantes was appointed earlier in the year to Minister of the Interior. Barreiro was personable, intelligent, and, from what Benes learned in his talks with Padrón and others, so eager to meet Casey that he was practically begged the visiting Americans to complete the arrangements quickly. For Benes's part, Casey's initiative surprised him, since the CIA had long been known for its failed efforts to overthrow Castro.

Because Tony de la Guardia was in Panama, Benes telephoned José Luis Padrón, using code words to inform the Cubans that Casey wanted to meet with his counterpart, Barreiro, and that the CIA's Bloomfield had messages to pass on to the Cubans. The first offered further talks between the CIA and its Cuban counterpart to "know each other and establish direct relations between the two institutions in direct and discreet ways." Bloomfield added that it might be timely to reopen the earlier negotiations. The location for the Barreiro-Casey meeting could be selected by the Cubans: Cancún, Key West, or Panama.[34]

The effort to bring Casey and Barreiro together possibly fit into the Reagan administration's efforts to negotiate with Mikhail Gorbachev, which were proceeding at this time, and possibly a CIA plan to upstage the Soviets by becoming friendly with Castro. On August 19, 1986, Bloomfield asked Benes and Guille to suggest that the meeting be held during the first half of September at an undisclosed military base in Panama, presumably at the request of the Cubans in earlier messages. Bloomfield also asked if the Cubans might be willing to fly to Maryland, in an airplane provided by the Americans, to meet Casey. There would be no agenda, the message stated. "The objective is to establish the connection and to talk about whatever each side wishes." It concluded with a telling statement: "This is a CIA initiative without any involvement for the moment with another United States 'department.'"[35]

On September 3, 1986, Guille and Benes flew to Havana at the invitation of the Cubans. They had two lengthy meetings with General Barreiro and Colonel Tony de la Guardia. The last directive for them to fly to Maryland to meet with Casey had surprised them. Fidel Castro, they were told, was visiting a non-aligned nations summit meeting in Zimbabwe but had earlier urged caution, communicating that any such meeting would require detailed thinking and the construction of a plan. Three hours later, the group produced a proposal they titled, "Meeting in the United States." They sent it to Castro and the next day received his reply: there should be a preliminary flight to the United States by Guille, Benes, de la Guardia, and Lieutenant Jesús Arboleya as an advance team. They reached no agreement, but the Cubans brought up an additional issue that bothered them. General Barreiro repeated what had been said before—that the Cuban government could not confirm Jim Bloomfield's identity although agents had checked with the intelligence services of several nations friendly to Castro.[36]

General Barreiro stayed in Guille and Benes's guesthouse #4 at Barlovento, across a canal from the home of fugitive financier, Robert Vesco, who had been given asylum by Castro earlier. Near the end of the general's two-day stay, he asked de la Guardia to prepare a gift of six hundred Cuban Cohiba cigars for Director Casey.[37] When the meeting concluded, Barreiro went to report to Raúl Castro.

Only a handful of Cubans knew about the invitation: Castro, Raúl, Abrantes, Barreiro himself, de la Guardia, and an officer named Gustavo Machín, the son of commander "Tavo" Machín, who died in Bolivia alongside Che Guevara. The date was set for September 15. Messages went back and forth to set an agenda. The Cubans proposed establishing a hotline between Havana and Washington. Wary, the Cubans mentioned twice that they were certain that the CIA ran agents in Cuba. Nonetheless they added, "We know that in these matters, the CIA is more than ethical, and as a result our personal safety will be better protected in the United States than in any other country in the world." Barreiro also complained about Armando Valladares's book, describing his years of imprisonment in Cuba, and called the Reverend Manuel Espinosa a "farce," saying further, "We failed." The general made a few off-the-record remarks (he had approved Benes's note taking) but mostly reiterated his "great desire" to meet with Casey.

Tony de la Guardia suggested that Benes and Guille first fly to Grand Cayman Island, then to Cayo Largo in Cuba, and then proceed to Havana. They also discussed meeting in Panama. "Fidel is suspicious," they said. Furthermore, Padrón warned, "if our friends [the Soviets] learn about [the] trip, things would be very bad for us."

But the meetings never occurred. Something happened, but Benes and Guille had no idea what it was. CIA Director Casey never contacted them again, nor, as Benes adds, did he learn whether Casey ever thanked Barreiro for the cigars. Some years later, William Casey's health deteriorated and ultimately, during the last stages of the congressional investigations on the CIA's role in the Iran-Contra affair, he died of heart failure. His Cuban counterparts also fared badly: General Abrantes died in prison after being fired from his post as interior minister;[38] General Barreiro became destitute and was kept under house arrest after his subordinate, Colonel Tony de la Guardia, General Arnaldo Ochoa and two others, including Amado Padrón, the former Cuban consul in Panama, 'confessed' their participation in drug trafficking and currency counterfeiting in a widely publicized trial in 1989. They died before a Cuban firing squad.[39] Ochoa had been one of the heroes of the anti-Batista struggle, and Tony de la Guardia was said by some to be "like a son" to Fidel Castro.[40] Cuba's Special Forces were disbanded. The shock of the news was so great among Cuba-watchers that many believed that Castro could not last more than a few more months, because the Special Forces were believed to be the "real power" within the government.[41] Once again, the experts proved wrong.

Castro's habit of repetition reveals how his mind worked at the time. Benes remembers three such examples. First, Castro told Benes and Dascal several times that "everything is negotiable—but if I have to, I will create more Camariocas." Secondly, he frequently praised President Jimmy Carter as a moral man worthy of international respect. In fact, Castro often made surprisingly positive remarks about the United States. One story circulating claimed that when Castro was a pre-teenager, he had written a letter to President Franklin D. Roosevelt asking him to send him a $10 bill with his signature. Apocryphal or not, this story, along with Castro's application to Harvard, suggests what Benes terms Castro's love-hate relationship with the United States. Thirdly, Castro repeated time and again that "when two countries come to agreement, they each should understand that the other will cooperate." Benes interpreted this phrase as meaning that each country would take steps to fulfill its obligations quietly, not with dramatic gestures.

Benes also attempted to reach former President Jimmy Carter to aid the plight of the *balseros*, whose numbers during 1995 were growing. The problem was that the Miami militant exiles lobbied against any formal agreement between Havana and Washington over the rafters, so that "*la lucha*" (the struggle) could continue. Benes took Max Lesnik with him to see Alfredo Durán, and the three of them facilitated communications between Castro and Carter, whom the Cuban leader had said he admired more than any other American president. Carter contacted the Cuban leader and explained why he should stop permitting the rafters to leave. Fewer than forty-eight hours later, the "rafter crisis" ceased.

At about this time, Benes read an article by Serge Schmemann in the *New York Times* that resonated with him. The article chronicled the extraordinary bond that had developed between Uri Savir, the head of the Israeli negotiators over the issue of the return of West Bank land, and Ahmed Korei (Khouri), the head of the Palestinian team, known by his *nom de guerre*, Abu Alaa. More than any of the other one hundred Arabs and one hundred Israelis who had been "virtually locked up together" in the same hotel in the remote southern tip of Israel, these two chief negotiators had grown close. Although at the negotiating table they constantly "fought and wrangled," away from it, they vacationed together and even phoned each other when one of them couldn't sleep.[42] Many years later, Bernardo Benes pulled out a yellowed clipping of the article, hinting that a similar bond had developed between himself and José Luis Padrón.

More recently, at an academic conference in Miami, Benes saw a gray-haired man seated in front of him who stood up and raised a question for the panel. Later, Benes asked who the man was, and when he learned that he was a former Cuban G–2 agent, he approached to the man and introduced himself. The man responded saying: "I know you, Dr. Benes. I was the guy assigned to open and go through your luggage when you arrived on your trips."[43]

ONE MORE MISSION?

In October 1995, Benes had, in his words, "a revelation" that he should travel again to Cuba. Some weeks before, Gustavo Godoy, a Cuban American journalist, had arranged for Benes to have breakfast with Richard Nuccio, President Clinton's advisor on Cuban affairs. Benes told Nuccio that he was toying with the idea of returning for the first time since 1986 to Cuba but that he worried about obtaining a Treasury Department visa. Nuccio informed him that he would have no problems. Benes did travel to Cuba that month, at the invitation of the Cuban government. On his return, he sent a faxed message to Peter Tarnoff at the State Department:

> The day Pres. Clinton spoke on Cuba, that same day, I visited the land of "El Tío" and spoke with R[icardo] Alarcón, Arbezú, and three other senior people. Stayed 3 days. Very interesting meetings, very frank and open. They invited me (all expenses paid). If you are interested, give me a call. By the way, there was a Cuban American rally yesterday in Miami against Pres. Clinton. I heard from one of the organizers, an Anglo Jewish Dade County commissioner, the following: "After hearing Pres. Clinton's policy on Cuba, I can tell you that he inhaled marijuana."[44]

Benes signed the fax: "Your friend who never talks to you, Bernardo," a reference to the fact that Tarnoff had stopped returning Benes's messages and calls.

Benes then telephoned Alfredo Guevara, the director of the Cuban Film Institute and a close associate of Castro. Flying through Cancún, Benes arrived in Havana, was met by Guevara and an aide, and taken to a spacious El Laguito guesthouse in West Havana. Guevara then told Benes that Ricardo Alarcón—one of the top members of the government and a fellow student with Benes at the University of Havana—would visit him before midnight.

Alarcón spoke with Benes until six in the morning, touching on such themes as opening permanent news bureaus in Havana (Alarcón said that he preferred this to temporary journalists writing stories after spending only a few days in Cuba), and the reasons for Cuba's refusal to permit the *Miami Herald* to send reporters. The next day, he met with José Arbezú, a diplomat who had participated during the 1978 negotiations. He was introduced to a young man with a black beard and his wife. She, it turned out, was the daughter of former General Germán Barreiro, and he, nicknamed "Fidelito," was the son of Fidel Castro's first wife, Mirta Diaz-Balart. The young man's name, then, was Fidel Castro Diaz-Balart, in the context of Miami an oxymoron, since the Diaz-Balarts in South Florida were ferverent anti-Castroites and increasingly powerful politically. The trip, in all, yielded little, but it paved the way for a more concrete initiative four years later.

In March 1999, at a conference at Miami's Florida International University organized by Lisandro Pérez, the director of the university's Institute for Cuban Studies, Benes ran into Richard Nuccio, the former White House advisor on Cuba. At the conference, Benes had lunch with Nuccio and Dr. José Raúl Alfonso, a former G–2 officer and later a political prisoner. After the meal ended, Nuccio asked Benes if he would be willing to meet a Norwegian diplomat who had ideas about improving Cuban–United States relations. Norway had taken the lead in establishing the Oslo peace talks between Israel and the Palestinians and evidently was interested in starting a similar process between Cuba and Washington.

A few weeks later, Benes flew to New York and went to an East Side hotel near United Nations headquarters. He brought with him an eight-page memorandum with background about his negotiating experiences with Cuban officials. The talks, which began at 4:00 P.M. and lasted for two hours, involved Benes and senior members of the Norwegian Royal Foreign Ministry who had flown from Oslo. They included Vaguer Strommer, the under-secretary of foreign affairs; Johan Vibe, an advisor; and Gro Nystuen, head of the legal division. The Norwegians said that they wanted to proceed with Richard Nuccio serving as contact person. To his credit, Nuccio told Benes that if he became an obstacle, he would withdraw from the process. Through a friend, Benes sent a message to the Cuban Foreign Ministry. But the proposal was not accepted, and the matter was dropped. Benes's third mission never materialized. During President Bill Clinton's first term, Benes spoke to him about possible new initiatives, and although the president behaved cordially and even followed up by asking Arturo Valenzuela, senior director for Inter-American Affairs of the National Security Council, for a written statement of Benes's ideas, no response ever came to Benes's reply.[45]

CHAPTER FIVE

THE MAKING OF A PARIAH

J ust weeks after his arrival in Miami in 1960, Bernardo Benes hurled himself into community causes and bridge building with the Anglo and African American segments of Miami's tripartite population. Numerous Miami Cubans considered him an outsider, and did not appreciate his efforts. But these slights proved trivial compared to the opprobrium he received after newspaper articles in late 1978 described his personal dialogues with Fidel Castro. Benes expected that the discussions with Castro would yield humanitarian benefits both for exiled Cubans and those under Castro; instead, they infuriated hardline Cuban Miamians and created such a poisonous atmosphere that even non-Cubans ostracized him.

Still, Benes remains proud of his accomplishments during the first phase, and laments that the younger generation isn't aware of them. For instance, he is proud of his work with the United Way, first convincing its officials to reach out to Miami Cubans by bringing them into the United Way organization, then giving United Way of America the idea of establishing international chapters. This effort proved successful throughout much of the world.

Benes was also a volunteer board member of the Comprehensive Health Planning Council for South Florida, and later board president. The unpaid job took "many hours of intense involvement," according to former Executive Director Wood McCue, who later became the national director of the Health Planning Association. At the 1977 meeting at which Benes was inaugurated as president of the national board, Senator Edward Kennedy was invited to be the keynote speaker, and Benes would introduce him. Benes's talk to the 1,500 delegates from across the United States earned him several standing ovations. When Kennedy came to the podium, he tore up his prepared remarks in sight of the audience, and delivered an impassioned extemporaneous address on the importance of making the American health system responsive to everyone's needs—Benes's introductory theme.

Additionally, Benes established Miami Beach's Cuban Hebrew Congregation, after local Jewish houses of worship essentially turned their backs on the more than ten thousand Spanish-speaking Cuban Jewish exiles. In 1969, he served as president, in honor of his father, who had passed away the year before. Moreover, he was the chairman of the Dade County School Volunteer Program, replacing the then-State Senator Bob Graham. During his two years of service, the number of Miami Cuban volunteers to be teachers' aides grew from three thousand to thirteen thousand. Additionally, he played an active role in the Greater Miami Coalition, a civic group to which he brought several hundred Cuban exiles and other Hispanics, including Paul Cejas, a wealthy economist and businessman who later became ambassador to Belgium, the economist Antonio Jorge, and the banker Luis Botifoll, one of the leaders of the exile community. Between 1970 and 1974, this group worked to improve conditions for Hispanics in Miami, until the management of the United Way group decided that the assistance was no longer necessary, and the special section was disbanded.

Despite setbacks, Benes pressed ahead to mobilize support in the Cuban refugee community for integration into Miami life. In 1966, *Fortune* magazine ran a story titled "Those Amazing Cuban Émigrés," bringing the story of the seven-year struggle in Miami to its readers nationwide. The article called Benes "restless and energetic," and chronicled his rise from clerk to vice-president within nine months of an institution with assets of $140 million. It pointed out how lawyers and physicians had suffered because of language problems and, for lawyers, the fact that Cuban law was based on the Napoleonic Code rather than common law, as practiced in the United States, made for difficulties. The article also mentioned that of the three hundred thousand Cubans who had come to the

5.1   Senator Edward M. Kennedy installing Benes as president of the American
Health Planning Association in Washington, D.C., June 1977.

United States since 1959, almost all had been from the "upper layers of
the old Cuban society." The article, however, sidestepped the tensions in
Miami: the mid-1960s saw the escalating Vietnam War, the workplace
displacement of African Americans by Cubans, isolated terrorist acts by

Cuban militants, and protests and anti-Castro rallies that puzzled the Anglo and black communities and provoked resentment.

Benes earlier had tried to cultivate friendships with leaders of Miami's Cuban community as well as the Anglo elite that ran the city. He and Dr. Ferdie Pacheco, the boxing physician and painter, had started a Tuesday noontime group they called the Sesquipedalians. They met at a Spanish restaurant, Las Cuevas de Sacramento, near the offices of the *Miami Herald*. In addition to such journalists as Edna Buchanan, Howard Kleinberg, David Kraslow (publisher of the *Miami News*), Pauline Winick, Larry Aberman, and telecaster Ralph Renick, Benes and Pacheco invited prominent Cubans from various points of the political spectrum.

Benes always crusaded to integrate Cubans into local social and charitable organizations and succeeded in adding the Centro Mater to the list of private social agencies assisted by the United Fund.[1] Benes also initiated a campaign against discrimination against the Cuban exiles by the Florida State Employment Services. Harry L. Tyson, the local FSES manager, bluntly admitted "a long standing policy . . . in Dade County that no alien, Cuban or otherwise, be referred to a job which could be filled by a citizen." Benes called the policy unjust, observing that by 1968 over 2,500 Cuban-owned businesses in Miami were paying local taxes.[2]

Benes organized a three-day "Forum for the Liberation of Cuba" (February 23–25, 1968), a closed-door summit of Miami Cuban leaders, which occurred at the Kings Bay Yacht and Country Club near Coral Gables, Florida. The forum, financed by Bacardí's Pepín Bosch, invited seventy-four exile leaders, forty of whom attended. Those present ranged from Carlos Prío Socarrás, the former Cuban president, and Emilio Núñez Portuondo, the former president of the United Nations Security Council, to CPA José M. Illan, who had served as treasury undersecretary in Castro's first government, to physician Antonio Maceo, the grandson of General Antonio Maceo, hero of Cuba's War for Independence.[3]

Most of the attendees were politically conservative, and all were intensely anti-Castro. But because José "Pepín" Bosch was a sponsor, the roster of participants represented an unprecedented convergence of members of the Cuban exile community at the highest levels of influence. The "Forum for the Liberation of Cuba" sought to lay the groundwork for a lobby to represent exile interests in a unified manner. With a touch of clairvoyance, Benes's opening remarks called for establishing a "dialogue" among leaders of Miami's Cuban community. Little did he realize that a decade later the word "dialogue" would undercut his career, split the exile community further, and confer on him the status of a leper. Unfortunately, little came of the forum because the right-wing exile groups ignored it, and it was eventually forgotten.

Benes's appointment to the five-man steering committee of the Study for the Fund for Human Settlements of the United Nations Environment Program was another achievement since it became the basis for a study proposing the establishment of the World Housing Bank.[4] Benes, in fact, was the only United States citizen selected for this top-level group.

Another significant achievement occurred in 1971. Benes invited Dr. Ernesto Freyre, who had negotiated with Castro for the release of the Bay of Pigs prisoners, and José M. Vidaña, president of the Miami Cuban Rotary Club, to help him raise money for a monument to be dedicated on the tenth anniversary of the ill-fated invasion in memory of the volunteers who had died fighting communism. Veterans of the Bay of Pigs Brigade served on the building committee, and the monument was designed by sculptor Mario Santí, and placed in Little Havana. Over the years, it became the favorite meeting place for convening demonstrations against Castro.

Two remaining items which mark Benes's service both within and outside of Florida merit mention. Benes was selected to the 1971 White House Conference on Youth; as late as 2000, he worked to combat gang and other youth violence. Finally, in April 16, 1973, the all-Anglo Dade County Commission adopted a historic resolution declaring the county a "bilingual and bicultural county." Cuban Americans had packed the meeting and demanded that a department or division of municipal government be established to supervise bilingual affairs. This was a coup for Benes. Mayor Jack Orr, a respected lawyer and politician, backed the ordinance—Spanish would be the county's "second language."

OUTRAGE

As soon as Benes's role in what the newspapers called "a story equally intriguing as anything that Graham Greene or John le Carré might fictionalize" became public, however, the man who had been called a hero in newspapers across the country in Miami became the target of threats from extremist anti-Castro exile organizations still waging "war" with Cuba. The attacks came over the air from Spanish-language radio stations, in Miami's *periodiquitos* (weekly newspapers distributed for free), and sometimes in person from persons encountering him on the street. At times, Benes's statements to the press were misconstrued, to his detriment. Other times, in his exuberance, Benes applied what today would be called "spin" to his stories, so that different versions exist but he always strove for honesty and continued to fight despite numerous setbacks.

Often what Benes said was misunderstood, taken in a different way from how it as intended, or simply twisted. In December 1978, for instance, he was quoted as saying that one hundred thousand visitors to Cuba from Florida might spend $500 million a year in purchases for their relatives. This made good sense to Benes, whose dream was to see Cuba opened up to the point at which relations between the two countries might become normalized, but some became enraged at the notion of tourist-exiles bolstering Castro's flagging economy. As it turned out, Benes had been conservative in his estimate of the number of visitors. In 1979 alone, one hundred and twenty thousand Cuban exiles returned to the island to visit their relatives.

The Cubans turned away from Benes, too, presumably because he failed to win over the Carter administration and the National Security Council. Castro had always been a manipulator, and although he devoted enormous energy to the prolonged negations, he brushed aside any feeling of closeness he might have felt by the time of the prisoner release. Benes realized this when he sent a private memo to Castro asking permission for José Luis Padrón and his new wife to attend the bar mitzvah of his youngest son, Edgar, scheduled for June 27, 1980. Castro never replied and Padrón never showed up.

Many exiles continued to express outrage at the Carter administration's willingness to deal with Castro. The 1970s had witnessed a wave of terrorist activity targeting Cuban diplomatic offices and other sites, as well as the doomed Cubana Airlines flight. The smaller exile groups likely were responsible for these acts of violence, while the Miami Cuban radio stations and press used intimidation against anyone who disagreed with them. No direct evidence points to who financed the acquisition of arms and the materials to make bombs. *Granma,* the official Cuban daily, accused the exile sugar barons in Florida of financing violent assaults against Cuban targets. But no evidence was ever produced to link any of the sugar growers to terrorism. Rather, they devoted their energies to help elect anti-Castro political candidates, contributing to the congressional campaigns of Miami's Ileana Ros-Lehtinen and Lincoln Diaz-Balart, as well as state races within Florida and the presidential campaigns of both major candidates.

Cynics claimed that these individuals and groups had become so powerful that they had created a de facto "Independent Republic of Miami."[5] Others pointed to Mas Canosa's alleged desire to succeed Castro as Cuban head of state and referred to Miami as "the State of North Cuba."

Many Miami Cubans, of course, resented these portrayals of their spokesmen as a "Miami Mafia." When rumors spread blaming these activists for such bizarre actions as the attempt to kill Castro with an exploding cigar, or to introduce nonlethal chemical agents over Cuban sugar fields to sicken workers, or to introduce African swine fever viruses to infect Cuba's cattle industry, Miami Cubans countered by explaining—correctly—that most of these acts were committed by the CIA.[6]

Through all of this, Benes continued to be attacked, almost daily. Roberto Cuitiño V. wrote in Spanish: "When the day of victory arrives, the traitors who attempted to deal with Castro in order to strengthen him had better be there. We refer specifically to Bernardo Benes, the banker who made mockery of the blood shed by our patriots through secret dealings with the [Cuban] butcher over a period of twenty years, following the orders of the bankers of the western world who have financed and supported Marxist regimes since the time of the Russian Revolution."[7]

In her book, *Guerrilla Prince,* Georgie Anne Geyer, known for her quickly written popular books about her travels, commented on what she termed "Pro-Castro Cubans in Miami, like the shadowy Bernardo Benes."[8] Generally, however, Benes's notoriety remained concentrated in the Cuban exile enclave in South Florida.

For his part, Benes told reporters that he felt undeterred. "This is a logical, historical step for us to take. The price of being a Cuban with a social conscience has been very high—even higher for a Cuban Jew like myself—but there is no need for political prisoners anywhere in this world. I have talked to hundreds of Cuban prisoners, and their situation is a major tragedy of our generation. Castro has been responsive, and it would be a shame for us not to expedite this by opening our doors to those who want to come here."[9]

Benes's reference to himself as a Cuban Jew may hold even more meaning than he himself understood. During the late 1940s, anti-Semitic haters of President Harry S Truman—who had supported the creation of the State of Israel—insisted that his middle name was "Solomon," although Truman was not Jewish, and his middle name was simply "S," without a period. Benes faced this kind of cruelty, too. For years, journalist Hermínio Portell Vilá insisted on writing Benes's name as "Bernardo Benes y Baikowitz." Portell Vila's diatribes were published not only in Miami, but in Spanish-language newspapers across the United States. In Boston's *El Mundo*, he attacked "Bernardo Benes y Baikowitz" (lest anyone fail to realize that Benes was Jewish) for meddling, and lied that Benes had not been born in Cuba. Benes and his Castro-days friends from his "*gatillo alegre*" (trigger-happy) days in Havana, Portell Vila added, had no right to represent the "800,000 Cubans scattered all over the United States and in Alaska and Hawaii." He offered one more parting shot: "Benes y Baikowitz," he said, had invited him to his 1968 "Forum on Liberating Cuba," but Portell Vila had refused to attend.[10]

Other Jews suffered attacks in the hardline Miami Cuban media as well. Max Lesnik, publisher of a weekly magazine, *Réplica*, who also supported the dialogue, received repeated attacks. "El Condor" in *El Expreso* wrote, behind his spineless *nom de plume*: "Lesnik is the puppet of the imbecile Benes."[11] A reporter for *Látigo* ("The Whip"), Nicolás Tolentino accused Max Lesnik of inventing Cuban-sounding names (Edgardo Menéndez, for example) for pro-dialogue bylines in reality written by himself. In January 1983, a bomb was found hidden in Lesnik's editorial offices, but it was inoperative.[12]

Látigo falsely attacked Miami Cuban Jews as profiteers in the newly established air link between Mexico's Yucatán Peninsula and Havana, a route accessible for Cubans abroad who wanted to visit their relatives under the 1978 negotiated arrangement.[13] This was pure invention. *Látigo* also brought up the frequently heard accusation that "the red" Benes and Castro had planned a deal whereby Cuba would export frozen lobsters and shrimp to Panama's Imperial Seafood Company, which would then ship them to Miami, a business windfall for the Miami banker. Benes issued a detailed statement to the press that the firm was Panamanian, and that the accusations against him amounted to slander.[14] Others pursued Dascal, the financier of most of the costs of traveling back and forth to Cuba during the process of negotiations. Dascal, the anonymous reporter "El Condor" wrote, sought to use Benes's trips to open commercial deals with Castro. When the president of his bank, Jorge Martínez, protested, "El Condor" assured his readers that Dascal, "in the height of his arrogance," fired Martínez for opposing the bank's treason.[15] In general, however, Dascal emerged unscathed. On January 25, 1980, the *periodiquito El Universal* headlined a story, "Benes and Dascal: Foreign Agents," and printed both men's photographs. The unsigned front-page article not only called Benes and Dascal Cuban communist agents, but lambasted government policy setters on Cuba in the State Department, and President Carter, as "blind, deaf hacks."[16]

Anti-Semitism among some Miami Cubans probably contributed to the coldness of many Cubans towards Benes during the 1960s and 1970s. Benes's personality was also distasteful to some people; certainly, animosity toward Bernardo as an outsider existed. In 1974, Benes received a typed postcard at his Miami Beach home on Normandie Island that read:

> The other day at a party, [an attendee] was talking about you. He says that he is willing to be cordial, but that you're not Cuban—you're a Zionist who shills for Israel. In addition to other things, it's sad to know that there are people who talk behind your back. They are laughing at your expense. Among the things he said, he mentioned that you stick your head into everything and that you have been able to fool some influential people by calling attention to yourself as being Jewish. You want everything, you totally lack shame. You want to be better than the rest and you are always looking over everyone's shoulder. But in Cuba nobody knew you, and you were nothing. With a sneer, he said that you want to be a writer, a banker, a professor and other things, even a witch doctor. And that you fool everybody but him. Ah well, why should I be telling you things you probably know. That you were a friend of the Batista dictatorship and an opportunist. But I suggest that you don't pay any attention to his jealousies. For what? He wants to know in what manner you are a doctor.

Sr. Bernardo Benes

John Hanson   Patriot

Sr. Benes: El otro dia en una fiesta   U.S.Postage 6¢
el ___ ___ ___ hablaba de usted. Dice que lo
trata socialmente, pero que usted no es cubano, sino
sionista que recauda para Israel. Ademas de otras co-
sas es penoso saber que hay gente que habla por detras
de otros. Se reian a su costa. Entre otras informaciones
que daba dice usted mete la cabeza por todas partes y
que ha podido engatusar a alguna gente influyente a ti-
tulo de judio. Aspira a todo, es osado a carta cabal.

5.2   Postcard received by Benes, 1974. Bernardo Benes collection.

The critic was referring to Benes's use of the title "Dr.," commonly used
by law school graduates throughout Latin America but not in the United
States. His Jewishness, however, set him apart even further from the mainstream of the Miami Cuban population, and may explain the extremity to
which other Miami Cubans made him into a pariah. Benes was an outsider,
a Jew, forcing himself on the Anglos as being better than the Cubans of the
Big Five clubs—more flexible, more willing to cooperate than the insiders.
Some came to abhor him for this. When he revealed in 1979 that he and
Dascal had paid every cent of their expenses themselves, mean-spirited individuals called him a liar; one said "a Jew would never spend his own
money for others."[17] The bitterness of the exile experience was likely to
have added fuel to the undercurrent of hostility against anyone not following the rigid anti-Castro line as demanded by the Spanish-language
media. Also, in Cuban society, family origin mattered as much or more
than material success. Even in Miami, well-connected Cuban bankers lent
money through "character loans," to those whom they recognized as inside
members of the exile upper stratum.[18] They were the Cubans who, during
Batista's years as head of state, had boasted that they had denied him entry
to the Havana Yacht Club because he was a mulatto.

In South Florida, the tables were turned. The Anglos neither cared about a person's privileged status in Cuba, nor came to Benes's defense after 1978. The more Benes tried to build bridges, the more he reached out to make friends, the more he became resented for not knowing his place. The harder he worked to cultivate the support of influential Anglos, the more he was despised, in part because in their eyes he clung to causes too tenaciously. The fact that many of his supporters and most of his business partners were Jewish made it even more difficult. It is telling that often when Benes was quoted in a newspaper article, the reporter felt compelled to describe him physically—his round face, his disheveled red hair, his "pot belly" showing through a shirt not fully buttoned. Articles belittled his Cuban accent and his incomplete mastery of spoken English; some mentioned that he used Yiddish phrases, and many referred to him as an outsider. He was constantly called "*el polaco*," a reference to his Eastern European Jewish origins that he considered pejorative. Marieta Fandiño, editor of *La Verdad* ("The Truth"), a Miami Cuban *periodiquito*, in an editorial titled "The Red Benes" wrote that "ruddy" Bernardo Benes was involved in "dirty games" and was a secret agent for the FBI.[19] Even reporters attempting to defend him called attention to his "atrocious accent in English."[20]

Some articles, invoking the racist stereotype that Jews are only motivated by money, accused him of starting the dialogue for his own personal profit, claiming that Benes planned to sell automobiles to Cuba, buy fish and seafood from the Cubans, and open shoe factories.[21] Others claimed that he lacked cultivated social skills or that he was a Jew who didn't look like one but whose mannerisms betrayed him. They commented at length on his habits, calling him a "table hopper," "an egomaniac," "a manipulator," and a man of "frenetic energy." More than one critic recalled that Benes, perhaps because of his insecurities about being an outsider, embellished the truth. Benes's personal appearance and mannerisms led people to see him as a caricature and as unattractive, and few realized Benes was, for instance, a witty conversationalist or an expert dancer. Jorge Luis Hernández, editor of *Regreso*, another *periodiquito*, mocked Benes for his "red hair, as well as skin," and insinuated that his politics were "red" as well.[22] Manuel Amor, in *El Expreso*, triumphantly announced Benes's election to the Hall of Infamy, calling him, in quotation marks, "this son of David."[23] But in the end, Benes's personal traits and appearance mattered less to the militants than the fact that he had audaciously negotiated with Fidel Castro, the devil incarnate.

Conversely, when reporters described "insiders," they did so with respect. Leslie Pantin, Sr., the descendant of a British diplomat turned planter and insurance magnate in Havana and a leading socialite, was described by the *Herald* as "tall, hazel-eyes, impeccably mannered . . . who spoke flawless English and said all the right things."[24] After his meetings with Castro, Benes became an outcast even in the eyes of Miami Beach's Cuban Jewish community. A 1979 gossip column in *La Nación* read:

> Half of the large exile community in Miami Beach . . . is Jewish. We send New Year's greetings to Isaac and Alberto Habif, to Jack Roisman, to Salvador Lew . . . to the Zacroisky family . . . and. . . . Why not? To Bernardo Benes in spite of the fact that Benes blundered into such an embarrassing mess.[25]

Author Joan Didion interviewed Benes at his house on Biscayne Bay for her book *Miami.* In contrast to other Cuban exiles she had met, she noted that from his arrival in 1960 he rejected the exile fixation on *la lucha*—the struggle against Castro—and saw Florida as a "kind of colonial opportunity, an India to be tapped." He shrugged off the cultural resistance which so many others were keeping alive. As a result, he became the first prominent exile, in Didion's words, "to travel what has been in provincial American cities a traditional road to assimilation, the visible doing of approved works, the act of making oneself available for this steering committee, for that kickoff dinner."[26] But Benes had not simply "made himself available"—he expected invitations. Without this kind of entrée, he had to do this, or he would have never gained access to the Anglo establishment. Benes told the writer:

> I am frank, I do not beat around the bush. Until 1977, 1978, I was "*The* Cuban" in Miami . . . the guerrilla in the establishment, the first person to bring other Cubans into the picture. And then came the big change in my life. I was no longer the first token Cuban in Miami. I was the *Capitán* Dreyfus of Miami. This is Miami. . . . Pure Miami. A million Cubans are blackmailed, totally controlled, by three radio stations. I feel sorry for the Cuban community in Miami. Because they have imposed on themselves

the same condition that Castro has imposed on Cuba: total intolerance.
And ours is worse because it is entirely voluntary.[27]

Benes had other reasons to be irritable as well. In mid-1979, Ricardo de
la Espriella, now president of Panama's National Bank and one of the
closest civilian advisors to General Omar Torrijos, the country's strongman, told Benes, during a flight to Washington, a shocking story. Benes's
G–2 (Intelligence Division) dossier maintained by then-Colonel Manuel
Noriega included a memorandum sent by a Noriega informant in Miami,
a Cuban named "El Gallego" Aldereguía. The informant claimed that
Benes had been responsible for the terrorist bombing of the Cubana Airlines plane that went down over Barbados on October 6, 1976, killing all
seventy-two of its passengers, most of them young Cuban athletes. Benes,
fearing that the Cubans would find out and might even believe the allegation, demanded to meet with Torrijos, and stated that he would not
leave Panama until he did. Some hours later, Benes received a call in-
forming him that Colonel Noriega would visit him at his hotel.

Noriega spent thirty minutes with Benes, assuring him that the entire
thing was a mistake, and that the memorandum had been removed from
the dossier. (According to de la Espriella, Torrijos had ordered Noriega to
remove it.) Later, Benes found out that Aldereguía's accusation had not
been sent to Panama as a part of a right-wing militant conspiracy; it occurred because Aldereguía was in the shrimp business, and had learned of
Benes's efforts to create a seafood export company with business colleagues in Panama City.

Some of the threats in Miami came from members of Omega 7. In actuality, Omega 7 was less an organization than a code name used by members of several different Miami-based exile militant groups. The name
Omega 7, according to an investigative report by the Herald, was simply
a new "calling card" for terrorists, recalling such earlier violent entities as
"Zero," the Pedro Luis Boitel Commandos, Condor, and CORU, the Co-
ordinated United Revolutionary Organizations. However, "Zeta," whose
black hooded and armed photograph graced the front page of Miami's El
Expreso, warned publicly (in an interview with a reporter in Puerto Rico)
that Omega 7 members were ready to "lay down their lives in the struggle against the Red enemy."[28] According to the FBI, terrorists using the

name Omega 7 had sent communiqués claiming responsibility for bombing the Soviet and Cuban diplomatic missions to the United Nations and a Russian airline office in New York City. In January, Omega 7 claimed responsibility for the vandalism between 1978 and 1982 and ultimately the bomb that blew up Padrón's business for its owner's having offered one of his cigars to Castro during the dialogue. No arrests were ever made. Omega 7's Eduardo Arocena, at his trial in New York for murder, admitted before a federal court in 1984 that four years earlier he had participated in a plan to introduce germs into Cuba.[29]

To protect Benes, the FBI placed not only the banker but also fifteen anti-Castro militants belonging to Omega 7 under watch. The new and mysterious Miami-based entity suddenly leaped into prominence when the FBI in New York named it "the most dangerous terrorist organization in the United States."[30] For Benes, humiliations continued without cease. One day during 1980, Benes invited his sister, Ana, who lived in Washington, to lunch at the Esquina de Tejas restaurant. It was named for a corner in Havana, and sits at the intersection of First Street and Southwest Twelfth Avenue, later co-named Ronald Reagan Avenue because he ate there three years later during a visit to Miami. As they were sitting at their table, the publisher of one of the dozens of *periodiquitos* distributed within the Cuban community entered with an armload of papers. The publisher saw Benes, approached his table, and violently threw a package containing several dozen of the newspapers; then began shouting obscenities about Bernardo and his sister. Not having lived in Miami for some time, Ana had no idea to what depths the expressions of hatred had descended.

Similar incidents occurred at the Cervantes Restaurant in Coral Gables, where Bernardo and his wife were dining with Alfredo Durán and his wife, Maria Elena Prío, and Pedro Ramón López, a banker, and his wife. As they were starting to leave, a short, burly man, apparently drunk, who knew all of the waiters, started shouting "Son of a whore, you are a communist and a Castro agent." He put his arm in his jacket, as if reaching for a gun, when three or four waiters jumped on him and wrestled him back to the bar. Benes gritted his teeth and exited with the others.

At El Bodegón de Castilla on Calle Ocho in Little Havana, the Beneses were dining with two couples, both childhood friends from Cuba. Late in the evening, two men approached them and one started shouting,

5.3   Bomb damage, Miami, 1979. *Miami Herald.*

"Communist! Castro agent!" interspersed with vulgar language. The owner and a couple of waiters removed the intruders. At Casa Juancho, an upscale Cuban restaurant on South West Eighth Street owned by Felipe Valls, Benes entered with a childhood friend. They had gone in for a drink and a light snack when they spotted several old acquaintances, including

Carlos Dascal and their bank's lawyer, Cesar Camacho, and a physician, well known in the community and Camacho's friend. When Benes extended his hand, the man turned his back, leaving Benes with his arm in the air. Benes became angered even further because neither Dascal nor Camacho said anything. At La Habana Vieja, a short, obese man who had been sitting with several other men approached Benes's table and whispered in his ear, "When you go to the parking lot, we will be waiting for you." Benes informed the owner, who called the Miami police, and soon two policemen escorted the Beneses and their guests to their cars.

Benes used to dine three or four nights a week at the brightly decorated Versailles Restaurant in Little Havana, known by the locals as "the Pentagon" because so much anti-Castro talk occurred there. He often chatted with Roberto Pertierra, who worked at the Versailles as a host. Pertierra had been a member of the family who had owned the Montmarte Night Club in Havana, and had also volunteered for Brigade 2506 in the Bay of Pigs invasion. When Pertierra died at the age of seventy-four, Benes went to pay his respects at the Caballero Funeral Home. After entering, Benes offered condolences to Roberto's children and nephew, a prominent Washington, D.C., lawyer. Then he walked through a corridor where a group of four or five men were standing. He recognized only one of them, but learned later that one of the others was Antonio Llama, a Brigade veteran and board member of the Cuban American National Foundation. In a loud voice so everyone could hear, Llama said: "What are you doing here?" Benes replied that Roberto had been a very close friend; Llama answered: "Impossible, he was a hero and you are a traitor." Some time later, when restaurateur Felipe Valls's wife died, Benes made another funeral-home visit, and with Manolo Reboso, the first Cuban elected to the city commission, entered to pay his respects. At that point, Llama approached and shook hands with everyone but Benes. Reboso started to introduce Benes, assuming that the two men did not know each other, but Llama turned away. Benes said to him: "Look, this is the second time you have done this to me. I want you to know that I will not tolerate a third time." Reboso very politely escorted Llama away from the group.

Some friends remained loyal to Benes, although they did not speak out. On Saturday, December 27, 1980, friends and family organized a birthday lunch for Bernardo and about one hundred invitees; almost half attended. Since it was before the New Year, many of the invitees declined because they would be traveling. The list of those who came to the lunch ranged from Carlos Dascal (now calling himself Charles), Max Lesnik, Sérgio Pereira, Ramón Mestre, Alfredo Durán of the Florida Democratic Party, Roberto Fabrício of the *Miami Herald*, CIA agent Larry Sternfield, Professor Antonio Jorge, and Polita Grau. Bobby Maduro was invited, but the old baseball team owner's telephone had been disconnected, and they did not know how to reach him to deliver the invitation.[31]

Benes offers his own analysis for the vicious reaction from the Miami Cuban exile leadership regarding his role in "dialoguing" with Castro:

> Curiously, although the *periodiquitos*, radio stations, and local Cuban "leaders" defiled me, I received not a single letter from individuals attacking me. On the contrary, I received hundreds of letters from people, some who knew me and others who did not. Many of these were from humble Cuban women and men who supported me. The fear instilled by a small minority of powerful militants who use much of the same tactics that Castro used has been a powerful psychological factor that has intimidated and controlled Cuban Miami for decades. If I had had more financial resources, I might have been able to hire the best Madison Avenue public relations firm to help me fight back. But I think that even such a campaign would have failed, because the militant exiles in Miami have cowed even high elected officials who seem afraid to stand up and say what is morally correct because they fear the wrath of the militants.[32]

Some friends snubbed Benes because they had to follow the unwritten laws of the Miami Cuban enclave. At one point during Benes's extended unemployment, Raúl Valdés-Fauli, a prominent Coral Gables attorney, invited Benes to join his law firm as its Cuban legislation expert. They met several times, and Benes received an office space, a part-time secretary, and supplies. A few days later, however, Valdés-Fauli called Benes into his office and told him that his father, also an attorney for the firm, had warned him that Benes's presence would cause problems because "Benes was very close to [the liberal] Jack Gordon." Valdés-Fauli felt terribly but had to heed his father. "This," Benes says, "is the power of the 'uncontrollable fear that holds Miami in its grip.'" Valdés-Fauli remained Benes's friend, although Valdés-Fauli joined the Republican Party.[33]

MORE TROUBLES

Even as the flights of political prisoners were landing in Miami in late 1978, exile groups demanded that the Cuban Reunification Operation (CRO), organized by Benes and Baptist Minister José Reyes, be stopped. The CRO's chartered American Airlines planes flew the prisoners out for two weeks after the first flight but then faced a challenge from a new group formed in Miami, Dignity Flights. Francisco Hernández, the president of the new group, charged that Benes, Reyes, and other invited delegates to the September 1978 dialogue in Havana had insisted to Castro that only CRO planes be permitted to transfer the prisoners. Monsignor Bryan Walsh of Miami's Roman Catholic diocese told reporters from the Atlanta *Constitution* that the "division" within the exile community saddened him.[34]

The journalists summarized the situation, explaining why the exiles had attempted to stop the CRO flights

> The old culture is kept intact. Cuban families intermarry. Spanish is spoken in many homes. Children are taught the history of Cuba. To many of these families, any acceptance of Castro is a loss of face, the abandonment of hope. The exiles' trips to Cuba have split the once-tight community. Spanish-language newspapers discuss the issue on editorial pages. Angry men debate it on street corners. The Reunification Operation, composed of members of the exile delegation that went to Cuba, is "pro-dialogue." The Dignity Committee wants to bring the prisoners home but is bitterly opposed to any dialogue with Cuba.[35]

Benes, quoted in the article, simply said: "I don't want to argue with anybody. I just want to bring the prisoners here." But his connection to the recovery operation made those angry with him even more irate.

In May 1979, investigative reporters revealed that Castro had not yet lived up to his bargain. He had promised to release 3,600 of his 3,663 political prisoners as well as 600 captured *lancheros*, Cubans convicted of trying to flee the island. Prisoners were to be released at a rate of 400 a month, and the oldest, sickest prisoners as well as the ones who spent the longest time in imprisonment would be the first to gain release. By May, however, few of the longest-term prisoners had been released, and none of the seriously ill or elderly prisoners had even been entered on the lists drawn up by Cuban officials. Because of paperwork delays on the United States side, furthermore, only 900 prisoners had been released, most of them serving light sentences for minor crimes, and 40 percent of whom had been in jail for five years or less. Of 34 women in this group, 24 had spent fewer than three years incarcerated. And there were virtually none of the 780 *plantados,* the hard-core dissenters who refused cooperation with prison officials who, rather than wear the same garb that was provided to genuine criminals, simply wore their underwear.

The most damning fact was that only 16 percent of those released by May 1979 were "historical" political prisoners, convicted by revolutionary tribunals in the first months after Castro assumed power. Many of these "historical" prisoners, sentenced to thirty-year terms because of alleged crimes committed under Castro, still sat in jail. In response to these facts, Benes could only reply that he didn't care whom the Cubans chose to release first as long as all gained their freedom in the end.[36] Most eventually did leave prison, but the Castro government's cat-and-mouse games about the sequence of releases added mental and physical anguish which was borne by the older and sicker prisoners who desperately wanted to see their families before death intervened.

The unrelenting barrage of personal attacks against Benes drained his family's energy. Continental Bank was picketed for weeks, even during severe rainstorms. Benes hired a photographer from *Réplica* to photograph the picketers, for his records. For a long weekend, Bernardo, Ricky, and their two younger children escaped from Miami to Gainesville, where the Beneses' oldest son was studying. They simply could not take the daily assault. Even when militants paid Benes backhanded compliments, they continued to slander him. "Everyone is talking about the miserable Bernardo Benes," wrote *A Patria*'s Alberto Rodríguez, a strident hardliner imprisoned on drug charges before his death:

> Of Benes, we have little to say. He has talked less than anyone else [about the dialogue] . . . he never asked anything from anyone; on the contrary, he told the tyrant [Castro] that the Carter administration was the one seeking better relations with Cuba. But the blunder of this ass-kisser (*guatacoide*) has affected all exiles still holding on to their pride. His bank was picketed and all of his friends have abandoned him, refusing even to talk or shake hands with him. Those who do not reject him, for reasons

```
          2

PAGE TWO DE RUEHFB 0115  C O N F I D E N T I A L
```

THAT A DOCUMENT SIGNED BY
"CONDOR" HAD BEEN PUBLISHED IN SEVERAL MIAMI BASED CUBAN
NEWSPAPERS INCLUDING SEVERAL LATIN RADIO STATIONS. THE
COMMUNIQUE ACCUSES CARLOS DASCAL, BERNARDO BENES AND MAX
LESNICK OF BEING RESPONSIBLE FOR THE CURRENT RAPPROACHMENT
BETWEEN THE UNITED STATES AND CUBA. IT THREATENS THEM WITH
"REVOLUTIONARY JUSTICE" AND IT ADDS THAT THERE ARE "A
SUFFICIENT NUMBER OF CEMETERIES IN MIAMI." THE COMMUNIQUE ENDS
BY STATING THAT ITS AUTHOR(S) HAS NO MORE PATIENCE. IT SHOULD
BE NOTED THAT IN INTERPRETING THE CUBAN WAY OF THINKING, THE
PHRASE "REVOLUTIONARY JUSTICE" AND THE REFERENCE TO "THE
NUMBER OF CEMETERIES IN MIAMI" IS ACCEPTED TO MEAN THAT A
SWIFT END WILL COME TO THOSE MENTIONED IN THE COMMUNIQUE.

5.4   Threats against dialoguers, 1978. Source: Benes FBI file. Photograph by
Robert M. Levine.

of self-interest, choose their places in which to encounter him . . . so as
not to be seen with the traitor who has stained the dignity of all Cuban
exiles.[37]

Not to be outdone, *La Nación* several days later published this byline-
less tidbit:

Roblejo Lorié and Bernardo Benes almost got into a fist fight [during the
dialogue in Havana]. Lorié had accused Benes of stealing the show at the
prisoner release process. Benes shouted hysterically: "If I do not obtain the
freedom of the prisoners I will commit suicide."

5.5   Picketing Benes, Continental National Bank, Little Havana, 1978. Robert M. Levine collection.

"Opinions remain divided," the anonymous journalist added, about whether this would be a good thing. "Doubts remain," he concluded.[38]

The Reverend Espinosa's role added a twist to an already bizarre tale. He was the man who had been arrested by Cuban officials for attempting to reach Castro to convince him to release prisoners. Groups of his Hialeah congregants had visited Havana to meet with their relatives well before the "Committee of the 75" had been formed. This man, who had said, "I'm no saint, but I'm no crook either," had now turned against Benes and the other would-be peacemakers in his acrimonious radio broadcasts and news conferences. His diatribes lasted for weeks, and, for the first time in Miami history, all of the Cuban radio stations simultaneously transmitted Espinosa's press conferences, each often lasting over three hours. In one statement, Espinosa pronounced:

> Bernardo Benes likes to appear most of the time as a jovial and gay guy, but he cannot avoid showing off his old "fidelism" and "liberalism" which has been infused into him by Senator Gordon, is a champion of pacifism

in the style of Jane Fonda. Every time he has a chance, he likes to express the thoughts of a man who left his brain in Cuba and lost his identity when he was sent into exile without knowing why he had to be exiled. It's a shame, because Bernardo Benes tries to be "simpático" and agreeable, and we have to confess that he achieves his purpose . . . except when he discloses his former pro-Castro feelings. Imagine . . . he left Castro and fell into Gordon's arms.[39]

After the first threats, Benes was immediately placed under protection by Miami Beach police officers at his home. At his bank, a bodyguard protected him, and he was strongly advised to purchase a bulletproof vest at a police equipment store, which he did. In addition, he remained under FBI surveillance, which assigned two agents to his case. Twice in one week, Miami's special agent in charge of the Miami FBI office, Arthur Nehrbass, held press conferences "warning against violence resulting from Espinosa's accusations. . . . Premature disclosure of intelligence information," he stated, "especially by one not privy to the whole intelligence picture, can seriously jeopardize intelligence operations."[40] He also forcefully confirmed that the FBI considered the charges that Benes was a Castro agent as totally without foundation.

On March 6, 1980, the *Herald* revealed that the FBI had broken up a plan to assassinate Bernardo Benes. Nehrbass confirmed that there were four suspects: one in Miami, an unnamed member of Omega 7, and three others hired to carry out the killing. The FBI agent also commented on the role of some Miamians in creating an atmosphere hostile to Benes, and began calling them "collaborators" and "agents" of the Castro government.[41]

FBI agents had arrested a Cuban American at Newark International Airport and charged him with unlawful possession of a firearm and with unlawful flight to avoid prosecution. Earlier, the same person had been freed on bond while awaiting trial for a killing in Miami. Special Agent Nehrbass,[42] a newspaper reported, "implied at a recent press conference that the suspect [had been under surveillance] in connection with an alleged plot to assassinate Dr. Bernardo Benes, a prominent Miami banker who initiated Cuban exile talks with the Castro government." The suspect denied everything, saying that he did not know Benes and that killing anyone is a "bad idea." He admitted having been one of the planners of the Bay of Pigs invasion.[43] No one, however, was ever charged with attempting to murder Benes.

The investigation of the plot against Benes was part of a larger FBI investigation at that time into other activities of Omega 7. For example, Miami FBI agents detained a twenty-five-year-old burglar alarm installer named Ramón Saúl Sánchez. Sánchez denied that he was a member of Omega 7, or that he had engaged in any unlawful conduct, although he said that he believed that Fidel Castro had long sought to kill him because of Sánchez's anti-Castro beliefs. "The truth is," he said, "if I hear that Castro lost a plane, if Castro lost an embassy, if Castro lost an ambassador, I won't cry. I will do anything—legally, of course—that will do harm to the Castro government." He admitted to the arresting agents that he had organized anti-Castro demonstrations and sent hostile letters to Cuba.[44] Sánchez also acknowledged that he had belonged to the Martí Insurrectional Movement, which, during the 1978 meetings in Havana had declared, "It was time for the machine gun instead of words." Sánchez, who had arrived on a Freedom Flight during the 1960s, recalled that one of his childhood friends in Matanzas had been executed by a firing squad by Castro's revolutionary government.[45]

Miami police officials contended that Sánchez had blocked a "plainclothes detective's auto" in the northern part of Little Havana. The undercover agent said that Sánchez had pointed a pistol at him, and threatened to shoot if he moved. The police also arrested a companion of Sánchez in connection with the incident, who had gained entry to the United States six years earlier by jumping over a fence into the Guantanamo Naval Base. "I don't see a great difference between a democracy using agents to follow us around and what happens in Cuba," the Herald quoted the companion as saying to the police.[46] An appeals court ultimately threw out the "charges" against Sanchez in connection with the incident.

In the court cases that arose out of the charges and countercharges in the exile community, Miami lawyer Ellis Rubin, drawn to high-profile cases like a moth to flame, represented the Reverend Manuel Espinosa. The Internal Revenue Service also investigated Espinosa's church, accused of carrying out profit-making activities having nothing to do with religion. Three of the dialogueros filed lawsuits against Manuel Espinosa for defamation of character after Espinosa repeatedly called them "Castro agents" on his radio broadcasts. Benes, however, never bothered to go to court.[47]

On May 27, 1983, at 10:57 P.M., a bomb exploded at the Continental National Bank. No one was injured, but damage was extensive. A man identifying himself as a member of Omega 7 called the *Herald* seventeen minutes later and claimed responsibility. Nelson Horta at the anti-Castro radio station WRHC received a similar call. Oddly, in spite of the conclusions drawn by the media and by the public, the local FBI chief informed Benes that "the bomb was not aimed at him."[48]

It was one thing to be castigated and branded a traitor by the militant exiles, but Benes felt equally betrayed by many of his former allies. Humberto Medrano, who had asked Benes to accompany him to the *Herald* over the plight of Cuban political prisoners, now turned on him, and publicly attacked him. Dr. Ernesto Freyre, who Benes had considered the most distinguished labor lawyer in Cuba before 1959, and as the president of the Miami exile group *Representación Cubana del Exilio* (RECE), had invited Benes to become an advisory board member. Now, Freyre, who worked for Benes in the Alliance for Progress housing projects in Latin America, rejected him, as did Bacardi's Pepín Bosch. Neither Freyre nor Bosch ever communicated again with Benes until their deaths. Yet, Benes wonders, why did the exiles accept Freyre, the chief negotiator with the Cuban government over the $53 million ransom of the Bay of Pigs prisoners, and continue to hold him in high esteem?

BRIDGES BUILT AND BRIDGES BURNED

The reason simply enough was that Freyre, Bosch, Mas Canosa, and the other exile leaders were insiders, while Benes was an outsider. Only a handful of outsiders within the Cuban exile community eventually bridged and won respect from both of Miami's main ethnic communities, the Cubans and the Anglos. One was Modesto Madique, the president of Florida International University, known to his friends as "Mitch." Bernardo never took (nor was given) an Anglo nickname. Another was Carlos de la Cruz, elected chair of the Board of Trustees of the University of Miami in 1999. A consummate insider, he was from one of the wealthiest families in Cuba and as a youth attended Andover Academy and then the University of Pennsylvania. Outsiders never made it in both worlds; Benes made it in neither.

Ostracism clearly negatively affects people, especially when they have healthy egos and crave recognition for their deeds. From Benes's perspective, he had achieved more for the Cuban American community than anyone else, and had been trusted by the Carter administration to negotiate with Castro. The *Miami Herald* called him "the Cuban Kissinger." Not only did Miami Cubans treat him like a leper, but the Anglo business community, to which he had forged so many ties, turned its back on him as well. The Miami of the early 1980s had fallen captive to the intimidating shouts of the exile right wing.

One example among many includes the following: Because of his friendship with various editors and reporters at the *Miami Herald*, Benes visited their offices fairly regularly, at least once a month. When the newspaper hired a Cuban American journalist, Roberto Fabrício, to cover the local community, Larry Jinks, the executive editor, said to Benes, "Take him under your wing." For two months, according to Benes, Fabrício spent most of the day with Benes at his bank, reviewing files and attending meetings with him. Years later, Benes helped Fabrício and fellow *Herald* reporter John Dorshner to get visas to visit Cuba for research on a book about Batista's last thirty days in power.

But when they returned, according to Benes, Fabrício turned on his mentor. He started referring to Benes and the others who had gone to Havana in 1978 as *dialogueros,* with a pejorative connotation. Meanwhile, Fabrício himself made a trip to Cuba for interviews, including one with Fidel Castro. Presumably, he did not consider himself a traitor.

One day in 1987, Benes received a call from *Herald* reporter Susan Sachs. She asked if he might drop in and chat with her about an article she was writing on the banking industry. As he entered the fifth floor, where reporters work, Fabrício confronted him. Now editor of *El Nuevo Herald,* an independent Spanish-language version of the *Herald,* Fabrício demanded that he leave the building. Reporter Sachs explained why Benes was there, but Fabrício did not listen. Out of the corner of his eye, Benes saw Richard Capen, the *Herald's* publisher (and former Under Secretary of Defense under Melvin Laird), walking to his office. Benes caught up with him and asked him what was happening; Capen made no response. A few minutes later, Fabrício came back with two security guards, and ordered them to "get him out of the building." Benes had no choice but to walk out between the uniformed guards, in full sight of dozens of reporters and staff members. More than ironically, it had been Benes, at a meeting of the new Florida International Foundation in 1972, who had said to the *Herald*'s Alvah Chapman, "it is very important that the *Herald* start a Spanish-language newspaper."[49]

Still, Benes plowed ahead. He continued his volunteer charitable work, for instance. When he learned that 100 children who had arrived via the Mariel boatlift could not afford the $6 fee for gym suits at Miami Beach's Nautilus Middle School, Continental National chipped in $600 to buy them. To reporter Michael Putney, Benes pointed out that these children had been stigmatized because of Mariel's bad name, and that something should be done to welcome them. He added that he hoped that other businesses and individuals would do the same for the other 13,000 Cuban and 2,000 Haitian children new to Dade Schools.[50] Few did. Only Benes, among the entire Miami Cuban enclave, spoke on behalf of Haitian immigrants as well as his fellow Cuban exiles.

Perhaps to bolster his shattered morale after his vilification in Miami, Benes corresponded with influential people who had supported his mission to Havana. Some responded generously. In May 1980, for example, Secretary of State Cyrus Vance sent Benes a friendly letter saying that he "was very happy to have worked for three years" with him.[51] Other letters arrived independently. In July 1981, he received a handwritten letter from Moisés Baldás, head of the remnant Jewish community of Cuba from 1960 to 1980 and executive director of the Coordinating Commission of Hebrew Religious Societies in Cuba. Previously hostile to the exiles, Jewish or not, Baldás acknowledged that Benes had been one of the two Jews who had "saved" the community. Later that same year, Benes flew to Havana to meet with Castro and several others, including United States Interests Section chief Wayne Smith. Benes claims that he personally convinced Castro to permit Cuban Jews still on the island to leave, since they were, for the most part, elderly and very poor. As soon as Benes returned from Havana, he contacted Jacobo Kovadloff, the vice-president of the American Jewish Committee and, as an Argentine, its Latin American specialist. Kovadloff arranged for the assistant to the president, Arthur Pruzan, of HIAS, the Jewish immigration aid agency, to visit Cuba to work out details. During the next few months, approximately one hundred Cuban Jews left for Venezuela.

In the summer of 1982, Benes floated the notion of running for Miami Beach mayor in the election to be held in the following year. The *Miami News'* Howard Kleinberg wrote: "Bernardo Benes—Miami banker, Miami Beach resident, refugee from Castro's Cuba, look-alike for old time movie comedian S. Z. (Cuddles) Sakall, and wit extraordinaire—has positioned himself in all segments of the community." Kleinberg added: "Benes's [human rights] rationale is still not widely accepted but much of the furor has died down."[52]

Perhaps. He did not run for mayor, although he raised $32,000 in campaign funds, which he returned to the donors. Donald Lefton, a close friend, convinced him not to run because there was another excellent candidate in the race. Nevertheless, Benes continued to remain busy. He wrote letters frequently to his former contacts and participated in academic meetings. At one of them, sponsored by the School of Advanced International Studies of the Johns Hopkins University, he was on the same program as Wayne S. Smith, Ambassador John Crimmins, and Senator Claiborne Pell (D-RI). In September 1984, he wrote to "S.P.," (Israeli leader Shimon Peres) that Fidel Castro a few months earlier had sent word to Benes asking if he could set up a "discreet" trip for two Cuban government officials to visit Israel to learn how the Israelis raised geese. "If you can arrange this," he concluded, "let me know through somebody in the U.S."[53]

By the mid-1990s, some Miamians expressed their belief that the community's wounds had started to heal, perhaps because members of the younger generation were becoming more prominent and because the economy was prospering. A business journalist quoted "Cuban experts" as saying that if the dialogue had occurred ten years later, community reaction likely would have been "mild," arguing that the Miami Cubans had "matured enough so politicians are no longer successful if they try to wrap themselves in the Cuban flag and shout 'communist' at opponents as a smokescreen to avoid real issues."[54] Benes was quoted as saying that he would have still carried out his missions even had he known of the response, although he added that the group that had met with Castro had

included some "bad apples," presumably referring especially to the difficult Hialeah evangelical pastor, Manuel Espinosa.

Provocations continued to surface. In September 1983, Mayor Norman Ciment and other members of the Miami Beach commission complained bitterly about the large numbers of Mariel refugees who settled in
their city. Ciment introduced an ordinance that would have set up road-
blocks on city streets and required that all Mariel refugees have legal
sponsors before being permitted to reside in Miami Beach. Benes, in a letter to *Herald* editor Jim Hampton, scolded Miami Beach commissioners
for having neglected to enforce its minimum-standard housing codes for
years. The result, he observed, was that Miami Beach had more decrepit
housing than anywhere else, so the refugees took advantage of the low
rents available.[55] Ciment and the others were reacting to the stories of
criminals and deviants among the Mariel refugees, and the state of fear
that had affected many of the city's older residents, now afraid to venture
out after dark. But in the end, the ordinance was not passed, and Ciment
chose not to run for reelection as mayor. A few years later, New
York–based real estate developers started to buy up undervalued properties south of Lincoln Road. As a result, SoBe (South Beach) blossomed as
one of the major upscale tourist destinations in Florida.

In 1983, Benes and a group of associates brought together over two
hundred Cubans at a Miami Beach reunion of the Zionist organization,
Hashomer Hatzair, that had been prominent among Cuban Jews in the
1940s and 1950s. Some came from Kibbutz Ga'ash, founded by Cuban
Jews in Israel. In 1986, Benes gave interviews to several newspapers in
which he attacked the Reagan administration's announcement that it
would no longer grant asylum to released Cuban political prisoners unless
Cuba reinstated an immigration agreement. "A big percentage of prisoners were there as a result of CIA-sponsored activities in the early 1960s,"
Benes said. "This is a betrayal."[56]

During the dialogue between the moderate exiles and the Cubans,
Benes's daughter Lishka went to Burdines department store to make a
purchase. She handed the clerk her father's credit card. The saleswoman,
a Cuban, handed it back and walked away.[57]

After he retired from the Continental National Bank over disagree-
ments with its management, Benes spent four years as an advisor to the

Universal National Bank, founded by his childhood friend George Feldenkreis. In 1992, Benes decided to pursue his civic work while embarking on new ventures. Teaming up with his old partner, Jefferson National Bank chairman Arthur Courshon, Benes was named executive director of the chairman's advisory committee and vice-chairman of its mortgage-lending branch, Jefferson Capital Corporation. But his personal financial standing continued to decline. In 1992, the Beneses sold their Bay Drive home on Miami Beach's Normandie Isle because their three children had grown up and married, and moved into an apartment in Surfside facing the ocean.

In that same year, both the Inter-American Press Association and the human rights organization, Americas Watch, criticized the Miami exile community for what they called growing violations of civil liberties. Much of the blame fell on the Cuban American National Foundation for its campaign of accusing editors at the *Miami Herald* as being propagandists for Castro because of an editorial opposing the Cuban Democracy (Helms-Burton) Act. They plastered the city with billboards and bus advertisements saying "*Yo no creo en el Herald*" (I do not believe in the *Herald*). Unknown individuals vandalized *Herald* vending machines throughout the city and sometimes smeared them with feces. *Herald* employees received death threats. The possibility for violence seemed palpable.

Benes responded by inviting four couples for dinner at his home: David Lawrence, the *Herald*'s publisher, and his wife; Doug Clifton, the executive editor, and his wife. Also invited were Congressman Dante Fascell and his wife; and Arthur Courshon, Benes's boss at Jefferson Bank and a close friend of Fascell, and Courshon's wife.

Benes tells what he recollects:

> I started the meeting by telling the group that the physical attacks against the *Herald* were un-American and therefore unacceptable and should be stopped. Looking at Dante, I said: "Dante, you are best person I know to talk to Jorge Mas Canosa because you helped him create his foundation." A few days later, the campaign against the *Herald* stopped abruptly.[58]

But when Mas Canosa died, the *El Herald,* now headed by half-Cuban, half–Puerto Rican Alberto Ibargüen, published a special edition in tribute to the man who had once led the boycott against the *Herald* newspapers.

Benes protested vehemently against Mas Conasa's recognition to the *Herald*'s David Lawrence. He reminded Lawrence of the dinner with Fascell at Benes's home that Mas Canosa's campaign had been "un-American" and that the CANF was the "biggest enemy" the *Herald* ever had.[59] But the *Herald*'s special issue, Benes said, undermined the earlier progress. "It is really *immoral,* and *not too smart,*" Benes wrote, "to play into the hands of your archenemy of thirty-five years to promote your newspaper." In response, Lawrence did not defend his editorial decision, but he met with Benes, Alberto Ibargüen, and Ramon Mestre for dinner to discuss the matter further and to try to explain his reasons.[60]

Benes reminded Lawrence that he and singer Gloria Estefan had begun to "free" the Miami Cuban silent majority, and that the militant Cuban radio stations had lost 50,000 listeners in the past year according to surveys. In 1991, 41 percent of Miami Cubans said they relied on the Spanish-language radio stations for their news. By 2000, the number had fallen to 14.4 percent.[61] But Radio Mambí remained the top station in Miami according to Arbitron, and remained the source of news for older Miami Cubans.

Benes volunteered to work for the first Clinton-Gore campaign, raising money and urging people to vote. Privately, he could not understand why so many fellow Cuban exiles had declared themselves Republicans. When he asked individuals, often they had no reply. Acknowledging that President Kennedy, a Democrat, had betrayed the Bay of Pigs invasion and imposed the embargo against Cuba, Benes reminded his friends that the politicians who most helped Cuban Americans were Lyndon B. Johnson, Jimmy Carter, and congressmen Claude Pepper and Dante Fascell. "The Republicans," he wrote in an op-ed piece in the *Miami Herald,* "have been better only in their anti-Castro rhetoric and in pandering, making fools out of the Cubans as they cast for votes by drinking espresso in Little Havana." Referring to the harsh Republican opposition to the proposed bilingual ordinance for Dade County, Benes offered his perspective. "As a Cuban," he wrote, "I am deeply hurt to think that, as a group, exiles consider themselves Republican when—because of the Republicans—a Hispanic policeman might not be allowed to speak Spanish to a Hispanic seeking assistance but unable to speak English. . . . [Lack of bilingual educational opportunities will] deny [Miami's] youth opportunities and financial aid; and many services might disappear."[62]

Benes also worked on the campaign to reelect Governor Lawton Chiles in Florida. He participated in programs held by the Carter Center at Emory University in Atlanta, especially those dealing with Panama (and its troubled elections). A long newspaper column in the *Diario de las Américas* by Luis V. Manrara attacking the State of Israel and its local supporters distinguished "Cuban Cubans" from the "Hebrew Cubans," and called Benes, as he did habitually, "my one-third compatriot."[63] After working for President Bill Clinton's reelection campaign, Benes arranged for Miami's Latin American Cafeteria to provide food for Cuban American attendees at the presidential inauguration on January 19, 1997. But the engraved invitation mailed out to Cuban Democrats omitted Benes's name. Instead, it read "Paul Cejas, Lula Rodríguez, and Maria Elena Toraño cordially invite you to Rhumba for Breakfast with Cuban American Democrats."[64] All three were major contributors to the Clinton campaign, but Benes's name was dropped probably to avoid offending anyone.

On some level, it remains puzzling why Benes was singled out for ostracism after 1978 for having dealt personally with Castro. Before the dialogue, Benes recalls being treated with respect; as soon as he returned from Havana with the first planeload of released political prisoners, he became an untouchable. Others who had participated in the 1978 dialogue did not suffer the same fate. Bobby Maduro, the highly respected baseball executive, had been a member of the six-member exile commission that spoke with Castro about setting up the dialogue, and sat on the same airplane as Benes with the first released political prisoners. But Maduro, who died in 1986, had Miami's baseball stadium named after him in his memory. Father Guillermo Arias of the Belén Jesuit School in Miami was a *dialoguero*, but he was never vilified or even publicly criticized. Ernesto Freyre, who died in 1987, was "instrumental in the negotiation process that led the Kennedy Administration to give the Castro government over $50 million in food and supplies to ransom the [Bay of Pigs] hostages," but neither Freyre nor any of the other Miami Cubans who petitioned the State Department to pay the ransom were considered traitors. And a Florida International University survey polling 670 Hispanic-surnamed residents of the city of Miami during the time of the dialogue revealed that almost 85 percent favored continued negotiations with the Castro government.[65]

The main reason for Benes being singled out as a disloyal traitor was his identification by the media as the architect of the dialogue. Benes's outspokenness led him to defend his long talks with Castro, acts that in the context of the Miami Cuban enclave's insistence on "political correctness" made him vulnerable to vilification. He and Dascal had spent more than a year in exhausting secret negotiations with the Cubans under the watchful eye of the Carter administration; the other *dialogueros* attended mostly for show, and, with some notable exceptions, did not suffer retribution.

Concurrently, right-wing revulsion against dialoguing with Castro intimidated Miami Cubans (if not Anglos as well) from acknowledging the astonishing achievement of the secret negations in securing release of most of Cuba's political prisoners and for opening the doors—for the first time in nearly two decades—to family reunifications. A high-level FBI agent who had maintained contact with Benes throughout the negotiations said, when asked to characterize Benes's personality during that time: "he was a walking lightening rod."[66] He added that Benes truly believed that he had accomplished something that had been an enormous success, but because he admitted publicly to having talked directly with Fidel Castro, he opened himself to venom.

APPOINTMENT IN SAMARA

The past continued to haunt Benes. A shock came in early August 1993. It turned out to be so remarkable that Meg Laughlin of the *Herald*'s Sunday *Tropic* Magazine wrote a story about it. One day, Benes received a telephone call from the brother-in-law of a distant cousin who told him that he had seen an advertisement in New York's *Jewish Weekly*. It was placed by the niece of Baruch Benes, Galina Sinelnikova, and she was seeking contact with any living relatives of Baruch Benes. Laughlin wrote:

> When Bernardo Benes was growing up, he wondered what he had done to make his father so miserable. His mother tried to tell him that his father's sorrow was history's fault, not his. Bernardo had always known the stark facts of what his father believed: His entire family, left behind in Russia, had died in Nazi concentration camps. But the subject was taboo in the house.[67]

In 1984, Galina discovered after her father's funeral, a photograph among her father's possessions. On the back, in Yiddish, was written "The family of Boruch [sic] Benes, Sept. 1960." The photograph showed a handsome family at some kind of social event—it turned out later to be the wedding of Bernardo's cousin, Anita Baikovitz—dressed in tuxedos and taffeta. The eyes of one of the men in the photograph, she observed, looked exactly like hers. Elated, she contacted the Cuban Embassy in Moscow, but doubted that she would receive any help, because the Beneses had abandoned their country. But the Cuban ambassador wrote back inviting her to talk with him, and Galina, a staff pediatrician at a children's hospital in Samara, made the nineteen hour trip east to Moscow.[68]

Based on the observation that the Benes family "looked wealthy" in the photo, the ambassador said that they had probably left for the United States or Costa Rica. He suggested that Galina contact the International Red Cross in Geneva. When this produced nothing, she wrote seven letters to the Immigration and Naturalization Service in Miami, but no one replied. In 1992, a colleague of her daughter's was to spend six months in New York, and Galina asked for assistance. When the woman returned six months later, she brought an application for an ad in the New York *Jewish Weekly* with her, for a section in which people searched for family members. In spring 1993, she mailed in the application along with the $25 fee. The ad, the journalist noted, ran in late July. It asked for information about "Boruch Benes, born about 1910 in Byelorussia and immigrated to the U.S. from Cuba after 1961, by his niece Galina Sinelnikova." Bernardo told the caller, choking back tears: "Someone is looking for my father. He thought his family in Russia had all been killed in the war."[69] Boris had died of cancer in 1968, and Bernardo had never told him that he thought that he understood the reason for Boris's lifelong depression. Finally, Bernardo finally received a letter from Galina. After he read it, he sat in his car and sobbed for hours. Among the things Galina explained was how his paternal grandparents had perished during the Second World War at the hands of the Nazis.

Bernardo, now fifty-nine, his wife Ricky, his older sister Ana, and her husband, David Anders, made plans to travel to Russia to visit their relatives as soon as possible. They departed on June 24, 1994, for Moscow.

Five family members met them at the airport after they cleared customs: their cousin Galina, her son, her daughter-in-law, and two grandchildren. There were hugs and tears, and close looks at faces to spot family resemblances. It was a beautiful day, with the sun shining and the poplar trees planted by Stalin as snow barriers were in full bloom. The next day they were tourists and visited Red Square, the Kremlin, Lenin's Tomb, and the tombs of well-known communists.

During the long train ride to Samara, Galina (through her son) related that after the Minsk bombings that had killed most of Boris's family, with their house on fire they began to walk east, forty-five miles a day, as part of an "endless stream" of refugees. "We had nothing: no coats, no food, no water. . . . We were thirsty, but all of the wells had been emptied by those who went before us," Galina revealed. "We sucked the wet sand on the bottom."[70]

Seventeen family members were waiting to greet Bernardo and Ana when the train arrived in Samara. They stayed at the Volga Hotel, which Ana described as "the pits" but everything else was wonderful. Laughlin continues the story:

> Some with red hair like Ana's and his. Some with sad, squinty eyes and dark complexions like their father's. They had huge bunches of flowers. They hugged him as if they had always loved him. At Galina's house they looked at old pictures, constructed a family tree, and stuffed themselves with Jewish and Russian food. They tangoed. They sang Yiddish songs. They drank champagne and vodka and made toasts: "To perestroika for opening up Russia." "To the family members who died in the war." "To America." "To Russia." "To the reunification of all families." "To peace."
>
> They argued politics: capitalism vs. communism. Benes told his cousins that he thought the former Soviet Union had had a "bad investment" in Cuba, wasting $110 billion over more than thirty years. He felt amazed at how unafraid they were to voice their opinions walking down the street and out in restaurants. He shocked them when he said: "You can't speak as freely in Miami as you can in Russia."
>
> One night after dinner, Bernardo broke into *God Bless America.* "Land that I love," sang the man who had to wear a bulletproof vest for two years in order to walk down the street. Everyone stood up and applauded.[71]

They learned that some of their relatives had "made *aliyah*" (emigrated) to Israel.

When they left, Ilusha, one of the children to whom Ana had given a little Post-it pad, stuck two of the yellow paper squares on the outside of the train window. They said, in English, "I love you" and "Write to us soon."

More of the Same

In an *Esquire*-style compilation of the 100 most influential Miamians in South Florida's history, the *Miami Herald,* in 1993, listed Benes eighty-eighth, but the essay's satirical undertone detracted from its potential weight.[72] More typical was the fact that even during the mid-1990s, Benes continued to be the subject of venomous criticism. Here is Benes's description of one such event:

> Although I was unemployed, I convinced Raúl Galindo, the founder and owner of the successful Latin American Cafeteria chain, to provide food to serve to all Cuban Americans attending President Bill Clinton's second inauguration in Washington. Following that, Galindo offered me a job as a consultant to help him diversify his company and to help it grow. I accepted, and started to work full-time as a consultant. I really liked the job![73]

Raúl, however, had as a neighbor Amancio Suarez, a Cuban who had become wealthy, according to Benes, buying electronic goods manufactured in China and re-selling them. Suarez also acquired Miami's three most popular Cuban radio stations and overnight became a very powerful figure in the exile community. In time, he sold the stations and started up a weekly newspaper, *Viva Semanal.* He gave that up, too, but in his final issue, October 23–29, 1996, he published a hostile article retelling the story of Benes and the 1978 dialogue with Castro. The newspaper concocted a sarcastic "interview" with Benes by a reporter named "Columpio Miguel," with tiny print under the byline reading, "The interviews by Columpio Miguel are imaginary and whatever similarities readers see in them are purely coincidental."

Shortly after the article appeared, Galindo asked Benes to leave the Latin American Cafeteria. Benes has always believed the criticism prompted his unceremonious discharge.

Benes continued:

He asked me to leave that very day, a Friday. I had to call a moving company to send a truck and had to pack all of my things in one hour. It was
one of the worst days in my life. My files were all over the floor, and I had
to drag my own desk to the truck. I felt like shit. This is what Miami,
U.S.A., is all about.[74]

Although he carried warm letters of recommendation from the editors
and publishers of the *Miami Herald* including David Lawrence, Congressman Dante Fascell, and others, Benes's enemies managed to blackball
him from employment in Miami.[75] Recipients wrote warmly of Benes;
Carnival Cruise Lines Chairman and CEO Micky Arison called him
"clearly a man of considerable accomplishment," but added, "I'm not sure
we presently have a need for someone with his skills."[76] Lawrence sent the
letter to Benes, accompanied by a banal note saying "*Mantenga la fé . . .*"
(Keep the Faith).[77]

Still, Benes persevered in trying to organize groups to confront community problems. In 1997, disturbed by the national media's coverage of
Miami as a corrupt "banana republic" dominated by Cubans, he worked
with the Washington, D.C.–based Center for Public Integrity (CPI), a
nonprofit research center co-founded by his nephew, Alex.[78] It investigated alleged abuses in government and reported its findings to the
media. In November 1997, he flew to the Center's Washington headquarters where he met with two of the center's senior officials. After two
hours of conversation about the existing level of corruption in Dade
County, he was put in touch with a similar organization in Chicago concerned with political corruption, the Better Government Association.

On his return to Miami, Benes contacted Parker Thomson, a prominent attorney and community leader, and Bryan O. Walsh, the head of
the Catholic Welfare Bureau. On February 6, 1998, the three met with
Alvah Chapman, retired chairman of Knight-Ridder Publishing Company
and perhaps the most influential community leader in Miami. Benes
sought support among Miami law firms and corporations, finally finding it
with Carlos Saladrigas, the Chairman of the Board of Vincam Group, Inc.
and the chairman of the Miami Cuban *Mesa Redonda*. Saladrigas invited
seventy people to a May 1998 luncheon at Florida International University to discuss the idea, and the initiative was launched—the program was

to be housed at the University of Miami School of Law. Benes was invited to the lunch but was in Los Angeles attending a family wedding. He never heard from the organization again because, he believes, he was still "too controversial" in Miami.[79] His sentence of ostracism imposed in 1978 remained a barrier in his efforts to serve the community. Meanwhile, Miami Cuban radio stations continued to insult him, and Spanish-language newspapers continued to impugn his character and motives.

In April 1998, Benes became an independent consultant to the Miami office of Washington-based Smith-Brandon International, a fast-growing risk analysis consulting firm dealing mostly with small and medium-sized firms interested in investing abroad. The match happened because Harry "Skip" Brandon had been former deputy assistant director of the FBI and had taken part in the events surrounding Benes's 1978 activities. In an interview about his appointment, Bernardo noted that because he had been trained at the University of Havana Law School, his schooling in Napoleonic law made reading Latin American bank documents, in his words, feel "just like I was back in my law firm in Havana."[80] But he remained active at Smith-Brandon only for eighteen months.

The snubs continued year after year. In 1998, Monsignor Bryan Walsh invited him to become a member of the board of the nonprofit Miami Catholic Hospice. He accepted and sent a copy of his résumé; when no response came, he called Walsh, who embarrassingly told Benes that he had not been accepted: The board had considered him too controversial.[81] Years later, Benes's dying mother spent twelve days in the hospice and received exceptional treatment before her death.

In August 2000, when Al Gore named Joe Lieberman as his running mate, Bernardo was invited to comment by Miami's Channel 23 and by several radio stations around Florida.[82] Even on the way to the first appointment, he heard anti-Semitic references to Lieberman and to Jews. Once again, his status as an "outsider" was being reinforced and rubbed in.

In November 2000, staff members of a Jewish agency in Miami wanted to hire a consultant having credentials like Benes's. When Benes was nominated, the agency's director pronounced that Benes would be unsuitable, because "rumors maintained" that members of the community knew that he had talked with Castro, and therefore could not be trusted.

5.6   Fidel Casto with Bernardo Benes in Cuba, October 1978. Miami *News*.

5.7   Benes and former political prisoner Juan Ferrer, Miami, 2000. Photograph by
Robert M. Levine.

Benes remained a *Capitán* Dreyfus even to his own people.[83] A few days later, Benes explained his reaction:

> As soon as I saw the way the director looked at me as we shook hands, I knew right then that I would never be offered the job. Over the last 20 years, I have learned to smell out when people try to hide their distaste for me. It is very difficult for others to understand the pain I have suffered in my twenty-two years of isolation.[84]

THE FIRST MISSION'S LEGACY

Over a million Cuban Americans visited their homeland under the agreement reached between Washington and Havana in 1978, as a result of Benes's negotiations and the subsequent dialogue. When they first arrived, the Miami Cubans were disoriented by what they saw: crumbling buildings, empty food markets, dark-skinned men and women in positions of authority. Their Cuban relatives felt another kind of shock: they had been told that the Cubans in exile lived in misery, but the returnees were dressed elegantly, exuded good health, and seemed eminently prosperous. Some Cubans cynically remarked: "the *gusanos* [worms] have become butterflies."[85] For their part, many Miami Cubans expected their long-suffering relatives to curse Castro in private, but in many cases the Cubans pronounced their fervent support of the revolution, regardless of the hardships caused by Cuba's economic distress.

Non-Cuban United States citizens—curiosity seekers, tourists and college-students seeking to see Cuba for themselves—have found it increasingly easy to enter and depart Cuba. At first, would-be visitors would have to travel to Canada, Jamaica, Mexico, or even Czechoslovakia to find reliable commercial flights to Cuba, and United States government agents photographed many of them as they boarded and disembarked. Cuban customs officials rarely stamped the passports of the Americans, so no proof (other than the clandestine photographs) existed of their visits. After 1978, however, direct charter flights made the trip from Miami to Havana and sometimes to other cities as well. These flights departed from unmarked gates often past midnight, lest they attract attention, but they became regular occurrences.

Passengers on these flights carried enormous quantities of clothing, medicines, and especially cash with them. Those who used intermediaries (*mulas*) sometimes learned later that the intermediaries removed some of the cash for themselves, but as time passed, it became more and more necessary for Cubans to have dollars, so they accepted the robberies as the cost of doing business. The *mulas*, of course, did not return to Florida empty-handed. Many brought back Cohiba cigars, which sold in Miami for $250 to $350 for a box of twenty-five. They bought them from the Cuban black market, in many cases paying for cigars stolen right from the factory.[86]

Most Miami Cubans accepted the opportunity to visit their relatives as a matter of fact, without thanking Benes in their hearts for making it possible. Not only did Benes's negotiations lead to family visits between Cuba and the United States, but the agreement exposed the fallacy of Che Guevara's "New Man" theory. The Cuban revolution, Che argued, would so reorganize social conditions that the next generation, unmarked by Batista's legacy, would emerge as virile, energetic builders of the community society. Instead, when the exiles visited their families, Cubans saw immediately from their clothing, robust health, and attitude that Cuba's revolution produced mostly poverty. Further, many children of fervent first-generation revolutionaries took advantage of opened doors to leave for Miami. They included the three children of René Anillo, Cuban ambassador to the Soviet Union; the son of Fructuoso Rodríguez, the fallen student leader; Osmel Francis de los Reyes, who left for the Canary Islands; Humberto Castello, son of a prominent physician and former student activist, and many others.

For over ten years, Benes sought under the Freedom of Information Act to obtain a copy of his FBI file. In 2000, amidst the turmoil of the Elián González tug-of-war, he sent faxes to fellow Miamian Janet Reno, the attorney general, to expedite his request. She never replied. Late in the year, however, Benes finally received a package from Washington containing hundreds of pages dealing with his dialogue activities and his missions to Cuba. Unfortunately, most of the pages were heavily blacked out, as if to suggest that Washington was still not ready to make the talks with Castro regarding normalization public.

In August 2000, similar scenes of family reunification were reenacted following the unprecedented meeting between the heads of state of North and South Korea, enemies as bitter as any on the face of the earth. The broadcast media around the world depicted the family reunifications in sensitive and compassionate ways. For some in the Miami Cuban community, these acts, too, represented betrayal.[87]

CHAPTER SIX

ONLY IN MIAMI

Since 1959, when Hispanics comprised less than 5 percent of its population, the city and surrounding area has absorbed newcomers from Latin America to the point at which Miami now has a sizeable Hispanic majority. Because the United States census does not break down its Hispanic category by country of origin, the total number of Cubans in Miami remains unknown, but the figure ranges between 650,000 to 700,000 today. From 1959 to the present, Anglos have departed for Broward and Palm Beach counties as waves of immigrants and refugees poured in from Cuba and many parts of Latin America. Cubans, who made up 90 percent of the Dade's Hispanic population in 1970, represented 60 percent in 1998. The first post-Castro-wave Cubans reoriented the local economy from seasonal tourism toward trade and banking, remaking Miami the de facto capital of Latin America. Yet the success story overlooked other issues. The 1980 Mariel boatlift and the flow of rafters who followed in their wake brought Cubans who were young, unprepared for the realities of life in the United States, and darker-complexioned than the elite Cubans of the first waves. These and other differences, caused a breach in the community; most earlier arrivals stood at arms' length from the newcomers, who had to rely more on family and government assistance because enclave sources of aid did not cover their needs.

Ironically, the success of Benes and Dascal's mission in 1978 in achieving freedom of travel back and forth to Cuba helped raise the expectations of many of those who would leave Cuba via Mariel two years later.

They had seen photographs of their relatives' lavish-appearing homes and cars but did not realize that such acquisitions meant mortgages, loans, and often working at two jobs. Some Cuban exiles had become enormously successful. Success stories among the newer arrivals occurred, but they were usually not on the same scale.

Still, the lack of support from earlier arrivals combined class snobbery, racial prejudice, and fear of the dangerous or dysfunctional Cubans that Castro had cynically forced onto the boats.[1] The original group of exiles also included some who built fortunes by exploiting off-the-books labor of the newer arrivals, the rafters. Miami in 1997 had the highest rate of unemployment of any United States city over a million in population—a circumstance that sent even more helpless new arrivals into the unprotected underground economy. In addition, scandal after scandal involving elected officials in the city and county, some Cuban, some Anglos, and some African American, portrayed Miami poorly as the stories of embezzlement, bribery, cronyism, and electoral fraud reached the media.

Perhaps the main characteristic of the diverse Cuban American community in Miami over the past forty years has been the domination by the exile minority waging permanent war against Castro. This, in turn, has turned the city into a one-issue community in which candidates for positions ranging from school boards to judges are assessed by their political beliefs regarding Cuba. As late as 2000, 77 percent of Miami Cubans polled in an independent survey said that they consider each candidate's position on Castro, regardless of the office sought.

The ramifications of the one-issue character of the community in turn have silenced the voices of many who might disagree and forced the majority to keep their feelings to themselves. It has yielded an odd paradox: Miami Cubans stand united as probably no other such group of newcomers to the United States, but only 4.5 percent belong to any single civic association, Cuban or citywide.[2] The sensitivity remains. Basilio V. Sikfo, a Cuban American and registered Democrat, complains that he spent nearly forty years becoming American, paying taxes, serving in Vietnam, and being sworn in as a citizen by Vice-President Bush at the Orange Bowl in 1984, and the minute he expressed his opinion against the Justice Department's rulings of the Elián González case he felt cheated, "reduced to an 'exile.'"[3]

The unity within the Miami Cuban community has lasted even though its founding members left Cuba for very different reasons. Some supported Batista; others risked their lives to defeat his regime, only to become angered at the new Cuban government that followed. What Damián J. Fernández calls the "politics of passion" common to all exile politics led to common ground: the maintenance of a moral vision of the lost homeland coupled with a crusade against Castro. "Return to *la patria* (the homeland) . . ." Fernández argues, "would legitimize the exiles' righteousness and pave the way for the moral rebirth of the Cuban nation."[4]

Some Miami Cubans have argued that in recent years there has been a turn toward moderation. If so, it shows more visibly within the Cuban community than outside. Miami Cubans remain deeply averse to being cast as outsiders within their enclave, so they do not air their dirty linen. "B'wanas," as Juan Carlos Espinosa calls the Anglo "experts" on Cuban American life and culture, in his eyes miss the fact that Cuban Miami today is far much more in touch with Cuba than anyone imagines. Five or six planes a day go back and forth to the island, and Little Havana shops sell CDs of the latest Cuban hits and videotapes of Cuban television variety shows sometimes less than a month after their screening in Cuba.[5]

Most Cubans in Miami, of course, bear the emotional trauma of exile, perceived betrayals, and culture shock, and most Cuban exiles brought with them complex emotional baggage. Although the wealthy lived American-style lives before 1959, Cuban culture in many ways reflected decades of anti-Americanism. It could be argued that the Cubans, although they practiced institutional discrimination against "outsiders," mostly of color or immigrant background, were far more tolerant on a personal basis than many racist North Americans. As late as 1990, only 1.5 percent of Cubans living in Miami classified themselves as black. Miami, an observer noted, "had a Little Havana rather than a Little Cuba" for a reason.[6] Yet Havana before 1950 had always been a multiracial city, although it was segregated psychologically as well as economically, exactly like cities in the northern United States. Even so, the Cubans' resistance to cast aside their cultural self-identity and cultural pride, as demanded by the "sand in the shoes" Anglo Floridians in the 1960s and after, produced alienation and confusion.

Yet both the "insiders" and "outsiders" within the Cuban population numbered only a tiny portion of the larger community. The rest of Miami's Cubans represented a silent majority, or, to be more exact, a silenced majority.[7] The pressure is felt not only by politicians but also among professional specialists on Cuba at some South Florida universities. There are examples of former liberals on the Cuban question turning into outspoken reactionaries. Such transformations rarely occurred in the other direction, although, as Juan Carlos Espinosa points out, the "liberal" position on Cuba—I would substitute the term "far left"—shows far too much willingness to excuse the excesses of Castro's regime.[8]

Benes complained to anyone who would listen that Miami Cubans acted little better than Cubans under Castro because both groups lined up like sheep and passively did whatever they were told but in Miami, the Cubans persisted in this behavior even when they had alternatives. The rhetoric of the Spanish-language radio stations and *periodiquitos*, he argued, sounded and read as if it were directed by the Cuban government, even to the point of calling for Miami Cubans to break up meetings or demonstrations by dissident groups—the same tactic employed in Cuba under Castro. Ramón Mestre, Sr., one of the most distinguished original political prisoners, blames Castro for the volatility of Miami Cubans. Tens of thousands of them, he explained to Benes, referring to post-1980 newer arrivals, had either served in Committees for the Defense of the Revolution, State Security, or in rapid-action brigades (*Brigadas de Respuesta Rápida*) before defecting, and therefore they were accustomed to following instructions blindly and turning against their neighbors.[9]

The conservative Spanish model—represented in Cuba by the *Diario de la Marina*, whose owners until his death had always supported Spain's Generalissimo Francisco Franco—influenced Cuban Miami extensively, even though in Cuba before Batista's 1952 coup, only about 10 percent of voters supported this position. Emilio "Millo" Ochoa, a founder of the Ortodoxo Party and respected former senator, now ninety-three years old and one of the two surviving members of the progressive 1940 Cuban constituent assembly, confirms this, charging that the Cuban exile lobby in Miami has tricked fellow Cubans into believing their political heritage to be right-wing. "The Cuban exiles have adopted an extreme right-wing posture, while during the June 1948 elections—Cuba's last—more than

70 percent of the voters cast ballots for one of the two progressive parties, the Ortodoxos and the Autenticos."[10] Only six members of the constituent assembly represented the communist P. S.P. and another six represented the far right. The large majority of the delegates represented progressive, pro-democratic positions. This fact may explain why the right-wing Miami Cuban exile message never penetrated Cuba.[11]

Miami Cubans loyal to the imagined universal right-wing past, including many of the exile leaders who emerged in the early 1980s, tended to view Cuba as a sacred abstraction, even sacrificial and, most telling of all, closed to debate.[12] This created the ground out of which right-wing groups—far less progressive than the majority of Cuban voters before Batista's 1952 coup—seized the high ground and won the power to speak for all of Cuban Miami. They never understood the truism that frantic orthodoxy is never rooted in faith but in doubt.[13] The major winner in this game has been the Cuban American National Foundation, modeled after the pro-Israel lobby, AIPAC, and headed by Jorge Mas Canosa from its creation in 1980 until Mas Canosa's death from cancer in 1997. The CANF maintained a strong record of successes in Congress. Its greatest victory was the passage of the controversial Torricelli and Helms-Burton (officially the Cuban Liberty and Democratic Solidarity Law) acts, both tightening the decades-old economic embargo. In response to Helms-Burton, whose second part amounted to no less then imposing an updated Platt Amendment on Cuba, on Christmas Eve 1996, the Cuban National Assembly of Popular Power passed the "Anti-Helms-Burton Law" (officially the Reaffirmation Law of Cuban Dignity and Sovereignty). This, of course, probably made CANF leaders laugh.

Brian Latell, an expert on Cuban–United States relations at Georgetown University and former CIA desk officer for Cuba, attributes the influence of the CANF most of all to the fact that its leadership, in his words, "was extraordinary." By the early 1980s, moreover, many of the original exiles had made personal fortunes and were willing to support the CANF financially. Its leaders supported political campaigns of both Republicans and Democrats. The Reagan administration's Cuba policy complemented the policies of Miami's exile lobby, and Castro's behavior during the Mariel boatlift significantly changed United States public and media opinion about him.[14]

It is telling to consider why Mas Canosa personally succeeded where, after 1978, Benes's efforts to normalize "dialogue" failed. William Aramony, the former CEO of United Way America, sums up Benes's personality:

> Bernardo, a man of passion and belief, is persistent. He can drive you crazy. He comes back again and again to make things happen. That "deficiency" was also his greatest strength. He had to "break through" and convince the decision-maker that something needed to get done. And he stayed on you until it got done. Bernardo was not easy to be with—he forced you off your agenda to his agenda. For a manager, this can be very upsetting. But if you bought into the vision, you accepted the pain so you could share the achievement.[15]

Benes's vulnerability opened him to scorn unlike the rich and power-ful, whose stature deflected criticism of their own personality flaws. The cliché is apt: Benes wore his heart on his sleeve which made it easy to brush him aside and not take him seriously. This situation dominated long before the volatile public "dialogue" issue surfaced. In 1968, Benes had or-ganized a group, the "Friends of Don José M. (Pepín) Bosch," and invited fifty persons to a catered lunch at the elegant waterfront Sheraton Four Ambassadors hotel. Bosch, the chairman of Bacardi Rum, was honored for "his dedication and efforts for the Liberation of Cuba." In 1970, Benes and *Herald* editor Don Shoemaker assembled a committee to raise funds to buy the "Freedom Tower," the old *News* building, which had served as a relief center for new Cuban arrivals in the early 1960s, and turn it into a public monument and museum. He pleaded with Representative Claude Pepper to send financial aid to the more than ten thousand Cubans in Spain and more in Mexico who were waiting out the up-to-two-year process for permanent resident visas to enter the United States, but who were suffering with scant resources. Few, however, remembered these and similar activities ten years later when Benes became the scourge of the community.

By contrast, Jorge Mas Canosa, as driven as Benes but more single-minded and better connected, started out as a deliveryman and laborer but eventually amassed a personal fortune. He became known for his toughness (his enemies called it ruthlessness), his ability to speak extem-poraneously, and his political acumen. A loan from an exile entrepreneur permitted him to purchase a construction firm—Church and Tower—from its Puerto Rican owners, Mr. Torre (a delegate of RECE in Puerto Rico) and Mr. Iglesias. By the late 1990s, Mas Canosa's Miami firm employed four hundred and had become a $62 million business. This gave him strong leverage in the city of Miami and in Dade County, where he forged contacts with other wealthy Cubans, as well as elected and appointed public officials. As a powerful businessman himself, he worked to collect and pool funds for political activities. His construction firm did extensive business with the city and county, and in the private sector won a major contract to lay cable for Southern Bell. His business ties with ATT and other major corporations impressed Washington insiders and added to the CANF's ability to influence legislation.

Unlike some of the other exile activists, such as Antonio Veciana, the founder of Alpha 66, Mas Canosa possessed a sophisticated command of public relations. Like Bernardo Benes, he wrote letters to important people. "I'd write letters to fifty congressmen and senators," Mas Canosa said, "telling them when I was coming, and I'd always get six or seven answers telling me to come and see them at such-and-such a time."[16] Before long, politicians at all levels of government deferred to him as spokesman for the Cuban-American community.

He helped swing South Florida voters away from support of New Deal Democrats to bloc voting for any office seeker militant against Castro, most of whom were Republicans. "It is the way we were raised," a forty-seven-year-old Miami Cuban told a reporter during the 2000 presidential campaign. "Being Cuban and of Cuban descent, we are all diehard Republicans."[17] Republicans or not, Miami Cubans grew highly conservative. In late 1999, the Cuban American National Foundation hired an "Anglo," Dennis Hayes, to be executive vice-president. Hayes had a solid anti-Castro record and had helped defeat a bill to pay pensions for the thousands of Cuban and Jamaican workers hired over the years to help run the Navy's Guantánamo base.[18]

The CANF backed hardline candidates for Congress, first winning the open seat left by the death of Claude Pepper and the rising numbers of newly registered Miami Cuban Republicans. Its lobbying and campaign support for candidates hostile to Castro transcended party lines: although the foundation usually supported Republicans, in 1988, through large campaign contributions to his opponent, Democrat Joseph Lieberman, it helped bring down moderate Republican Senator Lowell Weicker, who had met with Castro and who opposed CANF-backed legislation. "We have a very close relationship with Senator Lieberman," the foundation's Joe García told the press. "Throughout the years, he has been a great supporter of Radio Martí, TV Martí. . . . On every single one of the issues, Joe Lieberman has been a staunch ally of freedom for Cuba."[19]

Yet some of the old guard disagreed with the CANF about Lieberman. The day (August 14, 2000) that Bernardo Benes heard on the news that the Connecticut senator had been selected as Gore's running mate, Benes said that he anticipated remarks about "*judíos*" (Jews) within the Miami Cuban community.[20] At nine in the morning, Radio Mambí's Armando Pérez-Roura said: "Cubans, how can you vote for a Jew when Benes is a Jew, and he favors relations with Cuba?"[21] An hour later, the broadcaster was still pontificating about "the Jew Lieberman."

Cuban Jews reacted with controlled anger. Anita Stone, born in San Germán, in Oriente, in 1926 to a family of Lithuanian immigrants, and later married to a physician, making their home in Havana, wrote to Pérez-Roura:[22]

> I am Cuban, and of the Jewish religion. The only Cuban station I listen to is Radio Mambí. . . . Early this morning I heard your commentary about the selection of a running mate for Al Gore. You said: "The Jew Lieberman" . . . I do not remember hearing "The Catholic Jack Kennedy" or "the Protestant Cheney."
>
> My advanced age permits me to express myself more these days, casting off my inhibitions. I remember years ago in Cuba when a committee came to my house in Miramar to interview us and to determine our religion before considering the application of my husband and I to join the Miramar Yacht Club. When I heard you . . . this morning, my blood boiled. Thank you for your attention, Catholic Pérez-Roura.

She signed her name, "Anita Stone, Very Cuban and Jewish as well."[23]

Later, Mrs. Stone learned that Pérez-Roura had read her letter on the air. He dismissed her complaint by saying that she had "imagined in his statements an anti-Semitic content that was not intended." The writer, however, received many phone calls from Cuban friends praising her for her courage, and she feels that sending the letter provided "cathartic" for her own self-understanding of her "complicated ethnic and national components."[24]

Its support of Senator Lieberman illustrated how the CANF took a candidate or politician's position on Cuba as the sole basis for support or opposition. Although its leaders were staunchly Republican, they felt no contradiction in contributing to the campaign of a Democrat. The foundation flexed its lobbying muscles in other electoral contests as well. When six-term Senator Claiborne Pell (D-RI), opposed to Radio Martí and critical of the embargo against Cuba, faced an uphill reelection campaign, Mas Canosa met with him in Miami. After their conversations, Pell switched his position on an amendment offered by Florida's conservative Senator Connie Mack. Whatever Mas Canosa said must have been persuasive.[25]

In his memoirs, Wayne S. Smith said of Mas Canosa, "In a way, he's a credit to the American way. This guy has assimilated the American political system better than anyone else. He really knows how to use it. . . . He's head and shoulders above every other politician in terms of being effective."[26]

Exile organizations worked hard to elect Republican candidates for Congress, to erode Miami's bedrock Democratic base (86 percent of registered voters in 1960). Once Cubans became citizens, they overwhelmingly registered as Republicans. Still, it took until the late 1980s to win a major battle. The first Republican member elected to Congress from Dade County, and the first Hispanic woman from any state, was Ileana Ros-Lehtinen. In 1989, she won the seat vacated by the death of Claude Pepper in 1989. While she became more involved in community philanthropy than many other political leaders, she provided unwavering backing for every position on Cuba endorsed by the exile lobby.[27]

Lincoln Díaz-Balart, the second Cuban American Republican to take a previously Democratic seat, entered the House of Representatives in 1992. Reelected without opposition, he was appointed by the Republican leadership two years later to the powerful House Rules Committee. His family in Cuba had been political allies of Batista, although Mirta Díaz-Balart, his aunt, had married Fidel Castro in the early 1950s. This made Lincoln Díaz-Balart Fidel Castro's nephew by marriage. The family numbered among the first to flee the island after Castro assumed power in 1959. Diaz-Balart started out in Miami politics as president of the Young

Democrats of Florida, but he soon shifted to the Republican Party and became a tenacious defender of CANF policies in Congress.[28] In the confusion following the 2000 presidential race, he charged during a televised protest rally in front of county election headquarters that the Democrats had "stolen the election." He had thought that candidate Al Gore won.

On November 27, without an invitation, Díaz-Balart and three others, including Ana Carbonell, his office director, went to WQBA at eight in the morning to make a statement about the elections. The station, a subsidiary of the Hispanic Broadcasting Corporation (owner also of Radio Mambí and a hundred stations around the country), accepted his request, and the morning program's producer, Spanish-born Santiago Aroca, put him live on the air. As soon as Díaz-Balart stopped speaking, Aroca surprised him by asking for his comments on the audit of the Federal Election Commission, dated March 24, 2000, in which a discrepancy of $178,970 in campaign funds had been found, along with other irregularities. Díaz-Balart denied knowledge of the matter, although some of his staff had been subpoenaed.[29]

Spearheaded by the election not only of Ros-Lehtinen and Díaz-Balart to Congress but by the victory of ultra-conservative Republican Connie Mack to the Senate and increased Cuban representation in the Florida House of Representatives, the CANF won easy outlets for its policy positions. In the late 1980s, the CANF collaborated with the United States State Department to create Project Exodus, an arrangement to aid the immigration to the United States of Cubans trapped in other countries. The program sponsored the arrival of more than 9,500 Cubans between 1988 and 1993 and provided health care insurance and employment for the new arrivals. The federal government allocated about $2 million in funding. The negotiations to create Project Exodus proceeded in much the same way that Benes had conducted his business with Cuba, although CANF representatives did not meet directly with Castro, at least for the record.[30] If "outsiders" like Benes had worked to create Project Exodus, they likely would have been castigated as a tool of the communists and as disloyal Cubans.

While the Cuban American National Foundation played hard but within legal boundaries, its tacit support of preexisting militant exile organizations increased the chilling and intimidating effects of violence against those the anti-Castroites labeled communist. The CANF's political strength allowed Mas Canosa to tell the press in 1991 that he had personally carried out secret dialogues with Castro-government officials during the previous two years—the same actions that had turned Bernardo Benes into a target of the hardliners in 1978. Mas Canosa explained that his talks had centered on "exploring the possibilities of a Cuba after Castro,"[31] without offering further details about what Cuban "officials" would be willing to discuss on this topic.

Anchored by the CANF, Miami's Cuban exile leadership made few public efforts to bring the economically and socially diverse Cuban American community together. Groups devoted to planning the implementation of a stable banking system in Cuba's "transition to a free market," presumably did not include any people living in Cuba.[32] This attitude of Cuban exceptionalism hindered links to other Spanish-speaking groups and contributed to the enclave's isolation. Miami's exile leaders did not worry about how the larger community reacted to its policies and actions. The Orlando Bosch matter made the extent of the CANF's influence clear. In February 1988, Orlando Bosch Avila, one of the two suspected bombers of the Cubana Airlines plane over Barbados in 1976 who had been sentenced in Venezuela for the crime, escaped from prison and traveled to Miami, where INS officials arrested him as a fugitive from justice. Through the efforts of right-wing Cuban Miamians and others, Bosch gained his freedom on July 17, 1990. In reaction, the *New York Times* editorialized that the Justice Department had released him not for legal reasons but rather due to visible political pressure. It also observed that "while the United States had sent the air force to bomb Libya and the army to invade Panama in the name of combating terrorism, the Bush administration was now pampering one of the most notorious terrorists in the hemisphere."[33]

Luis Posada Carriles was the second suspect in the airline bombing. He escaped from a Venezuelan prison in 1985 while awaiting trial, and, disguised as a priest, made his way back to Miami. In his memoirs, *The Paths of the Warrior*, published in the late 1990s, Posada Carriles praised Jorge Mas Canosa for capably leading the anti-Castro fight and for sending Posada Carriles "a sufficient amount of money, which arrived regularly every month."[34] In 1997, Posada Carriles bragged that he had carried out a series of hotel bombings in Havana, and, in 2000, using false documents, slipped into Panama with the intent, according to the Cuban government, of assassinating Castro while attending a meeting of the Ibero-American summit. Panamanian police also picked up three other Cuban exiles, all former members of the defunct anti-Castro terrorist group Omega 7. One of them, Miami resident Gaspar Jiménez, while in prison in Mexico in 1981 for an attempted kidnapping five years earlier of Daniel Ferrer, the Cuban consul in Mérida, Mexico, had been secretly indicted along with another anti-Castro exile in Miami. The charge: wiring dynamite to Emilio Millián's car in 1976; after he turned his ignition key, the explosion succeeded in blasting his legs off.[35]

Reaction in Cuban Miami to the Panama arrests did not provoke public outrage. Emilio's son Alberto Millán, fresh from losing a bid to unseat Miami-Dade State Attorney Katherine Fernández Rundle, declared that linking Jiménez to a Castro assassination plot should be considered suspect, since the complaint had been Castro himself. "He has no moral authority to denounce the U.S. or anybody. It's absurd. If anyone should be charged with terrorism, it's [Castro]."[36] Ninoska Pérez Castellón, speaking for the CANF, called the allegation "ridiculous." Castro is like a rock star, she said, "who needs to call attention to himself."[37]

The effort to broadcast anti-Castro news and information to Cuba was always a priority of Cuban exile groups, with support from the CIA and other government agencies. In 1960, planners of the Bay of Pigs invasion planted radio transmitters to support the operation. After the fiasco, the transmitters were pressed into service as Radio Swan, which after a few years became Radio Americas before it stopped transmitting. Over the years, dozens of independent as well as United States government-supported stations kept up the attempt. In 1981, President Reagan declared his administration's intention to create a Radio Free Cuba on the models of the European Voice of America and Radio Liberty. In 1982, however, the Senate rejected a proposal for funds but it passed in the following year. Jorge Mas Canosa headed an advisory board named by the president to plan operations. Fidel Castro, as might be expected, protested, and threatened to broadcast Cuban programs to the United States using the same frequencies as commercial stations. When Radio Martí signed on the air on May 20, 1985, it operated professionally, not sending hostile programs aimed at attacking the Castro government but providing balanced news coverage along with broadcasts of interest to Cubans. On one hand, the timing of its start-up undermined the painstaking negotiation process being carried out by Benes, Guille, and the CIA's Jim Bloomfield. This group then found itself caught between congressional support for anti-Castro measures and the brief attempt within the executive branch for negotiations and improved relations. Benes, Guille, and Dascal all had been pawns whose moves were dictated by groups representing only certain individuals, albeit highly placed, in the United States government. Even the *New York Times* backed away from its initial criticism of Radio Martí, editorializing that "the station appears to have found a responsive audience and filled a void in Cubans' information. It had avoided propaganda and supplemented, not duplicated, commercial Spanish-language broadcasts from Florida."[38]

Almost everything changed in 1997, when the Office of Cuban Broadcasting (OCB) moved from Washington, D.C. to Miami. Management changed, too, and some of the new on-air broadcasters came from local exile radio stations. To many, Radio Martí has abandoned its standards of objectivity, accuracy, and balance. The station's share of listeners in Cuba fell precipitously, from 70 percent to barely 6 percent, and its programming, according to one journalist, has become so superficial that "Compared to Radio Martí, Radio Mambí [WAQI-AM] is National Public Radio." Critics also claimed that jobs at the radio station now awarded jobs as political patronage (*botella* in Cuban slang).[39] A former aide to unsuccessful mayoral candidate Miguel Díaz de la Portilla mailed a flier to two thousand members of the media and other "opinion makers" accusing Radio Mambí of "biased coverage and conflicts of interest." The missive also charged that the radio station denied equal time to candidates and refused to sell airtime to candidates it does not support—both violations of the Federal Communications Committee.[40]

Few voices of protest arose from the Miami Cuban community which from the beginning always sidestepped attacks on powerful community organizations. By this time, most Miami Cubans who had arrived before 1981 had settled into comfortable or even lavish existences. Many of the overlooked Miami Cuban lower class, the rafters and others, lived better lives than Cubans under Castro. Community pride exulted in the fact that Cuban exiles overall had become the most prosperous group of new arrivals ever to enter the United States. But the price of living in the Miami Cuban enclave was isolation.

One morning in 1997, those Miami Cubans who still read the *Herald*, notwithstanding the frequent virulent attacks against the city's daily newspaper by the Cuban American National Foundation and numerous other organizations and exile personalities, woke up to disturbing news. A national poll had found that Americans gave post-1980 Cuban arrivals a more negative rating than any other group of immigrants. More interesting than the finding itself was the reaction of many Miami Cubans which was a combination elements of disbelief, suspicion, outrage, and wounded pride.[41] The Cubans believed themselves to be model newcomers—indeed, their level of philanthropy was among the highest in South Florida—and the feeling of betrayal, always looming under the surface, became strengthened.[42]

This sense of betrayal only served to further motivate the exile lobby. The CANF, having prevailed over Radio Martí, faced a tougher fight over TV Martí. From the beginning, opponents claimed that the ease of jamming television signals would make the effort worthless, but year after year the CANF mobilized sufficient support to save the agency.[43] It also succeeded in moving the administrative operations to South Florida from Washington, and successfully resisted efforts by some members of Congress to force its governing board to broaden its representation.

In August 1998, Representative David Skaggs (D-CO) proposed cutting funds for TV Martí. Skaggs pointed out that ever since the first telecast in 1990 from a balloon over the Florida Keys, Cuban technicians had successfully jammed TV Martí. As a result, Skaggs said, the United States spent $100 million to telecast to Havana, but no one there had viewed a single program. And, he added, TV Martí required more than forty employees to get one hour on the air, and that program was always jammed. It was, he said, "a waste of taxpayers' money." The Republicans, led by representatives Harold Rogers (R-KY), Ileana Ros-Lehtinen, and Lincoln Díaz-Balart prevailed, blocking the measure to cut off funding. Ros-Lehtinen introduced, into the record, photographs of "children killed by Castro's thugs just a few years ago because they attempted to leave the island." She added:

The Cuban dictatorship realized from the onset that knowledge empowers, and it knew that if it controlled the flow of information, it would be possible to manipulate the Cuban people and forever imprison them in a parallel world created by Castro's lies and twisted propaganda.[44]

INTIMIDATION PAYS

Although the CANF did not disavow acts of intimidation and contributed to the atmosphere of confrontation with its campaign against the *Miami Herald*, it publicly stood above the fray when it came to extremism. It took others to point out this ugly side of Miami's history. Jim Mullin, the editor of *New Times*, the city's alternative newspaper, listed some of the most violent acts committed by some Cuban exiles in Miami, leaving off his list dozens of acts of violence and murder committed by Cuban exiles in other United States cities and at least sixteen foreign countries. "Completeness isn't the point," he wrote. "The point is to face the truth, no matter how difficult that may be. If Miami's Cuban exiles confront this shameful past—and resolutely disavow it—they will go a long way toward easing their neighbors' anxiety about a peaceful future."[45] Miami Cubans, proud of their heritage but not in support of terrorism, termed the *New Times* "Miami's Anglo-supremacist paper."[46] Others complained of "Cuban-bashing," revealing their anger at being tarred by the brush of militant extremism.

Yet none of Mullin's nearly one hundred listed terrorist acts—most carried out before 1980—was denied or refuted by his critics. The first occurred in 1968 when exile pediatrician Orlando Bosch's fired a bazooka at a Polish freighter from Miami's MacArthur Causeway (the City of Miami later created an "Orlando Bosch Day"). In 1972, singer Julio Iglesias, at a local nightclub, remarked that he would not mind performing in Cuba. His audience exploded in anger; the concert was canceled, and most Miami Cuban radio stations blacklisted Iglesias's recordings. The one that did not, *Radio Alegre*, received bomb threats.

Some of the bombings and murders resulted from internecine exile power struggles and may have involved infiltrated Castro agents. But whatever the cause, the steady pace of violence and intimidation widened the gap between Cubans and Anglos in the city. Prejudice and intolerance from Anglos did not, of course, help alleviate tensions. Letters such as this one, from Joseph T. Casavant, appeared in the *Herald*, the *News*, and the old *Miami Beach Sun*:

> There does not seem to be any happy medium with our Cuban population: they are either very nice or most rude. True, the Miami economy in general has benefited by the Cuban influx, but about one million of us Americans in Dade County do not benefit because we are not slum landlords or owners of central Miami's run-down business section real estate. Have any of our politicians who have been playing footsie with the Cubans ever thought of a modified code of behavior for those Cubans who are uneducated, inconsiderate, and arrogant?[47]

The Cuban Spanish-language radio stations continued to stir up anger among listeners. Politicians would speak reasonably to the *Herald* and the English-language media, then turn petulant and accusative over the radio. Spanish-language broadcasters freely called people communists and "fellow travelers," the old McCarthyite smear used against persons considered sympathetic to the far left. According to one listener, Francisco González Aruca, Miami's single leftist Spanish-language radio host who pays for his weekly one-hour show, several days before the book's release, attacked the co-authors of the book *Cuban Miami* as pawns of Miami's "evil industry" (right wing) although clearly he had not read it.[48] On Miami's Radio Mambí, Agustín Tamargo allegedly demanded a "three-day license" after the fall of Castro "to dole out retribution to all of those who stayed in Cuba and supported the regime."[49] Some justified this anger because Castro maintained hundreds of spies in Miami. Others blamed the Cuban government for prodding the fringe militants to commit violent acts, thereby feeding division and intolerance and keeping alive the image of the Miami exile community as dominated by fanatics.[50] This image became prevalent within the American Roman Catholic Church, even though the image was grossly exaggerated. During the Elián González tug of war, Monsignor Brian O. Walsh said that he had received scores of e-mails from priests offering moral support but also telling him that Miami had acquired a reputation for extremism so deep that the city would likely never recover.[51]

As recently as the end of 2000, Radio Mambí continued to boast the highest Arbitron ratings for listeners among AM stations in the Greater

Miami area. Young Miami Cubans tended to say that they listened to the music, not to the political commentary, but older listeners remained influenced by the station. To economist Antonio Jorge, a frequent participant on Spanish-language broadcasts dealing with Cuba, the stations have always played a positive role in "helping to maintain and galvanize the community's unity of purpose in opposing the Castro regime."[52]

Benes wasn't alone in receiving community opprobrium for his advocacy of dialogue with Cuba. In 1984, an African American caller to a local radio talk show—in the words of the *Herald*'s Guillermo Martínez—expressed dismay at the lack of gratitude that Cuban Americans in South Florida showed for the Reverend Jesse Jackson's efforts to release political prisoners from Cuban jails. Twenty-six political prisoners had been freed, and a prominent Cuban dissident was permitted to leave the country. Yet the Reverend Jackson, an outsider to the community, remained ignored.[53]

Even so, the more militant exile groups over the decades have diminished in overall influence. One reason was simply that the United States government, which since 1959 had been subsidizing them at a cost of tens of thousands of dollars a month, in mid-1966 substantially lowered or completely cut off the public subsidies. In the first of a series of weekly articles in the *Herald* called "The Cuban Beat," the columnist Carlos Martínez told the news about the curtailment of the subsidies, but added that some of those laid off received consolation bonuses at the end of their tenure.[54] The "fancy stationery" and "big air-conditioned offices," in his words, had become a thing of the past.

The Cuban Museum of Arts and Culture lost the support of the exiles in 1988 when at a fundraiser its director, Ramón Cernuda, included paintings by Cuban-based artists. After years of threats, bombings, and protests, the museum finally shut down. George Sánchez's art show ten years later honoring the veterans of the Bay of Pigs and featuring a huge pink balloon of a pig (many Bay of Pigs veterans cooperated with and supported the exhibition) was vandalized and completely ruined on its second day by persons presumably opposed to Sánchez's artistic expression of homage.

Armando Pérez-Roura still broadcasts from Radio Mambí that Miami remains on the front line of the war against Castro, whom he calls "this damned assassin . . . this demonic madman."[55] On November 16, 2000, *El Nuevo Herald* published a cover story celebrating Pérez-Roura and his

6.1   George Sánchez's controversial Bay of Pigs Memorial. Robert M. Levine collection.

intense desire to return to a free Cuba. Not one word was written about his fierce support of Batista during the late 1950s, his about-face embrace of the Castro revolution, or his powerful, bullying presence in Miami.[56]

Benes, in contrast, and those Miami Cubans seeking to resolve enmities and open dialogue, received little support. In 1992, a small group headed by Xiomara Almaguer and her husband, Eddy Levy, founded the Cuban American Defense League, in close cooperation with the American Civil Liberties Union (ACLU), to speak out against intimidation and to educate people of their right of free speech under the First Amendment. What spurred the group's creation was the attack by Miami Cubans on President Clinton's appointment of Afro-Cuban Washington attorney Mario Baeza to head the Cuba desk at the State Department. Because Baeza had visited Cuba representing his law firm, the anti-Castro lobby protested so furiously that Baeza withdrew his acceptance. In response, the Defense League held two or three fund raising dinners, honoring Cuban exiles who had been attacked for stating their views, but within a few years its activities ceased. One of the honorees was radio commentator Francisco González Aruca, but Benes wasn't included.[57] (As usual, members of the Cuban Defense League received threats and were called communists and fellow travelers by the right-wing Cuban media.)

After the Cuban community turned on Benes following his missions to Cuba to release political prisoners, Jack Gordon, who became an influential state senator, drew back. Benes found it increasingly difficult to raise money for his causes. Lamentably, many of the scores of people he had helped in the early 1960s turned their back on him after the mainstream Miami Cubans transformed him into a leper. Benes remembers being shunned by persons to whom he had devoted enormous energy and loyalty, one of them was Antonio Jorge. They had first met in early 1959 in Havana at the Treasury Ministry, where Benes was a legal counsel and Jorge the chief economist, one of the most important positions in the reorganized ministry. Jorge, along with many others, had appeared with Pérez-Roura and others at a rally in support after the attack on the presidential palace—but later became an ardent supporter of Castro's revolution after it assumed power. After he saw where it was going, however, Jorge departed for the United States with his large family. When Benes became chairman of the Spanish-Speaking Coalition of the Miami United

6.2   Batista and Pérez Roura at Havana rally celebrating defeat of student-led attack on presidential palace, 1957. Bernardo Benes collection.

Way, he hired Jorge as executive director, its only paid employee. They spent, Benes recalls, fifty to sixty hours a week working together, and became extremely close. When the United Way dissolved the coalition by integrating it into its own organization, Jorge lost his job, and Benes worked to find him a new one. Their close friendship continued until the news of Benes's role in the negotiations with Castro became public information in late 1978.[58] "At that moment," Benes says, "he disappeared from my life." Jorge never called again, not even, as Benes had hoped, to offer help if he needed it should the attacks worsen. Jorge did go on, however, to appear frequently on the radio shows of Armando Pérez-Roura, who Benes calls "the cancer of Miami." Benes also discovered later that Dr. Jorge's name was listed as one of the attendees at a massive rally held in support of Batista in 1957 after the failed attack on the presidential palace by Benes's fellow university students in which several died.[59]

   That Cubans could "celebrate" the death of students for overthrowing a dictator turned some people's stomachs, but Batista's media spokesmen turned the mass demonstration into a rally for conservative values.

6.3   Armando Pérez-Roura in Cuba, standing behind revolutionary Minister of
Labor, during the confiscation of CMQ radio and television, Havana, May 13,
1960. Bernardo Benes collection

Benes remembers Armando Pérez-Roura's past history; Pérez-Roura
is arguably the most influential Cuban radio voice, of all of the broadcasters, who have intimidated most of Miami's Cubans into fearing to
think independently. Pérez-Roura, Benes observes, has for decades been
a remarkable chameleon. He was Batista's official radio announcer in
the late 1950s until Castro's victory, when he abruptly became a passionate supporter of the revolution. He turned again after leaving Cuba,
becoming a self-appointed arbiter of whom in Miami is a communist and
who is not. But while he headed the new Castro government's radio
broadcasters' union, Pérez-Roura lambasted "American imperialism"
and what he called its pernicious influence on Cuban radio. On September 13, 1960, he and communist syndicalists—led by Augusto
Martínez Sánchez, the revolutionary Minister of Labor—invaded and
confiscated the privately owned CMQ, Cuba's leading radio and television voice.[60]

Following the takeover, Pérez-Roura proclaimed: "Cuban broadcasters will repeat again and again the goals of our Revolution: Facing imperialist aggression stands our unbreakable decision to be victorious or die: *PATRIA O MUERTE*."[61] Forty years later, Pérez-Roura, still not a United States citizen, twice rode with presidential candidate George W. Bush in his limousine in Miami.[62]

Confused and depressed by Miami Cubans' mean-spirited acceptance of the intimidating tactics of the Spanish radio and press, Benes became exhausted emotionally as well as physically. Throughout the 1980s and 1990s, he tried to rekindle old contacts, often unsuccessfully. Unlike many Cubans who had come to the United States before 1961, Benes never fully learned the conventions of American manners, although he is an extremely intelligent man. In an interview about Representative Dante Fascell's role in helping involve Cyrus Vance in the plans for the 1978 mission, he said, in print, "without the cooperation of that little Italian congressman, I would not have been able to have brought the first group of political prisoners."[63] Benes considered his remark a gesture of friendship, not realizing that it might be taken as patronizing.

By the mid-1990s, Benes spent long hours writing personal letters to the public figures for whom he had worked secretly. Dascal had put the missions behind him, but Benes, still humiliated by the lingering atmosphere of animosity toward him, wrote in search of solace. To former President Carter, he wrote:

> One of my dreams for this summer is to be able to have lunch with you in Atlanta. The purpose is simple. I was a supporter of yours from the time you were Jimmy who? I was Hispanic chairman for Florida. When you were president I devoted quite a few years to work for human rights in Cuba, and with your support we succeeded.[64]

Many of the individuals Benes had named to participate in the dialogue with Castro were outsiders like him—the owner of a cigar factory, a motel-keeper, and other businessmen—who added to the "suspicious and cynical attitude" of the Miami anti-Castroites, according to Margarita Esquiroz, a Florida Assistant Attorney General (and today a judge) quoted in the *New York Times*.[65]

In the aftermath of the dialogue, Benes had lost many of his old protectors and found few new ones. He drew up lists of people he might call upon as references in case some new opportunity came up, but these were people from his past. On an undated typewritten sheet compiled during the Carter years, Benes listed the following as "references": Cyrus Vance, Peter Tarnoff, Director Webster of the FBI, Senators Kennedy, Metzenbaum, and Chiles, Governor Bob Graham of Florida, as well as present and former heads of state from Costa Rica, Israel, Paraguay, Venezuela, Panama, and Peru, and many powerful business leaders and professionals.[66]

While some of Benes's community projects succeeded, others did not. The former director of the Greater Miami United Way, United Way International, and CEO of the United Way of America from 1970 to 1992—William Aramory—described the volunteer work Benes did for United Way in the 1960s and 1970s:

> The arrival of the Cuban exiles was near overwhelming to the facilities that were already taxed. The then established "white" community and the African American community were struggling with existing social problems. The Cuban arrival added enormous tensions to an already tense relationship. . . . Benes was a brilliant motivator, at his best in expressing ideas that people can comprehend. The incredible divide between the rich and others in Latin America provided the basis for establishing the mechanism of "common ground." . . . When I read about the attacks on Bernardo for being a "communist," it was just unbelievable. Here is a man who spent days convincing me that the only way to prevent communism and to defeat it was to build community infrastructure which engaged community leaders. He also convinced me that the voluntarism history of the United States could in fact be transferred to other cultures.[67]

During the early 1990s, Benes faced bleak prospects. He was nearly bankrupt, and the defamation he endured for over a decade had worn him out and instigated bouts of depression. His high sensitivity—the result of his intensity and commitment to social injustice—made it virtually impossible for him to listen to criticism and walk away from it.

Miami Beach Rabbi Sholom Lipskar believes that Benes has an "extraordinary righteous compass for social justice, and is always willing to put himself on the line to defend his cause. Because he is a driven person, however, his quests often produce deep angst. Sometimes this produces in him great creativity but other times brings him great consternation."[68]

Benes's role of dialogue-seeker was held against him during the 1960s when he worked unrelentingly to bring Cubans into American institutions, and in the late 1970s when the news of his negotiations with Castro emerged. Some in Miami resented Benes's ecumenism—his efforts to work with African Americans; to help Mexican migrant workers; his friendships with Roman Catholic leaders, especially Monsignor Walsh. In the tunnel vision of his opponents, who were perfectly content to live in their own enclave, this was annoying at best and traitorous at worst. Certainly, this accusation was not limited to Benes, and others experienced it as well. The 140 Cubans who had participated in meetings in November and December 1978 to discuss reconciliation were subject to varying degrees of harassment, even having bombs thrown at their homes and businesses. The careers of others languished on their return, and two key participants were murdered shortly after the dialogue. Exile terrorist groups claimed responsibility for the killings and, seemingly, the Anglo community yawned.[69]

Benes took on FIU president Charles E. Perry in 1963. Perry bristled with anger when Benes accused his institution of not hiring sufficient numbers of Hispanics (read: Cubans), and resented his demand that the contract of visiting economics professor Antonio Jorge be renewed. Accused of interfering in academic affairs, Benes replied that he lived by his conscience, quoting Andrew Jackson's "One brave man makes a majority."[70]

After his fall from grace in the late 1970s, although militants in Miami despised Benes, many dissidents in Cuba respected him. In September 1988, Ramon Cernuda, the Miami spokesman for the Cuban dissident association *Comisión de Derechos Humanos y Reconciliación Nacional*, headed by Elizardo Sánchez Santa Cruz, asked for a favor. Could Benes arrange for a meeting between Elizardo, who was briefly in Miami, and Senator Edward M. Kennedy? Within days, Senator Kennedy agreed, and spent an hour in his Washington office bombarding Elizardo with questions about labor unions, the condition of dissidents in Cuba, political prisoners, communication with international human rights organizations, the Cuban constitution, and other matters. Benes learned later that the photograph taken at the meeting with Senator Kennedy hangs in a prominent place in Elizardo's home in Havana.[71]

Even during his banishment from Miami Cuban affairs and the continuing campaign to deny him employment, journalists and broadcasters approached Benes for comments on events. In early 1993, for example, the *Herald* ran a story about Orestes Lorenzo Pérez, the Cuban air force pilot who landed his 1961 Cessna on a Cuban highway and rescued his family. Lorenzo became an instant celebrity, appearing on television with Larry King, Jay Leno, and various CNN reporters; he was named grand marshal of a parade at Disney World, riding with his wife and children on a fire truck. "Only in America," the *Herald* reporter said. Bernardo Benes's quoted comments typified his decades-long approach to the exile issue. "This one has hit the heart of America," he said. "The important thing is, it was not a political act. It was a very personal decision by a father to reunite with his children and wife."[72] In 1993, few readers of the *Herald* had any way of appreciating the irony of his statement about reuniting families in the light of the Elián Gonzalez saga seven years later.

ISOLATION

Over the years, Miami's Cuban residents remained so nostalgic and loyal to the country they had left that they never developed the capacity to embrace all Spanish-speaking Miamians in a multicultural political coalition. Many Miami Cubans, speaking in the name of their communities used the word "Hispanic" for the names given to their programs and organizations, but in reality the term represented an anodyne half-truth: in most cases, it meant Cubans. One may speculate that if Miami Cubans in the 1980s had reached out to the growing numbers of Colombians, Nicaraguans, Haitians, Peruvians, Brazilians, and other arrivals from the rest of the hemisphere, they might not have been seen by Anglos as a self-centered, single-issue, and privileged entity.

Miami by the mid-1980s had become the economic epicenter of Latin America. Corporations and businesses relocated to Miami from Latin America because conditions were more stable. Inflation had been brought under control, and a seemingly unlimited labor pool of Spanish speakers was available. Telecommunications and, later, dot.com firms came to Miami because they needed a reliable supply of electric power, immediate access to new technology, and institutions from which they could gain

credit and financing. The Cuban Miamians benefited from some of this—
especially the younger Cuban Americans who had become successful professionals—but most of the Latin American firms moving their
headquarters to Miami or Coral Gables retained their Mexican, Brazilian,
or Chilean identity. Some of the Spanish-language radio stations, entirely
Cuban for decades, were sold to business interests from other Latin American countries. Miami Cubans' psychological need to limit participation in
their businesses to family and close friends hindered expansion beyond
Greater Miami. Individual Cuban Americans, however, by the 1990s
began to leave their family's nests and—law or business degrees in
hand—take jobs elsewhere. The majority, though, stayed home.

Changing migration patterns, however, altered the character of the enclave. Cubans who arrived during the Mariel boatlift and after were rarely
professionals; more often they entered the United States labor market
with low-grade skills. Migration to South Florida from the rest of the
hemisphere at first included mostly lower-class Puerto Ricans, Haitian
boat people, and Mexican migrant farm laborers, but in the 1990s this
changed as lawyers, manufacturers, and businessmen began to arrive in
Miami, fleeing from political instability (Peru, Colombia, Venezuela) or
from economic decline (Argentina). These new immigrants, as well-edu-
cated as the Cubans who arrived between 1959 and 1961, may well challenge the local Cubans, especially if they form alliances with individuals
like themselves from other Latin American countries.

During the early 1990s, small groups began to emerge within Cuban
Miami representing views not in line with local political correctness. In
1992, moderates from the professional and academic arenas founded the
Cuban Committee for Democracy, headed today by Executive Director
Elena Freyre. The committee opposes the embargo and claims as its goal
the reconciliation of all Cubans regardless of where they reside; for the
most part, it has been left unbothered. But when a Cuban American political science professor at Florida International University, Dario
Moreno, a registered member of the Republican Party, gave an interview
in which he disparaged the city of Miami and the passionate intolerance
of Cubans, he received threats and outbursts of ire.

In late 1994, the Clinton administration refused to accept Cubans
fleeing their island, even during a brief period of time when Castro said

they could leave. Officials feared another Mariel: defending the administration's position, Attorney General Janet Reno referred to the rafters as "illegal migrants," setting the stage for their incarceration. Those who made it to the United States were returned as illegal aliens to Guantánamo Naval Base in southern Cuba, where they spent up to eighteen months under miserable conditions.[73] Some 50,000 Haitians and Cubans were already on the base; plans made to send them to larger camps in Honduras failed when the Honduran government balked.

When approximately 7,000 internees were flown from Guantánamo to the Panama Canal Zone, the terrible conditions in the new camps precipitated protests and ultimately riots in which one camp was burned down by its inmates. The internees were separated into several camps, some with only men. Rumors about being returned to Cuba spread wildly, adding to the tension and sense of helplessness. Researcher Elizabeth Campisi retells the events, based on extensive interviews with internees and others who had been present:

> After some time, a riot started in Camp One, which led to the fires. The internees were then dispersed to other camps, stripped and in flexicuffs. At Camp Two, where most of the rioters went, soldiers beat them and knocked down their tents. At dawn the next day, United States soldiers in camouflage gear and face paint dropped to the ground from helicopters. They beat people severely: many suffered broken arms, legs, or hips. Camp Two housed families, so children watched the punishments being carried out. Pregnant women were beaten as well. A group of women who were at the back of the camp were stripped and paraded around naked. In a show of spontaneous solidarity, internees kept their eyes down, while many people threw shirts at them, trying to cover them up. After being led through the camp, they were forced into the cafeteria, where the soldiers sat them down in front of breakfast trays. Later, many of the men were cuffed and dragged in their underwear to the camp jail, which was called Campo Loco. My interviewee's hands were purple before they let him out of the cuffs. The internees were held in Campo Loco without being allowed to bathe or shave for 2 weeks—in camps that were in the middle of the jungle. After this horrible abuse, none of the American military would talk to the Cubans. . . . Eventually the group was returned to Guantánamo but no one complained, because they were afraid that if they did, they would be sent back to Cuba.[74]

What some of the Guantánamo refugees said after finally gaining entry to the United States is telling: "I received worse treatment in Miami," psychologist Lidia González Prado confessed, "from Cubans than from Americans. Most people in Cuba thought America would be a paradise, that you would not have to work hard. I worked like a slave when I got here. Two things surprised me most about the U.S. In Cuba, I thought that we Cubans were the most highly stressed people in the world. I was wrong. The atmosphere is more stressful here. You are on your own, and you can only survive and improve yourself with very hard work. The second thing was that when I arrived I thought that people were made of stone, or of ice. Everyone was like this."[75]

From the first, Bernardo Benes threw himself into protesting the decision to send all new refugees to Guantánamo. He faxed urgent messages to Peter Tarnoff at the State Department and to Attorney General Janet Reno: "This is *insane*," he wrote Reno:

> I am willing to go to see F[idel] C [Castro] privately to look for a *real* solution. Peter Tarnoff, my very good friend, doesn't answer my phone calls (?). He knows me *well*. I was the first Cuban American supporter of President Clinton. I'd like to see Lawton [Chiles] re-elected but not at the price we are paying.

As far as the Miami Cuban militants are concerned, he wrote in a second fax, "they [represent] an industry that uses anti-Castro rhetoric for personal gain." He added a P.S.: "As you know, the militant Cubans in Miami have been using verbal terrorism for the last 35 years. Make your decisions based on what is in the best interests of the United States." Reno never responded.[76]

Benes's ire, however, had no impact on the Clinton administration's refugee policy. Marines guarded detainees in Guantánamo for up to a year and a half before permitting some but not all to enter the United States. Benes attempted everything he could, on one occasion sending a translated copy of a statement made by Cuba's new Roman Catholic cardinal, Jaime Ortega, who was about to visit Miami in late May 1995. "It would be very interesting to see the reaction of the protesters in Miami, the majority of whom are Catholics."[77] Benes also resigned from the Atlantic Council, a Washington-based organization sponsoring a "U. S. Relations with Cuba Working Group" because he learned that the group's report had been modified after receiving pressure from those he called "Right Wing Cuban Americans." He began to tell people that Miami was a crazy place, weakly caving in to intimidation. No longer daunted by the threats made against him years before, Benes became increasingly bold in his statements. Benes remained moderate on the Cuban issue, and less friendly to the regime than others—like his old friend, journalist Max Lesnik, who by the late 1990s had become so pro-Castro that he frequently wrote for Havana's afternoon newspaper, *Juventude Rebelde*.

Benes's reappearance in the news commenting on Clinton's new immigration policy led to renewed attacks on him as vicious as in 1978, seventeen years earlier. Never one to duck an opportunity to defend himself, Benes agreed to be interviewed live by Tomás García Fusté. He might as well have been speaking into a dead microphone. Fernando del Castillo, reviewing the interview a few days later in the Miami Cuban tabloid *La Verdad*, called Benes's statements "cheap words to assert that he is neither a communist or socialist." He quoted Benes as saying, "If I were a communist, I would hold a ministerial post in Cuba. It is not easy to be exiled and love one's country." And, del Castillo concluded, "if any doubts linger about Benes, the relentless *dialoguero*, consider his venomous final statement: Murdering Fidel is an impractical goal; it is a chimera."[78] In 1995, political correctness in Cuban Miami required, for the exile media, agreement that Castro merited assassination.

One of the major crises affecting the Cuban exile community in Miami occurred on February 24, 1996, when Cuban MiGs shot down two Cessnas flown by members of Brothers to the Rescue. This organization, founded in 1991 by José Basulto, a veteran of the School of the Americas, the Bay of Pigs invasion, and the CIA's war against the Nicaraguan contras, flew small planes based at the Opa-locka airport over the Florida Straits to rescue rafters (and sometimes dropped leaflets over Cuba). Despite thirteen protests filed by Cuban officials between May 1995 and February 1996, Brothers to the Rescue continued to fly, often diverging from their flight plans, a violation of the rules of the Federal Aviation Agency, in order to enter Cuban airspace. Testimony at a trial of accused Cuban spies later revealed that the FBI had intercepted clandestine radio communications between agents in Cuba and in South Florida "forecasting a potentially violent confrontation between Cuba and Brothers to the Rescue" more than a week before the shoot-downs, but the FBI kept the information to itself. Relations between the FBI and Basulto had been soured by his group's frequent diversions from their flight plans in order to drop leaflets over Havana, an action that likely precipitated Havana's anti-Brothers to the Rescue "Operation Scorpion," also referred to as Operation *Picada* "bite," fomenting acts of violence to be blamed on the Miami exile fliers.[79]

Two years later, in early 1998, declaring that helping the Cuban people would put additional pressure on the Castro government, President Bill Clinton ordered approval of increased humanitarian aid to Cuba and a reversal of a two-year-old ban on direct flights to Cuba. The exile community divided sharply over the issue. A resident of Little Havana was quoted as saying "I don't think the [Cuban] people themselves will ever see [the aid]." Miami's Representative Ros-Lehtinen declared in an interview that "for all practical purposes, there is no embargo against Cuba, and the United States should be tougher on Castro. . . . The people of Cuba are hungry," she said, "but they are hungry for democracy and freedom, and we wish that President Clinton would be a little tougher with the dictator instead of trying to normalize relations."[80] Other Miami Cubans argued that not to send food and medicine would be cruel, and that ending the embargo would remove one of Castro's main excuses for holding onto power. When Bernardo Benes emerged as a member of the Clinton election committee in Miami, disdain for him among the mostly hardline Miami Cuban community increased, although Clinton advocated as hard a line against Castro as did the Republicans. By this time, two out of every three Miami Cubans had registered in the Republican Party, so Benes's support of Clinton provided one more reason for him to be considered an outsider in the exile community.

During Clinton's campaign for a second term, Benes received an invitation to a reception at the Biltmore Hotel in Coral Gables where the president was staying. From there, Bernardo drove to the Versailles restaurant on Calle Ocho where he found Manolo Reboso—the first Cuban elected to public office in Miami—sitting with the parents of Alex Penelas, the mayor of Miami-Dade County. As soon as Benes joined them, they told him, "President Clinton is on his way here with a group of Cubans." Although Benes and Reboso had not been invited, the president walked over to greet them. Reboso whispered: "Bernardo, why don't you tell the joke I just told you—you are better at it." So when Clinton shook hands with them, Benes asked him if he would like to hear a Cuban joke. Clinton said yes:

> One day in Havana a man started to paint on the side of a building, but no sooner than he wrote, "Down with F," security police grabbed him and dragged him to their headquarters. Under interrogation, he was asked why he had dared to insult Fidel Castro. "No I didn't," the man said. "I was going to write 'Down with Flinton.'"

The president roared with laughter.

CHAPTER SEVEN

ELIÁN ELECTS A PRESIDENT

Arguably, the turning point for Cuban Miami was the Thanksgiving Day 1999 arrival of Elián González. Two men fishing off the coast of Fort Lauderdale spotted an inner tube holding a small boy, still alive, reportedly surrounded by dolphins. The boy was taken to a hospital and found to be five years old; his mother and a dozen others on their overcrowded seventeen-foot powerboat had drowned when the craft capsized, but they managed to lash Elián to a tube so that he might be rescued.

The events provoked an emotional crisis and ultimately a scenario by which Elián's relatives in Miami—the closest being a great-uncle—sought to keep the boy despite Cuban protests to return him to his father on the island. Hundreds of sympathizers kept vigil at the relative's small house in Little Havana, forming prayer circles, damning Attorney General Janet Reno for having declared that the family courts should rule on the case, and that there were no grounds for having others seek asylum in Elián's name. They also protested the government's refusal to permit Elián himself to appear at hearings.

Cuban Americans divided vociferously over the issue. According to the *New Republic*, Brothers to the Rescue's José Basulto at first "thought the boy should probably go back to his father in Cuba." But when Castro began demanding Elián's return, Basulto immediately changed his mind. Returning the boy would mean returning him to *el tirano*. As he reflected further about Elián's survival at sea, he told reporter Charles

Lane, he realized that only with God's help could Elián have been saved. The boy had been protected "as if he were one of heaven's own angels."[1]

Benes's own views were featured prominently in a probing article by Jim DeFede in Miami's weekly *New Times*. As he frequently did, Bernardo took an opposing stand:

> "This [Anglo] community opened its arms to Cubans," he says. Now Cubans are talking about shutting down the airport and the seaport, blocking traffic on causeways, and reviling Attorney General Janet Reno as a communist and a traitor. "Any gains made in bridging the gap between Cubans and non-Cubans," Benes says, "have been destroyed: What we have done in forty years has gone to hell in four months."
>
> [. . .]
>
> Benes believes the real tragedy of this event is that the Cuban American community is in fact making Castro stronger, not weaker. "Fidel Castro is laughing at all of this," he says. "Castro would like nothing better than to have Elián stay in the United States, because as long as the boy is in Miami, he has something to rail about and a rallying point for his countrymen. As long as the world's attention is focused on Elián and not on the repression of political dissidents in Cuba, Castro is thrilled." "Amazingly," Benes says, "this debacle over Elián has placed Castro in the role of being 'the great unifier of families' when the truth is he has always been a great destroyer of them. Elián is a tool for Castro and he is a tool for segments of the exile community. Both are using him to amass and maintain power within their respective constituencies. Yet few Cuban Americans are willing to publicly condemn the way politicians such as [Alex] Penelas and [Joe] Carollo exploit the fears and pain of their own people. It sickens me to see the old women, day after day, lining the barricades near Elián's Little Havana home, rosaries in hand, praying for a miracle. Their value to the politicians is that they vote; their weakness is that they are terrified at the prospect of dying in the United States and being buried in a cemetery on Flagler Street rather than in the towns where they were born."[2]

Meanwhile, anonymous donors gave the family a car, trips to Disney World, and a lavish assortment of toys and clothes for the bewildered boy. He was sent to a local Lincoln-Martí private school, one of a chain owned by a Demetrio Pérez, Jr., a hardline anti-Castroite and member of the Miami-Dade County school board. Because reporters and photographers hounded his every move, the boy had to be removed from school and kept at his great-uncle's home.

Attorney General Reno's decision to have the Immigration and Naturalization Service storm the house at 4:00 A.M. on Holy Saturday, April 22, proved traumatic for most Miami's Cubans—although around the country most of those polled agreed that he should be sent back to his father, who had come to the United States with his family and who, after initial negotiations to get them together in Miami failed, had settled into a house in Washington, D.C., to wait out the appeal process. In the meantime, Miami's already dubious national reputation diminished even further. The city's mayor Joe Corollo used municipal funds to fly to Washington to lobby Elián's case, and to protest the action of the federal government. Few within the Miami Cuban community publicly criticized Corollo, however, because they supported his role in the emotional Elián saga.

Hialeah's powerful mayor, Raúl Martínez, attacked the role of the federal government. Miami-Dade County Mayor Alex Penelas, considered a coming political star because of his moderate views and his articulateness (and chosen, a year earlier, as the "sexiest politician" in the country by the editors of *People* magazine), stunned Miami and the nation by vowing that if the INS dared to try and take Elián, he would order county police not to lend assistance.

Some younger Cuban Americans—self-described as Generation Ñ— had argued that the issue should be settled in family court. Older Cubans and others passionately hoped that the boy be permitted to remain, because his mother and stepfather had died attempting to bring him to freedom. Others, defenders of Elián's right to stay, noted the difference between law and justice, pointing out that the boy should not be sent back to Castro because in Cuba there are no parental rights at all.

Media coverage quickly became a feeding frenzy, with hundreds of photographers and reporters from all over the world camped across the street day and night. Their presence encouraged demonstrations, led by community leaders who besieged the crowds to defend Elián at all costs. A large exile crowd roughed up a radio talk show host from Portland, Oregon, who displayed a T-shirt stating "Send the Boy Home," before the police were able to intervene.

The Cuban radio stations never stopped covering the story. One emotionally distraught woman holding vigil in front of Elián's house said, on the air, that she was praying to God to punish Janet Reno by worsening the attorney general's Parkinson's disease. Local politician Javier Soto was urged by Salvador Lew, on the air, to present a bill to the county commission declaring Reno persona non grata in Miami, where she was born and raised.

A week later, ABC-TV's Ted Koppel came to Miami and broadcast live a town meeting, with the mayor sitting in the front row, and a young man in the audience declared, "Mr. Mayor . . . I want you to know that you left a lot of us incredibly disenfranchised from the community. And it is going to be very, very difficult to ever forgive you for that." The audience applauded energetically. Koppel asked the mayor if he would like to respond, but Penelas sat mute. Koppel asked a second time but Penelas just stared. "If not, we're going to take a break," he said, and when Peneles still did not respond, he ordered a commercial. Analysts later speculated that the mayor was so frightened of offending his political base that he could not get himself to say on television that he regretted what he had said about not permitting Miami police to cooperate with federal agents.[3]

This and other episodes involving statements by Miami elected officials outraged many in South Florida and beyond who wondered out loud how different the Miami Cubans were from their Castroite enemies regarding the use of intimidation and threats to disobey the law. The visual shock of the raid—exemplified by the photograph of a combat-outfitted government agent pointing his weapon at Elián and others, and of the boy being hustled away—enraged Miami Cubans. They saw the raid as a victory for Castro and further proof of their isolation, in the words of one reporter, "that the world is against them."[4] Many exiles agreed. Juan Pérez-Franco, president of Brigade 2506, the Bay of Pigs veterans' organization, remarked to the press, "From the onset, this has been a blackmail. Castro is playing a good card. He had threatened the United States if the boy was not returned within [seventy-two] hours."[5]

Cuban-born Harvard political science professor Jorge Domínguez argued that Castro could not have done a better job messing up the Elián case and using it for his own ends as did the Miami Cubans.[6] Castro, who previously had labeled every fleeing Cuban as a traitor and a *gusano*, suddenly made the boy into a hero and had hundreds of thousands of Cuban schoolchildren rally in mass support of the little boy, who turned six years old shortly after his miraculous rescue. The Elián González tragedy released years of stored up anger in a diversity of Miami Cubans, especially those who worked hard to suppress their bitterness toward Castro and to adjust to life in their new country. One Miami Cuban woman in her fifties confided:

> For years I put the past behind me. But now I feel rage at my [Anglo] neighbors, who want to send back that poor little boy to a life under communism. How can they talk of a father's rights when parents have no rights in Cuba? Before, I would forget the little slights at my accent, or that I always dressed more elegantly than my office colleagues, or the remarks I heard about the "pushy" Cubans. Now they are coming back to me in a rush, and I cry not only for Elián but also for myself.[7]

Members of the older generation of Miami Cubans painfully recalled their personal traumas: separation from their relatives, and the sudden loss of their homes and possessions. Elián himself embodied that reality, for he, too, was an innocent victim. Many felt confused: their leaders controlled much of Dade County; they had had the support of the Clinton administration and Congress, but the agony provoked by reuniting Elián with his father—and the publication of a photograph showing Elián in Washington wearing a Young Pioneer uniform—reopened wounds that had never entirely healed. These suppressed pockets of pain and memory may explain the persistence of the insider-outsider division within Miami Cuban society. Rejecting "outsiders" provides some measure of retribution, if not release.

Curiously, Jorge Mas Santos, the son of the late CANF chairman, "tried to broker an accord with Washington that would have allowed the boy to rejoin his father peacefully," but when the conflict intensified, Mas Santos retreated.[8] Earlier, during Pope John Paul II's visit to Cuba, the CANF leadership had suggested that surplus food from the United States be distributed to hungry Cubans, but its own members forced the idea to be dropped. The CANF and the Round Table, an association of Miami Hispanics, mostly Cubans, also successfully pressured the Archdiocese of Miami to cancel its plans for chartering a ship to take hundreds of devout Catholics in Miami to see the pope during his visit to Havana.

Among the thousands of Miami Cubans who filed by Elián's house before and after his seizure by federal agents, many felt there was a spiritual dimension to the saga. Tom Blackburn, writing in the *National Catholic Reporter*, observed that Miami Cuban Catholicism diverges from the form encouraged in Rome because miracles and miraculous interpretations are emphasized. That the boy survived the doomed voyage that killed his mother and six others "was, in secular metaphor, a miracle. Miami Cubans see it as a nonmetaphorical miracle." He added:

> It had a biblical echo of Moses among the bulrushes. To the basic story, dolphins were added to keep his inner tube afloat and sharks away. The boy, the dolphins and the Blessed Mother can be seen in a 15-foot mural quickly painted in the modest neighborhood where Elián's distant uncle lived. Elián González, 6, became "the miracle boy."[9]

Not soon after Elián arrived in the Little Havana home of his great-uncle, some of the neighbors whispered that Elián had been sent to Miami from heaven as a marvelous angel—a boy who would lead his flock against the hated *El Comandante* and repatriate the exiles to their homeland. On Saturday, March 25, 2000, crowds gathered around the front window of the Totalbank on Northwest Twenty-seventh Avenue, a few blocks from Elián's house, to view a cloud-like apparition of the Virgin Mary that was said to have appeared. So many people came that traffic halted in front of the bank. According to the *Herald*, "bank employees first spotted the luminous reflection—capped by an iridescent mixture of gold, purple and green. As word of the vision spread, and the colors failed to fade with repeated cleanings," the bank entrance became a shrine.

The *Herald* article, topped by a crude headline, "The Branch Miamians At It Again," continued: "Visitors ranged from the curious to the deeply religious. Some came in their sport-utility vehicles, waving the Cuban flag and carrying their camcorders. Some people rubbed their babies against the windowpane for good luck. Others scrubbed the surface with paper towels to see if they could make the image go away." Other bystanders scoffed: "It looks like what happens when you apply Windex and then get a rainbow pattern," Eulalia Ascencio, 29, commented. "I really think it is a reflection of the light." Some took the apparition as a sign that they should keep vigil outside of Elián's house. They camped outside the boy's home and said they were on a state of "high alert" awaiting word from exile leaders on when to mobilize a civil disobedience campaign in

Miami. "We are praying," one of the vigil keepers confided, "so that the heart of Señorita [Janet] Reno will become sweeter and she will see that Elián is a poor boy who cannot go back to Cuba."[10]

In early November 2000, Delfín Fernández, another of Elián's great-uncles who is a lobster fisherman in the Florida Keys, revealed that he had purchased the two-bedroom white stucco house on Northwest Second Street in which Elián and his American relatives had lived, to be converted into a permanent shrine, a haven for Elián's memory. After four months of remaining vacant—since the fateful April 22, 2000, Justice Department raid—the house was being converted into a shrine. A life-sized statue of Elián was planned for the front yard and tours would be conducted so that the public could see the room from which the boy was taken. Fernández told the media that he hoped that community members would assist him with his monthly mortgage payments.[11]

ELIÁN ELECTS A PRESIDENT

The official results of the bizarre 2000 presidential election, whose balance hung for weeks while lawyers and politicians jousted over recounts and validations in the State of Florida, delivered the election to George W. Bush by fewer than 300 votes out of 6 million cast in the state. The Cuban American community's perception of the Elián Gonzalez incident as a heinous federal government act generated so much anger that it put the Republican candidate over the top: at least half of the Miami Cubans who voted for Clinton in 1992 and 1996 voted for Bush in 2000. Andrés Oppenheimer, the Herald's respected specialist on inter-American affairs, observed that 82 percent of the 280,000 votes cast by Miami Cubans on November 7, 2000, went to the Republican candidate.[12] Even while the stalemated election's Florida ballots were still being counted, the Miami González family denounced the pro bono lawyer and former United States Attorney for Florida, Kendall Coffey, for the sin of representing the Gore campaign in the post-election legal contest. Political broker Armando Gutiérrez, the family's voluntary spokesman, accused Coffey of having been deceived by the Clinton-Gore administration.[13] Not only did they attack Coffey, but they also canceled a scheduled ceremony to honor the lawyers who had worked with him.

When Elián and his father returned home to Cuba in June, Benes looked back and saw that within the outpouring of emotion over Elián, there was the surfacing of painful frustrations that Miami Cubans, himself included, had endured for forty-one years. The lack of a "solution" to the Castro problem, and *El Comandante*'s uncanny ability to stay in power despite economic hardship, fuel this frustration. For those Miami Cubans separated from their relatives or who have lost loved ones, hatred of Castro never abated. This, in turn, has been exploited by politicians and by the Cuban Miami media to keep Cuban Miami a one-issue community and to decide what it should and should not be told.[14] On November 3, 2000, the *Miami Herald* (and probably hundreds of other newspapers around the United States) ran stories on candidate George W. Bush's DUI (driving under the influence of alcohol) conviction in Maine, revealed a week before the 2000 election. *El Nuevo Herald*, however, published not a single word about it until the next day, when a small item appeared on an inside page.[15]

Elsewhere in the United States, opinions about Elián González took a very different direction from those espoused by the majority of Miami Cubans. For the most part, non-Cuban Americans sympathized with the boy's father, not his distant Miami relatives. Staunch Republicans were torn between their opposition to the Castro regime and their oft-pronounced respect for parental rights and the integrity of the family. The aftermath of Elián's return, in fact, witnessed a sudden reversal of political positions. On July 21, two conservative Republican congressmen, Mark Sanford (R-SC) and Jerry Moran (R-KS) offered amendments designed to loosen the embargo on Cuban trade that had been in place for decades. In a passionate speech on the House floor arguing for opening doors to Cuba, Sanford argued that President Ronald Reagan's decision to let American students travel to Eastern Europe helped bring down the Berlin Wall. The way to increase contact between Cubans and Americans, Stanford said, would be by withholding allocations to federal agencies entrusted with enforcing the travel ban. This, however, was not to be.

The trade measure passed in the House of Representatives by 232 to 186 in favor of a liberalized travel provision and 301 to 116 supporting food and medicine sales. The Senate concurred on October 18, 2000. The debate over the bill yielded caustic reflections on the pressures from the Miami Cubans. "You're talking about seven percent of the electorate in [Florida]," said pro-trade Senator Pat Roberts (R-KS).[16] Pressed to explain their vote in the light of Cuban human-rights abuses, supporters of the bill countered by recalling that China had at least taken steps to liberalize its economy. But nothing was said at all about human rights and the right to dissent, ugly stains on the records of both Cuba and China.

The vote handed a victory of sorts to the coalition of farming interests, business groups, and Democrats trying to lift American sanctions, but also to the Miami Cuban lobby, which weakened the bill by barring grants of government or private credit to the Cubans to permit them to buy from the United States, and by making travel to Cuba more difficult.

The Cuban government reacted as it usually did in such circumstances. An estimated eight hundred thousand people—40 percent of Havana's population—marched down the Malecón coastal highway in protest of the bill, explained by the Cuban media as "a gross lie that the genocidal blockade has been softened." Fidel Castro walked in front, dressed in his usual olive fatigues but with white athletic shoes instead of boots, and holding a small Cuban flag in his hand. Some of the marchers held portraits of Abraham Lincoln, presumably selected to catch the attention of the foreign television cameras recording the protest.[17]

The lead story in the Communist Party's *Granma*—believed by some to have been written personally by Castro—bitterly denounced the effort of the United States Congress and the Clinton administration:

> Chaos reigns in U.S. politics. Our people have just witnessed how the Miami Cuban American terrorist mafia and the extreme right wing politicians occupying key congressional posts are capable of using the U.S. government and its Congress as instruments of their policies. That was already evident in the absurd sequence of events that surrounded the kidnapping of Cuban child Elián Gonzalez. . . . Now they want to recover their lost ground at any price. Their every pore exudes their hatred and their craving for revenge against our people. A long history of complicity and aggression on the part of successive administrations and a profusion of laws and legislation enacted over the past 40 years have made things easy for them and given them encouragement in their actions against Cuba.[18]

Among Miami Cubans, novel and, in some cases, inexplicably contradictory, opinions began to surface. A survey of 1,975 Miami residents conducted by researchers at Florida International University released on October 19, 2000, revealed that while 82 percent of Miami Cubans agreed that the community's reaction to the Elián Gonzalez affair had portrayed it in a negative light, 93.5 percent would do the same thing again. Seventy-three percent considered the embargo a failure, but 62 percent would maintain it. Although only 15 percent of Miami Cubans told pollsters that they intended to vote for Al Gore for president—no real surprise since only 17.2 percent of Miami Cubans holding citizenship were registered Democrats—a small majority (54.7 percent) favored permitting Cuban artists and musicians to perform in Miami, and 52 percent disagreed with the recently repealed county ordinance preventing the use of municipal funds for events with Cubans in attendance. Only 18.3 percent agreed with the statement that Miami possesses the characteristics of a "banana republic," referring to the city's constant stream of indictments of elected officials, while 43.7 percent of Anglos polled agreed. But while only 35.5 percent of those polled in 1991 had favored dialogue with the Cuban government, in 2000 the number rose to 51.8 percent, a startling figure considering Benes's twenty-two years of vilification for having done precisely that.[19]

The poll results punctured some myths, although some of its apparent paradoxes may not, in fact, have been contradictory. That a majority of Miami Cubans agreed that the embargo had not worked, and a larger majority stated their preference for it to be continued, represented not so much as illogic, as a principled and conscious decision to continue the community's united anti-Castro stand.

While the poll results showed growing signs of political liberalization among its Cuban American respondents, little changed in the actual numbers of followers of right-wing politicians. The 1980s had witnessed an astonishing political shift in Dade County, formerly a safe Democratic Party stronghold, to strong support for conservatives. In 1960, Miami and Miami Beach voters had favored the politics of Eleanor Roosevelt and Claude Pepper. Democrats represented 86 percent of the registered voters in Dade County; Republicans only 14 percent. By 1972, the Democratic percentage had slipped badly—Miami Cubans enthusiastically supported Richard Nixon, whose close friendship with Key Biscayne financier Bebe Rebozo was well known. On August 6, 2000, only 9.6 percent of Hispanics in Miami-Dade County registered as Democrats, half of them Miami Cubans.[20] In 2000, the Elián Gonzalez affair closed ranks within the city's Cuban community even more tightly than before. "I have never seen a community behave in such a monolithic fashion as it did around Elián," pollster Guillermo Grenier told the press.[21]

Many reasons contributed to the move to the right pole of the political spectrum. Exile politicians pounded the view home that one was either an anti-Castroite or a communist, and very few Miami Cubans dared any retort. Once in a while, when things were so extreme as to be ludicrous, a courageous publisher would print a discreet protest. Luis Tornes, for example, the director of *Impacto*, a weekly paper distributed in Little Havana and Hialeah, wrote in 1972:

> We have to be careful with the word communist, which we have the habit of using against people freely. Some people used to call Claude Pepper—a good friend of the Cuban people—a communist. Yet he was the only congressman who protested the presence of a Russian ship in Miami harbor. The same happens with Bernardo Benes, whom others call a communist because he has a different approach to the Cuban situation. And he is a friend of Claude Pepper. Gentlemen, it is about time that we grow up politically![22]

Yet less than a year later, the same newspaper directed by the same Luis Tornes published a front-page story attacking Benes. It carried tabloid-style headlines: "Russian Exposition in Benes's Bank." Two quarter-page photographs of a sign in Russian and a Moscow subway station filled out the remainder of the page. The accompanying story revealed that an exhibit of photographs from Russia—a fact not known by "the great majority of Miami Cubans"—had been placed in an "important" part of Washington Federal's vestibule. The remainder of the article attacked Benes for pretending to be the "voice" of Cuban exiles. "We do not know what the Cuban patrons of Washington Federal will think of this Soviet exhibition, all the more insulting because it is being shown during the week commemorating the birth of José Martí."[23] *Patria* added: "If things change tomorrow, the name of this bank would be Moscow Federal."[24]

In any case, the anti-communism heard ceaselessly in Miami played a major role in transforming Cuban Miami into a Republican Party bastion.

Interviewed by the *Herald* about her political feelings, seventy-year-old Elisa Perdomo told the *Herald* that she "didn't like what Clinton did in the White House." In George W. Bush, she sees "somebody who has a good family, a good life." "It's the way we were raised," observed Gilda Almeyda, forty-seven. "Being Cuban and of Cuban descent, we are all die-hard Republicans."[25] Ironically, as Benes points out, Cuban politics since the 1940s, and even during Batista's regime, has been highly progressive regarding social issues. But the turn of the Miami Cubans to the far right undercut Benes's and other moderates' community influence. On the wall of cartoonish caricatures of visiting celebrities at the Southwest Twenty-seventh Avenue Latin American [read: Cuban] Cafeteria, the portrait of Bill and Hillary Clinton is partially covered by a photograph of Elián. Further up on the same avenue, as well as in locations throughout Miami and in other cities across the United States, billboards carried a triptych showing Adolph Hitler, looking over the shoulder of an Aryan youth, Josef Stalin lurking behind a Russian child, and Fidel Castro in back of Elián. Viewers interpreted the images somewhat differently. Anglos tended to explain the billboard for what it portrayed specifically—brainwashing by hated dictators—while Cuban Americans responded more broadly, seeing personifications of evil in the billboard.[26]

In response to pressure from the rest of the country for the United States to ease the embargo to permit trade, the Cuban American National Foundation's Executive Director, Joe García, conceded to the *New York Times* that attitudes were changing. He pledged, however, that his organization would fight even harder to convince the American public to support the CANF's position. The *Times'* reporter referred to the CANF as "a lobby that long exerted virtual veto power over United States foreign policy, [and has] acknowledged losing critical ground."[27] But its influence remained strong. In recognition of the CANF's influence, Governor Lawton Chiles, toward the end of his term, appointed Joe García to the Public Service Commission.

When the Elián furor finally receded, many Americans outside Miami concluded that the right-wing voices in the Cuban American community, for years dwindling in number but still backed by a formidable political lobby, had lost prestige in the light of the national media coverage. But the reportage had been shallow and one-sided. "Rather than making an

7.1   Elián González billboard, Miami, 2000. Photograph by Robert M. Levine

effort to understand the background to the Cuban American reaction, most of those who covered the story insisted on portraying us as a faceless, incoherent mob," Cuban American scholar Luis Martínez Fernández observed. "What is represented as Cuban culture," he added, "is a reductionist caricature of what in reality is a very complex culture." Martínez-Fernández's view of his own place, shared by many of his countrymen in the United States, sheds light on the dilemma caused by Castro's four decades in power. "I do feel an outsider," he writes, "and that is fine because home is really Cuba. I am on loan in this country even if that loan may have already defaulted for all practical purposes. There is, by the way, a very long tradition of Cubans who have spent long periods of exile and never ceased to be Cuban: Saco, Martí, Varela, Estrada Palma. . . . Still, I am thankful for all the opportunities that this great country has afforded me and my family."[28]

Watching Elián flown to Cuba with his father only deepened the feelings of betrayal among Miami Cubans. On the first anniversary of Elián's rescue at sea, Miami's Spanish-language WLTV-Univision Channel 23 released a poll showing that Cubans disagreed with other ethnic groups in the city on almost every issue raised. Ten times the number of non-Hispanic whites and blacks, as opposed to Cuban Americans, said they supported Attorney General Reno's decision to remove Elián González forcibly from his relatives—83.5 percent versus 8 percent.[29]

Rare voices spoke out. Dr. Raúl de Velasco, president of Miami's Cuba Committee for Democracy, lamented in the *Miami Herald:*

> For years in Miami there has been a dramatic tension between the rhetoric of democracy—which at its core defends the freedom of expression—and the actions of many of our Cuban and Cuban American compatriots and the leaders we have allowed to speak for us. We have emphasized that we are exiles of a totalitarian regime that does not allow dissent. At the same time, however, we have been intolerant of different points of view in a way that has created an atmosphere of intimidation. Ironically, we have too often mirrored—with obvious differences—the system we all oppose. . . . The best way to change this cycle is with the courage of openness. This society offers us the legal space to act on this courage. What has happened here signals the beginning of a new era in Miami and—we can all hope—the possibility for change in Cuba.[30]

None other than Eloy Guitérrez Menoyo, the prisoner whose explosion of rage against his Cuban captors in 1978 had led to eight years additional jail time, wrote:

> Thousands of Miami Cubans do not feel they are represented by a vociferous minority that controls some of the local media. There is an evident divorce between these self-appointed leaders and a silent majority that travels to the island for family visits and defies rhetoric by showing generosity to those relatives left behind. This should send a clear message to Washington. The time for change is here.[31]

The Elián saga and its impact on Cuban Americans took its toll. Television viewers throughout the United States recoiled at filmed scenes of Cuban Americans burning the U.S. flag, setting fires, and impeding traffic in Miami. The *Washington Post*'s William Raspberry chastised the Miami Cubans for being a "single-issue constituency." "In their near-fanatic focus on a small tree named Elián," the journalist wrote, "the Miami Cubans may be jeopardizing their foreign policy forest."[32] An African American Congressman, Alcee Hastings (D-FL), in mockery introduced a bill to confer permanent residency on a six-year-old motherless Haitian boy, in his district of Miramar. "I have a long list of children . . . in similar or worse situations than Elián," he said. "Why should he receive preferential treatment?" Other reactions showed deep-seated resentment of Miami Cuban exceptionalism. "For years the U.S. has been returning children to countries with poverty and child labor that make Cuba look like a 5-star resort," stated a message on an Internet site hosted by the e-magazine *Slate,* "but we have never heard one peep out of the Miami Cubans. For years we have returned young women to countries where they are considered men's chattel, given ritual clitoridectomies and arranged marriages, but the Miami Cubans never lifted a finger."[33] "If this boy was from Haiti, Mexico, Guatemala, or from Senegal, Congo, or the Ivory Coast, he would have been returned to his father and his immediate family by the first plane available," wrote the president of the progressive International Association of Educators for World Peace.[34] "This child, who may have suffered permanent psychological trauma . . . continues to be forcibly retained in a foreign environment, surrounded by people he has never seen, turned into a celebrity and plunged into a media frenzy by the heartless, vengeful, ultraright Cuban American pseudo-politicians," fumed Alberto Jones. "In order to explain their absurd position, they are presenting the most bizarre, baseless arguments, as they perceive the well being of the child in direct relation to the availability of Nintendo . . . or McDonald's."[35]

In November 2000, an Anglo retired attorney, a longtime resident, stood up at a forum on Cuban Miami and charged that it is hypocritical and self-destructive for Cuban Americans to continue to call themselves "exiles." Seth Stopek argued that the vast majority of Cubans in Miami have long since assimilated and will not return to reside in Cuba, and Cubans forced to leave their country of origin are no different from numerous Americans and their ancestors who, for reasons of oppression left their countries and came to America, established new, permanent lives as Americans, and worked to free their former countrymen. Stopek stated that the fiction that Cuban Americans are "exiles" requiring special treatment only serves to alienate the rest of the country, and to weaken the support Cuban Americans would otherwise receive if reality prevailed. Further, he charged it is immoral and self-defeating to continue to isolate Cuba rather than to encourage routine person-to-person contact with all Americans. And it is particularly opportunistic and shameful that the

Miami Cuban leadership waves the bloody shirt of anti-Castro resistance with the likes of Jesse Helms, shows little interest in the welfare of the less-privileged Miami Latin and African American residents of their own city, and too often ironically suppresses a free and open dialogue of these issues using the very intimidation it seeks to fight in Cuba.

In response, a Cuban member of the panel answered that Cubans will always be exiles because they are not permitted to return to live, and because they have been made "non-persons" by the Cuban regime—their accomplishments wiped off the slate of Cuban culture and life.[36] This revealed a powerful aspect of the Cuban American dilemma: those who fled Cuba demand the right to consider themselves exiles because to them Castro has kidnapped not only their homeland but their identities.

Only in Miami

Most public discourse in Miami on issues related to Cuba invariably emphasized polemical viewpoints. Critics of the exile lobby charged that the "silent majority" Miami Cubans had been silenced by intimidation, and that in South Florida the right of free speech had been taken away. In 1992, in fact, two respected human rights groups, the Fund for Free Expression and Americas Watch, issued *Dangerous Dialogue: Attacks on Freedom of Expression in Miami's Cuban Exile Community*, a thirty-page report condemning Miami's atmosphere of fear, terror, and violence. Because of the tendency for public officials—especially Mayor Xavier Suarez—to make statements "that contribute to an impression that the city government is not ardently interested in the prosecution of terrorist acts," the report concluded, "[in Miami], moderation can be a dangerous position."[37] Popular radio broadcaster Armando Pérez-Roura replied by calling the report the work of "cowards, pinkos and hung-over leftists."[38]

Some argue that nothing has changed except for the downgraded influence of the CANF after founder Jorge Mas Canosa's death in 1997. Others point to evidence to the contrary.[39] While the younger generation may not possess the rage of their parents, Cuban exile organizations in Miami have deftly maintained their symbolic presence. On August 30, 1997, for example, a coalition of exile groups, *Generación de Relevo*, sponsored a motorcade from Key West as a memorial to the death of more than one hundred members of the Bay of Pigs invasion thirty-five years earlier. A white truck bearing the Cuban and American flags and playing Spanish marches led the line of cars. Runners representing Alpha 66 carried a torch along sections of South Dixie Highway (U.S.1). The motorcade stopped at Florida International University to pick up members of the Free Cuba Foundation, an anti-Castro student group. Key West is dear to all Cubans because José Martí issued his call for Cuban independence from the San Carlos Institute on Duval Street, and to Cuban Americans because so many *marielitos* and rafters (*balseros*) landed or were processed there.[40]

It has been said that the narrative of the Miami Cubans internalizes betrayal and defeat. Because they define themselves as victims, each with long memories of dispossession and disorientation, it becomes more difficult to shake off the memories of the past. The evolution of Alpha 66 represents a case in point; the group originated in the Escambray Mountains among anti-Batista guerrillas allied with Castro's July 26th revolutionary movement. When Castro came to power and began to speak Marxism-Leninism, many of the former Escambray fighters fled to Miami. Two of them, Front Commander Eloy Gutiérrez Menoyo and Andrés Nazario Sargén, founded Alpha 66 in 1960. Alpha, the first letter of the Greek alphabet, signaled that the group was the first to declare war against Castro, and 66 represented the original number of fighters in the Escambray front. On its own, Alpha 66 raided the island fourteen times during 1961 and 1962 and fired on a Soviet freighter in a Cuban port. Alpha 66's reputation for violence remained solid, even as the original members aged. In 1964, Gutiérrez Menoyo and three other Alpha members carried out a raid from the Dominican Republic in which they landed on Cuba's northeast coast, hoping to spark an insurrection. But they were captured after a month in hiding, and Gutiérrez Menoyo spent twenty-two years in prison.

Changes in attitude occurred slowly. For decades, Alpha 66 operated a short-wave radio program, *La Voz del Alpha,* using World War II–era transmitters. On Sundays, the older members started training volunteers as young as sixth-graders at Alpha 66's secluded South Dade camp, known as Rumbo Sur. Most recruits were older, in their twenties. But when Gutiérrez Menoyo was released from prison in 1986, he created a new group, Cambio Cubano, advocating dialogue as the only way to achieve democracy in Cuba.[41] He was quickly forced out of Alpha 66.

Other Alpha 66 members sat around their Little Havana clubhouse, across from the Bay of Pigs monument, telling war stories and occasionally napping. Some members remained belligerent: Field Commander Elvis Castellano said that either Castro will die "or we're going to kill him. I'm going to try to assassinate him. And if I don't, someone else will."[42]

Because Cuban American families are tightly knit and emotionally open, hatred of Castro's revolution is passed on to newer generations. Many still have relatives in Cuba who are enduring hardships. They blame Washington political leaders for being "soft" on Cuba, despite such measures as the Torricelli and Helms-Burton legislation. Basulto and other exile spokesmen criticized "the North American government" for not retaliating in 1996 when Cuban MiGs downed two Brothers to the Rescue aircraft in international airspace. "If Cuban blood does not flow in your veins," a protester caught up in the Elián saga said to a reporter, "you have no idea of what it is like to be us—all of our memories of what it is like under Castro and what it means to be separated from your homeland."[43]

What makes the hurt run so deeply in the Miami Cuban community is that the memories are real, as well as emotional. Cubans were betrayed by Batista when his coup tossed aside and outlawed the 1940 Constitution and cancelled elections. Castro and his 26th of July movement called them *gusanos* and forced them to leave, even though many had supported his nationalistic proclamations when he first took power. But the strident, threatening voices of Miami Cuban radio broadcasters accused nonconformist local Cubans of sympathizing with Castro or even working for him as secret agents. They felt betrayed by politicians who made friendly gestures toward Cuba, and they worked to unseat them from office, contributing money to their opponents in other states.

DIVERSITY IN A RISING GENERATION

New and not-so-new names of Miami Cubans have begun to replace the old guard. Unlike their parents' generation, the children of the first émigrés (called Generation "One-and-a-half" by Gustavo Pérez-Firmat),[44] and its successor, Generation Ñ, the second generation, tend to represent a broader and more diverse spectrum than the first wave of émigrés, although they have been no less committed to community causes. They live, in the words of Max J. Castro, in the midst of a "conflict-laden and asymmetric aspect of the relation Cuba(n)/America(n)."[45]

In 1976, Florida Republican delegate Al Cardenas drove to his party's convention in Kansas City and back, 36 hours in all because he could not afford a motel room. A friend of Jeb Bush since 1976, he was named by President Reagan as special ambassador to St. Kitts-Nevis, and now chairs Florida's Republican Party.[46] One of the first members of the new power elite linked to the Anglo establishment was Leslie Pantin, Jr., a public relations executive and charismatic figure in the Cuban community. The *Herald* wrote in 1988:

> Pantin bolts for his Ford Taurus and heads to the Kiwanis Club of Little Havana, his 13-year-old trampoline to the heights of prominence in Dade County. He was the founding president, and now, at age 39, he's its elder statesman. Tonight is the annual Christmas party, a time to sip Bacardi, talk Cuban talk, and plan one of the biggest street festivals in America [the annual Calle Ocho festival]. Shouts of "¡Pantin!" and "¡Ya llegó"—He's here!—echo his breathless stride through the Kiwanis' cramped office. Offhandedly, he declares: "I have to be downtown at 6." Nobody is offended by the announcement. The Hispanic lawyers, executives and CPAs who run today's Kiwanis know Pantin's schedule is the price of success—a kind few Cubans in this country can match.[47]

Pantin, together with his father, were joiners. Leslie Pantin, Sr. became the first Cuban on the Greater Miami Chamber of Commerce, the first Cuban on the Florida Insurance Commission, the first Cuban on the prestigious Orange Bowl Committee. In Cuba, the Pantin family had been extremely wealthy, starting with Leslie Sr.'s grandfather, who had come to Cuba from his native Trinidad in the 1880s as British vice-consul. He made a fortune as a tobacco dealer, sold out to the British, and then started an insurance business that would become the island's second largest. The Pantins were insiders, and they brought their social prominence with them from Cuba.

This was not Benes's case, because despite his efforts to be accepted, he remained the outsider, even before 1978. Once in Washington, Benes visited Elena Mederos, Castro's first Minister for Social Work in 1959, whose daughter, María Elena, Benes's classmate at the Ruston School, became head of "Of Human Rights," a small Cuban American organization. When the news of the dialogue became public, Benes asked Elena to work with Roman Catholic Bishop Eduardo Boza Masvidal to monitor Castro's release of his political prisoners. Benes reasoned that having more prominent exiles involved would help the cause. After a long conversation, Elena told Benes that she would call him, but she never did. Benes suspects that she was uncomfortable working on a project organized by an "outsider."[48]

On the other hand, while Miami Cuban leaders remained cautious about speaking out in public on political issues, many have quietly committed themselves to community and philanthropic activities. These men and women include members of the old generation as well as the new. Some are considered politically moderates, but they have made their mark in community service, not in the political arena. Some of their case studies follow.

Sylvia Iriondo, a Key Biscayne upscale real-estate broker and grandmother, founded Mothers and Women Against Repression in Cuba (MAR). Iriondo organizes anti-Castro demonstrations with members of her group dressed in black. One of the first was a vigil near the home of Magda Montiel Davis, a prominent Miami Cuban *dialoguera* who had been caught by a television camera embracing Castro during a 1994 conference in Havana. "To this day, I can't bear to repeat that woman's name," Iriondo told an interviewer.[49] As a participant in the Brothers to the Rescue exile pilot organization, she was a passenger in the Cessna flown by Jorge Basulto in February 1996 when Cuban MiGs shot two others down. Undeterred, she continues to ride on the rescue missions, scouring the waters of the Florida Straits to find rafters in trouble.

Mercedes Scopetta, a major figure in philanthropy in Miami today, was the daughter of Manolo Arca, one of the wealthiest Cubans in Oriente province, the owner of cattle ranches, rice plantations, and lumber and sugar mills. Mercedes was born in Manzanillo in 1926, studied at the Lestonac Academy in Havana, and for a year attended the Sacred Heart School. Her parents sent her to the United States to study, and she graduated in chemistry from Rosemont College in Philadelphia. There she met John Scopetta, a civil engineering student at Villanova University. They married in 1949 and moved to Miami for two years before leaving for Oriente, where John was hired by Mercedes's father as an engineer at his Estrada Palma sugar mill.

They fled to Miami in May 1960 along with their entire family. Mercedes took a master's degree in psychology from the University of Miami and in 1972 became the project director of the Miami Mental Health Center, created with a federal government grant for treatment of Hispanic addicts. After her retirement, she became director of the archbishop of Miami's lay volunteer center, and also maintained a private practice as a psychologist. Today she volunteers at the Mother of God community in Key Biscayne, a treatment center. She mentors young Hispanic psychologists and has influenced the thousands of people whose lives she has touched.

Manuel Balado was born in 1918 in the town of Bolondron, Matanzas; his family moved to Havana four years later. As a teenager, he left school to start his own business, and within a few years he owned three car repair and tire stores. Because of his success, the Firestone company invited him to visit its Akron, Ohio, tire factory. Eventually, he became one of the largest tire dealers in Cuba and a leader in the Cuban Automotive Chamber of Commerce.

The first round of confiscations after 1959 so worried Manuel that he and his wife sent their children to Miami via the Pedro Pan flights. Sixteen-year-old Alicia and fourteen-year-old Myriam arrived in 1961, and Balado and his wife flew to Panama in February 1962. Six months after reuniting his family in Miami, he received a fortunate break: he managed to acquire, without any cash, a tire retail store in Little Havana from a widow. At first the business languished, but with the arrival of tens of thousands of Cuban refugees, all of whom preferred to make their purchases within the Cuban exile enclave, he began to prosper. In 1968, he became founding president of the Latin American Chamber of Commerce (CAMACOL), and in 1974, he and some co-investors purchased a shopping center in Little Havana. By 1975, his annual sales exceeded $5 million. He then started a wholesale and export operation. Today, his business thrives, and CAMACOL claims two thousand members, wielding considerable influence in Miami business affairs.

Francisca "Paquita" Aldrich has played a quiet but effective role in community service. One of seventeen children born into a Havana family in 1925, her father was a successful restaurateur, and she attended elite schools. In 1948, she married Gaspar Aldrich, a lawyer. They moved to Miami in 1955, where they raised their children, who are all successful professionals today. In 1959, Paquita became one of the most active volunteers with the Catholic Charity Services, and during the 1960s, she co-founded Little Havana's first community-sponsored day-care center, the Centro Mater. She served as president for twenty years before turning her job over to younger volunteers. Centro Mater now provides services to eight hundred children in Little Havana (many of them not Cuban but from Nicaragua, Colombia, and other Latin American countries), and a second center in Hialeah. Her sister, a Catholic nun of the Order of the Sacred Heart, remained in Cuba to minister to Catholic students across the island.

In the midst of enormous public cynicism about ineffective and corrupt members of the city and county commissions, a relatively new commissioner, Jimmy L. Morales, emerged as a staunch defender of ethics in government and progressive causes. In 2000, Greater Miami's Chamber of Commerce awarded him a citation for taking the lead in government reform issues, including campaign finance and transportation oversight. Morales's father was Puerto Rican and his mother Cuban; both worked at Biscayne Elementary School, Miami Beach, as a janitor and cafeteria employee, respectively. Morales received his law degree at Harvard, for a while practicing international law in New York City, before returning to Miami and winning election to the Miami-Dade County Commission. Morales cast the deciding vote repealing the twenty-year-old anti-gay rights ordinance, passed as the result of conservative singer Anita Bryant's "Save our Children" crusade. He told the press: "When you unleash hatred, it's only natural that some people would run with it, and sometimes it becomes deadly."[50]

Others in the new generation preserved the community's sense of anger. Rafael Sánchez-Aballí, a thirty-six-year-old lawyer, helped craft the Helms-Burton Act. In an interview with reporter Jonathan Kandell, he explained his philosophy—"What's so extreme about wanting democracy and freedom for Cuba?"—but then went on to talk more darkly about Castro's reputed stock of biological weapons. "All he has to do is get a little Cessna with some of those weapons, make it crash in the Everglades, and South Florida is going to have a tremendous problem."[51]

Alvaro Fernández, a Democrat and president of the Citizens' Accountability Network, an organization affiliated with the League of Women Voters, in efforts to weed out government corruption and to enact strong campaign finance reforms, has sought an alternative political role. Running for county commissioner against a well-financed conservative opponent who trounced him in the election, Fernández told Miami voters that, from the beginning, he opposed the county ordinance barring municipal funds for any arts group "interacting with Cuba." Fernández vice-chairs the Miami Beach Cultural Arts Council, and he openly admits his desire for cultural exchange with Cuba. "People are tired of politics as usual in Miami-Dade,"[52] he contends. "You walk around this town and you hear people saying, 'I can't believe we lost the Grammys [and] the Pan-American Games [because of the threat of protests if island Cubans participated].' Not only are we hurting our stature with the rest of the country and our own cultural life," he adds, "but also our economy."[53] By 2000, booking agents for Cuban performing groups bypassed Miami in their tours—scheduling tour stops as near as Fort Lauderdale, West Palm Beach, and throughout the rest of the country. But the pressure from the militant right did not diminish. Miami-Dade County in the same year rescinded a grant to the Florida International University Film Festival for screening a Cuban film.[54]

But most cultural figures in the Miami Cuban community do not agree with Fernández. Ricardo Pau-Llosa, a highly regarded poet, represents the majority. He minces no words on the political issue: "I'm opposing that monster Fidel and I'm called a fascist by people who claim to be liberal. I feel like I'm Rigoletto and I've wandered onto a performance of *Tosca* and I'm being ordered off the stage: 'Get off! Get off! You lousy clown, you're spoiling the opera!' Well, I think I should be on stage because without me the opera makes no f—ing sense." Yet, Pau-Llosa keeps a memory alive of a romanticized Cuba he left when he was six. "We lost a tropical Venice," he says, "a Caribbean Florence, something worth so much more than those little pieces of lost real estate that so many exiles cry about."[55]

Carlos Saladrigas has emerged as a voice of practicality in the Cuban community. He is a fifty-two-year old former owner of the Vincam Group, which had annual revenues of almost $1 billion before he sold it. In some ways, he is the insider who has taken Benes's former role. A graduate of

Miami-Dade Community College and Harvard, he followed the fast track to community leadership. One of his specialties has been mediating between contentious groups, and he brings style and power to this role. Before the Cuban Museum went under, Saladrigas negotiated the transfer of much of its art to the University of Miami. He was one of the inside negotiators during the Elián case with the University of Miami's chairman of the board of trustees and president. In 1998, he helped organize the *Mesa Redonda* (Round Table), a dinner club involving members from other Latin American backgrounds but mostly Miami Cubans. Reporter Jonathan Kandell quoted Saladrigas on the subject: "We, as a community, have failed to put forth our best and our brightest in public office. When I was growing up in Cuba, I remember the phrase 'Decent people don't get involved in politics.' Maybe there's still that same mindset here." On Cuba, he proposes that Cubans abroad forget about Castro because he has become irrelevant. "Miami," he says, "should become the intellectual center to craft a new vision for Cubans in Cuba. There has to be more communication between our people here and over there. . . . We don't have to be afraid of ideas—Castro does."[56]

Beyond the political arena, some Miami Cubans adopted ingenious ways to preserve their family ties while adjusting to life in South Florida. A member of the younger generation explains:

> The idea started with my great-grandfather in Havana. He wanted to keep all his children and grandchildren near so he bought them all houses on the same block. Years after my family arrived in Miami, they all got together and bought some new houses that were being built on the same block in the Westchester area. When the families began to multiply, my father and my uncles bought a large parcel of land in the East Kendall area about 23 years ago. They divided the land into ten acres and each family built their own home. It is quite a unique setting because none of the houses have fences and we all share a common backyard. Needless to say, we all had an amazing childhood. So much so that at one point in time, there were 25 children under the age of 15 playing in the backyard after school. As all these kids grow older and start their own families, they have begun to buy the houses across the street whenever they come up for sale. Now there are 14 houses that belong to family members on the block.[57]

Although most first-generation Cuban Americans continue to live in Miami, some of them have settled throughout the rest of the United States, as well as in countries like Spain, Venezuela, Australia, and Israel. Each family's story, of course, proved unique. Exiles who settled far from Miami faced experiences much more like those of typical minority immigrants because they lacked the enclave support network provided in Miami.

Consider the experience of Tina Abich who was born in Miami in 1961 but relocated with her family to Oregon:

> My greatest difficulty . . . [was] feeling a loss of culture. My father introduced me to Cuban foods—*yuca* [manioc], *frijoles negros* [black beans]. On occasion he would play an old album recorded by Nat King Cole in Cuba, and he would tell me incredible stories of his childhood. He can remember stories from when he was three years old. I, however, grew up with out any Latino friends and only visited Miami briefly, maybe three times. I believe that because my father had assimilated and forced himself to let go much of his culture, there was little space for me to connect to it. I have always felt sad for my father's loss of connection with his culture.[58]

Regardless of political stance, a divide still separates the emerging political generation from its predecessor on one key issue: return to Cuba. Members of the older generations, like the Chinese who came to Taiwan with Chiang Kai-shek, have always expected to return; Miami, in fact, supports a flourishing mini-group of researchers who are paid to research deeds of ownership so that claims can be filed as soon as Castro dies. (That his inevitable demise does not necessarily mean that Cuba will immediately abandon its communist system is not usually taken into consideration in Miami.) But the new generation says *no hay regreso*—there is no return. This may be interpreted in different ways. To some, it may mean that reality has set in. To others, it may be a slogan, in Kandell's words, "of tenacious sullenness for having been forced to abandon a way of life that can never be resurrected."[59] In 2000, the Elián González trauma raised the national consciousness of Miami Cubans to the extent that 38 percent said they would return to Cuba to live after Castro leaves, 10 percent more than in 1997. It remains to be seen whether this gain will hold up in the coming years.

Another recent phrase, *amnesia y amnistía*—forget and forgive—is also heard frequently, but it also cannot be taken at face value. Those who use the term apply it only to post-Castro communists "who do not have blood on their hands."[60] Unlike Eastern Europe's former Soviet bloc, there will be no effort to put the past behind.

Fainter voices offer even more open positions about Cuba, but they're usually disregarded. Marifeli Pérez-Stable, a visiting professor at Florida International University in 1999–2000 and the author of an important book on the Cuban revolution, wrote an op-ed piece in the *Herald* arguing that Cuban Miamians are "too Castro centered," the same sentiment expressed by Carlos Saladrigas. She wrote:

> We need to build on our strengths—our remittances, our family visits, our dialogue with civil society—and avoid shouting matches that we are bound to lose. The choice is ours: Either we grope along the trodden paths or illuminate new ones that expose the regime's weaknesses. Let's put on our high beams and look beyond present obscurities toward the democratic Cuba that lies ahead![61]

Some signs of a diminishing militant backlash against *dialogueros* in Miami surfaced in early September 2000, where a delegation of left-leaning Cuban exiles met with Castro during his visit to the United Nations Millennial Summit. Among those attending the Cuban Mission to discuss continuing the dialogue process were Eddy Levy, the blind human rights activist; Magda Montiel Davis; Andrés Gómez of the Antonio Maceo Brigade, and publisher Max Lesnik. The *Herald* reported the exile group's opposition to the economic embargo. "We," Lesnik said, "are not pro-Castro or pro-government. What is certain is that we are publicly against the embargo."[62] The militant radio broadcasters carried on predictably, but little public debate ensued.

THE PRICE OF RESILIENCE

Bernardo Benes remains perplexed and hurt by the irrationality and cruelty he has endured as an outsider within Cuban Miami. Benes's politics on Cuba today stand to the right of many members of the Miami Cuban community, including Max Lesnik, the former publisher of *Réplica*. Benes recalls with sarcasm his experience at the closing luncheon at the Summit of the Americas, held in Miami in 1994. Pauline Winick, then the executive vice-president of the Miami Heat basketball team and later vice-president of Florida International University, invited Benes to sit with her. At the table were General Barry McCaffery and an intelligence specialist posted to the Southern Command, soon to be moved from Panama to Miami. After twenty minutes of conversation, Benes contends, the intelligence officer told him: "I don't understand the politicians in Washington. Can't they see the embargo does no good?"[63] But in South Florida, and in the minds of politicians in both major parties, this subject remained a sacred cow, something all feared touching lest their careers be jeopardized.

Those enlightened enough to understand the chilling effect of intimidation and constant threats in a city divided racially, ethnically, and by an enormous gap between rich and poor sympathized with Benes—most were Anglo or blacks. Tom Cunningham, the former president of the British Open University, wrote to Meg Laughlin, the *Tropic* magazine journalist who wrote about Benes's "appointment in Samara":

> [Benes] is a people leader who lives in the wrong place, maybe even the wrong time. He seems too sensitive and alert for the "morbid and thwarted" state of those individuals whose denunciations are all hiss and spittle. God! I wish they would get a pulse, maybe even a life. You can tell Mr. Benes, Meg, that his being/travels speaks/acts eloquently to me about faith and purpose. His is a life of the bumpy kind, edging towards the tragic, with heroic outlines; definitely noble. Gracious also comes to mind.[64]

Bernardo Benes could not have survived his four decades in Miami had it not been for his wife's constant support. Ricky Benes bears the weight of years of countless slights and, in many ways, is Benes's backbone and strength. When Joan Didion visited them in their Normandie Isle home, Ricky exploded in frustration because she was worried about the impact of what Benes was telling Didion. He replied that no Cubans will read what Didion says, suggesting that he was speaking to non-Cuban readers. "No Cubans will read what she writes," Bernardo Benes said in English. "You will be surprised," Ricky replied, in English as well. "Anything I say can be printed; that's the price of being married to me, and I'm a tough cookie." When her husband protested, she stated: "Just take out more life insurance."[65]

In a letter to his eight grandchildren, written so that they might learn about his life in a manner never revealed to him by his father or

7.2   Bernardo Benes on his balcony, October 2000. Photograph by Robert M. Levine.

grandfather, Benes says that first and foremost he dedicated his life pursuing social justice without compromising his fundamental values. "Maybe Cuba is not a part of you," he wrote, "but I have no problem with multiple loyalties." On his fellow "exiles" (a term he emphatically uses) he wrote:

> We came to Miami in great quantities. I'm sure it was frightening for many non-Cubans. Today Cuban Americans hold enormous power in the city's political and economic life. They have been manipulated by a small group of their leaders into believing that their legacy from Cuba was conservative, which is not true. The militants ruined my life after 1978 because they felt that the jailed political prisoners in Cuba were more useful to their cause as martyrs, and that it was also convenient to keep families separated because increased tension would somehow lead to more pressure on Fidel Castro. The intimidation in Miami is little different from the intimidation in Cuba, with the only difference being that in Miami we allow ourselves to be silenced by choice. To you, I repeat the words of Pope John Paul II to the Cuban people during his 1997 visit to their island: *No tengan miedo* [do not be afraid].[66]

Benes never fell victim to the so-called Stockholm syndrome, in which persons kidnapped for ransom sometimes take the side of their abductors. After 1972, Benes decided that negotiations were the only way to achieve change. Others in his position might have become more sympathetic after 150 hours one-on-one with a stubborn, moody, and self-made revolutionary.

Benes faults Fidel Castro for betraying his revolution even further in August 1993, when Cuba created a dual monetary system based on pesos and dollars. Those Cubans with relatives abroad willing to send them dollars did well, but the vast majority, regardless of their skills or professions, fell into impoverishment. Benes also observes that most Cubans who have dollar-sending relatives are white, because a disproportionate number of white Cubans left the island and succeeded financially. Cuban non-whites, despite their government's revolutionary rhetoric, continue to live at the bottom of the socioeconomic ladder, and one of the main reasons has little to do with racial prejudice. Benes offers an interesting illustration: Two twin brothers work in the same factory and earn the same salary in Cuban pesos. One of them has a wife with relatives in the United States; the other one's wife does not. If the first twin receives $50 a month from abroad, the difference between his standard of living and his brother's will be greater than the difference before 1959 between his father's standard of living and any of his 500 industrial employees.[67]

Although Benes was among the first Miami Cubans to declare publicly that the thirty-seven-year old embargo should be lifted, he demanded that in return Cuba restore or create mechanisms to create a just society, free from police repression and arbitrary justice. He reminds his fellow Cuban exiles that former House Speaker "Tip" O'Neill wrote in his memoirs that Dade County was the best represented in the United States, because of its three Democratic congressmen, Claude Pepper, Dante Fascell, and Bill Lehman. "How long," he asks, "are we going to fool and betray our children by not telling them that pre-Castro Cuba was overwhelmingly progressive, and that Jimmy Carter and Representative Carrie Meek, not Representative Lincoln Diaz-Balart and Senator Jesse Helms, should be the community's role models." Helms, Benes says, is probably the "most racist and despicable" senator in Congress. And, Benes adds, punitive legislation did not bring down the Berlin Wall; the people did.

"Why do we think in our arrogance that we can legislate measures to bring down the Cuban government? The Soviets did not fall because of any law passed in Washington."[68]

Benes believes that the three most powerful Cuban AM radio stations in Miami over the years—Radio Mambí, La Poderosa and WQBA—along with the *periodiquitos* and the diverse members of the anti-Castro lobby have, unlike any other city in the United States, silenced opposition through verbal intimidation. The *Miami Herald,* at the same time, has reduced its staff, becoming less innovative (and probing), and has reduced its Spanish-language newspaper, *El Nuevo Herald,* to being a vehicle for the Cuban right wing.

In most places outside of South Florida, Benes observes, two groups, government investigatory agencies and the media, often work hand-in-hand against corruption. In Cuban Miami, by contrast, the Spanish-language media has done no investigative reporting. When a Cuban elected or appointed politician is indicted, Cuban exile radio stations and newspapers, regardless of the charges, rush to the defense of the accused, claiming anti-Cuban conspiracy. This amounts not only to manipulation of the news but also serves to reinforce the contention that everything is black or white (or, in Miami's case, red or white).

While mainly Miami Cubans have been targeted for repudiation for their failure to follow the militant line publicly, some Anglos have also been reviled. Across the street from the popular Versailles restaurant in Little Havana, a graffito painted on the sidewalk remains: "Clinton H.P." ("Son of a Whore"). Among the Miami-born, Janet Reno now heads the list for her role in the Elián González affair, even though she, raised in Miami by a Danish immigrant father and a fiercely independent mother, a Floridian, in the most "inside" manner possible, has been recast as an enemy "outsider" by the militants. Reno, reared in a house built from the ground up by her mother, rode to prominence as a courageous public prosecutor, and served eight years in President Clinton's cabinet as attorney general. It is likely that she will remain an outsider in the minds of the exile community forever.

Some members of the Cuban American community disagree with the notion held not only by Benes's adversaries but by Benes himself that they will continue to consider themselves exiles until Castro and his government relinquishes power. Others, however, hold differing views. "Luis Salas," a Peter

7.3 *Periodiquito* rack, Versailles Restaurant, Little Havana. Photograph by Robert M. Levine.

Pan alumnus and career United States military officer, says that despite his background, he finds it "astonishing that there are many Cuban Americans who are United States citizens and still consider themselves exiles."[69]

The city's atmosphere of distrust among ethnic groups is, as Max J. Castro observes, "a situation in which no group feels completely secure, and everyone feels somehow aggrieved or deprived. Understanding the forces that create such feelings in their full complexity and confronting them are just as crucial as facing the facts and dispelling the myths."[70] A North Miami attorney, presumably an Anglo, wrote scathingly about his city, calling it filled with "impossibly obdurate and involuntary immigrants who have no clue or stake in the American values of reasoned discourse, free speech, and fair play and no desire to abandon the cultural attributes that have allowed them to suffer under one form of tyranny or another for a long, long time."[71] Coming together in Miami may take decades longer.

Many non-Cubans in Miami (and outside) believe that Cuban community leaders do not respect or fully understand the First Amendment— that when anyone says anything in public that is taken, correctly or incorrectly, as a pro-Castro statement, that person receives a barrage of attacks for being a communist sympathizer. Yet differences between Miami and Cuba remain palpable. María de los Angeles Torres offers a telling comparison between varieties of intolerance in Cuba and in Cuban Miami. In 1990, Cuban brigade members broke into the home of poet María Elena Cruz Varela, and, before carting her off to prison, tried to force her to eat leaflets she had written. Four years later, when Magda Montiel Davis was caught on camera embracing Castro, the Cuban government then sold copies of the videotape to the foreign press. The result yielded protests, death threats, and ostracism for Davis. But a major difference stood out. In Cuba, the government perpetuated the violence against the victim (as in setting up the hapless Ms. Davis to abuse, ignoring the fact that she naively had attempted to praise Castro), but in Cuban Miami, the residents created an atmosphere of violence in which the government intervened as a protective force for the victim.[72]

Cubans continued to risk their lives to find refuge in South Florida. Most arrived by raft or were smuggled in by professionals, but a few employed unusual methods. In late September 2000, thirty-six-year-old Angel Lenin Iglesias Hernández piloted a Russian-made Antonov AN–2 biplane used for crop dusting out of Cuban air space until it got lost trying to find Key West. It soon ran out of fuel and crashed into the sea off the Yucatán Peninsula after first spotting a Panamanian freighter and circling around it at least six times before crew members on the vessel acknowledged the pilot's emergency signal. Nine of the ten passengers survived, and despite the wet/dry rule (anyone actually walking on land won asylum), the Coast Guard officer to whose ship the passengers were transferred defied regulations and took his passengers to a hospital in Key West. A day later, Hernández was disclosed to the nephew of retired army colonel Joel Iglesias Leyva, who had once headed Cuba's *Asociación de Jovenes Rebelde* (Rebel Youth) and who had previously fought with Che Guevara in central Cuba, at one point saving Che's life by absorbing most of the blast from a grenade that exploded near both of them. But times have changed. One of the first things pilot Hernández asked when he met Armando Gutiérrez, the exile activist who had represented the González family during the Elián crisis, was whether he could legally drop "Lenin" from his legal name.[73]

But the stakes have remained high, and the lives of so many on both sides of the Florida Straits have been irretrievably damaged, as has South Florida itself. Allegations of vote-count improprieties during the 2000 election and the unexplained reluctance of Miami's Mayor Alex Penelas, a Democrat, to campaign for his party's presidential candidate added fuel to the fire. Discoveries of shady dealings continued to surface. Late in 2000, Miami's English-language press reported that candidates for office from mayor to city commissioner to state legislative posts routinely made payments to Spanish-language radio broadcasters and commentators for "campaign advice." It was also reported that commission candidate (and convicted felon) Humberto Hernández paid $22,476 to an advertising agency belonging to Radio Mambí's Marta Flores for political ads. This did not shock very many Miamians since they are inured to such political behavior in their city.[74] Journalists examining ballots in Miami-Dade County after the official recount stopped found in an examination of 138 of the county's 617 precincts at least 144 ballots cast illegally. In one instance, poll workers accepted a ballot in the name of a man who had died three years before.[75]

Before Elián González was rescued at sea, signs had appeared suggesting that perhaps the passage of four decades and the inevitable process of assimilation may have tempered the fierce pride of the Miami exile community. This pride set Cubans apart from their non-Cuban neighbors and kept alive an emotional fantasy of a pre-1959 Cuba overlooking the enormous gap between rich and poor, light-skinned and dark-skinned, and dominated by a benevolent hierarchy of status. But the process by which the American legal system determined that Elián had to return to Cuba with his father, and the insensitive way the removal was handled, released feelings of pain and anger that many Miami Cubans may not even have been aware of themselves. "I have never publicly displayed my feelings about being Cuban," a young attorney said, "until I saw what the American government did to Elián. I rushed out, bought Cuban flags, and draped them over my car and my front door. . . . I was so angry that when I saw cars driving by with American flags, I gave them the finger."[76]

What was not publicized as much as it should have been was the fact that non-Cubans performed acts of violence and hostility as well. Moisés Asís witnessed non-Cuban Hispanics, blacks, and Anglos burning Cuban flags in the lower-class neighborhood of Cutler Ridge. As bizarre as it sounds, witnesses also claimed to have watched the burning of a Ku Klux Klan cross to the applause of blacks, other non-Cubans, as well as policemen.[77] Anglos drove around Miami not only with American flags on their cars and trucks, but Confederate flags as well. Asís, a Cuban who defected in 1993, argues that some or all of the flag burnings may have been perpetrated by Cuban agents or persons sympathetic to Castro, because, he argues, "Cubans revere symbols of their country, especially the flag, and there has never been a documented example of burning an American flag in Castro's Cuba." He also believes that Castro himself, in his speeches to protesting Cubans in Havana, was the only source of the misinformation that Elián's family's house was filled with weapons—the reason that federal agents assaulted the house fully armed.[78]

Miami Cubans exulted when personnel of national repute took their side. During the 2000 Olympic Games in Sydney, Tommy Lasorda, a longtime Dodger manager, executive, and coach of the 2000 Olympic baseball squad, dedicated his team's gold medal victory to the Cuban exiles. That the Americans—their team made up of college players and cast-off minor leaguers—beat the heavily favored Cubans for the championship made the victory even sweeter.

Lasorda played winter ball in Cuba during the 1940s and 1950s and for years had visited Miami to see his friend Ron Fraser, coach of the University of Miami Hurricane baseball team. On October 15, 2000, some fifteen hundred Miami Cubans honored him at a public ceremony paid for by the City of Miami; the prominent *Herald* reporter, Liz Balmaseda, later confessed that she was moved to tears by this event. Lasorda received a Cuban flag, a white *guayabera*, a rendition of the nostalgic song "*Guantanamera*" from singer Celia Cruz, and ovations when he spoke Spanish to the crowd. "*Lasorda nos escuchó*"—"Lasorda heard us," a sign in the audience proclaimed. It was a play on words: in Spanish, the word *lasorda* means "the deaf one." The crowd started to chant: Lasordá, Lasordá. ¡Libertad! ¡Libertad! He received honorary membership in Brigade 2506, the Bay of Pigs veterans' group. Congressman Lincoln Diaz-Balart quoted from José Martí: "When there are many men without honor, there are some men who possess the honor of many." Lasorda brought the audience to its feet by proclaiming that "when we win gold" [at the Olympics] Castro "will send his players to cut sugar cane." Then the announcer called Orlando Bosch up to the stage who, in Balmaseda's words, is "a dark figure from exile Miami's violent past." Depending on one's viewpoint, however, he can also be considered the hero/terrorist of the early 1960s. Bosch received a rousing ovation. "People cheer him," the Pulitzer Prize-winning Cuban American journalist wrote, "and not because they think him innocent. . . . It was then," she concluded, "amid the chants of genuine gratitude to an American friend that I realized why this population remains in the trenches—a world apart."[79]

Miami Cubans themselves have only rarely addressed the issue raised by Balmaseda. The editorial in the spring 1993 issue of *Palenque* stated:

> Why have we Cubans insisted on living in a perpetual state of war? It is time that we demonstrate to the world, and especially to those who are living under the horror of tyranny, and above all to ourselves, that we have learned the lesson and that we are going to exile from our thoughts and actions the gratuitous intransigence and the absurd pretension that we are the sole possessors of the absolute truth.[80]

The exile community did not reply, for it had become accepted behavior not to show non-Cubans any cracks in the enclave. Yet through the end of 2000, Miami Cubans continued to wield enormous political influence. Representing only 4.3 percent of the nation's Hispanics, a group traditionally loyal to the Democratic Party, their lobbyists nonetheless influenced both major parties to endorse extreme hardline policies toward Cuba. Their overwhelming support of the Republican ticket in South Florida provided the difference in the election that delivered Florida, and therefore the presidency, to George W. Bush. Had Miami's Cubans voted comparably with other Hispanics around the United States, Al Gore would undoubtedly have won.

Miami Cubans did not themselves sabotage efforts for improved relations with Cuba because neither major presidential candidate espoused such a change. Both took a hard line, even though public opinion nationally remained at best indifferent to the economic embargo of nearly four decades. Bush, in fact, at the outset of the presidential campaign, said that he supported continuation of the existing (wet/dry) immigration policy toward Cubans—although this was never reported in the

Miami-Cuban media. After the Miami Cuban lobby reached him, Bush immediately changed his position.

As soon as Democrat Gore conceded in December following the Supreme Court's 5–4 decision to stop the recount process, South Florida Republicans predicted a hardened United States policy and increased support for dissidents in Cuba. "Nobody's saying that if we have a Republican administration in Washington, the Marines are going to be storming the ports of Cuba tomorrow," Congresswoman Ileana Ros-Lehtinen commented, but she did predict tougher talk, tougher restrictions on American business travel, and fewer contacts between Americans and nondissident Cubans to turn back the tide of what she called "a trickling, weakening of the United States embargo day-by-day during the Clinton administration."[81] Opposing her position were such groups as the libertarian Cato Institute; the powerful voice of the "establishment," the Council on Foreign Relations; and William Ratliff and Roger Fontaine of the conservative Hoover Institution at Stanford University. Facing one another, then, were the "dwindling, well-entrenched Cuban hard-liners" and "a growing, increasingly bipartisan and ideological set of embargo critics."[82]

In the aftermath of the 2000 election tug of war, some blamed past presidential candidates all the way back to the 1950s for having permitted themselves over the years to be held hostage to a bloc vote. "There is little chance for a rational and effective immigration policy toward Cuba," the Cuban exile scholar Max J. Castro wrote in 1999, "within the context of an irrational and ineffective foreign policy."[83] Yet for a leader known for his shrewdness, Castro never improved his understanding of the United States. He continued to turn a blind eye to human rights abuses in Cuba and ignored the chilling effects of his government's reliance on force and intimidation, despite the widespread support of the Cuban people. Nor did he acknowledge the democratic world's insistence that he hold open and free elections, something that, as an old-line Stalinist, he seemed to fear.

Many visitors to Cuba wore blinders and simply accepted what the Cuban government wanted them to see. Those who wandered outside the boundaries of Cuba's dollar-based tourist economy saw the real Cuban people—enthusiastic about life, cautious about speaking out, repressed by State Security, and, especially outside of Havana, enmired in poverty. Most foreign visitors behaved like the Brazilian Workers' Party leader Luis

Inácio da Silva ("Lula"). When he traveled to Cuba in December 2000, his hosts limited his itinerary to showcase schools and factories, and kept him inside the zones developed for tourists. He visited Lenin Park and admired the new statue of John Lennon dedicated to mark the twentieth anniversary of the musician's murder. In a press interview, Lula called Cuba "a democracy," even though its president, Fidel Castro, has been in power for over forty years. Castro's political base, Lula explained, represents an "organic" composite of the people's wishes. The press reported that Lula's eyes reddened with emotion when he spoke of his "pride in showing solidarity with Cuba."[84] The Brazilian national magazine's reporter's cynical account suggested that either Lula was a fool or had been brainwashed during his six-day stay.

Life across the Florida Straits in Miami imitated, in some ways, the patterns of revolutionary Cuba. The tenacious passion of Miami's Cuban Americans against Castro and for their collective national memory has maintained their enclave isolated from the rest of their new nation. Cuban American businesses in South Florida, some observers noted, limited their opportunities for growth because of their reluctance to expand beyond Miami's boundaries. Intimidation against open dialogue, whether from elected politicians or Spanish-language broadcasters, blinded decent, family-oriented Miami Cubans to broader-based American political values. Many other Cuban Americans in Miami, however, have energized the city, making significant contributions to charity, the arts, and to Miami's image as being fashionable and dynamic.

On April 2, 2001, anonymous persons paid to have small planes circle Miami's Pro Player Stadium for about twenty minutes at the start of the baseball season's opening day game between the Marlins and the Phillies. One trailed a message reading "AMERICANS EXERCISE YOUR RIGHT TO TRAVEL: VISIT CUBA"; the other, in skywriting shorthand, "CUBAN AMERICANS 4 LIFTING THE EMBARGO: CLAP" If anyone clapped in response, they were swallowed up by the sellout crowd filling up the stadium under the hot, unforgiving Miami sun.

NOTES

PREFACE

1. Guillermo Martinez, "The Exile Who Dared Talk to Castro," *Miami Herald*, July 20, 1984. Benes clipping file.
2. "Anglo" is a term widely used in Miami to denote white non-Hispanics.
3. Letter, Anita Stone to Armando Pérez-Roura, August 10, 2000. Courtesy of Anita Stone
4. Letter, no date, Benes clipping file.
5. E-mail from Wood McCue to Benes, October 19, 2000.
6. Letter, December 19, 1978. Benes clipping file.
7. Letter from Cousin Mary, Washington, D.C., December 7, 1978.
8. Mailgram, Ernest A. Iniguez, Hialeah Police Department, to Miles Frechette, Cuba Desk, State Department. no date. ca. 1978. Bernardo Benes collection.
9. Transcript of statement by Wayne S. Smith on WQBA, February 16, 1980. Bernardo Benes collection.
10. E-mail, Bernardo Benes to author, October 15, 2000.
11. Statement, Bernardo Benes to author, November 22, 2000.

CHAPTER ONE

1. Pons paid the $72, but Benes went back to the restaurant and asked for a signed copy of the receipt because he thought it might hold historical importance. Receipt, Club Panamar, August 22, 1977. Benes collection.
2. These events are based in part on detailed notes taken by Bernardo Benes and in his possession. Benes collection.
3. Interview, Bernardo Benes, July 6, 2000
4. See "Victims' Stories," www.cubanet.org/Cnews/y00/mar00/23el.htm
5. Interview with former president Ricardo de la Espriella and Bernardo Benes, Coconut Grove, October 6, 2000.
6. Statement to author from anonymous FBI agent assigned during the 1970s and 1980s to Cuban issues.
7. One of the automobile dealerships Dascal acquired was South Motors, a major Honda and BMW agency.

8. When asked about Dascal's role in the missions, Benes responded with a quote from Sir Harold Nicolson's *Diplomacy:* "There are two kinds of diplomats: the 'warrior or the heroic,' and 'the mercantile or shopkeeper.'" For Benes, he represented the former and Dascal the latter. Interview, Bernardo Benes, September 14, 2000.

9. Helga Silva, *Miami News*, November 13, 1978, 1A, 4A

10. Robert A. Pastor, *Whirlpool: U. S. Foreign Policy Towards Latin America and the Caribbean*, 52.

11. Public Papers, Carter, 1977, vol. 1, 903–09, cited by Robert A. Pastor, *Whirlpool: U. S. Foreign Policy Towards Latin America and the Caribbean* (Princeton: Princeton University Press, 1992), 52.

12. Dascal, for some reason, was not disguised. E-mail, Bernardo Benes, October 29, 2000.

13. Interview, Bernardo Benes, August 9, 2000. Benes later maintained that he said this as a joke.

14. Interview, Bernardo Benes, October 1, 2000.

15. Meg Laughlin, in *Tropic* Magazine, *Miami Herald*, November 6, 1994. Benes clipping file.

16. The episode was filmed and shown on the television news. Courtesy of Sara Sánchez, University of Miami Richter Library, November 17, 2000.

17. Letter, Fred Wahl to author, September 6, 2000. But he still failed to get transportation for his relatives. The Hamburg-American Line demanded $1,500 (a fortune in 1939) plus the cost of telegrams to Germany, and Wahl paid. But when his family arrived in Hamburg to board the ship, Nazi officials confiscated their belongings and told them to wait for another ship. None ever came, and the family perished in the Holocaust.

18. Interview, Leon A. Cuervo, Miami, November 17, 2000.

19. Courtesy of Sara Sánchez.

20. Obituary, Jesús Yáñez Pelletier, *Miami Herald*, September 20, 2000, 4B. Pelletier later fled into exile to the United States, where he helped purchase weapons for the 26th of July rebels. After Castro took power in 1959, he appointed Yánez his military aide. In 1960, however, Castro ordered him arrested and charged with treason. He served eleven of a fifteen-year sentence before gaining his release in 1971, but Cuban officials refused to issue him an exit visa. In the early 1980s, Yáñez became vice-president for the Cuban Commission for Human Rights, a dissident group. He died in Havana on September 19, 2000.

21. Jorge Mañach, among his many books, wrote *Martí the Apostle*. Despite the fact that the author left for the United States after Castro's takeover, and became a fervent anti-Castro voice in Miami, after he died in exile the Cuban government reedited and published a new edition of his Martí biography. Courtesy of Moisés Asís, Miami, September 20, 2000.

22. Castro's statement may have been paraphrased from Adolph Hitler's self-defense speech at his trial after the 1923 Munich putsch. Courtesy, Moisés Asís, September 20, 2000.

23. Fidel Castro, La *Historia me Absolverá* (Havana: Editorial de Ciencias Sociales, 1967), 42, quoted by Louis A. Pérez,Jr., *On Becoming Cuban* (Chapel Hill: University of North Carolina Press), 452.

24. See Mona Rosenthal, Inside the Revolution: Everyday Life in Socialist Cuba (Ithaca: Cornell University Press, 1997).

25. See Mark T. Gilderhus, *The Second Century: U.S. Latin American Relations Since 1889* (Wilmington, DE: SR Books, 2000), 163–65.

26. See Carlos Franqui, *Cuba: El libro de los doce* (Mexico City: ERA, 1966).

27. See Hugh Thomas, *Cuba: the Pursuit of Freedom* (DaCapo, 1998), the standard history of Batista's fall and Castro's rise.

28. Wayne S. Smith, *The Closest of Enemies: A Personal and Diplomatic History of the Castro Years* (New York: W. W. Norton, 1987), 16

29. See his history of Cuba, *Historia de Cuba desde Colon hasta Castro* (New York: Edwin Publishers, 1963).

30. During the Six-Day War in 1967, Benes organized a meeting to support the State of Israel. Members of all of the important Cuban groups in Miami attended. The meeting became so emotional that some of the men present volunteered to fight as soldiers for Israel, including Julio González Rebull, a Bay of Pigs veteran, who actually enlisted. Some days later, Benes received a letter from Primitivo Rodríguez apologizing for his anti-Semitic stance in the past. Letter in Benes collection.

31. Wayne S. Smith, *The Closest of Enemies*, 19.

32. María de los Angeles Torres, *In the Land of Mirrors: Cuban Exile Politics in the United States* (Ann Arbor: University of Michigan Press, 1999), 46–47.

33. Quoted by Wayne S. Smith, *The Closest of Enemies*, 23.

34. Wayne S. Smith, *The Closest of Enemies*, 34.

35. Interview, Bernardo Benes, September 29, 2000.

36. Interview, anonymous CIA official who was assigned to Cuban affairs during the late 1950s. September 7, 2000.

37. Harvard's dean of the Faculty of Arts and Sciences, McGeorge Bundy, confirmed this in an interview given in November 1994 to Alexsandr Fursenko and Timothy Naftali. See Fursenko and Naftali, *"One Hell of a Gamble": Khrushchev, Castro and Kennedy, 1958–1964* (New York: W. W. Norton and Company, 1997), 10.

38. Wayne S. Smith, *The Closest of Enemies*, 37.

39. See J. A. Sierra, at http://www.historyofcuba.com/history/batista.htm

40. Damián J. Fernandez, *Cuba and the Politics of Passion* (Austin: University of Texas Press, 2000), 71.

41. Jane Franklin, *Cuba and the United States: A Chronological History* (Melbourne, Australia: Ocean Press, 1997), 17–19.

42. Jane Franklin, *Cuba and the United States*, 20–21.

43. Bernardo Benes, interview with Margalit Bejarano, March 3, 1987. Transcript in Benes collection.

44. Confidential memorandum, Vice-president Richard M. Nixon to Senator Mike Mansfield, Washington, April 25, 1959. Cited by Jeffrey J. Stafford,

"The Nixon-Castro Meeting of 19 April 1959," *Diplomatic History* 4 (1980), 426–31.

45. Confidential memorandum, Vice-President Richard M. Nixon to Senator Mike Mansfield, Washington, April 25, 1959. Cited by Jeffrey J. Stafford, "The Nixon-Castro Meeting of 19 April 1959," 431.

46. Thomas Boswell and J. R. Curtis, *The Cuban American Experience* (Totowa, NJ: Rowman and Allenheld, 1984), 42.

47. Quoted from the *New York Times* by María de los Angeles Torres, *In the Land of Mirrors*, 51.

48. Later, according to Benes, Núñez left Cuba for the United States and became one of Miami's most successful businessmen.

49. Fursenko and Naftali, *"One Hell of a Gamble,"* 32–33; Robert E. Quirk, *Fidel Castro* (New York: W. W. Norton, 1993), 248–49, 264–65.

50. Maria de los Angeles Torres, *In the Land of Mirrors*, 4.

51. See Fursenko and Naftali, *"One Hell of a Gamble,"* 26.

52. Fursenko and Naftali, *"One Hell of a Gamble,"* 32

53. Fursenko and Naftali, *"One Hell of a Gamble,"* 32–33, 45, citing documents from Archive of the Secretariat of the Soviet Central Committee of the Communist Party, Folio 4, List 16, File 954, 169. See also Robert E. Quirk, *Fidel Castro*, 88.

54. Margalit Bejarano, interview with Bernardo Benes, March 3, 1987. Courtesy of Margalit Bejarano.

55. *Gaceta Oficial*, Havana, October 13, 1960, 4.

56. Interview, Dr. Leon A. Cuervo, Miami, November 17, 2000.

CHAPTER TWO

1. Alejandro Portes and Alex Stepick, *City on the Edge: The Transformation of Miami* (Berkeley: University of California Press, 1993), 97.

2. Ana Acle, "Salvaged Papers Shed Light on Former Cuban Dictator," *Miami Herald*, August 17, 2000, 1A, 11A.

3. Alejandro Portes and Robert L. Bach, *Latin Journey: Cuban and Mexican Immigrants in the United States* (Berkeley: University of California Press, 1985), 84.

4. Interview, Brian O. Walsh, Miami, November 22, 2000.

5. Interview, Brian O. Walsh, Miami, November 22, 2000. As a result of Voorhees's recommendation, however, the Eisenhower administration allocated $1 million for South Florida refugee relief.

6. Tom Blackburn, *National Catholic Reporter*, ca. February 2000, at www.natcath.com/NCR_Online/archives/050500/050500c.htm

7. Based on more than twenty interviews of Cuban Americans who arrived during the first post-1959 wave of exiles.

8. Louis A. Pérez, *Cuba: Between Reform and Revolution* (New York: Oxford University Press, 1995), 297–99.

9. Curiously, in Cuba the airlift is called "Peter Pan" while in Miami many Cubans call it "Pedro Pan."

10. Interview, former Pedro Pan official, Miami, September 30, 2000. Name withheld by request.

11. She died in Miami on March 22, 2000 at the age of eighty-four, her health having been broken in prison. See www.fiu.edu/fcf/politagrau.html

12. E-mail, Silvia J. Muñoz to author, November 6, 2000. Silvia was fortunate: her mother arrived only three months after she was placed in the camp.

13. Courtesy of Marcos Kerbel, one of the HIAS airlift children.

14. María Cristina García, *Havana USA* (Berkeley: University of California Press, 1996), 16–17.

15. Maria Cristina García, *Havana USA*, 17.

16. The events of this period are concisely summarized by Miguel González-Pando, *The Cuban Americans* (Westport, CT: Greenwood Press, 1998), 17–30.

17. Alejandro Portes and Alex Stepick, *City on the Edge*, 149.

18. Rafael Prohias and Lourdes Casal, *The Cuban Minority in the U.S.* (Boca Raton: Florida Atlantic University, 1973), 111.

19. Tom Blackburn, *The National Catholic Reporter*, May 5, 2000, at www.natcath.com/NCR_Online/archives/050500/050500c.htm.

20. Cuban Banking Study Group, Inc., *Cuba: Past, Present and Future of its Banking and Financial System* (Miami: CGSG, 1995), 7.

21. Letter, Rep. Emanuel Celler to Rep. Claude Pepper, December 24, 1970.

22. For example, *Miami Review*, Sept. 17, 1969. Benes clipping file.

23. United States Department of Commerce, Bureau of the Census. *County Business Patterns* (Washington, D.C.: United States Government Printing Office, 1959).

24. Melissa Soldani de Lemon, *Cuban Exile Bankers, International Banking, and Miami's Emergence as a Commercial Crossroads of the Americas* (Ph.D. dissertation, Florida State University, February 1998), 36.

25. Melissa Soldani de Lemon, *Cuban Exile Bankers*, 42.

26. *Loc. cit.*

27. Literally, "Anglo" refers to Anglo-Saxons, but over the years in Miami has come to include all person of Caucasian background.

28. Melissa Soldani de Lemon, *Cuban Exile Bankers*, 90–91

29. *Time*, November 12, 1965, 36–37.

30. Rev. Bryan O. Walsh, interview with Alex Stepick and Alejandro Portes, January 12, 1987, in *City on the Edge*, 144.

31. Aleksandr Fursenko and Timothy Naftali, *"One Hell of a Gamble": Khrushchev, Castro and Kennedy, 1958–1964* (New York: W. W. Norton & Company, 1997), 83.

32. Minutes of meeting of Flavio Bravo and Soviet officials Suslov and Koslov, March 3, 1961, Folio 3, List 871, Archive of the President of the Russian

Federation (APRF), cited by Aleksandr Fursenko and Timothy Naftali, *"One Hell of a Gamble,"* 87.

33. Aleksandr Fursenko and Timothy Naftali, *"One Hell of a Gamble,"* 97, on the meeting between Khrushchev and Castro on May 5, 1963; Zavidovo papers, Archives of the President of the Russian Federation.

34. John McMullan, editorial, *Miami Herald,* May 22, 1983, 2E.

35. The total cost of Castro's requested weapons was $193 million in United States dollars, a figure worth significantly more today. Soviet archive documentation cited by Fursenko and Naftali, *"One Hell of a Gamble,"* 373, note 20.

36. See Herman H. Dinsmore, *All the News that Fits: A Critical Analysis of the News and Editorial Content of the New York Times* (New Rochelle, NY: Arlington House, 1969, 220–24.

37. Later émigrés came during Mariel (1980); as part of a visa lottery deal between Havana and Washington; smuggled in via professional traffickers; and on rafts and hazardous vessels, many of which sank in the sea, taking with them their desperate passengers.

38. Interview with Bill Teck, publisher of *Generation Ñ* magazine, Coral Gables, October 10, 2000.

39. See Dorita Roca Mariña, "A Theoretical Discussion of What Changes and What Stays the Same in Cuban Immigrant Families," in José Szapocznik and María Cristina Herrera, eds., *Cuban Americans: Acculturation, Adjustment, and the Family* (Washington, D.C.: The National Coalition of Hispanic Mental Health and Human Services Organizations, 1978.)

40. E-mail, Silvia J. Muñoz to author, November 6, 2000.

41. E-mail, Silvia J. Muñoz to author, November 6, 2000.

42. Fabiola Santiago, "A Century of Learning," *Miami Herald,* November 6, 2000, 1E, 2E.

43. Fabiola Santiago, "A Century of Learning," 1E, 2E.

44. See Letter, Bobby Maduro to Benes, Jersey City, May 27, 1961; Tommy Devine, in the *Miami Herald,* June 2, 1961. Benes clipping file.

45. Interview, Jack Gordon, September 5, 2000.

46. Letter, Bernardo Benes, ca. 1970. Benes collection.

47. Edythe Schindler, "A Cold Day in Miami," *American Judaism,* 1964, 20, 59. Benes collection.

48. *Jew-Ban,* I:1 (January 1969). Interestingly, later issues were titled "JEW[in lower case, "ish"] -Cu [in lower case] BAN/." After the congregation's first ten years, it had 800 families as members, buried their dead at one of two cemeteries, sold Israel Bonds, and contributed extensively to the United Jewish Appeal campaigns. Services were held at first in rented offices, then in the auditorium of Washington Federal S&L courtesy of Jack Gordon, in the social hall of the DiLido Hotel, and finally at its own building and community center at Michigan Avenue and Seventeenth Street.

49. Testimony, Bernardo Benes, 1967, at Senate Judiciary Committee. Benes collection.

50. Larry Birger article in *American Savings and Loan Weekly*, ca. 1966. Benes collection.

51. Jaime Benes, letter to Charlotte *Observer*, ca. 1970. Benes clipping file.

52. Interview, Bernardo Benes, October 29, 2000.

53. *Beach Diary*, c. 1968. Benes clipping file.

54. Marshall Wise, "The Cuban Exile in Miami: Asset or Liability?" Talk presented June 2, 1966. Transcript in Benes collection.

55. Marshall Wise, "The Cuban Exile in Miami: Asset or Liability?"

56. Marshall Wise, "The Cuban Exile in Miami: Asset or Liability?"

57. Mike Abrams, "Beach Cubans Exist in Prejudice," Miami Beach *Sun*, June 28, 1969. Benes clipping file.

58. Letter, "Bilingual Problem of Miami Beach," ca. 1967. Newspaper not identified. Benes collection.

59. Clipping, Miami Beach *Sun*, ca. 1966. Benes clipping file.

60. Letter printed in unidentified newspaper not identified, ca. 1966. Benes clipping file.

61. Clipping, newspaper not identified, ca. 1967. Benes clipping file.

62. Letter from Evangelism Task Force, Miami, to Benes, December 12, 1967. Benes collection.

63. Letter from Primitivo Rodríguez, June 6, 1967, Benes collection. See also letter, Netenial Lorch, Secretary General of the Israeli Knesset, Jerusalem, to Benes, October 26, 1972. Benes collection.

64. Interview, Bernardo Benes, July 30, 2000. He donated all of the religious objects to appropriate organizations although one Torah remains on loan in his home.

65. Al Burt and Don Bohning, in the *Miami Herald*, February 17, 1968, 9A; *Miami Herald*. November 10, 1991; *New York Times*, October 24, 1976; burn.ucsd.edu/archives/ats–1/1997.Feb/0070.html/.

66. Helga Silva, *Miami Herald*, April 8, 1979, 22A.

67. See Norman Mailer, *Miami and the Siege of Chicago*, rev. ed., (New York: Primus, 1986).

68. See www.afrocubaweb.com/history2.htm

69. Mike Baxter, *Miami Herald*, May 24, 1970, 1, 13C. Benes clipping file.

70. Mike Baxter, *Miami Herald*, May 24, 1970, 1, 13C.

71. Letter, Bernardo Benes to Dr. Charles E. Perry, June 8, 1971. Benes collection.

72. Letter, Bernardo Benes to Dr. Charles E. Perry, July 22, 1972. Benes collection.

73. Interview, Bernardo Benes, September 16, 2000.

74. Interview, Bernardo Benes, October 22, 2000.

75. Aleksandr Fursenko and Timothy Naftali, *"One Hell of a Gamble"* 6.

76. Interview, Luis Salas, May 23, 2000.

77. Jennifer Suárez, statement at University of Miami forum on *Cubanidad,* September 27, 2000.

CHAPTER THREE

1. Lars Shoultz, *Beneath the United States: A History of U.S. Policy Toward Latin America* (Cambridge, MA: Harvard University Press, 1998), 356.
2. *New York Times,* October 21, 1960, 18, cited by Lars Shoultz, *Beneath the United States,* 356.
3. See Robert M. Levine and José Carlos Sebe Bom Meihy, *The Life and Death of Carolina Maria de Jesus* (Albuquerque: University of New Mexico Press, 1995).
4. Wayne S. Smith, *The Closest of Enemies: A Personal and Diplomatic History of the Castro Years* (New York: W. W. Norton, 1987), 85.
5. Wayne S. Smith, *The Closest of Enemies,* 86
6. E-mail, Bernardo Benes to author, November 13, 2000.
7. Wayne S. Smith, *The Closest of Enemies,* 113
8. Wayne S. Smith, *The Closest of Enemies,* 86–89
9. See Robert A. Pastor, *Whirlpool: U.S. Foreign Policy Towards Latin America and the Caribbean* (Princeton: Princeton University Press, 1992), 42–44.
10. Lars Shoultz, *Beneath the United States,* 362.
11. Robert A. Pastor, *Whirlpool,* 47.
12. *Miami Herald,* April 8, 1979, 22A.
13. María de los Angeles Torres, *In the Land of Mirrors: Cuban Exile Politics in the United States* (Ann Arbor: University of Michigan Press, 2001), 91.
14. *Miami Herald,* January 23, 1977. Benes clipping file.
15. U.S. Senate, Committee on Foreign Relations, *Nomination of Hon. Cyrus R. Vance To Be Secretary of State,* January 11, 1997, 17.
16. Cheryl Brownstein and Sam Jacobs, "Cubans React with Shock and Disgust," *Miami Herald,* February 2, 1977. Benes clipping file.
17. From Benes's notes of the meeting, February 14, 1978. Benes collection.
18. Benes's close friend, the owner of Miami Shoes, provided the boots at no cost. Benes told him the boots were for Panama's Omar Torrijos. Interviews, Bernardo Benes, October 31, 2000, November 22, 2000.
19. Interview with Senator Jack Gordon, July 18, 2000. Gordon years later traveled to Havana as part of a delegation and, when on the receiving line to meet Castro, asked him if he still had Benes's boots. Castro laughed and said that he did.
20. Marshal Timoshenko served in the Russian civil war of 1918–20 as a cavalry commander and subsequently rose in the Soviet army. He commanded the Soviet troops in their final victorious offensive in the Finnish-Soviet War (1940). In May 1940, he succeeded General Voroshilov as commissar for defense and held that position until it was assumed by Joseph Stalin in July, 1941. He led the recapture (November 1941) of Rostov from the Germans and helped in the relief of Moscow.

Later he commanded on the northwest front (1942), in the Caucasus (1943), and in Bessarabia (1944). After the war, he served as chief of the Belorussian military.

21. Interview, Bernardo Benes, November 5, 2000.

22. Interview, Bernardo Benes, July 29, 2000.

23. Memorandum. Bernardo Benes to Zbigniew Brzezinski, Benes collection.

24. Interview, Bernardo Benes, August 21, 2000.

25. Notes taken at meeting with Zbigniew Brzezinski. Benes collection.

26. Telephone interview, Zbigniew Brzezinski, October 5, 2000. Dr Brzezinski recalled that the Benes-Dascal mission was "well-intended" and "promising," but that Robert A. Pastor took over the negotiations after the prisoner release.

27. Interview, Bernardo Benes, July 6, 2000. Benes also told Castro that he suspected that Castro was descended on his father's side from crypto-Jews forcibly converted to Catholicism by the legal action of the Spanish crown. According to Benes, Castro agreed that this might well have been possible. In 1984, Castro explained to Benes something he had done "because of my Jewish ancestors." He was likely joking.

28. Interview, Bernardo Benes, September 24, 2000. The message, as all others, was passed on verbally, not in writing. Also, telephone conversation with Peter Tarnoff, December 15, 2000.

29. Interview, Bernardo Benes, September 20, 2000.

30. Interview, Bernardo Benes, September 20, 2000.

31. Telephone interview, Robert A. Pastor, October 12, 2000.

32. Telephone interview, Robert A. Pastor, October 12, 2000. Both Pastor and Wayne Smith minimize the roles played by Benes and Dascal. "I do not believe that Benes and Dascal influenced Castro at all," Smith wrote (e-mails to author, November 2 and 3, 2000), "or that they influenced us. Essentially, they were emissaries."

33. The afternoon paper may have been more lively, but it hewed to the party line as assiduously as did *Granma.*

34. Interview, Bernardo Benes, August 22, 2000.

35. Interviews, Bernardo Benes, September 24, 2000; Moisés Asís, November 25, 2000. The Soviet advisors were readmitted afterwards in some areas.

36. United States Judiciary Committee, "Hearings before the Subcommittee to Investigate the Administration of the Internal Security Act and other Internal Security Laws, Part 6, First Session, July 30, 1975, 379.

37. Reported by Mimi Whitfield, *Miami Herald,* February 16, 1994, 13.

38. Rep. Dante Fascell (D-FL) quoted by Meg Laughlin, *Tropic* Magazine, *Miami Herald,* November 6, 1994.

39. Wayne S. Smith, *The Closest of Enemies,* 14

40. Wayne S. Smith, e-mail to author, November 3, 2000. Smith added: "[W]hile I never got to know Dascal very well, I did develop a friendship with Benes. I had high regard for him and believe his principal objective was to bring about a more sensible relationship between the two countries that would benefit both."

41. Taken from Bernardo Benes's handwritten notes, Benes collection.

42. Taken from Bernardo Benes's handwritten notes, Benes collection.

43. Interview, Bernardo Benes, July 18, 2000.

44. Helga Silva, *Miami News,* November 16, 1978, 2A.

45. Interview, Bernardo Benes, July 29, 2000.

46. Verbatim note in Benes collection.

47. E-mail, Bernardo Benes to author, October 29, 2000.

48. http://www.cambiocubano.com/consev.html, drawn from Fabiola Santiago, "Old Conspirators Never Die," *Tropic* Magazine, Miami Herald, October 8, 1995.

49. Cynthia Corzo, "Brigada 2506 sentenciara a los defensores de diálogo," *El Nuevo Herald,* November 18, 1995, 1A, 4A.

50. *Miami News,* October 23, 1978, 1.

51. Affidavit, Emilio Rangel, November 8, 2000.

52. Merwin Sigale, *The Washington Post,* October 22, 1978, 1. Thousands more stood outside the auditorium as well.

53. William Tucker, *Miami News,* October 23, 1978, 4A.

54. Interview, Bernardo Benes, September 9, 2000.

55. Guy Gugliotta and Helga Silva, *Miami Herald,* April 9, 1979, 1.

56. Moreno, along with Benes, seemed to have been singled out for attack by the Reverend Manuel Espinosa. Three of Espinosa's radio speeches were transcribed and printed by the Miami Radio Monitoring Service. Benes collection.

57. Merwin Sigale, *The Washington Post,* October 22, 1978, 1.

58. Benes quoted by Zita Arocha, in *Miami Herald,* October 24, 1978, 1, 2C

59. Fernández Caubí, "Pamplinas," *Pla,* December 15, 1978, n.p. Benes clipping file.

60. Statement, Bernardo Benes to author, November 28, 2000.

61. E-mail from Bernardo Benes, December 17, 2000.

62. Memorandum, Benes and Alfredo Durán to Phil Wise, White House, September 21, 1979. Benes collection.

63. Benes had known the pre-1959 owner, Juanito Zarzavitoria, who later opened a Centro Vasco in Miami, although it closed in the early 1990s.

64. Interview, Bernardo Benes, August 13, 2000.

65. Guy Gugliotta and Helga Silva, *Miami Herald,* April 9, 1979, 1.

66. William R. Long, "Even Some of the Reporter Couldn't Hide their Emotions," *Miami Herald,* Sept. 9, 1978.

67. Ana Veciana, *Miami News,* December 28, 1978, 5A.

68. Telegram, *The Washington Post* to Bernardo Benes, December 3, 1978, carrying text of story. Benes collection.

69. Telegram, *The Washington Post* to Bernardo Benes, December 3, 1978, carrying text of story. Benes collection.

70. See, for example, letter, Ramón Sánchez-Parodi, Jefe Sección de Intereses de Cuba en Washington, to Benes, August 22, 1979. Benes collection.

71. Juan Almeida, Sergio del Valle, Osmani Cienfuegos, José Machado Ventura, Jaime Crombert, Ricardo Alarcón, Aleida March, and René Rodríguez. Source: "Acta Final," Consejo de Estado, Havana, December 8, 1978.

72. Author's emphasis.

73. Otherwise, Benes did not say one word during the dialogue between the Miami Cubans and the Cubans.

74. Source: typed report based on notes taken by Benes at November 21, 1978 meeting. Benes collection.

75. Fernando Villaverde, *Miami Herald,* December 14, 1978. Benes clipping file.

76. *The Voice,* November 21, 1978, cited by Guy Gugliotta in the *Miami Herald,* no date, Benes clipping file.

77. Memorandum. Benes and Alfredo Durán to Phil Wise, White House, September 21, 1979. Benes collection; *New York Times,* December 27, 1978, 1.

78. Interview, Bernardo Benes, September 9, 2000.

79. Editorial, *New York Times,* November 24, 1978. Benes clipping file. See also the *Washington Post,* November 25, 1978, editorial, A14.

80. Quoted by Jon Nordheimer, *New York Times,* December 10, 1978. n.p., Benes clipping file.

81. Bonnie M. Anderson, *Miami Herald,* December 10, 1978, 1.

82. Howell Raines, *New York Times,* December 27, 1978, 1.

83. Bonnie M. Anderson, *Miami Herald,* ca. November 18, 1978, Benes clipping file.

84. Bill Brubaker, in the *Miami News,* April 16, 1979.

85. Editorial, *Miami Herald,* Sept. 2, 1978, 6A.

86. Letter, March 1, 1979, from Continental National Bank of Miami. Benes collection.

87. Quote recorded by Meg Laughlin, *Tropic* Magazine, *Miami Herald,* November 6, 1994. Benes clipping file.

88. Quote recorded by Meg Laughlin, *Tropic* Magazine, *Miami Herald,* November 6, 1994. Benes clipping file.

89. Helga Silva and Guy Gugliotta, *Miami Herald,* April 8, 1979, 1A, 22A

90. Helga Silva and Guy Gugliotta, *Miami Herald,* April 8, 1979, 1A, 22A

91. Agenda, Friday, September 14, 1979. Benes collection.

92. Bernardo Benes, memorandum, "Frechette's Visit to Miami," October 31, 1979. Benes collection. Years later, when Frechette was ambassador to Colombia, an American Airlines plane crashed. All of the passengers died, including the son and daughter-in-law of Miami Mayor Maurice Ferré. Benes called Frechette, who consoled Ferré's wife and did everything possible in Colombia to help.

93. Telephone Interview, Peter Tarnoff, December 15, 2000.

94. Robert A. Pastor, *Whirlpool,* 53.

95. Interview, Bernardo Benes, September 23, 2000.

96. Handwritten note from J. A. Regalado and family, no date, Benes collection.

97. Guillermo Martínez and Guy Gugliotta, "The Trauma of Separation and Reunion," *Miami Herald,* December 11, 1983. Benes clipping file.

98. Editorial, *Miami Herald,* October 24, 1978, 6A.

99. Liz Balmaseda, in the *Miami Herald,* April 23, 2000.

100. Liz Balmaseda, in the *Miami Herald,* April 23, 2000.

101. Interview, Bernardo Benes, September 20, 2000.

102. Interview, Bernardo Benes and Ricardo de la Espriella, October 6, 2000. Former president Ricardo de la Espriella added: "Tragically, this was the exact neighborhood bombed by the Americans when, under the Bush administration, they invaded Panama City to retrieve General Manuel Noriega. There was no connection whatsoever between the *barrio* and Noriega, but the bombings and the brief military occupation of the neighborhood resulted in the deaths of hundreds of innocent people. American soldiers shot and killed Panamanians at random. The American press minimized the details of the assault, so the American public barely knew the details." De la Espriella, feeling that he had to do something, telephoned Spain's Prime Minister Felipe González, who then personally called President Bush to register a strong protest.

103. Government of Cuba, *Reclamaciones Norteamericanas por Orden Alfabetico,* Book 3, October 1980.

104. *Reclamaciones Norteamericanas por orden Alfabetico General* (Havana, October 1980). Benes possesses Ejemplar N. 3 (Copy #3).Benes collection.

105. List in Benes collection.

106. Benes, quoted by Ward Sinclair, *The Washington Post,* November 21, 1978, A10.

107. Robert A. Pastor, *Whirlpool,* 53.

108. E-mail message, Ambassador Ambler H. Moss, Jr., to author, September 13, 2000. Benes offers a somewhat different description: he recalls that the meeting with de la Espriella took place at the Miami International Airport and that furthermore de la Espriella never issued any denial.

109. E-mail messages from Ricardo de la Espriella, September 29, 2000 and confirming telephone conversation, October 1, 2000, supporting Benes's recollections.

110. From Bernardo Benes's written notes. Benes collection.

111. Tad Szulc, "Shah's Incredible Journey," reprinted in the *Miami News,* ca. April 1980. Benes clipping file. See also his biography of Castro, *Fidel: A Critical Portrait* (New York: Avon Books, 1986).

112. Statement, Luis Pozo, Miami, October 15, 1999. Benes collection.

113. Liz Balmaseda, in the *Miami Herald,* April 23, 2000.

CHAPTER FOUR

1. Wayne S. Smith, *The Closest of Enemies* (New York: W. W. Norton, 1987), 212.

2. María de los Angeles Torres, *In the Land of Mirrors* (Ann Arbor: University of Michigan Press, 2001), 112–113.

3. Twenty years later, in 2000, Roger Fontaine joined the small but growing chorus of conservative Republicans calling for an end to the economic embargo on Cuba.

4. Telephone conversation with Ambassador Vernon A. Walters, September 13, 2000, West Palm Beach to Coral Gables.

5. Telephone conversation with Ambassador Vernon A. Walters, September 13, 2000. By this time, General Walters had stepped down from his post at the CIA and been named ambassador-at-large.

6. The name assigned to Dascal has been forgotten.

7. María de los Angeles Torres, *In the Land of Mirrors*, 11.

8. Telephone interview, Ambassador Vernon A. Walters, with author, September 13, 2000. See also General Vernon A. Walters's memoirs, *Silent Missions* (Washington, D.C., no publisher listed), released in 1978 and his forthcoming book of essays, *The Mighty and the Meek*, to be published in Great Britain by Little, Brown.

9. Wayne S. Smith, *The Closest of Enemies*, 253.

10. E-mail to author from Wayne S. Smith, November 2, 2000.

11. Wayne S. Smith, *The Closest of Enemies*, 257–58.

12. Wayne S. Smith, *The Closest of Enemies*, 264.

13. Interview, Mercedes María de la Espriella, Coconut Grove, October 6, 2000. Jokingly, she told Benes: "I could shoot you for that." Benes was so close to the de la Espriellas that he regularly stayed in their home when he visited Panama. Once, Mercedes remembers, she was holding a formal tea for ambassadors' wives in her home when Benes, dressed only in a bathing suit and carrying a cigar, walked through the room. The First Lady was not happy at the scene.

14. Interview, President Ricardo de la Espriella, Coconut Grove, October 6, 2000.

15. Geoffrey Tomb, "Presidents, Paper Plates, and Protocol," *Miami Herald*, October 6, 1982. Benes clipping file. While in Washington, Ricky Benes had asked the State Department's chief of protocol whether their guests in Miami could be served on paper plates. He replied: "Okay for all the guests except the President." Ricky ignored him and served de la Espriella *arroz con pollo* on paper plates, the same as everyone else.

16. From notes taken by Bernardo Benes. Benes collection.

17. Helga Silva and Liz Balmaceda, *Miami Herald*, May 21, 1983, 1A.

18. Liz Balmaseda, *Miami Herald*, May 21, 1983, 8A.

19. Alfonso Chardy, *Miami Herald*, May 21, 1983, 1A.

20. In a telephone response on August 24, 2000, to a letter sent to James Baker asking for information about that meeting, Mr. Baker's assistant told the author that Baker "has no recollection" of such a meeting.

21. Information about the meeting was conveyed by Guille to Benes.

22. Verbatim notes taken by Bernardo Benes, December 24, 1984. Some paraphrasing of translation by author.

23. Memorandum, Jim Bloomfield to Benes, May 13, 1985. Benes collection.

24. See Edwin Meese, *With Reagan* (New York: Gateway, 1992). For a more skeptical view, see Johnson Haynes, *Sleepwalking Through History* (New York: W.W. Norton & Company, 1991).

25. Notes, Benes collection.

26. Notes of message in Benes collection.

27. Bernardo Benes, notes from conversation of April 25, 1985, 8:30 A.M. Benes collection.

28. See Donald T. Regan, *For the Record: From Wall Street to Washington* (New York: Harcourt Brace Jovanovich, 1988), 368–73.

29. E-mail to author, Washington, October 11, 2000, name held confidential.

30. Nick Grace, "Radio Martí," February 8, 1998, www.qsl.net/yb0rmi/marti.htm

31. Brett Sokol, "Out with the Geezers," Miami *New Times,* September 7–13, 2000, 20.

32. Reconstructed from Bernardo Benes's personal notes by author.

33. When the writing of this book commenced in mid-2000, Benes wrote a note to Governor Jeb Bush asking that he provide clarification, but no response came.

34. Text of message, Jim Bloomfield to José Luis Padrón and Tony de la Guardia, June 25, 1986. Benes collection.

35. Taken from Bernardo Benes's handwritten notes, 1986. Benes collection.

36. Taken from Bernardo Benes's handwritten notes, 1986. Benes collection.

37. Interview, Bernardo Benes, September 9, 2000.

38. Interview, Moisés Asís, September 21, 2000.

39. Compiled from detailed notes taken by Bernardo Benes. Benes collection.

40. Interview, President Ricardo de la Espriella, Coconut Grove, October 6, 2000.

41. See *New York Times,* October 5, 2000, A13.

42. Serge Schmemann, "Negotiators, Arab and Israeli, Built Friendship from Mistrust," *New York Times,* Sept. 28, 1995, A1, A6.

43. Interview, Bernardo Benes, September 14, 2000.

44. Handwritten faxed message, Bernardo Benes to Peter Tarnoff, October 16, 1995. Benes collection.

45. Benes collection.

Chapter Five

1. See letter, Bernardo Benes to Madre Margarita Miranda, September 19, 1969. Benes collection.

2. Clipping dated 1968, probably from the *Miami Herald.* Benes clipping file.

3. Others present included Jorge Mas Canosa; the lawyer Luis Botifoll; Abel Mestre, who had been the director of the largest radio and television enterprise in Cuba; Raúl Martínez Araras who was a veteran of the attack on the Moncada barracks; Joaquin Martínez Saenz, a former political prisoner, who had been president of the National Bank of Cuba. Additionally,

Alberto Blanco, a respected professor of law in Havana, was present, as was Jorge Garcia Montes, the former prime minister under Batista, and Eduardo Suarez Rivas, who had been a distinguished senator in Cuba. Also attending the forum were Vicente Rubiera, former president of the telephone workers' union, Dr. Guillermo Martínez Márquez, who had been the owner of the confiscated newspaper *El País* and former president of the Interamerican Press Association, and, finally, Eusébio Mujal, who had been general secretary of the Confederation of Cuban Labor Unions.

4. The housing bank, however, never materialized. Interview, Bernardo Benes, March 10, 2001.

5. www.afrocubaweb.com/SugarSultans.htm

6. www.hartford-hwp.com/archives/43b/070.html

7. Roberto Cuitiño V., "¡Victoria del Pueblo Cubano!," ca. 1998. Benes clipping file.

8. Georgie Anne Geyer, *Guerrilla Prince: The Untold Story of Fidel Castro*, reprint, (New York: Andrews McMeel Publishing Company, 1986), 361.

9. Telegram, Washington *Post* to Bernardo Benes, December 3, 1978, carrying the text of Ward Sinclair's story to be published the following day. Benes collection.

10. Herminio Portell Vilá, "Los Comisionados," *El Mundo* (Boston), April 12, 1978. Sent to Benes by the law offices of Lazar Lowinger, J.D., December 4, 1978.

11. "El Condor," in *El Expreso*, November 17, 1978.

12. In 1974, *Réplica*'s offices were firebombed for having angered unknown militant exiles.

13. "Polaco" was the name pejoratively used in Cuba for East European Jews. See *Látigo*, February 1979. Benes clipping file.

14. Nicolás Tolentino, "Apologia de los Traidores," *Látigo*, December 1978, Benes clipping file. See also Benes's counterstatement, "Declaraciones a la Prensa del Dr. Bernardo Benes," Benes papers, Cuban Heritage Collection, University of Miami.

15. "El Condor," *El Universal*, November 23, 1978. Benes clipping file.

16. *El Universal*, January 25, 1980, 1.

17. Interview, Calixto Nieves, Miami, July 28, 2000, who asserts that he heard the allegation made denying that Benes and Dascal paid for their own expenses.

18. Melissa Soldani de Lemon, "Cuban Exile Bankers, International Banking, and Miami's Emergence as a Commercial Crossroads of the Américas," Ph.D. dissertation, Florida State University, 1998, vi.

19. "El 'Rojo' Benes," *La Verdad*, March 3, 1980. Benes clipping file.

20. Guillermo Martínez, "The Exile Who Dared Talk to Castro," *Miami Herald*, ca. 1984. Benes clipping file.

21. Manuel Amor, Entrelineas, *El Universal*, March 7, 1980, 1.

22. Jorge Luis Hernández, in *Regreso*, July 29, 1972. Benes clipping file.

23. Manuel Amor, "Entre Lineas," *El Expreso*, November 17, 1978.

24. *Miami Herald*, Feb. 6, 1988, 1A.
25. Jacobo Saif, "Cositas Sueltas," *La Nación*, September 28, 1979. Benes clipping file.
26. Joan Didion, *Miami* (New York: Vintage Books, 1986), 109–113.
27. Joan Didion, *Miami*, 113.
28. "Afirma Zeta," *El Expreso*, November 11, 1978. Benes clipping file.
29. www.hartford-hwp.com/archives/43b/070.html
30. Dan Williams and Joan Fleischman, *Miami Herald*, no date. Benes clipping file.
31. List of invited guests from Benes collection.
32. Interview, Bernardo Benes, September 14, 2000.
33. Statement from Bernardo Benes, November 26, 2000.
34. Ana Venencia and Bob Dart, Atlanta *Constitution*, 1979, Benes clipping file.
35. Ana Venencia and Bob Dart, Atlanta *Constitution*, 1979, Benes clipping file.
36. Bonnie M. Anderson, *Miami Herald*, May 6, 1979, 1B.
37. Alberto Rodríguez, "Infames Anecdotas," *Patria*, October 11, 1978.
38. *La Nación*, November 22, 1978. Benes clipping file.
39. Transcript translated and notarized by Amaury Cruz of the American Translator's Association and notarized on March 17, 1980.
40. Undated article, "FBI: Espinosa Charges Led to Plot," Benes clipping file.
41. Dan Williams and Joan Fleischman, *Miami Herald*, March 6, 1980, 1–2.
42. *Miami Herald*, April 5, 1980. Benes clipping file.
43. Gene Miller and Dan Williams, *El Herald*, March 7, 1980, 1. Benes clipping file.
44. Dan Williams and Joan Fleischman, *Miami Herald*, no date. Benes clipping file
45. Years later, Sánchez, released from prison after serving a sentence for refusing to testify before a grand jury, became coordinator of the "Democracia Movement" that claims as its mentors Mahatma Gandhi and Martin Luther King.
46. Dan Williams and Joan Fleischman, *Miami Herald*, no date. Benes clipping file
47. See Howard Kleinberg, "When is a 'Dialogue' Acceptable?," *Miami Herald*, June 4, 1991. Benes clipping file.
48. Mary Vorobil and Sandra Dibble, "Bank in Little Havana Bombed: Key Officer had Angered Some Exiles," *Miami Herald*, May 28, 1983. Benes clipping file.
49. Bernardo Benes, written statement to author, September 2, 2000. That night, at 10:00 P.M., editor Jim Hampton telephoned Benes to offer his support, and the next day Benes went to publisher Alvah Chapman to tell him what had happened. But in the end, no remedy emerged. Benes purchased a share of *Herald* stock to be able to attend the next stockholder's meeting, but for some reason he never attended.
50. Michael Putney, in *Miami Herald*, September 22, 1980, 5D.

51. Letter, Cyrus Vance, Washington, D.C. to Benes, May 15, 1980. Benes collection.

52. Howard Kleinberg, The *Miami News*, December 13, 1982. Benes collection.

53. Handwritten memo, "B." to "S. P." September 18, 1984, Benes collection.

54. Linda Rodriguez Bernfeld, *Miami Today*, October 6, 19988, 22B.

55. Letter, Benes to Jim Hampton, September 23, 1983.

56. Lourdes Meluza, *Miami Herald*, June 11, 1986, 1B.

57. Joan Didion, *Miami*, 115.

58. Interview, Bernardo Benes, March 10, 2001.

59. Statement, Bernardo Benes to author, November 22, 2000.

60. Letters, Bernardo Benes to David Lawrence, December 4, 1997; David Lawrence to Bernardo Benes, December 5, 1997. Benes collection.

61. FIU poll, October 2000.

62. Bernardo Benes, in *Miami Herald*, January 12, 1996, 23A.

63. Luis V. Manrara, "Los Portentosos Hebreos," in *Diário de las Américas*, July 19, 1972, 5.

64. Engraved invitation to Rhumba for Breakfast, January 19, 1997.

65. Howard Kleinberg, *Miami Herald*, April 6, 1991. Benes clipping file.

66. Interview, former FBI official, September 19, 2000. The name of the agent is not revealed by mutual agreement.

67. Meg Laughlin, *Tropic* Magazine, *Miami Herald*, November 6, 1994. Benes clipping file.

68. Meg Laughlin, *Tropic* Magazine, *Miami Herald*, November 6, 1994. Benes clipping file.

69. Meg Laughlin, *Tropic* Magazine, *Miami Herald*, November 6, 1994. Benes clipping file.

70. Meg Laughlin, *Tropic* Magazine, *Miami Herald*, November 6, 1994. Benes clipping file.

71. Meg Laughlin, *Tropic* Magazine, *Miami Herald*, November 6, 1994. Benes clipping file.

72. "The 100: A Ranking of the Most Influential People in South Florida History," *Miami Herald*, February 7, 1993, 4J.

73. *Viva Semanal*, Oct. 23–29, 1996. 19.

74. Bernardo Benes, handwritten statement to author, September 2, 2000. See also *Viva Semanal*, October 23–29, 1996. 19.

75. See, for example, letters written on Benes's behalf from Representative Dante Fascell to Bill Clinton, Hillary Clinton, and many others, saying, among other things: "Dr. Benes is a remarkable person whom I have known for over 30 years." Copies of all letters in Benes collection.

76. Letter, Micky Arison to David Lawrence, Miami, February 12, 1996. Benes collection.

77. Letter, David Lawrence to Bernardo Benes, February 15, 1996. Benes collection.

78. Alex Benes later became president of NBC News.

79. Letter, Carlos A. Saladrigas to community leaders, May 19, 1998. Benes collection.

80. Mimi Whitefield, *Miami Herald*, April 20, 1998, Business Section, 11.
81. E-mail, Bernardo Benes, November 23, 2000; Interview, Msgr. Bryan O. Walsh, Miami, November 22, 2000.
82. Interview, Bernardo Benes, August 9, 2000.
83. Anonymous interview with author, November 17, 2000.
84. E-mail, Bernardo Benes to author, November 20, 2000.
85. See Robert M. Levine and Moisés Asís, *Cuban Miami* (New Brunswick: Rutgers University Press, 2000)
86. Kathy Glasgow, "Family Baggage," Miami *New Times*, September 18, 1997, from www.miaminewtimes.com.
87. Interview, Ramón Arteaga, Miami, August 20, 2000. Newly-inaugurated president George W. Bush allied with the far right wing when in March 2001 his administration dashed the hopes of the South Koreans, whose president had won the 2000 Nobel Peace Prize for his efforts, by reversing the policy of the Clinton administration favoring rapprochement.

CHAPTER SIX

1. Interview, Juan Carlos Espinosa, Coral Gables, November 10, 2000. Cubans arriving on the 20,000 visas per year issued by the United States Immigration and Naturalization Service fared much better because most had relatives waiting for them.
2. Guillermo Grenier and Hugh Gladwin, *2000 FIU/Cuba Poll*, Cuban Research Institute, Florida International University, October 19, 2000.
3. E-mail, Basilio V. Sifko to author, November 21, 2000.
4. Damián J. Fernández, *Cuba and the Politics of Passion* (Austin: University of Texas Press, 2000),142–43.
5. Interview, Juan Carlos Espinosa, Coral Gables, November 10, 2000.
6. Max J. Castro, "The Trouble with Collusion," in *Cuba, the Elusive Nation: Interpretations of National Identity*, eds. Damián J. Fernández and Madeline Cámara Betancourt (Gainesville: University Press of Florida, 2000), 303.
7. The phrase is the author's, based on more than seventy-five interviews conducted among a broad spectrum of Cuban American residents of Miami.
8. Letter, Juan Carlos Espinosa, Miami, to author, December 1, 2000.
9. Reported by Bernardo Benes, October 13, 2000.
10. Interview, Dr. Emilio Ochoa, October 15, 2000.
11. Signed statement to author by Dr. Emilio Ochoa, October 20, 2000.
12. See Joan Didion, *Miami*, paperback ed., (New York: Vintage Books, 1998), 110.
13. The phrase was coined by theologian Reinhold Niebuhr.
14. E-mail, Brian Latell, Washington, D.C., to author, October 11, 2000.
15. Letter, William Aramony, to author, October 10, 2000.
16. http://cuban-exile.com/doc063.htm
17. *Miami Herald*, July 24, 2000, 3L-3L

18. Alberto Jones, The Alberto Jones Column II, www.afrocubaweb.com/Alberto Jones2.htm. Jones, a black Cuban, spent many years at Guantánamo and later moved to northern Florida.
19. Mark Silva, in *Miami Herald*, August 8, 2000, 19A.
20. Bernardo Benes, statement to author, September 16, 2000.
21. Bernardo Benes, statement to author, August 24, 2000. Also, Affidavit, Dr. José Raúl Alfonso, confirming under oath that at 9:00 in the morning on August 14, 2000, he heard Armando Pérez-Roura say over Radio Mambí the following (verbatim): "The Cubans shouldn't vote for Lieberman, because he is a Jew the same as Bernardo Benes, who seeks to dialogue with Cuba."
22. Letter, Anita Stone to Armando Pérez-Roura, August 10, 2000. Courtesy of Anita Stone.
23. Interview, Anita Stone, Miami, October 7, 2000.
24. Interview, Anita Stone, Miami, October 7, 2000.
25. Interview. Msgr. Bryan O. Walsh, Miami, November 22, 2000.
26. Quoted by Gaeton Fonzi, http://cuban-exile.com/doc063.htm. Smith also allegedly said that "he's also sinister. I don't think he understands democracy any more than Castro does."
27. http://www.house.gov/ros-lehtinen/bio.html. Some editing by author.
28. http://www.house.gov/Díaz-balart/bio.htm. Some editing by author.
29. See Federal Election Committee, "Report of the Audit Division on Lincoln Díaz-Balart for Congress Committee, March 24, 2000"; E-mail, Santiago Aroca to author, November 28, 2000.
30. Felix Roberto Masud-Piloto, *From Welcomed Exiles to Illegal Immigrants: Cuban Migration to the U.S., 1959–1995* (Totowa, NJ: Rowman and Littlefield Publishers, Inc., 1996). 132–33.
31. Howard Kleinberg, *Miami Herald*, April 6, 1991. Benes clipping file.
32. Fernando Capablanca, remarks at meeting of the CBSG, October 19, 2000.
33. *New York Times*, July 20, 1990, A1.
34. Luis Posada Carriles, The *Paths of the Warrior* (published in Spanish as *Caminos del Gurrero*, city and publisher unknown, 1994).
35. See Glenn Garvin, *Miami Herald*, November 25, 2000, 3A.
36. Quoted by Glenn Garvin and Francis Robles, *Miami Herald*, November 21, 2000, 1A, 2A.
37. Glenn Garvin, "Castro Says Exiles Planned to Kill Him," *Miami Herald*, November 18, 2000, 11A.
38. Courtesy of Nick Grace.
39. Kathy Glasgow, "Broadcast Blunder," Miami *New Times*, August 31-September 6, 2000), 23–29.
40. Joseph Tanfani, in *Miami Herald*, October 26, 2000, 3B.
41. Max J. Castro, "The Trouble with Collusion," in *Cuba, the Elusive Nation*, 299.
42. Max J. Castro, "The Trouble with Collusion," 298–301.

43. See Allen C. Hansen, *USIA: Public Diplomacy in the Computer Age* (New York: Praeger, 1989), 120–21.

44. www.westword.com/extra/martidebate.html

45. Jim Mullin, Miami *New Times*, April 27, 2000.

46. Anonymous statement to author, October 30, 2000.

47. Joseph T. Casavant, letter to the Herald, June 21, 1970. Benes collection. He added: "Here are what I consider the most important DO NOT's. Refrain from blowing auto horns to beckon people from their homes, day or night; No double parking to converse with people on the sidewalk; No parking on or across sidewalks; Tone down heated discussions while driving; no four people in an auto with eight hands in the air; Refrain from carrying on loud conversations during church services and allowing church to be a playground for their youngsters; Do not congregate on sidewalks in large groups, compelling passersby to get off the sidewalk to get by."

48. Interview, Moisés Asís, April 26, 2000. The broadcaster was referring to Robert M. Levine and Moisés Asís, *Cuban Miami* (New Brunswick: Rutgers University Press, 2000).

49. www.afrocubaweb.com/AlbertoJones2.htm

50. Interview, Moisés Asís, September 1, 2000. Asís came to Miami in 1993.

51. See Jim Mullin, "The Burden of a Violent History," Miami *New Times*, April 27, 2000.

52. Interview, Antonio Jorge, Miami, November 17, 2000.

53. Guillermo Martínez, "The Exile Who Dared to Talk to Castro," *Miami Herald*, ca. 1984. Benes clipping file.

54. Carlos Martínez, "The Cuban Beat," *Miami Herald*, October 9, 1967, 4.

55. Jonathan Kandell, "City of Exiles," *Cigar Aficionado*, July-August 2000, 62–81.

56. Elelio Taillacq, "Armando Pérez-Roura: Con la Audiencia en un Puño," *El Nuevo Herald*, November 16, 2000, 9D.

57. Courtesy of Elena Freyre, the head of newly-revived Cuban American Defense League. No reason was given for Benes not having been honored. Interview, Elena Freyre, February 26, 2001.

58. Professor Jorge, on the other hand, recalls that he counseled Benes not to get involved in any dialogue with Castro *before* the flights started. He maintains that he personally defended Benes's "Cubanness" and his honest intentions publicly after Benes returned to vilification. Interview, Antonio Jorge, November 17, 2000, Miami.

59. Interview, Bernardo Benes, October 28, 2000.

60. Interview, Bernardo Benes, September 5, 2000. Benes cites as the source Goar Mestre, chairman of the station, in a talk at his club in Buenos Aires in 1965.

61. Armando Pérez-Roura, "De la Junta de Gobierno del Colegio Nacional de Locutores," *Periódico Revolución* (a precursor to *Granma*), Havana, December 16, 1960.

62. Statement, Bernardo Benes, November 23, 2000.

63. Quoted by Helga Silva, *Miami Herald*, c. 1979. Benes clipping file.
64. Letter, Bernardo Benes to [former] President Jimmy Carter, June 6, 1995. Benes collection.
65. Quoted by Howell Raines, *New York Times*, December 13, 1978, A16.
66. "References," Benes collection.
67. Letter, William Aramony to author, October 10, 2000.
68. Interview, Rabbi Sholom Lipskar, October 23, 2000.
69. *Miami Herald*, April 19, 1994, 6A.
70. Statement, Bernardo Benes, November 22, 2000.
71. Interview, Bernardo Benes, October 4, 2000.
72. Mike Wilson, *Miami Herald*, January 2, 1993, www.fiu.edu/fcf/lorenzo.escape.html.
73. Interview by Moisés Asís and Robert M. Levine for the book *Cuban Miami*.
74. Statement courtesy of Elizabeth Campisi, February 26, 2001.
75. Interview, March 6, 1999.
76. In late 2000, Benes finally received his FBI file under the Freedom of Information Act. He had first requested in ten years earlier.
77. Bernardo Benes, faxed letter to Peter Tarnoff, Department of State, May 24, 1995.
78. Fernando del Castillo, "Avispas Peligrosas y . . . ¡Bernardo Benes!" *La Verdad*, September 14, 1995, 4.
79. Gail Epstein Nieves, "Messages May Have Warned of Shoot-down," *Miami Herald*, December 23, 2000, 1A, 2A.
80. Cited on www.cnn.com/WORLD/9803/20/cuban.americans

CHAPTER SEVEN

1. Charles Lane, "And a Child Shall Lead Them," *The New Republic*, January 24, 2000, posted on www.thenewrepublic.com/012400/coverstory 012400.html
2. Jim de Fede, "The Not Ready for Prime Time Mayor," *Miami New Times*, August 24–30, 2000, 22–23.
3. Jim de Fede, "The Not Ready for Prime Time Mayor," 22–23.
4. Tom Blackburn, *National Catholic Reporter*, April 2000.
5. www.cubanet.org/Cnews/y00/mar00/23e1.htm
6. *Harvard Magazine*, July-August 2000, 35–39.
7. Interview, Maria Mendoza Muxo (pseudonym), Miami, March 11, 2000.
8. Jonathan Kandell, "City of Exiles," 69.
9. Tom Blackburn, *The National Catholic Reporter*, April 2000.
10. Sandra M. García, *Miami Herald*, March 26, 2000, 1. Another "miracle" of sorts occurred in late August 2000. Shortly before she shot herself to death, a fifty-seven-year-old devout woman in Oklahoma, whose ninety-one-year-old mother had just died, rewrote her $500,000 will, giving half to the Miami relatives of Elián González and the other half to a husband and wife in Massachusetts believed by some to have been

falsely convicted of a lurid crime. She had never met either family but disinherited her own relatives in order to provide for her new inheritors. See Ana Acle, "Bequest Names Elián's Family," *Miami Herald*, August 27, 2000, 1A.

11. Luisa Yañez, *Miami Herald*, November 3, 2000, 1B, 4B.

12. Andrés Oppenheimer, "Growing Hispanic Vote Among the Big Election Winners," *Miami Herald*, November 8, 2000, 22A.

13. Howard Kleinberg, "Miami Cubans Still Fighting the Elián War," Cox News Services, November 19, 2000.

14. Interview, Bernardo Benes, September 14, 2000.

15. *Miami Herald*, November 3, 2000, 1A; *El Nuevo Herald*, November 3 and 4, 2000.

16. Quoted in *New York Times*, October 19, 2000, A15.

17. Associated Press release, quoted in the *New York Times*, October 19, 2000, A15.

18. *Granma*, story on its web site, October 20, 2000.

19. Guillermo Grenier and Hugh Gladwin, *2000 FIU/Cuba Poll*, Cuban Research Institute, Florida International University, October 19, 2000.

20. Compiled from Voter Registration Summaries, Dade County, 1990–2000.

21. *Miami Herald*, October 20, 2000, B1.

22. *Impacto*, 1:16, April 4, 1972, 1.

23. *Impacto*, 2:31, January 27, 1973, 1, 5.

24. *Patria*, January 11, 1973, Benes collection.

25. *Miami Herald*, July 24, 2000, 2L-3L

26. Based on twelve interviews on site conducted by author, December 4, 2000. One of the Cuban Americans interviewed, said that the billboard demonstrated that Stalin was worse than Hitler and that Castro was worse than Stalin.

27. Christopher Marquis, *New York Times*, July 22, 2000, A3

28. Luis Martínez Fernández, e-mail to author, December 22, 2000.

29. WTLV-Univision 23 poll, in *Miami Herald*, November 4, 2000, 1B,2B.

30. *Miami Herald*, July 16, 2000, 5L.

31. Statement by Eloy Gutiérrez Menoyo, President of Cambio Cubano, Miami, February 4, 2000.

32. www.wilmingtonstar.com/daily/04252000/editorial/14216.htm

33. bbs.slate.msn.com/bbs/slate-historylesson/popsts/vq/437.asp

34. Charles Mercieca, "Plight of Elián González: American Obsession with Cuba," www.gcty/com/pathtofreedom/plight.html

35. www.afrocubaweb.com/AlbertoJones2.htm

36. E-mail, Seth Stopek to author, November 21, 2000.

37. Quoted by Andres Viglucci and David Hancock, *Miami Herald*, August 4, 1992, 1A.

38. Quoted by Joel Gutierrez and Ana E. Santiago, *Miami Herald*, August 6, 1992, 4B.

39. A random survey taken in late 2000 among Cuban Americans reveals, however, a broader spectrum of opinions than might have been expected. It posed seven short questions to persons representing a cross-section of the Cuban American community and included both women and men. A sampling of two questions from the survey follows.

   Question 1: When Elián González was in Miami, do you think the media handled the story with fairness?

   "Reasonably."

   "I think the English-language press did a fair job of handling the story as it unfolded. After he was taken from his home, as seems to happen when there is community unrest of any kind, the press concentrated on showing the few areas of trouble and did not give enough importance to the Cubans who quietly wept, prayed, or otherwise sought answers to what we though a great injustice. The Spanish-language press went, as expected, to the extreme and seemed to 'fan the flames' when the need for calm was greatest."

   "No. Anglo media coverage ranged from the circus like coverage by [local] Channel 7 to responsible analysis in the *Herald* and Fort Lauderdale *Sun Sentinel. El Nuevo Herald,* however, fanned flames of hysteria."

   Question 2: Do you as a Cuban American feel fully accepted by non-Cuban Miamians or are there areas in which you feel uncomfortable?

   "I feel well accepted."

   "I have felt let out or discriminated against . . . Having lived in the US for 40 years, it never occurred to me what I could be looked at as anything other than an 'American.' It was a very rude awakening, one that drove me to stay home from work on the day the Miami Cuban American community called for it."

   "I am completely at home in Miami. In a completely Anglo society, I would feel like an outsider. In Miami I can be very Cuban one day and very Anglo the next."

   "It depends on the circumstances. When I am talking Spanish (or Spanglish) with my friends, I get dirty looks, especially from blacks and working-class whites."

40. Ilene Goldenberg, "In the Cause of Freedom," *The Key West Citizen,* August 31, 1997, 1A.

41. Kirk Nelson, "Alpha Males," Miami *New Times,* August 27, 1998, from www.miamitimes.com.

42. Kirk Nelson, "Alpha Males."

43. Charles Lane, "And a Child Shall Lead Them," *The New Republic,* January 24, 2000, posted on www.thenewrepublic.com/012400/coverstory012400.html.

44. Gustavo Pérez-Firmat, *Life on the Hyphen: The Cuban American Way* (Austin: University of Texas Press, 1994).

45. Max J. Castro, "The Trouble with Collusion," in *Cuba, the Elusive Nation,* 292–310.

46. Fort Lauderdale *Sun Sentinel,* August 1, 2000, 8A.

47. Luis Feldstein Soto, *Miami Herald,* Feb. 6, 1988, 1A.

48. Boza Masvidal turned out to be in Venezuela, and no contact was made with him after Mederos refused Benes's proposal. E-mail, Bernardo Benes to author, October 29, 2000.

49. Jonathan Kandell, "City of Exiles," 71

50. http://www.dakini.org/news/98/44.html

51. Jonathan Kandell, "City of Exiles," 64

52. In the mid-1990s, presumably as a public relations' measure, commissioners changed the name of Dade County to Miami-Dade County.

53. Quoted by Brett Sokol, Miami *New Times,* August 10–16, 2000, 19.

54. Brett Sokol, "Kulchur," Miami *New Times,* October 12–18, 2000. 21–23.

55. Jonathan Kandell, "City of Exiles," 74

56. Jonathan Kandell, "City of Exiles," 80.

57. E-mail from "P. Arias" to author, Miami, November 21, 2000.

58. Letter, Tina María Abich to author, Portland, Oregon, August 11, 2000.

59. Jonathan Kandell, "City of Exiles," 64.

60. Quoted by Jonathan Kandell, "City of Exiles," 69.

61. Marifeli Pérez Stable, *Miami Herald,* July 24, 2000, 5L.

62. Francis Robles, "Castro Aide, Exiles, Exchange Ideas," *Miami Herald,* September 10, 2000, 11A.

63. Reported by Bernardo Benes, August 24, 2000. Names have been omitted for the sake of confidentiality.

64. Letter, "Tom" (Dr. Thomas Cunningham) to Meg Laughlin, November 11, 1994. Benes collection.

65. Paraphrased from Joan Didion, *Miami,* paperback edition (New York: Vintage Books, 1998), 115.

66. Paraphrased from statement from Benes to his grandchildren, Miami Beach, November 28, 2000.

67. Ironically, in 2000 the Cuban *Confederación de Trabajadores* (Workers' Federation) took the same stance publicly.

68. Interview, Bernardo Benes, October 29, 2000.

69. E-mail, "Luis Salas" to author, November 7, 2000.

70. Max J. Castro, "Don't Give in to Myths," *Miami Herald,* September 12, 2000, 7B.

71. Review by "Oyez" of Joan Didion, *Miami,* www.amazon.com

72. María de los Angeles Torres, *In the Land of Mirrors* (Ann Arbor: University of Michigan Press, 2001), 20–21.

73. Paul Brinkley-Rodgers, "Escaped Cuban Pilot Kin to Revolutionaries," *Miami Herald,* September 23, 2000, 1A, 17A; Sandra Marquez Garcia and Paul Brinkley-Rogers, "Cubans Recount Harrowing Flight," *Miami Herald,* September 23, 2000, 17A.

74. Joseph Tanfani and Manny Garcia, "Radio Commentators Get Campaign Cash," *Miami Herald,* September 25, 2000, 1A, 13A; Lyssa Graham, "Stations, Politics a Sleazy Mix," *Street* (published by the *Miami Herald*), October 6–12, 2000, 9.

75. Manny Garcia and Tom Dubocq, *Miami Herald*, December 24, 2000, 1A, 18A.
76. Interview, (name withheld by request), Miami, April 22, 2000.
77. Statement, Moisés Asís, November 25, 2000.
78. Statement, Moisés Asís, November 25, 2000.
79. Liz Balmaseda, "Lasorda Scores Big with Exiles," *Miami Herald*, October 16, 2000, 1B,2B
80. Editorial, *Palenque*, Spring 1993, 3. Translation by María Cristina García in *Havana USA: Cuban Exiles and Cuban Americans in South Florida, 1959–1994* (Berkeley: University of California Press, 1996), 165.
81. Carol Rosenberg, "Hardening of Cuba policy is expected from Bush," *Miami Herald*, December 19, 2000, 3A.
82. Max Castro, "Will Bush Follow Nixon's Example?" *Miami Herald*, December 19, 2000, 7B.
83. Max Castro, "A Sensible Cuban Immigration Policy," *Miami Herald*, July 7, 1999, 4A.
84. "A Cuba de Lula," *Veja* (São Paulo, December 6, 2000), 49; *Japan Post*, December 15, 2000, 3.

INDEX